ISON

ATION

TITLE III

DISCARD

THE AMERICAN NOVEL

1789-1939

THE AMERICAN NOVEL

1789-1939

by Carl Van Doren

Revised and Enlarged Edition

New York

THE MACMILLAN COMPANY

THE MACMILLAN COMPANY, NEW YORK
COLLIER-MACMILLAN CANADA, LTD., TORONTO, ONTARIO

PRINTED IN THE UNITED STATES OF AMERICA

PREFACE

THE FIRST edition of this book in 1921 announced a further volume, which appeared the next year as *Contemporary American Novelists: 1900-1920*. That volume, parts of which have been absorbed in the present work, is no longer either contemporary or satisfactory and now goes out of print. In the revised edition, which is nearly double the length of the original, an effort has been made to present the history of the American novel for a hundred and fifty years on the same scale throughout. If some later novelists have been given less space than some of the earlier ones it is because the biographies of the later are not available and their work is not complete. If later novels appear in much greater number than the earlier it is not only because many more have been written, but also because more later ones, however likely to be some day forgotten, have not yet been. The revised edition, like the first, is meant to serve as a record of the national imagination as exhibited in the progress of native fiction. Though it incidentally takes into account poems and plays and short stories, as well as national myths and legends and traditions and aspirations, it concerns itself primarily with novels: here defined simply as long prose narratives in which the element of fact is on the whole less than the element of fiction.

In general outline *The American Novel* in its first edition followed the chapters on fiction which I had contributed to *The Cambridge History of American Literature*. With the permission of the publishers, The Macmillan Company, this larger version is still considerably indebted to those chapters. I have in other sections, also with the permission of the various publishers, made some use of other writings of mine: *Stephen Crane* in *The American Mercury* for January 1924

PREFACE

(Alfred A. Knopf); *Lucifer from Nantucket in The Century Magazine* for August 1925 (D. Appleton-Century Company); *James Branch Cabell*, 1925, revised 1932 (Robert M. McBride & Company); *Sinclair Lewis: A Biographical Sketch*, 1933 (Doubleday, Doran & Company); *What Is American Literature?* 1935 (William Morrow and Company). Much of what I have written about recent novelists comes from what they themselves have told me.

Carl Van Doren

December, 1939

CONTENTS

THE AMERICAN NOVEL

1789-1939

I

BEGINNINGS OF FICTION

1~Arguments and Experiments

Prose fiction, before the American Revolution already a popular form of literature in Europe, had as yet a small and insecure reputation in the English colonies which subsequently became the United States. Not only were there still no native novels, but the great English masters of the art had little vogue. Richardson's *Pamela*, read everywhere as much for its piety as for its power to entertain, had been printed—the first novel in America—in 1744 by that shrewd judge of public taste and private profits, Benjamin Franklin, and there were editions the same year at New York and Boston. But Richardson's later novels, like Fielding's *Joseph Andrews* and *Tom Jones*, did not appear for more than forty years, when all of them were brought out in abridged editions in 1786. Even *Robinson Crusoe* had to wait nearly fifty years for an American printer, while *Rasselas* and *The Vicar of Wakefield* only tardily crossed the Atlantic. English editions, of course, had some circulation, but it could not have been great or a keener rivalry would have been awakened among the printers in such towns as Boston and Philadelphia in spite of the coldness of utilitarians and Puritans. Probably the Southern and Middle colonies read more novels than New England. William Byrd of Virginia, owner of one of the largest private libraries in America, possessed novels by Defoe, Fielding, Smollett, Le Sage, and Cervantes (who as satirist and moralist was widely admired), as well as more trivial performances. The Library Company of Philadelphia, founded by Franklin's Junto in 1731, bought *Robinson Crusoe* and *Gulliver's Travels* among their earlier though not their

(3)

earliest books. And New England was by no means innocent of novels. Jonathan Edwards himself, conspicuous among the saints, read *Sir Charles Grandison*, with such interest that he resolved to correct his own hitherto neglected style upon the example of Richardson; while Stephen Burroughs, as conspicuous among the sinners, later charged many of his offenses to his early reading of such books as *Guy, Earl of Warwick*, which he read about the time of the Revolution.

In part this apathy to fiction was due to the common colonial tendency to lag behind in matters of taste and culture. Pope in poetry and Addison in prose long sufficed for models among the Americans, and theological and political discussion proceeded with little reference to prevailing modes in imaginative literature. But even more important than mere apathy was the positive antipathy which showed itself when, soon after the Revolution, novel reading began to increase with great rapidity, and native novelists appeared in respectable numbers. The moralists were aroused and exclaimed against the change—their cries appearing in the magazines of the day side by side with moral tales. Nearly every grade of sophistication applied itself to the problem. The dullest critics contended that novels were lies; the pious, that they served no virtuous purpose; the strenuous, that they softened sturdy minds; the utilitarian, that they crowded out more useful books; the realistic, that they painted adventure too romantic and love too vehement; the patriotic, that, dealing with European manners, they tended to confuse and dissatisfy republican youth. In the face of such censure American novelists came forward late and apologetically, armed for the most part with the plea that they told the truth, pointed to heaven, or devoutly believed in the new republic. Before 1800 the sweeping abuse of the older school had been forced to share the field of criticism with occasional efforts to distinguish good novels from bad. The relative merits of Fielding and Smollett were discussed almost as frequently as, fifty years later, were those of Dickens and Thackeray, and in much the same confusion of ethical and æsthetic considerations. Fielding was of course preferred by the enlightened, Smollett by the robustious, Sterne by the sensitive, and Richardson, most popular of all it will be seen, by the domestic and sentimental. Indeed, to the influence of Richardson, with something from Sterne, must be credited the first regular American novel, *The Power of Sympathy*, a thin and stilted narrative in epistolary form which was published anonymously by William Hill Brown at Boston in 1789.

Political allegory, however, had already begun to prepare the way for invented narratives. The eighteenth century would have been less than itself had it brought forth in America only sentimental romances. Franklin, creating the character of Poor Richard and writing his hoaxes and bagatelles, was full of pleasant fictions. Francis Hopkinson, also of Philadelphia, produced an allegory which lies nearly as close to fiction as to history. In *A Pretty Story* (1774) he set forth, after the fashion earlier established by Dr. Arbuthnot, the history of a certain nobleman (the king) who had an old farm (England) and a new farm (the colonies) in the management of which his wife (Parliament) and his steward (the ministry) constantly interfered to the annoyance of his sons (the colonists) and to the great derangement of his own affairs. The story breaks off abruptly with Jack (Boston) shut up in his farm and turning for help to his brothers. The satire was without much bitterness or indignation, and perhaps for that reason all the more effective through its diverting narrative. Jeremy Belknap, the learned historian of New Hampshire, likewise tried his hand at allegory in *The Foresters* (1792, enlarged 1796). His foresters are the colonists, whose career he follows in a mild comic history, consistently allegorized, from the days of settlement, through the colonial wars, the Revolution, the Confederation, the Constitution, the establishment of the Republic, and the polemic episode of Citizen Genêt.

Neither Hopkinson nor Belknap is to be compared, for comic force and satirical point and power of observation, to the Pennsylvanian Hugh Henry Brackenridge (1748-1816), who between 1792 and 1815 published the various installments of his satirical novel *Modern Chivalry*. It is indicative of the changing taste of his time that he began his book in 1788-89 in the meter of *Hudibras*, recently employed with such success in Trumbull's *McFingal*, but later changed to prose. He coveted, he said, and followed the style of Hume, Swift, and Fielding—like Swift in *A Tale of a Tub* alternating chapters of narrative with ironical essays on all manner of subjects. Captain Farrago, the hero, is a new Don Quixote, who takes it into his head to leave his farm in western Pennsylvania "and ride about the world a little, with his man Teague at his heels, to see how things were going on here and there, and to observe human nature." As a description of manners in the early days of the Republic the book is unapproached by any other. Races, elections, rural conjurors, pseudo-scientists, inns, duels and challenges, treaties with Indians, the American Philosophical Society, the Society of the Cincinnati, hedge parsons, brothels, colleges, Congress, Quakers, lawyers, theaters, law courts, Presidential levees, dancing masters, excise officers, tar and feathers, insurrections: all these are displayed in the first part of the book with verisimilitude and spirit. Much of the action of this part is furnished by the doings of Teague, a grotesque and witless Sancho Panza, whose impudent ambition survives the most ludicrous and painful misadventures. Brackenridge regarded him as typical of the political upstarts of the period, and his triumphs as an accusation properly to be brought against the public which followed such sorry leaders. In Part II Captain Farrago, after a brief hiatus spent on his farm, resumes his travels, which at first do not take him beyond the limits of the nearest village, with its newspaper, academy, coffee house, lunatic asylum, and fair, but which eventually bring him to a settlement in the back country of which he becomes governor. The remainder of the book, ostensibly a chronicle of the new settlement, is virtually a burlesque of the history of America in the years following the Revolution. The settlers war with the Indians and make a constitution. They legislate like half-mad tyros, under the guidance of a visionary from Washington who holds that beasts should have the vote as well as men, and actually persuades his fellow-citizens to commission a monkey clerk of the court and admit a hound to the bar.

Brackenridge, himself a firm democrat of the classic school, aimed his satire primarily at doctrinaires and demagogues, but he laid his whip on almost all current follies and affectations, extending and revising his work through seven volumes, finally collected in two, to keep pace with new absurdities. Learned and pugnacious, as well as humorous, he had a popular audience in mind. "It is Tom, Dick, and Harry, in the woods, that I want to read my book." He understood that fiction may be as true as history, and thought that "little of the historical kind, in point of truth," was superior to such novels as *Roderick Random* or *Gil Blas*. For half a century *Modern Chivalry* was a good deal read, nowhere more so than along the very frontier which it satirized. One of the first books published west of the Alleghenies, it is the only early American novel which is still entertaining, and it is a lasting document on its confused time.

Satire had to be helped by sentiment, however, before fiction could win the largest audience. Indeed, until Scott had definitely established a new mode of fiction for the world, the potent influence in American fiction was Richardson. The amiable ladies who produced most of the early sentimental novels commonly held, like Mrs. Rowson, that their knowledge of life had been "simply gleaned from pure nature," because they dealt with facts which had come under their own observation; but like other amateurs they saw in nature what art had assured them would be there. Nature and Richardson they found the same. Whatever bias they gave this Richardsonian universe was due to a pervading consciousness that their narratives would be followed chiefly by women. The result was a highly domestic world, limited in outlook, where the talk was of careless husbands, of grief for dead children, of the peril of many childbirths, of the sentiment and the religion without which it used to be thought women could not endure their sex's destiny. Over all hangs the unceasing menace of the seducer, who appears in such multitudes that modern readers might think that age one of the most illicit on record if they did not understand that Richardson's Lovelace is merely being repeated in different colors and proportions. It is true, however, that the two most important novels of this sort, as well as *The Power of Sympathy*, were based on actual happenings. Hannah Webster Foster's *The Coquette* (1797) recorded the tragic career of Elizabeth Whitman of Hartford, who, having coquetted with the Rev. Joseph Buckminster, was seduced by a mysterious rake identified by gossips with Jonathan Edwards's son Pierpont, and died in misery at the Old Bell Tavern in Danvers, Massachusetts, in 1788. *The Coquette* saw thirteen editions in forty years, and was known in almost every household of the Connecticut Valley. It did not survive as long as Susannah Haswell Rowson's *Charlotte* (1794), one of the most popular novels ever published in the United States. Mrs. Rowson, an American only by immigration, had written the novel in England (where it was published in 1791), but *Charlotte Temple*, to call it by its later title, was thoroughly naturalized. It persuaded an increasingly naïve underworld of fiction readers to buy more than two hundred editions running into the twentieth century, and built up a legend about a not too authentic tomb in Trinity Churchyard, New York, which at least since about 1845 has borne the name Charlotte Temple in concession to the legend but which probably contains the ashes of a certain Charlotte Stanley whom John Montrésor seduced from her home in England and deserted in New York, much as in the novel. This simple story Mrs. Rowson embroidered with every device known to the romancer: bathos, easy tears, high-flying language, melodrama, moralizings without stint or number; and yet something universal in the theme long kept it, in its way, alive without the concurrence of critics or historians of literature.

The tradition that Abigail Stanley, mother of Elizabeth Whitman, was a cousin of Charlotte, serves to illustrate the process by which *Charlotte Temple* and *The Coquette* won a hearing from a community which winced at fiction: like sagas they stole upon their readers in the company of facts. A similar companionship appears in Royall Tyler's *The Algerine Captive* (1797). The hero, Updike Underhill, after an account of his youth and education in the backwoods of New England, and of his experiences as a schoolmaster there, goes on to Boston, begins the practice of medicine, proceeds to Philadelphia, where he meets Franklin, and to Virginia, where he is shocked at encountering a figure quite unknown to New England, a sporting parson; later he goes to sea, visits London, tells of Tom Paine, observes the horrors of a slave ship, and is captured by the Algerines, among whom he spends the six years recounted in the second volume. The value of the book lies largely in its report of facts, which it gives clearly and freshly. That Tyler thought of the traveler and the novelist as about equally his models appears from his preface, upon which the fame of *The Algerine Captive* principally depends. In 1787, it should be remembered, he had produced a comedy, *The Contrast*, opposing to foreign affectations the rustic worth of the first stage Yankee. Now ten years later he renewed his demand for nativism, while pointing out that the status of fiction had greatly changed in the interim. Formerly, he says, "books of Biography, Travels, Novels, and modern Romances, were confined to our sea ports; or, if known in the country, were read only in the families of Clergymen, Physicians, and

Lawyers; while certain funeral discourses, the last words and dying speeches of Bryan Shaheen, and Levi Ames, and some dreary somebody's Day of Doom, formed the most diverting part of the farmer's library." But "no sooner was a taste for amusing literature diffused than all orders of country life, with one accord, forsook the sober sermons and Practical Pieties of the fathers, for the gay stories and splendid impieties of the Traveller and the Novelist. The worthy farmer no longer fatigued himself with Bunyan's Pilgrim up the 'hill of difficulty' or through the 'slough of despond'; but quaffed wine with Brydone in the hermitage of Vesuvius, sported with Bruce on the fairy land of Abyssinia: while Dolly, the diary [sic] maid, and Jonathan, the hired man, threw aside the ballad of the cruel stepmother, over which they had so often wept in concert, and now amused themselves into so agreeable a terrour, with the haunted houses and hobgoblins of Mrs. Ratcliffe [sic], that they were both afraid to sleep alone." Such addiction to romance, Tyler argued, was too exciting for plain Americans; their novels like their clothes ought to be homespun.

It was in the very year of Royall Tyler's preface that the first American to make authorship his sole profession decided upon fiction as the chief form he should undertake. Charles Brockden Brown (1770-1810) of Philadelphia as a schoolboy aspired to be an epic poet, and contemplated epics on Columbus, Pizarro, and Cortez, possibly desiring to rival Timothy Dwight, whose Conquest of Canaan appeared in 1785, or Joel Barlow, whose Vision of Columbus followed two years later. But after ardently reading various French and English revolutionary philosophers, particularly William Godwin, Brown formed a new ambition. He would be a philosophical novelist, perhaps like Godwin in Caleb Williams (1794). Brown would patriotically write about America, and of course he would lay stress on the moral tendency of his stories. But in addition he hoped "to enchain the attention and ravish the souls of those who study and reflect." At the same time, he was too good a democrat to write for geniuses alone. He believed that while they were being stirred by the ideas of a novel, ordinary readers could be captured by the plot.

Brown's important books were written in a few vivid months, spent mostly in New York. His specific indebtedness to Godwin appears chiefly in a fondness for the central situation of *Caleb Williams:* an innocent and somewhat helpless youth in the grasp of a patron turned enemy. The parallel is exact in *Arthur Mervyn* (1799-1800), which brings a young man of that name to Philadelphia, makes him blunder into the secret of a murder, and subjects him to elaborate persecutions from the murderer. A surviving fragment of the lost *Sky-Walk* (written in 1797) shows that Brown there varied the Godwin situation by making the patron a woman. In *Ormond* (1799) by still another variation a woman is the victim: Constantia Dudley, pursued by the enthusiast and revolutionary Ormond until in self-defense she is obliged to kill him. Constantia won the passionate regard of a greater among Godwin's disciples, Shelley, to whom she was the type of virtuous humanity oppressed by evil custom. But Brown's victims do not have to undergo the cumulative agony of Godwin's, for the reason that Brown worked too violently to be able to organize a scheme of circumstances all converging upon any single victim. And more than his vehement methods of work handicapped him in his rivalry with Godwin: to be a master of the art of calm and deliberate narrative he must have had Godwin's cold and consistent philosophy of life, which Brown had not.

The Godwinian elements in Brown now seem less impressive than certain effects he was able to produce by the use of native material. In 1793 he had fled with his family to the country to escape the epidemic of yellow fever which then visited Philadelphia; five years later he had gone through a similar invasion of the plague at New York. His letters show

how deeply he was moved by the only personal contact he ever
had with such affairs of danger and terror as he chose to write
about. Composing *Ormond* almost before the pestilence had
receded, Brown transferred his impressions from the New York
of 1798 to the Philadelphia of 1793, as he did in *Arthur
Mervyn*, perhaps for some gain in perspective; but in both
he wrote with an eye on the fact as nowhere else in his books.
With unsparing, not to say sickening, veracity, he reproduced
the physical horrors of the plague and the general moral collapse. Less successful than these experiments was that in
Edgar Huntly (1799), wherein he turned to the material
which beyond any other was to be celebrated in American
fiction for half a century: frontier adventure. Brown claimed
for this book the merit "of calling forth the passions and
engaging the sympathy of the reader by means hitherto unemployed by preceding authors. Puerile superstition and exploded
manners, Gothic castles and chimeras, are the materials usually employed for this end. The incidents of Indian hostility,
and the perils of the Western wilderness, are far more suitable;
and for a native of America to overlook these would admit of
no apology." Brown knew little of the frontier, either its
scenery or its customs, and no more of the Indians than he
could have picked up from books or casual meetings in the
towns. But he found new devices for calling forth much the
same passions and sympathies as had been addressed by the
older Gothic romances. His wild regions and his wild adventures are all seen through an intensely romantic temperament
with only occasional intervals of realism. He set forth grisly
details of blood and suffering, and he treated his Indians without the glamor with which they were already being invested
by certain sentimentalists. The visible Indians are none of
them so memorable as the old woman called Queen Mab,
who never appears in person and who exists chiefly as a symbol of a race vanquished yet still clinging to its old domains
with a tenacity that is poetic. In Huntly's feverish nocturnal

wanderings, without much aim or sequence, Brown's sham-
bling narrative methods dull the edge of the story.

As a rationalist Brown tried to solve the mystery of *Edgar
Huntly* by explaining that both Clithero, the suspected villain, and Huntly were addicted to sleep-walking, a subject
which was just then under discussion and much debated. In
another attempt to fuse mystery with science, *Wieland*
(1798), Brown's most compact, most psychological, most
powerful novel, made use of ventriloquism. The plot was
founded upon the deed of an actual religious fanatic of Tom-
hannock, New York, who in a mad vision had heard himself
commanded to destroy all his idols, and had murdered his
wife and children with ferocious brutality. With this theme
Brown involved the story of Carwin, the biloquist, to make
the voices seem less incredible than in the original. It may
be assumed that ventriloquism did not seem a pinchbeck solution in 1798, when it was a trick little known or practised;
and Brown, too much an artist to make his ventriloquist a
mere instigator to murder, made him out a hero-villain whose
tragedy it is that he has to sin, not as the old morality had
it, because of mere wickedness, but because of the driving
power of the spirit of evil which no man can resist and from
which only the weak are immune. Yet though Carwin by his
irresponsible acts of ventriloquism in and out of season
actually sets going in Theodore Wieland's mind the train of
thought which terminates in the crimes, he does no more
than to arouse from unsuspected depths a frenzy already
sleeping in Wieland's nature. These were cases of speculative
pathology which Brown had met in his Godwinian twilights,
beings who had for him the reality he knew best, that of
dream and passion; from them comes the fever in the climate
which gives the book its power. To a notable extent *Wieland*
fulfills the rules Brown had laid down in his announcement
of *Sky-Walk*. Ventriloquism, religious murder, and a case of
spontaneous combustion make up the "contexture of facts

capable of suspending the faculties of every soul in curiosity."
These were for the unlearned. The apparent scene of action
is laid upon the banks of the Schuylkill; this was patriotic
realism. But for those of his readers who might have "soaring
passions and intellectual energy," as Brown had, the absorbing thing was the clash of mighty forces, the din of good and
evil, which after so many years now still awkwardly resound
through this old story of old ghosts.

2~Three Matters of American Romance

Except for the work of Irving, who deliberately chose short
stories to avoid any rivalry with Scott, the first twenty years
of the nineteenth century produced no memorable fiction
besides Brackenridge's in the United States. Even the example
of Scott, who was immensely popular, at first failed to arouse
imitators. The brilliance of his achievement served to dis-
courage his warmest admirers. Such learning, such experience,
such humor, such abundance as the Author of Waverley displayed: who dared match his powers against them? Moreover, the elements which gave Scott his vogue, and which for
a time seemed the essential elements of fiction, were not easily
transportable to another soil. The attitude of Americans in
the matter was well set forth by John Bristed in his book on
The Resources of the United States in 1818: "Of native novels
we have no great stock, and none good; our democratic institutions placing all the people on a dead level of political equality; and the pretty equal diffusion of property throughout the
country affords but little room for varieties, and contrasts of
character; nor is there much scope for fiction, as the country
is quite new, and all that has happened from the first settlement to the present hour, respecting it, is known to every
one. There is, to be sure, some traditionary romance about
the Indians; but a novel describing these miserable barbarians,

(14)

their squaws, and papooses, would not be very interesting to the present race of American readers." To Bristed, as to most contemporaries, it seemed impossible for the novel to flourish in a country which had no aristocracy, no distinct classes of society, no wide range of poverty and wealth, no legendary and semi-legendary lore like that of the English-Scottish border.

A genuine task challenged the American imagination before any considerable body of fiction could be achieved. Whatever man of genius might appear, there was still the problem of reaching a public taught that fiction belonged to the Old World, fact to the New; taught to look for the pleasures of the imagination on the soil where they had long existed and to which even the most self-conscious and politically independent American had been accustomed to look back with admiration, with some vague nostalgia of the spirit. Yet at the very moment when Bristed wrote, national passions were awake which within a half-dozen years had not only elicited a great romancer but had shown a popular imagination unexpectedly prepared for him. Out of such emotions come, in the proper ages, ballads and epic lays. In the United States, though prose fiction was the form at hand, the narratives were all romantic, and the literary process but repeated the processes of romantic ages. As in medieval France there were three matters of romance,

De France, et de Bretagne, et de Rome la grant,

so in the United States there were also three: the Revolution, the Settlement, and the Frontier.

The Revolutionary generation had been an age of myth-making. Washington, for instance, to his very face was apotheosized by his followers with a passion of language that notoriously embarrassed him. Almost before his bones were cold appeared Mason Locke Weems's astounding tract, mis-

(15)

called a biography, to catch the popular fancy at once and to establish the legend of Washington's superhuman virtues. "Private life," Weems avowed, "is real life"; and though, lacking first-hand knowledge, he was obliged to invent, he seemed intimate and credible to an audience somewhat overwhelmed by the heavy splendor of the more official orations and odes and sermons called forth by Washington's death. Thereafter the legend grew unchecked, until the pious Catherine Maria Sedgwick, in 1835, apologizing for the introduction of the hero in her novel *The Linwoods*, could write "in extenuation of what may seem presumption, that whenever the writer has mentioned Washington, she has felt a sentiment resembling the awe of the pious Israelite when he approached the ark of the Lord." The legends of Arthur and Charlemagne grew no more rapidly in the most legend-breeding age—indeed, did not grow so rapidly as this. And around Washington, as around Arthur his knights and around Charlemagne his peers, were speedily grouped such minor heroes as Francis Marion, whose life also was written by Weems; Israel Putnam, whom David Humphreys celebrated; Patrick Henry, whose biographer William Wirt was Attorney-General of the United States; Ethan Allen, who wrote his own record; and others whose fame or infamy (as in the case of Benedict Arnold) depended less specifically upon books. As all these heroes were consistently whitened by their biographers, so was the cause for which they fought; until the second generation after the Revolution had hardly a chance to suspect—at least so far as popular literature was concerned—that the Revolution had been anything but a melodrama victoriously waged by stainless Continental heroes against atrocious villains in British scarlet, followed by a victory without ugly revenges and crowned by a reconstruction culminating in the divinely-inspired Constitution. George Bancroft himself, a scholar of large attainments, could write as late as 1860 such words as these concerning the Declaration of Independence: "This im-

(16)

mortal state paper, which for its composer was the aurora of enduring fame, was 'the genuine effusion of the soul of the country at that time,' the revelation of its mind, when in its youth, its enthusiasm, its sublime confronting of danger, it rose to the highest creative powers of which man is capable. The bill of rights which it promulgates, is of rights that are older than human institutions, and spring from the eternal justice that is anterior to the state. Two political theories divided the world; one founded the commonwealth on the reason of state, the policy of expediency; the other on the immutable principles of morals: the new republic, as it took its place among the powers of the world, proclaimed its faith in the truth and reality and unchangeableness of freedom, virtue, and right. The heart of Jefferson in writing the declaration, and of congress in adopting it, beat for all humanity; the assertion of right was made for the entire world of mankind and all coming generations, without any exception whatever; for the proposition which admits of exceptions can never be self-evident. As it was put forth in the name of the ascendent people of that time, it was sure to make the circuit of the world, passing everywhere through the despotic countries of Europe; and the astonished nations as they read that all men are created equal, started out of their lethargy, like those who have been exiles from childhood, when they suddenly hear the dimly remembered accents of their mother tongue." This, the most patriotic American must now admit, is the language of romance.

The deeds and personages of the Revolution, steadily growing in the popular imagination under the stimulus of an exultant and hopeful independence, were naturally first expressed and most highly regarded of the new national themes. But side by side with them, in part aroused and drawn along by the Revolution, went the matter of the Settlement, consisting of the tales told in every state about its colonial days. Here again Weems took a hand and wrote folk-books about

William Penn and Benjamin Franklin. Weems, a Virginian, in his choice of these Pennsylvania worthies as subjects for his art illustrates the national feeling which gradually superseded the old colonial memories and prejudices. The new states no sooner pooled their national resources than they began unconsciously to pool their resources of tradition, of legend, of local poetry. Their wealth was as unequal in this respect as in any other, and widely different in quality. Certain themes from the first assumed a prominence that attracted to them the national imagination as it was attracted to no others. The landing of the Pilgrims, the witchcraft mania at Salem, Connecticut and its Charter Oak, the Dutch on the Hudson, Penn's liberality and tolerance, the settlement at Jamestown, Pocahontas and her career, Bacon's Rebellion, John Locke's schemes for the Carolinas, the debtors in Georgia, and, somewhat later, the siege of Louisbourg and Braddock's defeat: each of these early became the center of an increasing legend. Particularly important was a theme which in some form or other belonged to every colony—the warfare with the Indians for undisturbed possession of the soil from which they had been driven. So long as the natives had been dangerous to the invaders there had existed that bitterness of race-hatred which goes along with race-menace, and which kept out of the records of the old Indian wars any general magnanimity or sympathy for the dispossessed owners of the land. They were as paynims to Christian knights, as the sons and daughters of Amalek to the invaders of Canaan. King Philip's War in New England having begotten books, it lived in the popular memory more vividly than did the equally bitter and important but unrecorded Tuscarora and Yemassee wars in the Carolinas, for instance. The Deerfield raid, in large measure because of the Rev. John Williams's narrative of his capitivity, became classic while similar episodes elsewhere were forgotten. The treaties between various colonies and the Six Nations, though these were diplomatic dramas of genuine literary merit and Pennsylvania's were printed in memorable folios by Franklin, were lost sight of among the books dealing with wars and captivities. Toward the end of the eighteenth century, however, when the Indian was no longer a present menace, he began to be freshly sentimentalized by admirers of the natural man, with whom he was commonly identified by Europeans, and not infrequently by the descendants of the very Americans who had hated him so bitterly a century before.

The Indian was a link connecting the matter of the Settlement with the matter of the Frontier, the only one which had a contemporary aspect. It was the frontier not as remembered from the beginnings but as reported from the more distant territories where it still lay in the early years of the new century. Even before the Revolution not a few imaginations had turned inland. The settlement of Kentucky had excited the seaboard, and Daniel Boone, though not the greatest of the pioneers, before 1800 was already beginning to be the most famous of all of them, a true folk-hero. Literature unquestionably did him this service, in the person of the eccentric schoolmaster John Filson, who wrote for Boone his *Adventures* in 1784. Later the Louisiana Purchase drew still more eyes to the West, while the government expedition conducted by Lewis and Clark, rather less through its reports than through busy rumor, had an influence upon the popular imagination perhaps larger than that ever produced by any other American exploring venture. As contrasted with the tradition of the Settlement or of the Revolution, the reports concerning the contemporary frontier came as news, but there was still about them the haze of distance: distance in miles if not in years. The Great Lakes, the prairies, the plains and mountains beyond, the fever lands of the lower Mississippi, and especially the broad rivers and bluegrass of Kentucky: all of these constituted a sort of hinterland for the national imagination which writers of fiction were not slow to take advantage of. Nor did the frontier lie entirely inland. The sea also was a frontier. From every port of the New England coast, and from the Atlantic coast generally, ships went to every corner of the world, particularly to the mysterious Pacific, with its strange calms and rich pastures for fishermen, and to the exotic countries beyond, but also to the crowded Mediterranean, the banks of Newfoundland, the neighborly West Indies. The new nation was setting out to become acquainted with its own immense domain and to establish communications between it and all the rest of the world, real or imagined.

Such potentialities, of course, still ran a long way before the facts at the time Bristed made his unhopeful prophecy. What he said of existing American fiction suited its recent examples accurately enough. John Davis, a visiting Englishman, had taken a fancy to the Pocahontas legend and had dealt with it in three versions in his *Travels* (1803), *Captain Smith and Princess Pocahontas* (1805), and *The First Settlers of Virginia* (1805). Preposterous as they all are, they are interesting as the first treatment of one of the most persistent of American legends. A rollicking anti-romance, *Female Quixotism* (1801) by Tabitha Tenney, which made fun of the novels of the day by showing into how many follies its heroine could blunder by taking the manners of such novels for her guide, was far less popular than Isaac Mitchell's Gothic tale *The Asylum* (1811), which achieved at least a score of editions and exhibits the worst qualities of Mrs. Radcliffe with none of the less bad. The Gothic mode had enough followers to call forth an ingenious anonymous parody in 1817: *The Hero, or The Adventures of a Night. A Romance translated from the Arabic into Iroquese; from the Iroquese into Hottentot, from the Hottentot into French, and from the French into English.* Yet what turned the public from the absurd fictions fashionable for a time was not parody, but the coming of a true and great story-teller in Fenimore Cooper.

II

JAMES FENIMORE COOPER

THE TASK of becoming the principal romancer of the new nation might have weighed heavily upon Cooper if he had entered his career as a novelist in any self-conscious way. Instead, he fell almost accidentally into authorship. Unlike the bookish Brown, Cooper was trained in the world of action and adventure. Born at Burlington, New Jersey, in 1789, the son of Judge William Cooper and Susan Fenimore, Cooper was taken when a baby to Cooperstown, the raw central village of a pioneer settlement recently established by his father on Otsego Lake, New York. Here the boy saw at first hand the varied life of the border, observed its shifts and contrivances, and learned to feel the mystery of the dark forest which lay beyond the cleared circle of his own life: a mystery which must be taken into account in any attempt to understand the American character in its frontier aspects. Judge Cooper, less a typical backwoodsman than a kind of warden of the New York marches, like Judge Templeton in *The Pioneers*, did not keep his son in the woods but sent him first to the rector of St. Peter's in Albany, who grounded him in Latin and Anglican theology, and then to Yale, where he wore his college duties so lightly as to be dismissed in his third year. Thinking the navy might furnish better discipline than Yale, Judge Cooper shipped his son before the mast on a merchant vessel to learn the art of seamanship which there was then no naval academy to teach. On his first voyage the ship was chased by pirates and stopped by British searching parties, incidents Cooper never forgot. Commissioned in 1808 as midshipman, he first served on the Atlantic and later in the same year was sent with a party to Lake Ontario to build a brig for service against the British on inland waters. He visited Niagara, served for a time on Lake Champlain, and in 1809 was ordered back to the ocean. In the natural order of events he would have fought in the War of 1812, but having been married in 1811 to Susan Augusta DeLancey, he resigned his commission, gave up all hope of a naval career, and began the quiet life of a country proprietor.

During the nine years that followed there is no evidence that Cooper ever thought of authorship, even as an amusement, much less as a profession. Except for three years at Cooperstown, where he stood more or less as heir to the manor, he lived in his wife's native county of Westchester. He inherited a substantial fortune from his father, though much of this was wasted by the elder brothers before the estate could be divided. James Cooper owned the chief share in a whaler which made profitable voyages, and he seems to have engaged in other shipping ventures. But for the most part Cooper's life was like that of many contemporary squires. Westchester had been favored by the gentry in colonial days and still cherished aristocratic traditions. Here Cooper was further confirmed in his theological opinions, which were orthodox and grew steadily stronger, not to say more intolerant; in his political doctrines, by which he belonged with few reservations to the idealistic, irascible, downright, and class-conscious older democracy which had achieved the Revolution; and in his social prejudices, which were what might have been expected from a man of his theology and politics. He took a propertied governing class for granted, the subordination of the lower orders, and clear-cut caste distinctions. Rank, according to his opinions, naturally demanded of the men who possessed it a proper dignity, magnanimity, courage, knowledge, public service, and chivalry toward women; women of rank he expected to be less positive but to unite to domestic competence and loyalty a certain elaborate yet timid decorum. Toward the less fortunate classes Cooper believed he had the feelings of a good American democrat: he was full of that condescension which the eighteenth century mistook for a virtue. He tended to admit humbler personages to his fiction for the diversity they brought and to admire them for their devotion to their superiors. Even his greatest characters drawn from the people, Harvey Birch, Natty Bumppo, and Long Tom Coffin, have about them each some touch of the faithful body-servant, though they are saved by a larger element of loyalty to a cause, Birch to the Revolution, Bumppo to the life of unspoiled nature, and Coffin to the deep sea. Besides the typical opinions of his class, Cooper had also its typical information. He read the accepted classics, interested more in modern than in ancient literature, and concerned more with history and biography than with poetry, philosophy, or science. He knew little of the fine arts. Later something of a traveler in Europe, during his formative years he saw, except upon his ocean voyages, only America, and little besides New York, its cities and its frontier. American history generally —and particularly that of New York, including its antiquities and topography—Cooper knew unusually well, though here again his knowledge came from the commoner sources. He knew a good deal of English history, rather less of French. In seamanship, his actual profession, he was better trained than any man who had ever used the ocean as the scene of a novel.

The accident which threw Cooper into fiction was a challenge which his wife made him to write a better novel than one which he had been reading with disgust. He accepted the challenge, wrote an unimportant domestic-sentimental romance, *Precaution* (1820), and found himself so much attracted by authorship that within three years he had written three of his best novels, each of them in one of the types he later clung to, and had completed his experimental stage. In *The Spy* (1821) American fiction may be said to have come of age with a tale of the recent Revolution. Love of country is its theme, and its hero a spy who had served John Jay against the British, as Jay himself had told Cooper, with singular purity of motive. The share of historical fact in it is not large, but the action takes place so near to great events that the characters are all invested with something of the dusky light of heroes, while the figure of Washington, disguised as Mr. Harper and yet always looming gigantically through his disguise, moves among the other personages like a half-suspected god. Such a quality in the novel might have gone with impossible partiality for the Americans had not Cooper's wife belonged to a family which had been loyalist during the struggle for independence. As it was, Cooper made his loyalists not necessarily knaves and fools. It is clear the British are enemies worth fighting. Perhaps by chance, Cooper here hit upon a type of plot at which he excelled, a struggle between contending forces, not badly matched, arranged as a pursuit in which the pursued are, as a rule, favored by author and reader. In the management of such a device Cooper's invention, which was naturally great and now was thoroughly aroused, worked easily, and the flights of Birch from friend and foe alike exhibit a power to carry on plots with sustained sweep which belongs to none but the masters of narration. To rapid movement Cooper added the virtue of a very real setting. He knew Westchester, where his scene was laid, the Neutral Ground of the Revolution, as Scott knew his own border; the topography of *The Spy* is drawn with a firm and accurate hand. In the characters Cooper was not so successful—by strict canons of realism was not successful at all. Cherishing an aristocratic and traditional conception of women, he accepted for his narrative the romantic ideals of the day, the ideals of Scott and Byron. Writing of violent events in which ladies could play but a small part, he cast his heroines into the straitest mold of helplessness and propriety. With the less sheltered classes, such as were represented by Betty Flanagan the sutler, Cooper could be more veracious. Of the men who appear in *The Spy*, most are mere gentlemen, mere heroes, although Captain Lawton, the Virginia dragoon, is drawn with spirit and truth, and here and there among the inferior soldiers and the slaves appear a few individual characteristics. Harvey Birch, however, peddler and patriot, outwardly no hero at all and yet surpassingly heroic of soul as he prowls about on his subtle errands, is memorable and arresting. The skill with which he is presented, gaunt, weather-beaten, canny, mysterious, should not conceal the fact that his patriotism is actually as supernatural as are the dæmonic impulses of Brown's characters. Patriotism drives Birch relentlessly to his destiny, at once wrecking and honoring him. This same romantic fate condemns him to be sad and lonely, a dedicated soul who captures attention by his secrecy and holds it by his adventures. All this is pure romance, but it is romance vigorously realized.

Cooper's imagination, having worked first upon Revolutionary material and having succeeded with an historical romance which won the loudest applause, was approved on the American stage, and promptly reached European readers, now turned with characteristic energy in another direction, to the matter of the Frontier. *The Pioneers*, with a bumptious, challenging preface, was published early in 1823. Technically this book made no advance upon *The Spy*. Cooper had only the method of improvisation, then or later. With a few characters and the outlines of a situation in mind, he began composition, perhaps not even aware what the outcome would be, and then found himself swept forward with impetuous haste. In one respect *The Pioneers* falls behind its predecessors in interest: it has no definite scheme of pursuit and flight, and consequently, though it has certain thrilling moments, no general suspense. But in another respect it was a more important experiment than *The Spy*: now for the first time Cooper had set himself to the realistic representation of American manners. Dealing as he did with the Otsego settlement where his boyhood had been spent, and with a time (1793) partly within his memory, he could write largely with his eye upon the fact. Whatever romance there is in the story lies less in its plot, which is a conventional story of a worthy line for the moment dispossessed but eventually to be restored again; or in its characters, which are, for the most part, studied under a dry light with a good deal of caustic judgment—less in these things than in the essential wonder of a pioneer life. In its costumes and gestures the novel is not so heroic as *The Spy*. Indian John, the last of his proud race, is old and broken, corrupted by the settlements; only his death dignifies him. Natty Bumppo, a composite from many Cooperstown suggestions but in his main outlines undoubtedly suggested by Daniel Boone, is nobler than Indian John because he has not yielded but carries into the deeper forest his virtues, which even in Cooper's boyhood were becoming archaic along the New York frontier, and now in 1823 had become a legend. Natty stands as a protest, on behalf of simplicity and perfect freedom, against encroaching law and order. In *The Pioneers* he is not of the proportions which he later assumed, and only at the end, when he withdraws from the field of his defeat by civilization, does he make his full appeal; but he is of the tribe of heroes to which Harvey Birch had belonged, lowly men of lofty virtues.

At the time Cooper seems to have seen no larger possibilities in his pioneer than in his spy. He was still experimenting. *The Pilot*, later in 1823, took him to another region of the frontier which he knew: the sea. The instigating motive was his desire to surpass Scott's *Pirate* in seamanship, but Cooper's imagination caught fire no less remarkably than when he had decided to write a purely American tale of heroism or to make a record of his youthful environment. Like *The Spy*, his new novel made use of the Revolutionary matter; like *The Pioneers*, it was full of realistic detail from his own experience.

(26)

Not only did he outdo Scott in sheer accuracy, but he created a new literary type, the tale of adventure on the sea, in which, though he was to have many followers in almost every modern language, he has not been seriously surpassed for vigor and swift rush of narrative. Smollett had already discovered the racy humors of seamen, but it remained for Cooper to capture for fiction the mystery and beauty, the shock and thrill of the sea. Experts say that his technical knowledge was sound; what is more important, he wrote in *The Pilot* a story about sailing vessels which convinces landsmen even in days of steam. The novel has its conventional element: its hero, John Paul Jones, who is always dark and secret, always Byronic, always brooding upon a dark past and a darker fate. As in the earlier stories, much is made of chase and escape, complicated by the fact that here ships, not merely men or horses, must be manœuvered, in a time of bitter war, among the rocks and storms of the Scottish coast. And once more, too, the central personage is a democratic hero, Long Tom Coffin of Nantucket, who lives and dies by the sea which has made him, as love of country made Harvey Birch and love of the forest made Natty Bumppo. Long Tom is as real as an oak; he is also as romantic as storms and tides. Thus at the outset of his career Cooper made clear his conviction—one of the most important of all the convictions which lie back of his work—that character is shaped by occupation. Aristocratic though he might be in his own prejudices, he understood the rich diversities which may be brought into fiction by the representation of men drawn from different callings, which, at least as much as different ages or landscapes, produce differences among men.

These three successes made Cooper a national figure, though New England, where criticism was solemn, still condescended to him. He moved with his household in 1822 from Westchester to New York. He founded the Bread and Cheese Club, a literary society of which he was the moving spirit; he took a prominent part in the reception of Lafayette, who returned to a magnificent welcome in 1824. In the same year Columbia College made Cooper honorary Master of Arts. He changed his name to Fenimore-Cooper in 1826, but soon dropped the hyphen. In the excitement of being a national romancer he planned a series of Legends of the Thirteen Republics, aimed to celebrate each of the original states, but he gave up his scheme after *Lionel Lincoln* (1825), dealing with Boston in the days of Bunker Hill, failed to please as his earlier novels had done. His account of the battle is in his best vein; but for the rest, Cooper was too unsympathetic towards the New England character and, in spite of his research, too little at home in Massachusetts for his imagination to be fired by this material. Beguiling as his conception of the series was, Cooper was not fitted, by breadth either of knowledge or of temper, to succeed in it; and his initial failure seems his ultimate good fortune. His future did not lie along the path of history which he had taken in *The Spy*, but along the path of frontier adventure which he had strayed into with *The Pioneers*.

The persuasion of friends led him to resume his narrative of Natty Bumppo, and in Cooper's next two years and his next two novels he reached the highest point of his career. With *The Last of the Mohicans* (1826) he undertook to show the days of Natty's prime, and with *The Prairie* (1827) his old age and final end. In each case Cooper projected the old hunter out of the world of remembered Otsego, into the dark forest which was giving up its secrets to the ax and the plow in 1793, or into the mighty prairies which stretched, in Cooper's mind's eye, for endless miles behind the forest, another mystery and another refuge. Natty, called Hawkeye in *The Last of the Mohicans*, no longer has the hardness which marred his disgruntled age in *The Pioneers*. He appears instead as erect, swift, shrewd, contented, and wise. With all his virtues of hand and head he combines a nobility of spirit

(28)

which the woods have fostered in a mind never spoiled by contact with human meanness and injustice. He has grown nobler as he has grown more remote from quarreling Otsego, more the poet and the hero as the world in which he moves has become more wholly his own. Chingachgook has undergone even a greater change, has got back all the cunning and pride which had been deadened in that victim of civilization, Indian John. Both Hawkeye and Chingachgook are of course considerably limited by their former conduct in *The Pioneers:* one must still be the canny reasoner, the other saddened with the passing years. The purest romance of the tale lies in Uncas, the forest's youngest son, gallant, skillful, courteous, a lover for whom there is no hope, the last of the proud race of the Mohicans. That Uncas was idealized Cooper then and always admitted; Homer, he suggested, had his heroes. And it is clear that upon Uncas were bestowed the standard virtues which the philosophers of the age had taught the world to find in a state of nature. Still, after a century many who can smile at ideas about the state of nature are yet able to find in Uncas the perennial appeal of youth cut off in the flower. The action and the setting of the novel are on the same imaginative plane with the characters. The forest, in which all its events take place, surrounds them with a changeless majesty, a venerable calm, a depth of significance that sharpens, by contrast, the restless sense of danger. Pursuit makes almost the whole plot. The pursued party moving from Fort Edward to Fort William Henry has two girls to handicap its flight and to increase the tragedy of its capture. Later the girls have been captured, and sympathy passes, a thing unusual in Cooper, to the pursuing rescuers. In these tasks Hawkeye and the Mohicans are opposed by the fierce capacity of the Huron Magua, who plays villain to Uncas's hero, in physical qualities Uncas's match, in moral qualities his opposite. There is never any relaxation of suspense; there are certain high moments which belong with the most thrilling episodes in fiction.

The Prairie has less swiftness than *The Last of the Mohicans* but more poetry. In it Natty appears again, twenty years older than in *The Pioneers*, far away in the plains beyond the Mississippi, where the popular mind knew that Daniel Boone had recently died. Natty owns his defeat and he still grieves over the murdered forest, but he has given up anger for the peace of old age. To him it seems that all his virtues are gone. Once valiant he must now be crafty; his arms are feeble; his eyes have so far failed him that, no longer the perfect marksman, he has sunk to the calling of a trapper. There is a pathos in his resignation which would be too painful were it not merely a phase of his grave and noble wisdom. He is more than ever what Cooper called him: "a philosopher of the wilderness." The only change is that Natty has left the perils and delights of the forest and has been subdued to the eloquent monotony of the plains. Nowhere else did Cooper show such sheer imaginative power as in the handling of this mighty landscape. He had never seen a prairie; indeed, it is clear that, like many travelers before him, he thought of the prairie as an ocean of land and described it partly by analogy. But he managed to endow the huge empty distances he had not seen with a presence as haunting as that of the populous forest he had intimately known in his impressionable youth. And the old trapper, though he thinks of himself as an exile, has learned the secret of the new scene and seems naturally to belong to it. It is his knowledge that makes him essential to the action, which is again made up of flight and pursuit. Once more there are girls to be rescued, from fiercer white men as well as from fierce Indians. There is another Magua in the Sioux Mahtoree, another Uncas in the Pawnee Hard-Heart. These Indians ride horses; the flat prairies afford few places of concealment. But the trapper is as ready as ever with new arts, and the flight ends as

(30)

romance prescribes. The final scene, the death of the trapper in the arms of his young friends, is touching and fine, yet reticently handled. Thackeray imitated it in the famous death of Colonel Newcome. For the most part, the minor characters, the lovers and the pedant, are not new to Cooper and are not notable. The family of Ishmael Bush, the squatter, however, make up a new element, as realistic as the rougher sort in *The Pioneers,* but more sinister, more important in Cooper's criticism of the frontier. Bush and his giant sons have been forced out of civilization by its virtues, as the trapper by its vices. They have strength without nobility and activity without wisdom. Except when aroused they are as sluggish as a prairie river, and like it they appear muddy and aimless. Ishmael Bush always conveys the impression of terrific forces lying vaguely in ambush. His wife is nearly the most memorable figure among Cooper's women. She clings to her mate and cubs with a tigerish instinct that leaves her, when she has lost son and brother and retreats dumbly from the scene in a vast silent grief, still lingering in the mind, a shabby, inarticulate prairie Hecuba.

The Last of the Mohicans and *The Prairie,* and the praise they won, did not convince Cooper that the frontier was his true province. His next novel, *The Red Rover* (1828), written in France, turned to the noisy Atlantic between New England and the West Indies. Feeling that he must take care in writing of nautical affairs to avoid the themes and characters preferred by Smollett, Cooper was at some pains to invent all his details "without looking for the smallest aid from traditions or facts." His plot, however, follows the romantic mode: an imperial-souled hero, wounded in his sensibilities, has long been a successful pirate under the scarlet flag, but, in spite of his evil deeds, has so much conscience left that he can be converted in a dramatic moment, subsequently to expiate his sins by services to the Revolution. This story could not have made *The Red Rover* one of Cooper's best tales. There must be taken into account also the solid basis of reality exhibited in the book's seamanship and, less remarkably, in the characters of the old tar Dick Fid and the slave Scipio Africanus. The excitement is less sustained than in *The Pilot*, but portions of the narrative, particularly those dealing with storms, are tremendous. The ocean here plays as great a part as Cooper had lately assigned to the prairie. One voices the calm of nature, the other its tumult; both tend to the shaping and discipline of man. If the theme of *The Red Rover* is conventional, so is that of *The Wept of Wish-ton-Wish* (1829), an episode of King Philip's War, in which frontier material indeed appears but in which it is overmuch involved with colonial history and with Cooper's anti-Puritan prejudices.

What may be called his first period had come decisively to an end. Since 1826, when he went with his family to Europe for a foreign residence of seven years, Cooper had been growing steadily more critical and less romantic. His universe was enlarging. He found his books well known in Europe and people disposed to make much of him. In Paris he fraternized with Scott, who enjoyed and approved his American rival. Parts of Cooper's stay were in England, Holland, Germany, Switzerland, which delighted and astonished him, and Italy, which he loved. Most of his time, however, he passed at Paris, charmed with a gayer and more brilliant society than he had known before. At first his nationalism was intensified. Unabashedly, outspokenly American, he had obtained from Henry Clay the post of consul at Lyons, that he might not seem, during his travels, a man without a country. As consul, though his position was purely nominal, he felt called upon to resent the ignorance everywhere shown by Europeans regarding his native land, and he set himself the task of educating them in sounder views. Cooper was not Franklin. *Notions of the Americans* (1828), while full of information and a rich mine of American opinion for that day, was too obviously partisan to convince those at whom it was aimed. Its proper audience was homesick Americans. He indulged, too, in some controversy at Paris over the relative cost of French and American government which pleased neither nation. Finally, he applied his art to the problem and wrote three novels "in which American opinion should be brought to bear on European facts." That is, in *The Bravo* (1831), *The Heidenmauer* (1832), and *The Headsman* (1833) he meant to show by proper instances the superiority of democracy to aristocracy as regards general happiness and justice. He claimed to be writing for his countrymen alone, some of whom, in that day of one-sided comparisons between Europe and America, must have been thrilled to come across a passage like "a fairer morning never dawned upon the Alleghanies than that which illumined the Alps"; but he was not sufficiently master of his material, stout as his opinions might be, to make good romances out of it.

He had, however, caught the contagion of the critical spirit, and he returned to New York in 1833 in no mood to lend his voice to the loud chorus of national self-approval then generally sounding—nor, at the same time, to the humility towards Europe displayed by certain Americans who at heart were still colonial, as Cooper was not. He found himself a cosmopolitan patriot in the republic he had been justifying abroad for seven years. He sought to qualify too sweeping statements about the United States in America precisely as he had in Europe. But he had not learned tact while becoming a citizen of the world, and he promptly angered the public he had only meant to correct. The result was the acrid wrangling which clouded the remainder of his life. If he had attended the dinner planned in his honor on his return he might have found his welcome warmer than he thought it. If he had been an observer at once keen and tolerant enough, he must have seen that the new phases of democracy which he disliked under Andrew Jackson were in large measure a gift to the old seaboard of that very frontier of which Cooper had been painter and annalist. But he did not see these things, and so he took to argument, often as right in his contentions as he was unfortunate in his manner. From Cooperstown, his residence except for a few winters in New York, to the end of his life he argued. His *Letter to his Countrymen* (1834), stating his position, and *The Monikins* (1835), an unbelievably dull satire, established the controversy. He followed these with five books dealing with his European travels and irritating to both continents. He engaged in altercation with his fellow-townsmen over the right to a piece of land which they had come to think of as a public park though it certainly belonged to the Cooper estate. In 1838 he published a fictitious record, *Homeward Bound* and its sequel *Home as Found*, of the disappointment of some Americans who return from Europe with a passion like that with which he had recently returned, and who find America what he had found it; but he appears not to have realized that the colossal priggishness of his returning Effinghams would make them seem more obnoxious than any qualities he could expose in the Americans at large. With something of the same tactlessness he proclaimed his political philosophy in *The American Democrat* (1838), a searching study of the times. Of a true democratic gentleman Cooper said: "The same principles and manliness that would induce him to depose a royal despot, would induce him to resist a vulgar tyrant." Attacked by furious newspapers throughout New York, Cooper went up and down the state suing those that had libeled him. He won most of the suits, but though he silenced his opponents he had put his fame into the hands of persons who, taught not to abuse him, could learn to neglect him.

All these controversies checked Cooper's tendency away from romance and towards realism. How strong that tendency was has not been frequently remarked; as a matter of fact, several of his later novels are packed with the most valuable information concerning the manners, opinions, speech, and costumes of their periods. But with Cooper, to be critical was too often to be contentious, and as a result those very novels and others still more largely abound in prejudices and arguments that continually break the strong current of romantic narrative or disturb the broad picture of reality. All his better achievements after 1830 came on those occasions when he could escape from contemporary New York to the ocean or to the old frontier. The ocean was an important relief. In 1839 he published his solid and long-standard *History of the Navy of the United States*, and followed it with various naval biographies. The *History* led to another libel suit; but generally Cooper left his quarrels behind him when he went upon the sea. As a cosmopolitan, he felt freer on the public highway of the nations. His novels of this period and theme are uneven in merit. *The Two Admirals* (1842) contains one of his best naval battles; *The Wing-and-Wing* (1842) ranks high among his sea tales, richly romantic and glowing with the splendors of the Mediterranean, and yet charged with the theological bigotry which latterly possessed Cooper. The two parts of *Afloat and Ashore* (1844), dealing powerfully as they do with the evils of impressment, are notable also for sea fights and chases. And the inland frontier was quite as much a relief. *Wyandotté* (1843), its scene on the upper Susquehanna, and its subject the siege of a blockhouse, though clumsily told is full of interesting matter. *The Oak Openings* (1848), fruit of a journey which Cooper made to the West in 1847, is a tale of bee-hunting and Indian fighting on Lake Michigan which has not deserved to be so much obscured as it has been by his greatest frontier stories.

Obscured it and its fellows have been, however, by *The Pathfinder* (1840) and *The Deerslayer* (1841), which he turned aside long enough to write in the midst of his hottest litigation. The forest even more than the ocean was for Cooper a romantic sanctuary, as it was for Pathfinder the true temple, full of the "holy calm of nature," the teacher of beauty, virtue, laws. Returning to these solemn, dim woods Cooper was subdued once more to the spirit which had attended his first great days. The fighting years through which he had passed had made him more critical, but so had they made him more mellow in the hours when he could forget his daily conflicts. He had now gone far enough from the original conception of Leather-Stocking to become aware of traits which should be brought out or explained. It was too late to make his hero entirely consistent for the series, but Cooper apparently saw the chance to fill out the general outline, and he did it with such skill that those who read the five novels in the order of events will notice relatively few discrepancies, since *The Deerslayer* prepares for nearly all that follows. In *The Pathfinder*, undertaken to show Natty in love and to combine the forest and a ship in the same tale, Cooper took unusual pains to point out how Pathfinder's candor, self-reliance, justice, and fidelity have been developed by the life he has led in the forest. Leather-Stocking, more talkative than before, may not seem more conscious of his special gifts, but Cooper does. Again there is abundant action: another flight through the woods with a timorous maiden, somewhat too nearly resembling the flight in *The Last of the Mohicans*; another siege at a blockhouse, very much like that in *The Wept of Wish-ton-Wish* and *Wyandotté*; and the more novel element of a storm on Lake Ontario which calls for a seamanship quite different from that learned on salt water. A romancer less realistic than Cooper might have shown Pathfinder behaving on shipboard with the masterful competence he had on land; but Cooper did not. A romancer more sentimental than Cooper, too, would hardly have dared to let Pathfinder love the heroine in vain; but Cooper did. Even though it is with a somewhat grandiose gesture that Pathfinder is made to surrender the young girl to a more suitable lover of her own choice, much more than a gesture was in Cooper's mind. He was drawing a sharp, true line around Pathfinder's character. Marriage would have domesticated the scout, whereas this sacrifice restores him to the forest solitude in which he essentially belongs.

For the final book of the series, *The Deerslayer*, Cooper could do nothing less than to undertake the hard task of representing the scout in the fresh morning of his youth. Love appears in this story also, but Deerslayer, unable to love a girl who has been corrupted by the settlements, even though Judith Hutter seems the most real and desirable of all Cooper's heroines, turns to the forest with his best devotion. He is naïve, friendly, virtuous with the engaging awkwardness of twenty, bound with a boy's affection to his companion and brother-in-arms, the young Chingachgook. The book is the tale of Natty's coming of age. Already a hunter, he here kills his first man and thus enters the long career which lies before him. That career, however, had already been traced by Cooper, and the distress with which Deerslayer realizes that he has human blood on his hands, becomes, in the light of his future, immensely eloquent. It gives the figure of the man almost a new dimension; one remembers the deaths Natty has yet to deal. In other matters he is nearer his later self, for he starts life with a steady if simple philosophy which, through all his many adventures, keeps him to the end the son of nature he was at the beginning.

"If anything from the pen of the writer of these romances is at all to outlive himself," Cooper declared, "it is, unquestionably, the series of *The Leather-Stocking Tales*." The series is still accepted as the quintessence of his achievement, and Leather-Stocking by any large ballot—both national and international—would be voted among the most eminent of all American characters of fiction. In Cooper's most definite summary, Natty was "simple-minded, faithful, utterly without fear, and yet prudent, foremost in all warrantable enterprises, or what the opinion of the day considered as such . . . The most surprising peculiarity about the man himself was the entire indifference with which he regarded all distinctions that did not depend on personal merit. . . . His feelings appeared to possess the freshness and nature of the forest in which he passed so much of his time, and no casuist could have made clearer decisions in matters relating to right and wrong; yet he was not without his prejudices, which, though few, and colored by the character and usages of the individual, were deep-rooted, and had almost got to form a part of his nature. . . . In short . . . he was a fair example of what a just-minded and pure man might be, while untempted by unruly or ambitious desires, and left to follow the bias of his feelings, amid the solitary grandeur and ennobling influences of a sublime nature." Nature in America is no longer so solitary, and no longer so ennobling, but much of this older simplicity, downrightness, courage, competence, unsophistication, and virgin prejudice still marks the national type. Generation after generation of American boys has read these romances as they have read no others. Boys of other nations and races have admired in Leather-Stocking qualities generously transcending merely national ones. Cooper's failure to write a sixth novel, as he at one time planned, which should show Natty in the Revolution, may be taken as a sign that he felt the difficulty of endowing the scout with the virtue of patriotism in the partisan degree which must have been demanded from that hero in that day and which would surely have been alien to the cool philosopher of the woods. Justice, not partisanship, is Leather-Stocking's essential trait: justice as conceived, somewhat out of space and out of time, by the universal spirit of youth. Being so universal, Leather-Stocking has naturally too simple a soul to call for minute analysis, and needs no more than the opportunity, which Cooper gave him, to move through a long succession of events aimed to display his valor and test his virtues. There was thus produced the panorama of the American frontier which at once became and has remained the classic record of an heroic age.

The classic record of an heroic age—although not classic at all in the stricter sense of fidelity to all the circumstances of the frontier. And yet in spite of the many charges that have been brought against Cooper's accuracy, charges well founded and well proved, his fame holds steadily up. He may not have recorded his universe at all points exactly, but he created one. His mighty landscapes lie still unshaken in a secure district of the human imagination. Over such mountains through such dim and terrifying forests to such glorious lakes the mind still marches, for the moment convinced. His Indians, whatever their authenticity, are securely established in the world's romantic memory as a picture of those belated and unfortunate men of the stone age who were fated to oppose the ruthless advance of a more complex civilization. It is poetic justice that those red savages, unjustly as they were dealt with while alive, should be a little honored with a chivalrous reputation when dead or conquered. In this manner all peoples remember their ancient defeated enemies. And later studies of the eastern Indians, especially of the Six Nations of the Iroquois, have shown clearly enough that the race possessed, if not exactly the qualities Cooper ascribed to them, at least a fineness and elevation of mind which are closer to Cooper's representation of them than to the picture as corrected by subsequent critics who called the Indians squalid devils. That Natty Bumppo, to the contemporary eye doubtless hard and crude enough, should have been made a hero is no more remarkable than that the same fortune should have come to Daniel Boone or Robinson Crusoe, plain men who like Natty clung to the dearest human virtues in the face of a nature which would as readily have destroyed as dignified them.

The Pathfinder and The Deerslayer seem to have left Cooper nearly exhausted, for his last decade saw him rise but once above the sensationalism which always menaced the romancers of his school and the contentiousness which grew upon him. Most of the novels of the period do not deserve

(39)

even to be called by name. He had still enough energy, however, to undertake and to complete his trilogy of Littlepage Manuscripts: *Satanstoe* (1845), *The Chainbearer* (1845), and *The Redskins* (1846). Having tried the autobiographical method with Miles Wallingford in *Afloat and Ashore*, Cooper now repeated it through three generations of a New York family. In the last he involved himself deeply in the question of anti-rentism then stirring, took his stand on the side of the landlords who Cooper thought should be supported in the interests of the whole society, and produced a book which is dull except as a document. The second is better by one of Cooper's most powerful figures, the squatter Thousandacres, another backwoods Titan of the breed of Ishmael Bush. The first, if a little aside from Cooper's best work, is so only because he was never quite at his best but when he dealt with Leather-Stocking and his fortunes. No other novel by Cooper, or by any other writer, gives so firm and convincing a picture of colonial New York, when Pinkster, the annual holiday of the slaves, was still a great day in Manhattan; when at Albany the Patroon still kept up something like baronial state; and when throughout the province a traditional order still went normally unchallenged. Even Cooper has no more exciting struggle than that of Corny Littlepage with the icy Hudson. But the special virtue of *Satanstoe* is a quality Cooper nowhere else displays, a positive charm in the way Littlepage unfolds his memories (now sweetened by many years) and his humorous crotchets in the same words. Unfortunately Cooper did not carry this vein further. With his family and a few friends he lived his latter days in honor and affection, but he held the public at a sour distance, and before his death in 1851 set his face against a reconciliation even in the future by forbidding any biography to be authorized. The publication of his correspondence after seventy years and of an authorized life after eighty came so late that his character is less familiar to the general world than that of any other American writer of equal rank.

This might be somewhat strange, since Cooper was lavish of intrusions into his novels, were it not that he wrote him-self down, when he spoke in his own person, as not only a powerful and independent man but also a scolding, angry man, and thus made his most revealing novels his most for-bidding ones. One thinks of Scott, who when he shows him-self most wins most love. The difference further characterizes the two men. In breadth of sympathies, humanity, geniality, humor, Cooper is less than Scott. He himself, in his review of Lockhart, said that Scott's great ability lay in taking a legend or historical episode, such as Scotland furnished in a splendid profusion that Cooper envied, and reproducing it with mar-velous grace and tact. "This faculty of creating a *vraisem-blance*, is next to that of a high invention, in a novelist." It is clear that Cooper felt his own inferiority to Scott in "creat-ing a *vraisemblance*" and that he was always conscious of the relative barrenness of American life; it is also tolerably clear that he himself aimed at what he thought the higher quality of invention. Of Leather-Stocking Cooper specifically said: "In a physical sense, different individuals known to the writer in early life certainly presented themselves as models, through his recollections; but in a moral sense this man of the forest is purely a creation." Cooper's invention, however, though his highest claim to greatness, is not without a solid basis; he is not to be neglected as a historian. No man better sums up in fiction the older type of republican—rather than democrat—which established the United States. No one—unless possibly Irving—fixed the current heroic conditions of his day more firmly to actual places. Though Cooper might have supplied more facts to the great legend of the frontier, no one else supplied so many. Certainly it was his superior technical knowledge of ships and sailors which helped him to write such sea tales as set him, in that province of romance, still high among many followers. Cooper had not Scott's resources of historical learning to fall back upon when his invention flagged, any more than he had Scott's good-nature when he became involved in argument; but when his invention escaped from the world of settled customs on which Scott's art was built up, Cooper did with his invention alone what Scott, with his subsidiary qualities, could not outdo. After all else that can be said, one returns to Cooper's invention, which is almost supreme among romancers, and which lifts him solidly above all his faults of clumsiness, prolixity, conventional characterizations, and ill-temper. Merely the multiplication of incidents could not have preserved him. Merely his good fortune in being first to celebrate the frontier would not have been enough. There had to be in him that intensity by virtue of which he so completely realized imagined, and often imaginary, events. How far this quality of his raises the quality of his invention may be observed in certain of his recognition scenes—scenes of that kind which Aristotle considered to be of the very essence of dramatic effect. Uncas revealing himself to the Delawares, the old trapper discovered on the prairie by the grandson of his former comrade: surely Euripides, if he had been a writer of hasty prose romances, might have taken pride in scenes like these.

III

ROMANCES OF ADVENTURE

VIEWED HISTORICALLY Cooper emerges from among his contemporaries as few of them could have realized he would
after a century. Every one of the great matters of his day—
the Settlement, the Revolution, the Frontier on land and
water—he touched with a masterly hand, and in essential
popularity he distanced all his rivals. It is of course mere coincidence that he was born in the year which produced *The
Power of Sympathy* and that when he died *Uncle Tom's
Cabin* was passing through its serial stage; yet the limits of
Cooper's life do mark almost exactly the first large period of
American fiction. Neal, Thompson, Paulding, Kennedy,
Simms—to mention no slighter figures—outlived him, but not,
as a current fashion, the type of romance which had flourished
under Cooper. Although by 1851 tales of adventure, as Cooper
and his school conceived adventure, had begun to seem anti-
quated, they had rendered a large service to the course of literature: they had removed the stigma, for the most part, from
the word novel. For the brutal scrapes of eighteenth-century
fiction the new romance, of Scott and Cooper, had substituted
deeds of chivalrous doings; it had supplanted the blunt flesh-
liness of Fielding and Smollett with a chaste and courtly love.
Familiar life, frequently shown in low settings, had been succeeded by remote life, generally idealized; historical detail had
been brought in to instruct readers who were being enter-
tained, not without some sense of guilt in their entertainment.
Cooper, like Scott, was more realistic than the Gothic romancers, more human than Godwin or Brown. The two most
common charges against the older fiction, that it pleased

(43)

wickedly and that it taught nothing, had broken down before the discovery, except in illiberal sects, that the novel is fitted for both honest use and pleasure.

In Europe, at Cooper's death, a new vogue of realism had set in, but America still had little but romance. The presence of the frontier as a contemporary fact as well as a matter of fiction accounts for this condition quite as much as does the absence at the time of any strong realistic bent among American writers. With that vast, mysterious hinterland free to any one who might come to take it, novelists, like farmers, were less prompt in America than in Europe to settle down to the intensive cultivation of known fields. There was a close analogy between the geographic and the imaginative frontier of the United States. As the first advanced, thin, straggling, from the Atlantic to the Pacific, widening from Canada to Mexico, and reaching out in ships, the other followed, also thin and straggling but with an incessant purpose to find out new territories which the imagination could play over and claim for its own. "Until now," wrote Cooper in 1828, "the Americans have been tracing the outline of their great national picture. The work of filling up has just seriously commenced." He had in mind only the physical process, but his image applies as well to that other process in which he was the most effective pioneer. Two years after his death the outline of the national picture, at least of contiguous territory, was established, and the nation gave itself to the problem of occupation. In fiction, too, after the death of Cooper, the main tendency for nearly a generation was away from the conquest of new borders to the closer cultivation, east of the Mississippi, of ground already marked.

As late as 1825 Jared Sparks thought ten American novels a striking output for one year, but during the second quarter of the century Cooper had many helpers in his task. For the most part they were more limited than he to particular sections. In New England, Neal, Thompson, and Judd had already set outposts before Hawthorne, at first a writer of short stories, came definitely with his greater novels to capture that section for classic ground. Paulding assisted Cooper in New York, and took Swedish Delaware for himself; for Pennsylvania, Bird was Brown's chief successor; Maryland had Kennedy; Virginia, without many native novels, began to undergo, in the hands of almost every romancer who dealt with either the Settlement or the Revolution, an idealization which made it seem the most romantic of American states; South Carolina passed into the pages of Simms; Georgia and the lower South brought forth a school of native humorists who abounded in the truth as well as in the fun of that border; the Mississippi and the Ohio advanced to a place in the imagination with the Hudson, the Susquehanna, the Potomac, and the James. North of the Ohio romance achieved comparatively little and the epic of the Great Lakes remained —as it still remains—unsung; but on the southern bank of the Ohio, Kentucky—Dark and Bloody Ground—rivaled its mother Virginia. Bird ventured into Mexico at a time when Irving and Prescott were writing romantic histories of the Spanish discovery and conquest. Nor did the romancers of the period confine themselves entirely to native borders, though the exceptions are relatively unimportant: various narratives by various narrators of the life and voyages of Columbus; the African tales of Mayo; the one story of classical antiquity, Mrs. Child's gentle, ignorant *Philothea* (1836); the Biblical romances of William Ware; and George Tucker's satirical *Voyage to the Moon* (1827).

The topographical arrangement is the natural arrangement of this body of romance, for as regards style, method, attitude toward the American past, present, future, general criticism of life, or individual distinction, the different novels exhibit but in rare cases any such qualities as would make classification significant or even possible. Again medieval France furnishes a parallel in the *chansons de geste*, which differ from

(45)

these old American romances in little besides their anonymity and their meter. Were the names of the American authors transposed it would be noticed, if at all, only by experts. Almost all of these tales employ a more or less standardized idiom and terminology, tending to the heroic and inflated in the dialogue and to the verbose in narrative and description. Swift improvisation underlies the method, with a large but heedless handling of groups of characters and blocks of material, and with Providence and coincidence involved as lightly as in the most romantic ages. Although there is a plethora of incident, the plots play continual variations upon a few themes and personages. In those dealing with the matter of the Revolution the war against the British never slackens; nor in those dealing with the Settlement and the Frontier, the war against the stubborn aborigines. Types of character are strongly opposed and slightly shaded, as suits an atmosphere habitually tinged with conflict. Children hardly exist on the scene, and the women rarely rise above the pretty and elegant and helpless except when now and then one of them assumes the virago, often with comic effect. So far as the characters have a psychology, it is restricted to a few single motives: with the women, a passive readiness to be wooed, a meek endurance of husbands, and a tearful solicitude for children—again except for the viragoes, who anticipate their suitors, nag their husbands, and beat or savagely protect their young; with the men, intense patriotism, a burning confidence in the national destiny, a passion for fighting and hardships, considerable insensibility to pain, in themselves and others, which finds expression in stoicism, cruelty, and heavy pranks; and chivalric love remarkably sexless in any but the villains. The moral standards implied belong to conventional ethics, Christianity being professed and war practised in the ordinary mixture. While some strained points of honor appear, especially arising from the codes of the gaming table and the duel, there is little of that casuistry which in the medieval courtly romances plays so large a part. There might be more of it were there not a tolerably constant strain of humor, though more often the characteristic American good humoi than wit or comedy. Burlesque frequently shows its head, as a rule in connection with the lower order of characters, who, as with Scott, are more likely to be conceived as amusing than as heroic. Such non-English elements in the population as the Irish, German, and French commonly play comic rôles; the Negroes have hardly ever any character but that of faithful slaves; and the Indians stand normally at one extreme or other of the scale —fierce savages to be exterminated without mercy or amiable sons and daughters of nature. Towards history most of the romancers took the attitude that it existed for the edification or for the elevation of their readers, and they did not hesitate to enlarge it at will. On the whole the most realistic elements in the entire tradition are the geography, which almost never becomes hazy and casual as in medieval romance, and the landscape, which though grandiose and elaborate, is little more so in the novels than it was in fact at a time when the great forest and mountains and prairies of the continent were still immense as compared with the settled regions. A certain largeness about the physical horizons went a long way for Cooper's generation toward tempting readers to forget the countless conventional elements in this early fiction. Without their sense of that largeness these novelists could hardly have possessed the rough narrative energy which is their highest quality.

Only a few of them need to be specially characterized. John Neal of Maine, the first obvious and confessed imitator of Cooper, when *The Spy* appeared took fire at the example. Neal's real master, however, was Byron, whom he followed with a fury of rant and fustian which would have made him, had he been gifted with taste and humor as well, no weak follower. *The Down-Easters* (1833), though promising at first to be a real picture of native life and character, soon

(47)

runs amuck into raving melodrama. The Rev. Sylvester Judd in 1845 published a novel, *Margaret*, which Lowell declared had the soul of Down East in it; but the soul of the book has not proved immortal. Written to show that the Unitarians could produce imaginative literature as well as the more orthodox sects, *Margaret* is badly constructed and it wanders, toward the close, into a region of misty transcendentalisms where characters and plot are lost; and yet it has genuine merits in its vivid fidelity to the life of rural Massachusetts just after the Revolution, in its thorough, loving familiarity with the New England temper and scene, and in a kind of spiritual ardor which pervades it throughout. Judge Daniel Pierce Thompson knew the Vermont frontier as Cooper knew that of New York. After many struggles with the bitterest poverty he got to college, studied law, became a prominent official of his native state, and somewhat accidentally took to fiction. Of his half dozen novels, which all possess a good share of honest realism, *Locke Amsden* (1847) gives perhaps the most truthful record of frontier life, but *The Green Mountain Boys* (1839) is the classic of Vermont. It is concerned with the struggles of the Vermonters for independence first from New York and second from Great Britain; its hero is the famous Ethan Allen. Thompson had none of Cooper's poetry and was little concerned with the magic of nature; he took over most of the tricks of the older novelists and their stock types and sentiments. But he made little effort to preach, he could tell a straight story plainly and rapidly, and he touched action with rhetoric in just the proportion needed to sell fifty printings of the book by 1860 and to make it a standard book for boys: the most popular romance of the immediate school of Cooper.

There was a school of Irving, too, which touched the novel. James Kirke Paulding, Irving's friend, had considerable merit as a novelist, particularly in the matter of comedy. He enjoyed burlesque and he laughed at what he called Blood-Pudding

Literature. He was too facile in lending his pen, as parodist or follower, to whatever fashion prevailed at any given moment to do any very individual work, but *The Dutchman's Fireside* (1831), his masterpiece, deserves to be mentioned with Cooper's *Satanstoe*, considerably its superior, as a worthy record of the Settlement along the Hudson; and his *Westward Ho!* (1832) significantly reveals the charm which the West—especially Kentucky, in which the scene of this novel is chiefly laid—had for the natives of the older states. Other writers of Eastern birth, resident for a time in the new settlements, cheerfully or romantically undertook the representation of manners not known to the seaboard. The wittiest was Caroline Matilda Stansbury Kirkland, a native of New York, who wrote from the Michigan frontier, among other lesser books, *A New Home—Who'll Follow?* (1839), a volume of keen and sprightly letters avowedly in the manner of Miss Mitford, an English imitator of Irving. Still closer to Irving was Judge James Hall of Pennsylvania, who went west in search of adventure, lived in Illinois and Ohio, and by his various literary enterprises served as an interpreter between West and East much as Irving did between America and Europe. Hall's manner is like Irving's in its leisurely, genial narrative, its abundant descriptions, and its affection for supernatural legends which could be handled smilingly. He had real powers of fidelity, the only merit he claimed, to the life he knew, but he had also a florid style and a vein of romantic sentiment which have denied his best book, *The Wilderness and the Warpath* (1846), a permanent vitality. Nearest of all to Irving, however, was his friend and admirer, John Pendleton Kennedy. Of excellent Virginia connections, but born in Baltimore, he served as bloodlessly as Irving in the War of 1812, like him was admitted to the bar, and like him lived merrily thereafter in his native town. His *Red Book* (1818-19) was a Baltimore *Salmagundi* in prose and verse; his *Swallow Barn* (1832), an amiable and admirable record of life on a Virginia plantation, was a Virginia *Bracebridge Hall*, even to certain incidents and characters which give the effect of having been introduced rather because Kennedy had observed them in Irving than because he had observed them in Virginia. But Kennedy's easy humor and real skill at description and characterization make the book distinguished in its own right. His *Horse-Shoe Robinson* (1835), in which he deals with the Revolution in the Carolinas, is nearer Cooper, with the difference that Kennedy depended, as in *Swallow Barn*, on fact rather than invention for much of his action as well as for his details of topography and costume. He founded the career of Horse-Shoe Robinson upon that of an actual Revolutionary partisan with such care that the man is said later to have approved the record as authentic. In *Rob of the Bowl* (1838) Kennedy turned back to seventeenth-century Maryland and a lively romantic manner which was at last his own, neither Irving's nor Cooper's. But Kennedy's gift, like Irving's, was for enriching actual or typical events with a finer grace and culture than most contemporary romancers could command.

Cooper's closest rival—in some respects his superior—among the romancers of his school of romance was William Gilmore Simms (1806-70) of South Carolina. Born in Charleston, outside the ruling class of that nearly feudal city, Simms got but a scanty schooling. He seems during his youth to have been as bookish as Charles Brockden Brown, but it was romantic poetry and history which fascinated him, not romantic speculation. From his grandmother he heard innumerable legends of the Revolution, South Carolina's epic age, and cherished them with a poetic, patriotic devotion. When he was eighteen he went to visit his father, who having lost his money and his business had left Charleston, become friend and follower of Andrew Jackson, and settled on a plantation in Mississippi. The young poet had a chance to see the rough manners of a frontier which corresponded, in several ways, to that of Cooper, and he seems, during extended travels, to have observed its violent comedy and violent melodrama with sharp eyes. But the border—the matter of the Frontier—was not Simms's first love as it had been Cooper's, and the inalienable Carolinian went back, against his father's advice, to the traditions and dreams of Charleston. There he was admitted to the bar, and there he published the first of his many volumes of verse.

It is unnecessary to say more of the miscellaneous literary tasks of Simms than that, somewhat after the fashion of Sir Walter Scott on a smaller scale, he wrote moderate poetry to the end of his life, including three verse tragedies; that he edited the apocryphal plays of Shakespeare; that he produced popular histories of South Carolina and popular biographies of Francis Marion, Captain John Smith, the Chevalier Bayard, and Nathanael Greene; and that he kept up a ceaseless flood of contributions to periodicals. His range of interest and information was large, but he commonly dealt with American, and particularly Southern, affairs. Though he made visits to the North he liked it no better than the West. His really significant work, as a romancer, he began in 1833 with a Godwinian tale of crime, *Martin Faber*, which was so well received that he followed it in 1834 with *Guy Rivers* and in 1835 with *The Yemassee*, two romances in which almost the full extent of his powers was early displayed. *Guy Rivers*, conventional as regards the love affair which makes a part of the plot, is a tale of deadly strife between the laws of Georgia and a border bandit. A born story-teller, like Cooper, Simms was as casual as Cooper in regard to structure, but he was too rapid to be dull and he revealed to Americans a new section of their adventurous frontier. His concern with colonial South Carolina bore fruit in *The Yemassee*, a moving tale of the Yemassee War of 1715 which has been his most famous, and which is as a whole his best, work. Once again Simms took hints from current romances, but when he set himself to

describing the rich landscape of South Carolina or to recounting its annals, he was more fully master of his material than
in *Guy Rivers* and more admirable in proportion as his subject was more congenial to him. He gave his Indians the
dignity and courage which he said they must have had at an
earlier period; he invented for them a mythology. But his
triumph comes from the bold and truthful variation he here
plays upon the theme used by Cooper in *The Last of the
Mohicans*. Occonestoga, the Uncas of this drama, has been
corrupted by contact with the whites and has betrayed his
people; Sanutee, his father, like another Brutus, denounces
the renegade; Matiwan, his mother, with a more than Roman
fortitude, kills him with her own hands to save him from
the dishonor which his tribe could inflict only upon a living
man. The older American romance has no more dramatic
moment. The various white and black characters in *The
Yemassee* have somewhat less heroic dimensions than the
red, but they are done with great vigor and considerable
realism.

   Having succeeded with the matters of the Frontier and
the Settlement, Simms now turned to the Revolution and
wrote *The Partisan* (1835), designed as the first member of
a trilogy which should properly celebrate those valorous times.
He later wavered in his scheme, and though he finally called
Mellichampe (1836) and *Katherine Walton* (1851) the other
members of his trilogy, he grouped round them four more
novels that have obvious marks of kinship. *The Partisan* traces
events from the fall of Charleston to Gates's defeat at Camden; the action of *Mellichampe*, which is nearly parallel to
that of *Katherine Walton*, the proper sequel of *The Partisan*,
takes place in the interval between Camden and the coming
of Greene; *The Scout*, originally called *The Kinsmen* (1841),
illustrates the period of Greene's first victories; *The Sword and
the Distaff* (1852), later known as *Woodcraft*, furnishes a
kind of comic afterpiece to the series. Simms subsequently

returned to the body of his theme and produced *The Forayers* (1855) and its sequel *Eutaw* (1856), to do honor to the American successes of the year 1781. Of these *The Scout* is perhaps the poorest, because of the large admixture of Simms's cardinal defect, horrible melodrama; *Woodcraft* is on many grounds the best, by reason of its close-built plot and the high spirits with which it tells of the pranks and courtship, after the war, of Captain Porgy, the most truly comic character ever created by this school of American romance. But neither of these two works is quite representative of the series; neither has quite the dignity which Simms imparted to his work when he was most under the spell of the Carolina tradition. That always warmed him; at times he seems drunk with history. He had a tendency to overload his tales with solid blocks of fact derived from his wide researches, forgetting, in his passionate antiquarianism, his own belief that "the chief value of history consists in its proper employment for the purposes of art"; or, rather, he was too much thrilled by bare events to perceive that they needed to be colored into fiction if they were to fit his narratives. Simms never took his art as a mere technical enterprise. He held that "modern romance is the substitute which the people of the present day offer for the ancient epic," and his heart beat to be another Homer. His seven novels are his epic of the Revolution. Marion, the Agamemnon of these wars, had already become a legend in the popular memory with the help of Weems's fantastic ardor, but it remained for Simms to show a whole society engaged in Marion's task. The defect of Simms was that he relied too much upon one plot for each of his tales—a partisan and a loyalist contending for the hand of the same girl—and that he repeated certain stock scenes and personages again and again. His virtue was not only that he handled the actual warfare with interest and power but that he managed to multiply episodes with huge fecundity. He described, in a surge of rhetoric, his favorite material:

(53)

"Partisan warfare, itself, is that irregular and desultory sort of life, which is unavoidably suggestive of the deeds and feelings of chivalry—such as gave the peculiar character, and much of the charm, to the history of the middle ages. The sudden onslaught—the retreat as sudden—the midnight tramp—the moonlight *bivouack*—the swift surprise, the desperate defence—the cruel slaughter and the headlong flight—and, amid the fierce and bitter warfare, always, like a sweet star shining above the gloom, the faithful love, the constant prayer, the devoted homage and fond allegiance of the maiden heart!"

The passage is almost a generalized epitome of his Revolutionary romances. It also betrays the fact that the epic for Simms lay decidedly nearer to Froissart than to Homer. If Simms is more sanguinary than Cooper, he is quite as sentimental. His women, though Nelly Floyd in *Eutaw* is pathetic and mysterious, and Matiwan in *The Yemassee* is nearly as tragic as formal romance can make her, are almost all fragile and colorless. Even more than Cooper, Simms was tediously old-school toward his women. He was also too often condescending toward his common men. Yet it was chiefly with his common men, rather than with his wooden gentlemen, that he was most successful. His days on the border had given him a knowledge of high-handed, high-hearted blackguards, and he put such characters freely into the Revolutionary novels to season the epic story with their wild deeds done out of doors, their boisterous jokes, and their rich, rank speech. The Falstaffian Porgy, first shown in *The Partisan*, runs through the series, never tired, never tiresome. In comedy Simms surpassed Cooper, whom he equals if not surpasses in the description of landscapes, which in Simms range from the sterile wastes of Georgia to the luxuriant Carolina swamps in which the partisans find a refuge—descriptions full of reality and gusto, but with little emphasis on the poetry or philosophy of nature.

Simms was at his best in dealing with the matter of the

Revolution; he was less happy with the Frontier. Perhaps the earlier frontier had been intrinsically more dignified than the one which Simms had observed along the Mississippi and which had a contemporary comic hero in the very real David Crockett. Certainly Cooper's frontier, lying deeper under the shadow of the past, had been romanticized more than Simms's. Simms grew more melodramatic, rather than more realistic, the further he ventured from the regions of law and order. *Richard Hurdis* (1838), *Border Beagles* (1840), *Beauchampe* (1842), and its sequel *Charlemont* (1856) are amazingly sensational—bloody and tearful and barbarously ornate. Nor was Simms happier when he abandoned native for foreign history, as in *Pelayo* (1838), *The Damsel of Darien* (1839), *Count Julian* (1845), and *Vasconselos* (1853). He constantly turned aside to put his pen to the service of the distracted times through which he lived. As the agitation which led to civil war grew more heated, he plunged into stormy apologetics for the grounds and virtues of slavery, as passionately conservative as Dr. Johnson or Sir Walter Scott. Just on the eve of the struggle Simms produced a romance of seventeenth-century Carolina, *The Cassique of Kiawah* (1859), a stirring, varied story which, however generally neglected, must be ranked with his best books. The war ruined and broke him, and though he wrote stoutly on till his death he never regained his earlier powers or his earlier prestige. If he has never quite regained it since, it is primarily because of a conflict in his literary character. By nature a realist, with a flair for picaresque audacity, he let himself be limited by a romantic tradition which did not seem to him to justify and call for his natural gifts. It was more or less in spite of his conscious aims that he now and then wrote about striking characters and situations through vivid pages in simple, nervous, racy language.

Robert Montgomery Bird of Delaware, in his Mexican romances recalling Irving and in his novels of New Jersey and

Pennsylvania nearer to Cooper, has survived solely—if dimly —as the author of *Nick of the Woods* (1837), an exciting tale of the Kentucky frontier of 1782, in which Bird attempted to correct Cooper's heroic drawing of the Indian by presenting him as a fierce and filthy savage utterly undeserving of sentimental sympathy. The book celebrates a type of character frequently spoken of in frontier annals, the white man who, crazed by Indian atrocities, gave his whole life to a career of ruthless vengeance. As critical a disposition as Bird's rarely appeared outside of Cooper, but it appeared in *The Partisan Leader* (1836) by Judge Nathaniel Beverley Tucker of Virginia, a novel which was made the vehicle of criticism. Remembered chiefly because it prophesied disunion and civil war, the book deserves note also for its classical restraint, its pride, its intense, conscious Virginianism. Distinction of another sort belongs to the Rev. William Ware of Massachusetts, whose *Zenobia* (1837), *Aurelian* (1838), and *Julian* (1841), Unitarian, diffuse, and monotonous, continued to be read for almost a century by persons to whom books dealing with the age of Christian origins were equally duty and delight. And there is another distinction still in *Kaloolah* (1849), by William Starbuck Mayo of New York, a romance which contains a strange mixture of satire and romance in its account of an African Utopia visited by the Yankee hero Jonathan Romer.

Besides the novelists who can here be characterized or even named there were, or had been, by 1851 many others whom it would avail little to catalogue: authors for children, authors preaching causes, authors celebrating fashionable or Bohemian life in New York; writers of domestic stories with shudderingly sensational plots. Longfellow lamented the success which attended the flashy labors of Joseph Holt Ingraham. E. Z. C. Judson (Ned Buntline) and Emerson Bennett began their energetic, sub-literary careers. Timothy Flint wrote novels dealing with the Southwest as well as his valuable *Recollec-*

tions. Henry William Herbert (Frank Forester), born in England, wrote in America about American field sports in *The Warwick Woodlands* (1845) and other sporting novels. As the century advanced there was undoubtedly an increase in the amount of trivial fiction produced. The rise of the great Victorian novelists in England was not paralleled in America. Their works in the absence of any copyright could be sold by American publishers more cheaply than native novels could be with the incumbrance of royalties to native authors. Some Americans avoided competition by preferring short stories; others by sinking to a lower level and manufacturing a cheap domestic grade of entertainment. All the more, then, do such figures as Cooper and Simms emerge from among the minor romancers of the half-century.

NATHANIEL HAWTHORNE

So FAR THE cause of the American novel had enlisted no man who came primarily for the sake of art. Brown had been a radical journalist, Cooper a stentorian man of action, Simms a passionate antiquarian; all of them had been technically improvisatores. The art of fiction was being studied in the United States during this half century chiefly in connection with the short story, which Irving had invested with his amused and amusing charm, of which Poe had discovered secrets of structure and effect not heretofore analyzed, and into which Hawthorne as the century advanced was pouring a deeper and deeper strain of intellectual and moral significance. Neither Irving nor Poe undertook a novel in any strict sense of the word, nearly as Irving's versions of history in works like *The Conquest of Granada* or *Astoria* approach the manner and color of contemporary romance; or bulky as was Poe's *Narrative of Arthur Gordon Pym, of Nantucket* (1838), which pretended to be a veracious book of travels though it was not. Nor do such pleasant divagations as Longfellow's *Hyperion* (1839) and *Kavanagh* (1849) or Whittier's *Margaret Smith's Journal* (1849), though not without invention, take any conspicuous position in the history of the American novel. When Hawthorne published *The Scarlet Letter* in 1850 he could not profit by a long series of native experiments in the art of the novel but had to initiate the mode in which he has since seemed supreme.

And yet *The Scarlet Letter* represents in Hawthorne's own career the fruit of an apprenticeship to art the like of which no other American man of letters had demanded of himself.

For twenty-five years a disposition which Hawthorne generally encouraged had held him to a task of preparation. Born in Salem, Massachusetts, in 1804, he came of a line of substantial citizens settled in the town since its earliest days. Once prominent, the line had become less so, but all its generations had busied themselves with affairs, latterly on the sea. Nathaniel Hawthorne, who could not point to even a clergyman among his ancestors, was the first of his name to be sedentary. As a boy he was robust, handsome, athletic, no particular student, but rather more of a reader of general literature than has been ordinarily noted, ranging easily from *The Faerie Queene* to *The Newgate Calendar*. When he was fourteen, Hawthorne proceeded to less literary adventures, and spent a year in the deep seclusion of the Maine woods along Lake Sebago. "It was there," he later declared, "I got my cursed habits of solitude." At the time he took a keen and wild delight in his exposure to the forest, which eventually played a larger part in his imaginative life than the sea which his fathers had followed and to which he himself at first wanted to go. He spent four years at Bowdoin College, which was then scarcely more than a clearing on the edge of the frontier, although it was also an average country college for the day and included among its students, besides Hawthorne and his particular friend Horatio Bridge, a future president and a future poet— Franklin Pierce and Longfellow. After graduation in 1825 Hawthorne returned to Salem not yet finally decided upon a profession but evidently with a stronger drift, perhaps even a stronger determination, toward authorship than he was accustomed to admit.

The records of his life between this and the appearance of *Twice-Told Tales* (1837) are dusky and brief. His mother, since her widowhood in 1808, had lived in a rigid seclusion which naturally influenced the entire family, confirming in her son an original bent. "I had very few acquaintances in Salem," he afterward said, "and during the nine or ten years that I spent there, in this solitary way, I doubt whether so much as twenty people in the town were aware of my existence." He rarely left the house except by twilight, but endlessly read and reflected, instructing himself in the dim Puritan past and absorbing into his imagination the residuum of its spirit, even while he grew increasingly critical of its doctrines. The gestures of sentimental asceticism with which the hero of his first book, the smooth but undistinguished *Fanshawe* (1828), in the conclusion waves aside a proposal of marriage from the heroine only himself to die interestingly of consumption within two paragraphs, could have come naturally from Hawthorne's pen during but an inconsiderable period, for though solitary he was not morbid, and he developed in the grave sunniness of his temper as clearly as in any other quality he possessed. Viewing the matter subsequently, when love and ambition had plucked him from his first solitude, he did not disapprove of it; "if I had sooner made my escape into the world, I should have grown hard and rough, and been covered with earthly dust, and my heart might have become callous by rude encounters with the multitude. . . . But living in solitude till the fulness of time was come, I still kept the dew of my youth with the freshness of my heart." From a less genuine man this would sound priggish enough. Hawthorne held aloof not because he thought himself too precious or merely because he knew himself too shy for general society, but in part also because of an opinion which governed his early behavior as an artist. "I used to think I could imagine all passions, all feelings, and states of the heart and mind." So competent was his imagination to interest and sustain him, so pervasive if not powerful, in its silent way so full of vitality, that he did not starve during his twelve lonely years but gradually ripened into a spirit that was no less strong than tender, no less sane than original, no less massive and secure than delicate and sympathetic.

Nor must his imagination be thought of as feeding solely

(60)

upon itself. At least once a year it was his habit to rouse himself for a season and make excursions here and there through his native section, an alert and observant traveler. The journal which he regularly kept and various of his tales and sketches bear witness to these journeys. The White Mountains are the scene of *The Great Carbuncle* and *The Ambitious Guest*; somewhere north of Boston Hawthorne laid the meeting genially recorded in *The Seven Vagabonds*; at Martha's Vineyard he met the village sculptor of *Chippings with a Chisel*; upon a visit to the Shaker community at Canterbury, New Hampshire, he based *The Canterbury Pilgrims* and *The Shaker Bridal*, though the action of the latter story takes place elsewhere; the shaggy flanks of Greylock in the Berkshires furnish the wild setting for the wilder story of *Ethan Brand*; and in other sketches and journal entries Hawthorne wrote of other regions in Vermont and Connecticut and New York to which he wandered, once as far as to Niagara and possibly still farther to Detroit. In none of these does there appear that elaboration of local color which was to characterize American short stories a generation or so later, but neither was Hawthorne inattentive to the outward manners of his age. He is a prime source for modern knowledge of them. Somewhat unexpectedly, he had a decided taste for the low life which he encountered, for peddlers, drovers, tawdry hawkers of amusement, stage-agents, and tavern-haunters. Fielding would have known them better, but Hawthorne knew them.

At the same time he invaded the past of New England, hunting for pictures with which to enlarge his consciousness of that age. From the very first, as in his sketches of Sir William Phips and Mrs. Hutchinson, he neglected analysis or historical narrative for the sake of constructing definite little scenes out of this material. "And now, having arranged these preliminaries," he says after two or three pages, "we shall attempt to picture forth a day of Sir William's life."

And similarly after the briefest discussion of Mrs. Hutchinson: "We shall endeavor to give a more practical idea of this part of her course": a crisp little vignette of the trial. To the end of Hawthorne's apprenticeship this was his historical method, perhaps best displayed in the vivid and diversified panorama of Salem, from its founding to the present, which he set forth in *Main Street*. He was not content to represent scenes for themselves, but sought assiduously for moments of drama, little episodes of controversy, clashes between the parties and ideas which divided old New England. In *The Gentle Boy* he exhibited the tragedy of the Quaker persecutions; in *The Gray Champion* the spirit of the Settlement flashing out against the aggressions of Governor Andros; in *The Maypole of Merry Mount* the conflict between the Pilgrims and the Merry Mounters, which Hawthorne deliberately symbolized. "The future complexion of New England was involved in this important quarrel. Should the grizzly saints establish their jurisdiction over the gay sinners, then would their spirits darken all the clime, and make it a land of clouded visages, of hard toil, of sermon and psalm forever. But should the banner staff of Merry Mount be fortunate, sunshine would break upon the hills, and flowers would beautify the forest, and late posterity do homage to the Maypole." To compare a tale like *The Canterbury Pilgrims*, a simple though significant description of the meeting of certain persons going to join a Shaker community and certain others just leaving it, with *Young Goodman Brown*, the somber account of how a witches' sabbath in the dark woods around early Salem tempted an honest man from his duty and his peace of mind, is to discover with what poise Hawthorne stood at the center of his world and sent his imagination out on subtle errands equally into the past and the present, exploring everywhere, and with accurate instinct seizing upon the matters which were proper to his art.

Both these last-named stories are concerned with a theme

which Hawthorne touched again and again and which rose from a deep inner experience: the conflict in a soul between the pride which would contract it to harsh and narrow limits and the affections which would reach out and bind it to the natural society of its kind. It is the theme also of *Wakefield*, *Rappaccini's Daughter*, *The Artist of the Beautiful*, and *Ethan Brand*, as well as many others. Always Hawthorne stands with society and sunshine against pride and gloom. Much as he had inherited from his Puritan ancestors of the knowledge of the secret heart, which in New England, from once seeking incessantly within itself for signs of a light from God, had formed habits of dwelling too constantly there; and much as he employed the secrets he had found in his own buried researches, Hawthorne was little of a Puritan. His sympathies in the historical tales are steadily with the radical movements away from the domination of the straiter sects, and in his contemporary pieces he regularly demolishes the austerities which had come down from the Fathers. In all his tales he is nowhere more engaging than in *The Seven Vagabonds*, wherein he—or the teller of the story—falls in with a chance assembly of traveling entertainers, the minstrels and jongleurs of New England, and plans to accompany them as a sort of peripatetic novelist. This is a conception of Hawthorne amazingly unlike that which sees him as a reflective owl blinking in his dingy garret, but it is not far from the conception of himself which he more than once cherished, and which he embodied in his original scheme for *Twice-Told Tales*. This collection he wanted to call *The Story-Teller* and to present as a series of narratives in a framework describing the adventures and observations of just such a novelist errant on his varied rounds. The publisher would not agree; the tales appeared without the framework in 1837, Horatio Bridge having guaranteed the expenses; and Hawthorne came promptly into a small but gratifying reputation decisively helped by approving reviews from Longfellow and, a little later, from Poe.

That he had heretofore been, as he not quite correctly said, "the obscurest man of letters in America," elicits the less complaint over the blindness of his contemporaries since he had worn anonymity as a regular garment and had addressed the public, for the most part, from the pages of very modest magazines or annuals among the dying birds and weeping willows which made up the fauna and flora of those periodicals in that period. A touch of fame stirred him to rather greater activity; and he was stirred still more by falling in love, very soon after the publication of his book, with Sophia Amelia Peabody, whom he married in 1842 and with whom he subsequently led a life of exquisite felicity. "We are but shadows," he wrote during his engagement; "we are not endowed with real life, and all that seems most real about us is but the thinnest substance of a dream,—till the heart be touched. That touch creates us,—then we begin to be,—thereby we are beings of reality and inheritors of eternity." Now he so far emerged from his solitude as to look about for some livelihood which would make marriage possible. Appointed by George Bancroft to be weigher and gauger at the Boston Custom House early in 1839, he served there two years and then entered the community at Brook Farm, not because he was a communist or a transcendentalist but because he was a lover who hoped that the experiment would help him to become a husband. A year sufficed to make it plain that his art could not flourish under such conditions. He left Brook Farm, issued a second series (1842) of *Twice-Told Tales*, was married, and went to live at the Old Manse in Concord, in the neighborhood of Emerson and Thoreau. There Hawthorne lived for three years, until he returned to Salem as surveyor of the Custom House for three years more; in Concord he wrote, beside certain hack pieces, the *Mosses from an Old Manse* (1846); there he rounded out his years of preparation for the greater novels.

The differences between the *Twice-Told Tales* and the *Mosses* are not important, nor are the stories of the later collection always later in composition, but it should at least be noted that whereas the *Tales* contains a larger number of vivid pictures from past or present, the range of the *Mosses* is on the whole the greater. Here may be found those profound studies of conscience, *Young Goodman Brown*, *Rappaccini's Daughter*, *The Christmas Banquet*, and *Roger Malvin's Burial*; while side by side with them are smiling and elusive exercises of Hawthorne's fancy, *The Celestial Railroad* and *Feathertop*. *Rappaccini's Daughter* is longer than any tale Hawthorne had written since *The Gentle Boy* a dozen years before; the average sketch or story in the *Mosses* is nearly twice as long as in the *Tales*; and here, moreover, may be found all of those singular narratives—*A Select Party*, *The Hall of Fantasy*, *The Procession of Life*, *The New Adam and Eve*, *The Intelligence Office*, *Earth's Holocaust*, *A Virtuoso's Collection*—written between 1842 and 1844 in which Hawthorne assembles upon some fanciful scheme a gallery of personages or symbols or ideas among which he moves as showman or spectator commenting upon the varieties of life and legend. Perhaps without being aware of it he was growing ready for larger flights and a wider scene. At the same time he imparts an artful unity to the *Mosses* by the preface which conducts to the stories as an avenue of trees conducts to the Old Manse itself and which concentrates attention upon his themes as the cylinder of a telescope concentrates attention upon the object covered by the lens.

A similar function is performed for *The Scarlet Letter*, written in Salem during the winter of 1849-50, by the introductory essay on the Custom House where Hawthorne had recently, as he thought, been wasting his time. The essay understandably surprised his late associates, who, though the gravest of citizens, learned now that they had been for Hawthorne little more than the characters of a farce; and it still surprises those of his readers who, knowing his reputation better than his veritable self, find in it a humor so chuckling, an eye for personal traits so sharp, a hand so deft at whimsical caricature, an intelligence so shrewd in its grasp of concrete realities. It was not for lack of talent in that direction that Hawthorne overlooked the surfaces of life; it was for lack of interest in matters not central to the serious concerns of the soul. In being a Puritan to the extent that he rarely lifted his gaze from the human spirit in its sincerest hours, he was also a universal poet. He who during a long experimental stage had brooded over the confused spectacle of mankind, posing for himself various of the soul's problems and translating them into lucid forms of beauty, had now posed a larger problem on a larger scale. To make a novel out of his material instead of a brief tale Hawthorne did not increase it, as he might have done, out of his antiquarian knowledge of early Salem: as regards such decorations his story is almost naked. Nor did he increase it by adding to his cast of characters: he need not have named, he need hardly have referred to, others than the four who hold the tense center of his stage. Nor yet again did he increase it by any multiplication of events: few events and half a dozen acts suffice him. With an austere economy that must have seemed parsimony had Hawthorne's vision and his style been less rich, he discarded all but the essential cruxes of his argument. His tableaux succeed one another almost without the links of narrative which ordinarily distinguish the novel from the play; yet as the curtain dimly rises upon each new tableau there is the sense of something transacted since the last—a sense conveyed by subtle hints so numerous as to betray how much more Hawthorne knew about his characters than he had space to put into words. With the same parsimony he narrows the physical bounds of his action to a little strip of seacoast between the Atlantic which signifies all the memories of Salem and the forest which spells its obstinate expectations. Only supreme skill could have exhibited within these limits the seven years of action which have to seem at once long enough to constitute a cycle of penance and brief enough to present a drama of which all the parts knit solidly together under the spectator's eye. Something more than mere technical devices, however, rounds out and compacts the story—something more than the scrupulous disposition of tableaux and the recurrence of that overshadowing symbol which is sewed upon Hester's bosom and burned upon Dimmesdale's; which is significantly and exquisitely woven into Pearl's very nature, and which, rather too artificially, is once blazoned upon the sky. Hawthorne gives every evidence of having moved through his first and greatest long romance with an unfaltering stride, never obliged to consider how he should construct because the story grew almost of itself, and never at a loss for substance because his mind was perfectly stored—neither too much nor too little—with the finest materials of observation and reflection gathered during a lifetime. For three years he had written almost nothing; now all the power that he had unconsciously hoarded freed itself and flowed into his book; now all the quarter-century of discipline in form and texture effortlessly shaped an abundant flood.

The historian should not hint at too much that is merely mystical in the making of *The Scarlet Letter*; it is an achievement of deliberate art grown competent and unconscious by careful exercise. At the same time, the impact which the story makes may be traced back of Hawthorne's own art and personality to the Puritan tradition which, much as he might disagree with it on occasion, he had none the less inherited. An ancestral strain accounts for this conception of adultery as an affair not of the civil order but of the immortal soul. The same strain in his constitution, moreover, led him to make of these circumstances more than the familiar triangle. A Frenchman might have painted the joy of Dimmesdale, the lover, with his forbidden mistress; an Italian might have traced the fierce course of Chillingworth, the husband, to a justified revenge; a German might have exhibited Hester, the offending wife, as actually achieving an outer freedom to match that one within. Hawthorne transfers the action to an entirely different plane. Let the persons in the triple conflict be involved as they may with one another, each of them stands essentially apart from the remaining two, because each is occupied with a still vaster conflict, with good and evil as the rival elements which continually tug at the poor human creature. Small wonder, then, that the flesh, to which the sin was superficially due, should go unsung; that the bliss of the senses should hardly once be alluded to. After such fleeting pleasures comes the inexorable judgment, which is of the spirit not of the body. To the Puritan imagination, journeys begin not end in lovers meeting. The tragedy of Dimmesdale lies in his defeat by evil through the temptation of cowardice and hypocrisy, which are sins. Chillingworth tragically, and sinfully, chooses evil when he decides to take a treacherous vengeance into his own hands, though vengeance, he knows, is another's. Hester alone emerges from her guilt through her public expiation and the long practice of virtue afterward.

So far *The Scarlet Letter* agrees with the doctrines of the Puritans. Its broader implications critically transcend them. In what dark slumber during these seven years has that Jehovah wrapped himself whom the elder Puritans invoked day and night about all their business, praying for the remission of sins through the merciful affection of his son? What prayers go up? Who counts upon the treasury of grace from which any sinner might hope to obtain salvation if his repentance were only sore enough? The theology which for seventeenth-century men was almost as real as religion itself had come to be for their descendant no more authoritative than some remote mythology except as it shadowed forth a cosmic and moral order which Hawthorne had himself observed. In one respect he seems sterner than the elder Puritans, for he admits into his narrative no hope of any providential intervention which might set these jangled bells again into accord. Dimmesdale will not encourage Hester to hope for a compensating future life even. The consequences of deeds live forever. At the same time Hawthorne has drawn the action down from heaven's pavement, where Milton would have conducted it, to earth and has humanized it to the extent that he centers it in human bosoms. The newest schools of psychology cannot object to a reading of sin which shows Dimmesdale and Chillingworth as the victims of instincts and antipathies which fester because unnaturally repressed while Hester Prynne is cleansed through the discovery of her offense and grows healthier by her confession. All the Christian centuries have known the truth here represented. But only certain of those centuries—and not the Puritan seventeenth—have been capable of viewing love as Hawthorne views it and unfolds its tragedy. To the actual contemporaries of Hester and Dimmesdale it would have seemed a blasphemy worse than adultery for the lovers to agree, in their meeting at the brookside, that "what we did had a consecration of its own." These are Hester's words, and so it was to Hester that eventually "it seemed a fouler offense committed by Roger Chillingworth, than any which had since been done him, that, in the time when her heart knew no better, he had persuaded her to fancy herself happy by his side." Hester thus becomes the type—subtly individualized but yet a type— of the moving principle of life which different societies in different ways may constrain but which in itself irresistibly endures. She feels the ignominy which attends her own irregular behavior and accepts her fate as the reward of evil, but she does not understand it so far as to wish uncommitted the act which her society calls a sin. A harder woman might have become an active rebel; a softer woman might have sunk passively down into unavailing penitence. Hester stands erect, and thinks. She asks herself whether woman, as life was constituted, could be really happy, even the happiest woman. "As concerned her own individual existence, she had long ago decided in the negative, and dismissed the point as settled." Yet her mind, though dismissing her particular case as a malady without a cure, still ranges the universe for some cure for the injustice her sex inherits. "The world's law was no law for her mind." In this manner those whom the world crushes always take their surest revenge. Hester finds no speculative answer; and so she turns to action, plays her necessary part, and gives herself to the nurture of her child, no less a mother than if approved by every human ordinance. She was the first important heroine in the American novel, which had neglected women, laughed at them, sentimentalized them, but never profoundly thought about them or greatly imagined any woman. New England had had no fatal Helens or glamorous Ninons, nor had it admiringly invented them. Hester is already a mother when she first appears, and an outlaw. But in the midst of austere Salem she has such radiance of beauty and magnificence of nature that she grows there till she cracks the stiff frame of the age's code.

Against a background so somber all the more do the fantastic elements stand out. They are summed up in the crimson brand which Hester wears as the statutory label of her offense but which she embroiders and illuminates until it is a token of the "rich, voluptuous, Oriental" luxuriance of her spirit. The idea of such a label and its consequences for the wearer had long haunted Hawthorne, at least since he introduced it in 1837 into his story of *Endicott and the Red Cross*. It haunted him, indeed, so impressively at last as now and then almost to detach itself from the matter symbolized and to assume an entity of its own—a kind of frozen fancy. What saved Hawthorne here was his felicitous conception of Pearl, the child of such wayward passion and defiant tenderness, as a reality sprung from a symbol, as the scarlet letter incarnate. Of this little creature, all brilliance and beauty yet all caprice and unaccountability, Hester "felt like one who has evoked a spirit, but, by some irregularity in the process of conjuration, has failed to win the master-word that should control this new and incomprehensible intelligence." Pearl lends this story its note of exquisiteness: she is the light that flashes across the gloom, the color that warms the sober tapestry, the wings that wake the scene when intensity has arrested movement. Nothing better than the figure of Pearl illustrates the intimate connection between Hawthorne's most delicate fancy and the closely scrutinized actuality upon which he founded his art. When he shaped her he must have been thinking constantly of his little daughter Una, who during the composition of the book, while his mother lay dying in his house, frolicked before his eyes like a bright fairy at the doors of a tomb. It was of Pearl that he says: "Hester could not help questioning, at such moments, whether Pearl were a human child. She seemed rather an airy sprite, which, after playing its fantastic sports for awhile upon the cottage floor, would flit away with a mocking smile." It was of Una at nearly the same time that Hawthorne wrote in his diary, among many other comments which suggest the qualities of Pearl: "there is something that almost frightens me about the child,—I know not whether elfish or angelic, but, at all events, supernatural. She steps so boldly into the midst of everything, shrinks from nothing, has such a comprehension of everything, seems at times to have but little delicacy, and anon shows that she possesses the finest essence of it,—now so hard, now so tender; now so perfectly unreasonable, soon again so wise. In short, I now and then catch an aspect of her in which I cannot believe her to be my own human child, but a spirit strangely mingled with good and evil, haunting the house where I dwell."

The Scarlet Letter was an immediate success. Hawthorne's fame was henceforth assured, and it helped stir him during the next three years to an activity he had never shown before.

In the summer of 1850 he went to the Berkshire village of Lenox, where Herman Melville was his neighbor. That fall Hawthorne began *The House of the Seven Gables*, completed and published early in the following year. In 1851 he wrote *A Wonder-Book for Girls and Boys* (1852) and collected various scattered pieces in *The Snow-Image, and Other Twice-Told Tales* (1852); that winter, now removed to West Newton, he produced *The Blithedale Romance* (1852); the next summer, finally established at The Wayside, a house he had bought in Concord, he wrote his campaign *Life of Franklin Pierce* (1852), then candidate for the presidency; and in the winter of 1852-53, his *Tanglewood Tales* (1853), completed just before he left for England, where upon Pierce's grateful appointment he was to be United States consul at Liverpool. The life of Pierce was written out of friendship but against the grain, since Hawthorne had almost no interest in politics. The *Wonder-Book* and *Tanglewood Tales*, with their versions of Greek myths quaintly medievalized and gently Puritanized by a passage through Hawthorne's imagination, in becoming unchallenged classics for all children have perpetuated the grace of his attitude toward his own and continue to exhale the light and sweetness which Hawthorne seems to have distilled into them in the sunny intervals between his profounder studies of these years. The *Snow-Image* volume, besides earlier writings some of great merit and some of little, boasts in the title story, *The Great Stone Face*, and *Ethan Brand*, three late tales that are among his best. The most considerable achievement of the period, however, is of course the two novels, *The House of the Seven Gables* and *The Blithedale Romance*.

Writing in the preface to the first of these Hawthorne distinguished between the Romance and the Novel. "The latter form of composition is presumed to aim at a very minute fidelity, not merely to the possible, but to the probable and ordinary course of man's experience. The former—

while, as a work of art, it must rigidly subject itself to laws, and while it sins unpardonably so far as it may swerve aside from the truth of the human heart—has fairly a right to present that truth under circumstances, to a great extent of the writer's own choosing or creation. If he think fit, also, he may so manage his atmospherical medium as to bring out or mellow the lights and deepen and enrich the shadows of the picture." Hawthorne, who called *The House of the Seven Gables* a Romance, assumed the full license to which he thought himself entitled, but it is with respect to the "atmospherical medium" that his powers were most successfully employed. If *The Scarlet Letter* springs from the faculty which had earlier created *Young Goodman Brown* and *Rappaccini's Daughter* and *Ethan Brand*, *The House of the Seven Gables* springs from the descriptive faculty which had set down *The Seven Vagabonds* and *The Toll-Gatherer's Day* and *Main Street*. By some inexplicable alchemy practised upon color it multiplies and combines shades of gray until they become—if it is not too fanciful to say so—silver and rose, faded green and dull crimson. The House itself, though the brisk daily life of Salem swirls naturally about it, contrives to stand invested in a cloud of omen projected from the dusky interior which has been innocent of sunshine, physical or moral, for two centuries. Ghosts crowd it, the ghosts of extinct grandeurs which have left dim tokens in portraits and furnishings too valuable for the present fortunes of the Pyncheon stock, and yet fiercely cherished by old Hepzibah, whose pride is a token hardly less dim. All the elements of the story center in these dusky chambers: the ancestral curse upon the founder, the treasure hidden in some forgotten cranny, the faded old brother and sister who when they try to escape are drawn irresistibly back, even the antique and hereditary flowers in the garden and the almost exanimate poultry whose queer, rusty, withered aspect parallels somewhat oversignificantly the appearance of their human owners. The

(73)

groundwork of this narrative is more richly woven than that of *The Scarlet Letter*, more full of details which Hawthorne had personally observed, but in picture and atmosphere it is no less finely unified.

The characters and action suffer a little from the perfection of the background. At certain moments they fade into it and grow indistinct, like men speaking out of dark corners in muted voices. When Hepzibah ventures so far from the recesses of the Pyncheon pride as to begin keeping her poor little shop, the light strikes her and she becomes pathetically real, and again when she puts forth her timid efforts to cheer her brother; but most of the time she is half hidden against the background. So with Clifford, who actually first appears in a darkened room which he has not been seen to enter and who continues to inhabit shadows. It is because of the particularly withered look of these older Pyncheons and of the house which becomes them that Phœbe shines, rather than because of any superlative vitality in herself. Externally the most natural of Hawthorne's women, she proves upon analysis to be scarcely more than a pleasant young girl deliberately introduced for the sake of contrast. The same purpose accounts for the daguerreotypist Holgrave, who in a rented gable of the old mansion nurses opinions which challenge the authority of the past here lying so heavily upon the present. What Phœbe personifies Holgrave argues: the need and right of living beings to throw off the burdens they inherit; but Phœbe has only the instincts of youth and Holgrave argues without activity. Their marriage at the end, while promising a renewal of energy for two decaying stocks, does not contradict the moral which Hawthorne had in mind: "the truth, namely, that the wrong-doing of one generation lives into the successive ones, and, divesting itself of every temporary advantage, becomes a pure and uncontrollable mischief." Clifford by his unjust imprisonment has been broken in mind and body until even his former love of beauty has turned to a sporadic gluttony, and Hepzibah has wasted her whole life waiting in poverty for her brother's release. Nothing now can recompense them for what they have lost; in them the moral sternly and veraciously shows its head. Elsewhere, however, the tragedy wears thinner. Judge Pyncheon, who has oppressed his kinsfolk and falls himself under the family curse, belongs too much to the stage—or to Dickens. The curse hangs vaguely over the action, a part of the house's furniture, an element thickening the shadow, but still a thing with little life apart from that preserved by the Pyncheon belief—and pride—in it. As in *The Scarlet Letter* the implications frequently go beyond the doctrine, so in *The House of the Seven Gables* the picture, with its softness of texture and depth of atmosphere, frequently overpowers the argument. The picture is the memorable aspect of the book.

Of *The Blithedale Romance* Hawthorne declared that he had "occasionally availed himself of his actual reminiscences" of Brook Farm—"essentially a day-dream, and yet a fact"—"merely to establish a theatre, a little removed from the highway of ordinary travel, where the creatures of his brain may play their phantasmagorical antics without exposing them to too close a comparison with the actual events of real lives." The personages of his romance he said were all imaginary. Conjecture has persisted in identifying Zenobia with Margaret Fuller and Miles Coverdale with Hawthorne himself; and research, since the publication of various portions of Hawthorne's diary, has found numerous sources for *Blithedale*, such as the masquerade in the woods, which actually occurred at Brook Farm, the little seamstress there from Boston, whose appearance must have suggested Priscilla's, and the woman drowned at Concord in 1843, whose fate is known to have suggested that of Zenobia. These, and many other items of actuality which might be added, are all subordinated to the central invention, enough so that in spite of them the romance has often been called the most shadowy Hawthorne ever wrote. But William Dean Howells preferred *The Blithedale Romance* to the others, and Henry James thought it "the lightest, the brightest, the liveliest" of them all. It lacks any such mastering theme as that in *The Scarlet Letter*, or any such brocaded vestures as is worn by *The House of the Seven Gables*. Its particular excellence must be looked for in a touching charm that springs from the very tenuousness of its substance—a tenuousness greater than life's even when Hawthorne was writing about matters he had seen with his physical eye, because the entire action of the novel is represented through the medium of its narrator, Coverdale the minor poet, who daintily eyes the moving world without ever coming close to it. Because Coverdale has no means of knowing all the history of the principal characters, Hawthorne waives the right of omniscience and omits certain hidden motives and submerged links of the story. Coverdale, too, being in love with Priscilla, suffers the confusion and limitation of vision natural to his state. While Hawthorne doubtless did not calculate all the consequences of his device, he was enough of a dramatist to incur them. The story flickers, lightens up, broadens, deepens, contracts, almost disappears, flares forth again, as it would have done in the perceptions of a real Coverdale; and the whole is seen through a misty illusion comparable in effect to those curtains of gauze let down at theaters to soften a scene. Through that wavering veil Coverdale sees enacted, against scenery which truthfully represents a community like Brook Farm, the tragedy of Hollingsworth the philanthropist and the two women who interrupt his career to love him. Through the figure of Hollingsworth project some of the bones of Hawthorne's reasoning; the man who blindly sacrifices actual hearts for an abstract cause is himself here something of an abstraction, though he eventually recognizes his fault with a human sincerity. Priscilla, outwardly so visible because so closely studied from the little seamstress at Brook Farm, is never quite impressive; she has been refined to a point which brings her too near the bloodless decorum of her decade. It is in Zenobia that the rather wintry senses of Coverdale—and readers of all degrees of vitality after him—detect the fullest flood of life, fire and color, passion and experience. Hester Prynne had been of this stature. Both of them come into Hawthorne's New England from other regions; both to be gorgeous have to be exotic. This may perhaps be taken as his tacit accusation that magnificence of personality did not ripen on the rock-bound coast. At least his imagination had gone out and found abundance and ripeness where they dwelt.

The seven years which Hawthorne spent in Europe removed him for the first time from the village atmosphere which—except in his imagination—was all he had known heretofore. His journals in England, France, and Italy throw quite as much light backward upon his earlier days as upon those of which he sedulously records the very modest happenings. A man of genius, already a classic, nearly fifty years old when he left America, he had yet to make his acquaintance with architecture, music, painting, and sculpture on their native ground, had yet to study the remains of great antiquity or to encounter a brilliant society. Any such society he conspicuously missed; he met few men of letters of real distinction; and he never felt more at home than among the other American and British expatriates in Florence. With the eagerness of a very young American he tasted the delights of antiquity in the routine quarters. With the patience of a man long withheld from masterpieces he gorged cathedrals and galleries. Very often he was bored. At the end of his journey he could still seriously condemn the representation of the nude in art. But his consistent provincialism is saved from being disagreeable by his exquisite honesty. What far smaller men learn early Hawthorne was learning late, but he gave himself without stealth or affectation to the task of mastering a new world, as observant, sensitive, and masculine in spirit as he had been in familiar New England. How good his temper was in the new circumstances appears from *Our Old Home* (1863), an account of his English stay subsequently refined from his English note-books: a book both beautiful and shrewd and nicely touched with international satire. A still more eminent, though hardly a more characteristic, product of his European experience was the romance which he himself always thought his best: *The Marble Faun*, begun at Rome in 1859 and finished the next year in England.

The established comment on *The Marble Faun* says that it is a guidebook to Rome—the Rome, of course, of the tourist who studies the city as a glorious mausoleum without much attention to the living inhabitants unless they appear in carnival or procession. Learning and observation went into the rich, smooth, trustworthy, and often penetrating descriptions which adorn the tale, but the atmosphere lacks the golden depth and substantial intimacy which Hawthorne had caught for *The House of the Seven Gables*. Though the Rome he saw was older than his Salem by millenniums to centuries, he had lived more years in Salem than months in Rome. The sole new quality he could impart to his Italian romance was the sense of crowds of people filling the scene, constantly stirring in variegated abundance, and providing a new privacy in the midst of which his important characters might take refuge. From these crowds the atmosphere derives more density than from the works of art and the landscapes, which just miss overloading the narrative. It is perhaps the best proof of Hawthorne's capaciousness of mind that he could have admitted so much still life into his action without confusing it. Elaborate as the background is, and stiff and difficult as it must have been to handle, the few essential persons of the drama move as freely and naturally as in the earlier novels with their almost empty stages.

The idea of the romance occurred to Hawthorne when he first saw the Faun of Praxiteles in the gallery at the Capitol and thought "that a story, with all sorts of fun and pathos in it, might be contrived on the idea of [the faun's] species having become intermingled with the human race; a family with the faun blood in them having prolonged itself from the classic era till our own days." Originally struck, it seems by the fanciful possibilities of his theme, Hawthorne afterward deepened it into another Paradise Lost—of a sort. Donatello, descendant of a faun and in spite of centuries of intermixture almost a faun himself, through sin estranges himself from his careless Eden and enters the human fraternity of guilt in the companionship of the more experienced Miriam, on whose behalf he sins, and who, by not preventing him, sins with him. Having thus shared a sin they find themselves indissolubly married by its spiritual consequences, whatever their outer fortunes may be. An accidental witness of the murder, Hilda, whose conscience grew in New England, in another degree also acquires the responsibility, which tortures her until she rises above her Puritan prejudices to a universal mood and unburdens herself at the confessional which her own creed has disallowed. The fourth character, Kenyon, has only technical duties to perform; to be a chorus in some scenes and a not-too-impassioned witness in others, and to marry Hilda at the end. *The Marble Faun*, though twice as long as *The Scarlet Letter*, has an equal unity—if not an equal depth—of tone and a still higher concentration of events. Donatello from his ancestral tower among the Apennines and Miriam and Hilda and Kenyon from their several birthplaces, their previous lives only hinted at, come together in the easy society of Rome, where the tragedy overtakes them. They act it with the swiftness of drama and then vanish, going as mysteriously as they came, so mysteriously as to vex all but those readers who are competent to perceive how much the strength of the central impression depends upon the obscurity which hides the past and future of the characters.

Though set in an environment so amply pagan and Catholic, *The Marble Faun* is in some respects the most Puritan of all Hawthorne's romances. He who in New England had created Hester and Zenobia, when he came to a world in which they and their kind might have grown to their intended stature, seems to have turned partially back to an austerer code. Among the children of the Renaissance he missed that sense of sin which in his native province had been as regularly present as sea and hills. Genial as were the pagan survivals in this many-stranded city, cheerful as were the Roman Christians, light-hearted as were the artists, Hawthorne's imagination would not expand unreservedly. It asked itself what would happen if sin and conscience should invade these charming precincts. Once more pagan than the Puritans, he was now more Puritan than the pagans. He would not let even Donatello play forever, believing that as generous youth died out of the faun he would "become sensual, addicted to gross pleasures, heavy, unsympathizing, and insulated within the narrow limits of a surly selfishness." There is more than Puritanism in such a prophecy. There is more than Puritanism in the speculation of Kenyon, which shocks Hilda but which touches the theme very sharply: "Sin has educated Donatello, and elevated him. Is sin, then, . . . like sorrow, merely an element of human education, through which we struggle to a higher and purer state than we could otherwise have attained?" This is almost as much as to wonder whether experience itself, evil as well as good, does not civilize us, as it civilized Donatello. Hawthorne's language is the language of sin and conscience which he had inherited, but here as in all his romances lurk certain questions the answers to which conduct to the most spacious regions of morals and imagination.

From his return in 1860 to his death four years later Hawthorne accomplished no remarkable work except *Our Old Home*. Another theme for romance constantly tempted him, or rather, two: the idea of an elixir of life and that of the return to England of an American heir to some hereditary estate; but though he experimented with them in four fragments, *The Ancestral Footstep, Septimius Felton, Dr. Grimshawe's Secret,* and *The Dolliver Romance,* Hawthorne could not fuse or complete them. Not only had the Civil War fatally interrupted his reflections but his imagination was dissolving, his vitality breaking up, along with the New England era of which he had been, among its romancers, the consummate flower. Had he survived he must have seemed an outlived figure in a community which after the war turned its eyes increasingly to Europe and to the American West, through emigration losing its compact strength, and as a result of larger connections with the rest of the world losing its stout old self-sufficiency. Although *The House of the Seven Gables* points forward to a whole school of prose elegists recording the New England decline, Hawthorne himself wrote while his corner of the country was still thriving and busy. Among men confident of the future of New England he could survey its past without the sense that life about him had diminished and so could utilize it without clutching it too closely as a compensation for the present. But though New England was still strong, it had softened its former iron theology to a more endurable set of beliefs and under the kind uses of prosperity had considerably enriched its life with secular culture. And yet so recent were the fires of that passion which had refined the spirit of the elder Puritans that the spirit of their descendants was still fine, though in a new way. In all but the sturdiest this modern spirit tended to be thin, frail, flat, merely a gentility of the intellect and disposition. Hawthorne was of the sturdiest. To a full heritage of the traditional inwardness he added wide reading and wide speculation and not a little observation of the color and costume of his province; he had talked with vagabonds and lived with transcendentalists. Of the little group at Concord—Hawthorne, Thoreau, Emerson—which with the passage of time stands up so unmistakably above the Long-fellows and Lowells and Holmeses of the Cambridge-Boston tradition, Emerson enunciated a larger diversity of maxims, and Thoreau most vividly lived the Yankee life; but Hawthorne alone shaped the stuff of his meditations into visible forms and living creatures.

Thus he may be said to sum up and body forth the inner vision of his age and section so far as that was done by any imaginative writer. What he insufficiently reflects is the homelier, coarser qualities of New England: its tough rustic fiber, its hickory-hearted endurance, its canniness yoked with dreams, its dry, knowing humor, its crackling dialect, its home-bred complacency, the fearful silence and obstinacy of which it is capable when crossed too long, the potentialities within it of degenerating when the stronger impulses weaken. Such of these as were surface matters Hawthorne eschewed as merely so much dialect—things not essential to the heart of his investigations. He took them for granted, without comment, and went deeper. In a world, he asked himself, where human instincts are continually at war with human laws, and where laws, once broken, pursue the offender even more fiercely than they hedged him before, how are any but the more docile spirits to hold their course without calamity? The Puritan Fathers at the same inquiry, which they asked hardly more frequently than Hawthorne, could point in answer to election and atonement and divine grace. Hawthorne had inherited the old questions but not the old answers. He did not free himself from the Puritan mode of believing that to break a law is to commit a sin, or that to commit a sin is to play havoc with the soul; but he changed the terms and considered the sin as a violation less of some supernatural law than of the natural integrity of the soul. Whereas another romancer by tracking the course of the instincts which lead to what is called sin might have sought to justify them as native to the offender and so inescapable,

(82)

Hawthorne accepts sin without a question and studies the consequences: in the souls of Hester and Dimmesdale, who sinned through love; of Chillingworth, who sinned through malice; of Judge Pyncheon, who sinned through covetousness; of Hollingsworth, who sinned through pride; of Donatello, who sinned, one may say, through chivalry; of Miriam, who sinned through the passion to escape her past; and of Pearl and Hepzibah and Clifford and Zenobia and Hilda, who are only the victims of sin in others. Although Hawthorne of course touches other themes than the consequences of sin, he touched it most importantly. He brought to his representation of the theme sanity without cynicism and tenderness without softness; he brought also, what is rarer than depth of moralism, an art finely rounded, a rich, graceful style, a spirit sweet and clear. He found a substance apparently as unpromising as the original soil upon which the Pilgrims established their commonwealth, and no less than they with their stony province he tamed and civilized it— going beyond them, moreover, by lifting it into enduring loveliness.

V

HERMAN MELVILLE

OUTWARDLY THE romances of Herman Melville were concerned with adventure in remote places, but he stood aside from his adventurous contemporaries, and has come—with Thoreau and Whitman—to stand above them all, by reason of his bold and energetic speculations and a style which is at once lofty and witty. Grandson of the picturesque old Boston conservative about whom Holmes wrote *The Last Leaf,* Melville was grandson also of a Revolutionary general of Dutch stock long settled in Albany. But Herman Melville's father, an unsuccessful merchant both in New York, where the son was born in 1819, and in Albany, died young and left his large family almost destitute. Herman Melville had only a brief schooling at the Albany Academy, tried his hand at clerkships, school-teaching, and living in the country with prosperous relatives, and at seventeen went as cabin-boy on a voyage to Liverpool. Restless at home, he found he had an instinct for the sea, as several of his kinsmen had had. After his return, and three more obscure years given in part to teaching and immature writing, he shipped early in 1841 on a whaler bound for the Pacific. Upon the experiences of that long, interrupted voyage his principal work is based. When the *Acushnet* after eighteen months reached the Marquesas Melville, tired of the hardships of whaling, escaped with a companion called Toby to the island of Nukuheva (Nukuhiva) and strayed into the cannibal valley of Typee (Taipi). There Melville spent perhaps four or five weeks, which he later represented as four months of indulgent captivity among the savages. Rescued, as he says, by an Australian whaler, Melville in Tahiti joined a mutiny, took once more to land, lived as a beachcomber in that and other islands of the Society group, and in 1843 had made his way to Honolulu, where he signed as ordinary seaman on the flagship *United States*. The frigate spent nearly a year in the Pacific and came around the Horn to Boston in October 1844. "Until I was twenty-five," Melville later told Hawthorne, "I had no development at all. From my twenty-fifth year I date my life." He quickly began to write, and in half a dozen years had published the four autobiographical books of his adventures: *Redburn* (1849), his voyage to Liverpool; *Typee* (1846), his days among the cannibals; *Omoo* (1847), his rovings as a beachcomber; *White Jacket* (1850), his service in the Navy.

The two which were first published had a hearty vogue and all were taken to have less fiction in them than they had. The English publisher of *Typee* believed it was pure fact, and many others ranked it with *Two Years Before the Mast* (1840) as a transcript from life. But Melville was a speculative romancer as well as a traveler. He fused his memories with his opinions and his wide reading, and enlarged or deleted as he liked. *Redburn* is possibly the nearest to a plain record. *White Jacket*, long thought to be that, now appears to have dealt freely with existence on a man-of-war, altering, elaborating, inventing. Neither book equals the *Typee-Omoo* pair in charm. *Typee* was the earliest romance dealing with the South Seas, since then made as familiar to novel readers as any exotic quarter of the globe. Merely as history the book has genuine value, with its sharp, sympathetic notes on Marquesan customs and its rich descriptions. It is, however, as fiction that *Typee* is usually read, as a romance of the life led by a civilized man in savage, exquisite surroundings. The valley of Typee becomes, in Melville's hands, a region of pleasant languors which stir the senses with the fragrance and color of the landscape and the gay beauty of the brown cannibal girls. While in his account of it he is shrewd and smiling, he valued that simple state of nature as much as he enjoyed it, and learned to think more highly of the human race than he ever had before. *Omoo* (the word is Polynesian for rover or beachcomber) carries Melville through still more cheerful vicissitudes to Tahiti; it is packed with activity and comedy. His racy sailors seem real, his consuls and vagabonds, and his irresponsible natives hovering between cannibalism and a half-comprehended Christianity. Melville's references to missionaries led to some controversy with members of their profession, and he was, indeed, caustic and contemptuous. The tale is dramatic; the teller had just emerged from a world of Edenic grace; and his recollection of the little world gave point to his judgments of the tawdry figures he met on the borders of civilization. Melville was something of a partisan of paradises, as *Typee* shows; but *Omoo* takes its quality, its keen edge, not so much from his satirical opinions as from the comic force with which he hits off the manners and persons of a heterogeneous community.

The charge that he had been writing romance led Melville to deserve the accusation deliberately, and he wrote *Mardi* (1849) which was romantic to the borders of chaos. As in *Typee*, two sailors escape from a whaling vessel in the Pacific and seek their fortune on the open sea, where they finally discover the mysterious archipelago of Mardi, a paradise which is more rich and sultry than the Marquesas and which becomes, as the story goes on, a wilderness of adventure and allegory. They encounter a magical white girl, Yillah, wander with her for a time, lose her, and spend the rest of the book in a blind search through the amazing archipelago. At one later point Mardi appears to signify the planet Earth. The seekers circumnavigate it, visiting its continents as Mardi's islands: Porpheero (Europe), Kolumbo (America both North and South), Orienda (Asia), and Hamora (Africa). Great Britain is Dominora, the United States is

Vivenza. There has been an uprising in Franko (France) which resembles that of 1848. Vivenza is troubled over slavery. The allegory is not so explicit as this for long, but becomes a transcendental hunt for perfect happiness and knowledge. Full of sumptuous inventions, it is a miscellany of ideas on countless themes. Occasional moods of satire bring realism into the narrative. The chapter Dedicated to the College of Physicians and Surgeons is one of the wittiest in English, that on Dreams one of the most beautiful. Again and again Melville achieves the epic prose of his later masterpiece. But this is epic prose without an epic story, and so is often hollow. Without a large, clear, powerful subject Melville with all his gifts could make no more of Mardi than a magnificent failure.

In *Redburn* the same year he was straightforward, and in *White Jacket* the next he kept within intelligible bounds, however much he poured a dramatic passion into his materials. In particular he stressed the cruelty of flogging, at a moment when there was a bill before Congress to abolish that punishment in the Navy. The tumult of his racing imagination did not too much disturb Melville's firm grasp of tangible human affairs. He was a man as well as a romancer. Married in 1847 to Elizabeth Shaw, daughter of the chief-justice of Massachusetts, Melville lived for nearly three years in New York, with a visit to London and Paris in the winter of 1849-50, and the following October established his family on a farm at Pittsfield, near Hawthorne who had recently come to live at Lenox, a few miles away. The two men became friends, but Melville did not find in Hawthorne the ardors he had expected. Hawthorne was fifteen years older, and serene in melancholy rather than violent in bitterness, as Melville was. Hawthorne at Lenox was writing *The House of the Seven Gables* while Melville at Pittsfield was writing *Moby Dick* (1851). "Shall I send you a fin of the *Whale* by way of a specimen mouthful?" Melville asked Hawthorne while his novel was in the press. "The tail is not yet cooked,

(87)

though the hell-fire in which the whole book is broiled might not unreasonably have cooked it before this. This is the book's motto (the secret one): *Ego non baptiso te in nomine*—but make out the rest yourself."

The substance of Melville's autobiographical narratives and the passion of *Mardi* met in *Moby Dick* to make it a masterpiece. The times were propitious for such an epic. The golden age of the whalers was growing toward a close, and the native imagination had been roused by tales of many whaling adventures. A minor literature had grown up around the theme, chiefly the records of actual voyages and a few novels, like J. C. Hart's *Miriam Coffin* (1834). New England, turning from her rocky pastures, had sought the more hospitable acres of the sea and had brought the art and science of whale-catching to a pitch never equaled before or since. Not only New England but all the northeastern United States looked often to the Pacific. Inland youths followed their instincts to the ports and set sail on vessels which, after interminable voyages, came home reeking of blubber. Men who stayed behind wished they might go with the greasy Argonauts and listened to their yarns wherever a returned whaler talked. California invited in another direction, and Kansas had its prospects of adventure. But the sea still filled a great part of the horizon of escape. It was the highway leading out of monotony. It was the purge of desperate moods. "With a philosophical flourish," says Ishmael in *Moby Dick*, "Cato throws himself upon his sword; I quietly take to the ship." Melville could feel sure that others would have shared his imagined impulse and would be interested in his information. He knew that a whole body of tradition had grown up, especially along the seaboard, and that it was waiting to be used. He attached his fable to a creature already fabulous. There had been rumors of a white whale, known to earlier chroniclers as Mocha Dick, which had lived for years as a villain of the deep and which, though it had eventually been conquered, might naturally be chosen as a symbol of the perils of the whaler's calling. Melville hardly changed the name. And as he took Moby Dick more or less from the life, so did he take from fact the details of whaling which, remote now, were then familiar.

Though a transcendentalist, Melville was also a sailor and a scholar, and he wrote his book as if to make all its rivals unnecessary. It is a treatise packed with erudition. "The classification of the constituents of a chaos, nothing less is here essayed. . . . My object . . . is simply to project the draught of a systematization of cetology. I am the architect, not the builder. . . . I have swum through whole libraries and sailed through oceans; I have had to do with whales with these visible hands; I am in earnest; and I will try." He classifies whales and names them. He pauses in his narrative to tell ancient stories or to deny mistaken ones. He describes the manners of his beasts not only when they are in conflict with their pursuers but, so far as he can learn, when they are at peace. Only a little less systematically does Melville undertake to present the manners of men on whaling voyages. He explains the construction of their ships, the discipline of their ordinary routine, the methods of their fierce assaults, their treatment of their prizes, the devices which comfort their hours of leisure, the punctilio which governs the society of ships in the whaling fields. He exhibits the characters of the men who are brought together in such a venture, reports their speech, and catches up items of their previous careers to round out the picture. He comments upon the antiquities and landscape and habits of the Pacific.

Often enough his information is interruption to his central plot, or lavish digression. *Moby Dick* may be read at random for splendid, salty passages. When, for example, Melville touches on mastheads, he has a cheerful fling through time to prove that "the business of standing mast-heads, afloat or ashore, is a very ancient and interesting one." He goes back to the Egyptians and the builders of Babel, and comes by way of St. Simeon Stylites down to the "modern standers-of-mast-heads" whom he finds "but a lifeless set; mere stone, iron, and bronze men; who, though well capable of facing out a stiff gale, are still entirely incompetent to the business of singing out upon discovering any strange sight." They are only statues of heroes. "Neither great Washington, nor Napoleon, nor Nelson, will answer a single hail from below, however madly invoked to befriend by their counsels the distracted decks upon which they gaze; however it may be surmised, that their spirits penetrate through the thick haze of the future, and descry what shoals and what rocks must be shunned."

Neither the incidental embroideries nor the solid substratum of fact would alone, or both together, make *Moby Dick* the masterpiece it is. The book is first of all a great story. The plot might, in other handlings, have been simple or farcical. Ahab, the captain of the whaler *Pequod*, has lost one of his legs in an encounter with Moby Dick and has vowed to have revenge. In the imagination of Melville, transcendentalist as well as sailor and scholar, the matter becomes a tragic, even a cosmic issue. On his own cruise he had, he hints, begun to brood over symbols. "Lulled into such an opium-like listlessness of vacant, unconscious reverie is this absent-minded youth by the blending cadences of waves with thoughts, that at last he loses his identity; takes the mystic ocean at his feet for the visible image of that deep, blue, bottomless soul, pervading mankind and nature; and every strange, half-seen, gliding, beautiful thing that eludes him; every dimly-discovered, uprising fin of some undiscernible form, seems to him the embodiment of those elusive thoughts that only people the soul by continually flitting through it. . . . There is no life in thee, now, except that rocking life imparted by a gently rolling ship; by her, borrowed from the sea; by the sea, from the inscrutable tides of God. But while

(90)

this sleep, this dream, is on ye, move your foot or hand an inch; slip your hand at all; and your identity comes back in horror. Over Descartian vortices you hover. And perhaps, at mid-day, in the fairest weather, with one half-throttled shriek you drop through that transparent air into the summer sea, no more to rise for ever. Heed it well, ye Pantheists."

Because the story seemed cosmic to Melville, it had to be tragic. An obscure distemper gnawed forever at the core of his peace. His unsettled youth had been due to a natural rebellion which sprang from his animal spirits. Then, after his return to land, he had grown more speculative. The general tendency of his speculations is fairly clear in outline, if not in their details. They move all in the direction of disillusionment. He looked—as with Hawthorne—for a friendship which should combine a perfect fusion of the friends with a perfect independence of the persons involved. He looked— as apparently with his wife—for a love which should be at once a white rapture and a fiery ecstasy, at once a lightning flash and an eternity. He wanted to find life profound and stable and yet infinitely varied. He set himself to reduce the mystery of the world to some simple formula, and then to master the formula. In all these things he had been, inevitably, disappointed. Nor was he able to explain his disappointment by reasoning that he must have given too docile a belief to the lessons of idealism. Instead, he clung to his own values and gradually made up his mind to the notion that diabolism was rampant in the universe. How else could he account for the estrangement of friends and the numbing of lovers, for the insecurity and boredom of life, for the multiplied obstinate riddles of the cosmos he inhabited? In Ahab he found an opportunity to project a drama with which he could intensely sympathize. Once Melville had hit upon this fundamental scheme, he could enlarge it with violent thought, as he enlarged his setting with piled erudition.

Ahab is the Yankee Lucifer. Another of his Nantucket kind,

accustomed to the dangers of his occupation, might have been expected to regard the loss of his leg as a mere accident for which nothing could be blamed. Still another, accustomed to the doctrine of predestination, might have been expected to regard his loss as some act of God, working mysteriously. But Ahab cannot be reconciled by either of the orthodoxies in which he has been bred. As he cherishes his mad hatred within him he becomes aware, by its hot light, of depths below depths of fury. "Ahab, in his hidden self, raved on. Human madness is oftentimes a cunning and most feline thing. When you think it fled, it may have but become transfigured into some still subtler form. Ahab's full lunacy subsided not, but deepeningly contracted; like the unabated Hudson, when that noble Northman flows narrowly, but unfathomably through the Highland gorge. But, as in his narrow-flowing monomania, not one jot of Ahab's broad madness had been left behind; so, in that broad madness, not one jot of his great natural intellect had perished. . . . If such a furious trope may stand, his special lunacy stormed his general sanity, and carried it, and turned all its concentrated cannon upon its own mad mark; so that far from having lost his strength, Ahab, to that one end, did now possess a thousand-fold more potency than ever he had sanely brought to bear upon any reasonable object." Ahab in his monomania had raised the white whale to a dignity which alone could justify this rage. "That intangible malignity which has been from the beginning; to whose dominion even the modern Christians ascribe one half of the worlds, which the ancient Ophites of the East reverenced in their statue devil;—Ahab did not fall down and worship it like them; but deliriously transferring its idea to the abhorred white whale, he pitted himself, all mutilated, against it. All that most maddens and torments; all that stirs up the lees of things; all truth with malice in it; all that cracks the sinews and cakes the brain; all the subtle demonisms of life and thought; all evil, to crazy

Ahab, were visibly personified and made practically assailable in Moby Dick. He piled upon the whale's white hump the sum of all general rage and hate felt by his whole race from Adam down; and then, as if his chest had been a mortar, he burst his hot heart's shell upon it."

No wonder that Ahab carries his desire for vengeance to lengths which for his creed meant blasphemy. He vows to know the cause of his misfortune and to pay back blow for blow. He is in absolute rebellion against whatever god or godless chaos has wrought this havoc upon him, against whatever it is that Moby Dick represents, against whatever is outside the wall within which mankind is hemmed. "How can the prisoner reach outside except by thrusting through the wall? To me, the white whale is that wall, shoved near to me. Sometimes I think there's naught behind. But 'tis enough. He tasks me; he heaps me; I see in him outrageous strength, with an inscrutable malice sinewing it. That inscrutable thing is chiefly what I hate; and be the white whale agent, or be the white whale principal, I will wreak that hate upon him. Talk not to me of blasphemy, man; I'd strike the sun if it insulted me. For could the sun do that, then could I do the other; since there is ever a sort of fair play herein, jealously presiding over all creations." "The prophecy was that I should be dismembered; and—ay! I lost this leg. I now prophesy that I will dismember my dismemberer. Now, then, be the prophet and the fulfiller one. That's more than ye, great gods, ever were."

Thus Ahab, lifted by his fury to a sense of equality with the gods, goes on his long hunt. Like Jonah, stifling in the belly of the whale, the prisoner of the universe fumbles for the whale's proud heart, to destroy it. Nor is Ahab alone. He commands a little world, men of all races and colors, and ruthlessly employs them to weight his blow. Gradually, as he withdraws from the land where they were free creatures, he infects them with his horrid will, until they are one fist

(93)

and one harpoon. The *Pequod*, which insolently sets sail on Christmas day, becomes an entity, a consolidated will insanely questing for a black grail, as if parodying some holy quest. For all its delays in the earlier chapters, the story increases its tempo as it advances, and becomes sulphurous at the close. The gods, disturbed upon both their upper and their nether thrones, invoke, it seems, thunder, ocean, and the hugest of the brutes of creation to put down this impious man who has tried to crowd so close upon their secrets. Moby Dick, white and silent, still inscrutable, turns upon his enemies and sinks their ship before he glides away, unharmed and unperturbed, in the unconcerned Pacific. The *Pequod* goes down, a skyhawk nailed to her mast. With her, for the moment, the hopes of man appear to sink before triumphant evil.

It is not clear how far Melville meant *Moby Dick* to be taken as symbolical. "I had some vague idea while writing it," he told Hawthorne's wife, "that the whole book was susceptible of an allegoric construction, and also that *parts* of it were—but the speciality of many of the particular subordinate allegories were first revealed to me after reading Mr. Hawthorne's letter which, without citing any particular examples, yet intimated the part-and-parcel allegoricalness of the whole." The conception of Ahab had its origin, it cannot be doubted, in Melville's own heart. Ahab is created with such passion because Melville was partly, or felt he might have become, another Ahab. Melville had inherited the creed of orthodox Christianity, with its scheme of rewards and punishments and its assumption that the universe was beneficent toward mankind. He must have noted exceptions to these rules while he was cruising through the Pacific, perhaps without generalizing about them. On dry land again, writing of his adventures, he had reflected bitterly upon the world at large. "I am like one of those seeds," he said, "taken out of the Egyptian pyramids, which, after being three thousand years a seed and nothing but a seed, being planted in English soil, it developed itself, grew to greenness, and then fell to mold. So I." He had, he thought, begun to grow during his year in the Navy. "Three weeks have scarcely passed, at any time between then and now [1851], that I have not unfolded within myself. But now I feel that I am come to the inmost leaf of the bulb, and that shortly the flower must fall to the mold."

Writing to Hawthorne in the midst of *Moby Dick*, Melville threw his own light on his seven best years. Transcendental thinking had poured fire into his veins. It had lifted him to a sense of wider human and divine horizons and had made him believe that the center of those horizons, if not their rims, lay within himself. But no orthodoxy satisfied him. Though both his earlier and his later doctrines taught him that the cosmos had a meaning, and that the meaning was simple and good, his experience denied the conclusion. He had found in the world a thousand malevolent contradictions. Blind chance, heedless of the interests of men, seemed to rule there; and blind chance, Melville thought, could come from nothing less than the activity of the devil. And where within his own self were those serene, virtuous regions about which he had heard and read? His heart was a region of storms and cross-currents. The deeper he went into his reflections, the more he was aware of fierce, dire things. Only a little more, and he could imagine himself a mad Ahab, fixed in a wild rebellion, setting out to scour the unfathomable universe which had wronged him and against which he had vowed an absolute 1evenge. For all Melville's realism, he never arrived at the idea that perhaps the universe has no meaning, as men understand meaning, or that it has many meanings, all equally satisfactory to different finite intelligences. As to the dark impulses which he found within himself, he seems only dimly to have realized that they were the survivors of functions and processes in which human nature had been engaged through millenniums of prehistoric and historic experience. Whatever his first-hand knowledge of the world and of human nature, he could not entirely free himself of the moral formulas which he had been taught. Between his knowledge and his formulas arose the conflict which muddied the streams of his own life. That conflict, however, begat Ahab. In Ahab Melville was creating higher than he knew. He came to no passionate, serene decision, either that God is always just, however incomprehensible, or that nature, however habitable to man, lacks any interest in his fortunes. But Melville, exhibiting Ahab's hatred of evil, reveals a profound truth: that men, hating too much, become what they hate. In the end it is Ahab that is evil, not the white whale going about his business in the order of his nature.

The passion in *Moby Dick* makes the language always high, often toplofty, whether the chapters in their changing sequence are given over to speculation, information, poetry, or comedy. The book is far more unified and more intelligible than *Mardi*. The story, in its enormous way, marches. "Call me Ishmael," the narrator says in the first sentence, cutting himself off from the ordinary, friendly world. He goes to New Bedford, takes up with a cannibal harpooner, joins the crew of the *Pequod* at Nantucket, and is at sea before he suspects the purposes of Ahab. They become evident to Ishmael but slowly. In the interval, while the ship makes its way toward the action, he has time to expound the technique of his calling and to describe the characters who are engaged in it with him. Even on the Pacific the *Pequod* cannot go directly to its mark. It must move through dull delays, while the illusion of its single, unavoidable aim gathers strength. Its path crosses that of many another vessel, and they exchange the news of the ocean till there has been woven of their crossings and communications a solid fabric of knowledge concerning all that goes on there. Finally, when it comes to the struggle with Moby Dick, the mad captain and his fated crew have built up such anticipations that this seems to be the focus of the universe, actual as well as symbolical. With the catastrophe the fable comes to the end in the vortex of a drowning world. It is with a sudden surprise that the reader learns in an appended paragraph that Ishmael survived, as he must have done to be able to tell the story.

Moby Dick is the epic of America's unquiet mind, but Melville's age did not recognize itself in that stormy mirror. Though the allegory was noted here and there, the book was read chiefly as a sea tale which had eccentric elements in it. The grandeur of its conception and execution was overlooked. "Though I wrote the Gospels in this century," Melville said while he was in the midst of his book, "I should die in the gutter." Nor did he improve his fortunes with his next romance, which was like an Elizabethan tragedy of blood. *Pierre* (1852) dealt with states of mind which suggest rather the age of Freud than the middle of the nineteenth century. The conflict between the hero and his mother, the attraction between him and his half-sister, both have a candor of insight and a neurotic intensity then unprecedented in novels in the English language. Contemporary readers were repelled where they were not obtuse to the hectic implications of the story. No one seemed, as later critics have mistakenly done, to take the story for autobiography and nose through it. The book was merely disliked or disregarded. Melville was thought to have changed his early witty style for the heavy splendors of Sir Thomas Browne or the welter and tumult of Rabelais, or to have lost himself in the mystifying clouds of transcendentalism. A fire in a publisher's warehouse in 1853 destroyed the unsold books Melville had written, and interrupted the spread of his reputation. In six years he had published seven books; he let three years pass before his eighth.

These three years deserve to have been considered more memorable in Melville's history than they have been. In 1854 he contributed to a magazine his superb description, *The En-*

cantadas, of the Galapagos Islands. He had visited them early in his cruise on the *Acushnet*, and besides remembering he had read about them in the work of other writers, including Charles Darwin. But it was Melville who first caught in words the sense of antediluvian desolation which all later travelers have felt in the Galapagos, though none since him has reproduced it so well. During 1854-55 he turned from the Pacific to American history, and retold the story of Israel Potter, a Revolutionary soldier whose *Life and Remarkable Adventures* (1828) had appeared as an obscure chap-book. For something like a third of his book Melville kept more or less close to the original, but in the rest he gave his powerful, bitter imagination free rein. Israel goes to Paris with messages to Franklin: "Jack of all trades, master of each and mastered by none—the type and genius of his land," as Melville characterized him. Franklin introduces Israel to John Paul Jones, and Israel serves on the *Bonhomme Richard*. In a British prison Israel later meets Ethan Allen. Here are three very different heroes. Melville with equal felicity brings each of them to rich and glowing, if romantic, life. A magnificent tale of adventure ends, deliberately, with the gloom and misery of Israel's last neglected days. Melville dedicated his book to the Bunker Hill Monument, the only reward that Israel, who had fought at the battle, had ever received for his services to his country.

The *Encantadas* has no central narrative, *Israel Potter* is in part, as Melville called it, "a dilapidated old tombstone retouched." *Benito Cereno*, first issued in a magazine in 1855, is for suspense and unity unsurpassed by any other short novel in any language. Once more Melville had an earlier source, in Amassa Delano's *Narrative of Voyages and Travels* (1817). The Delano in the novel, like the Delano of the *Narrative*, encounters a Spanish ship in distress off the coast of Chile, and goes on board from his own ship to offer assistance. He finds the Spanish captain, Benito Cereno, mysteriously sick in body and will and utterly dependent on a Negro servant who never leaves his side. Circumstance after circumstance bewilders the downright American visitor, to whom the whole management of the San Dominick seems a headless confusion. Only just as he is leaving does he suddenly understand that the Spaniard has been in the power of savage, sly Negro mutineers, led by Don Benito's ostensible servant. At once light falls upon the mystery and all its confusion turns to a dreadful meaning which is made clear in detail in the deposition with which the story closes. If it was like Melville to have taken his plot where he found it, it was like him also to have immensely enriched and completely realized the episode. Step by step the danger grows on the reader, faster than it reveals itself to Delano, so that the reader is concerned for the American's safety as well as for the Spaniard's. Early in the novel Melville has created an atmosphere of general horror over the whole scene, out of which the special horrors emerge, with almost unbearable dark menace, until the climax pounces. Though the incidental symbolism of the story should not be overstressed, it is impossible not to feel that primitive deeps have malignly stirred and risen to overwhelm their customary masters. Yet the story nowhere runs into metaphysics. It is somehow humanized by being seen through the blunt eyes of Captain Delano and finally explained in the matter-of-fact language of a legal document. Melville wrote it like a poet who was a man of the substantial world.

He did not write like that again till nearly the end of his life. Israel Potter (1855) had three editions in its first year, but the Piazza Tales (1856), though it included The Encantadas and Benito Cereno, was as little read as the wild and whirling satire of The Confidence Man (1857). Melville was now overworked, ill, and in debt to publishers and relatives. Failing to obtain a position in the consular service, as Hawthorne had done, Melville made, on borrowed money, the journey to Egypt, Palestine, Greece, and Italy of which he left a record in *Clarel* (1876), two volumes of troubled but occasionally striking verse. At home he lectured on his travels, made a voyage to San Francisco, and in 1863 settled with his family in New York. Never, as he said, "a blind adherent" to either side during the Civil War, he was temperate in his war poems, collected as *Battle Pieces* (1866). That year he became an inspector of customs and remained in that minor post for nearly twenty years, almost forgotten by the reading world which saw hardly one of his books reprinted till after his death in 1891. He issued *John Marr* (1888) and *Timoleon* (1891), both verse, privately in very small editions. He left *Billy Budd*, written 1888-91 after his retirement from the customs, in manuscript, not finally revised and not published till 1924.

There have been many explanations for the long eclipse of a romancer who could write *Moby Dick* at thirty-two and then in forty years more produce so little else of high merit. Chagrin over the reception of *Pierre* and the books following may have had something to do with it. His shift from romance to theological speculation may have had more. "It is strange," Hawthorne commented after a walk with his friend in 1856, "how he persists—and has persisted ever since I knew him, and probably long before—in wandering to and fro over these deserts, as dismal and monotonous as the sandhills amid which we were sitting. He can neither believe, nor be comfortable in his unbelief; and he is too honest and courageous not to try to do one or the other." Whatever the cause or causes of his brooding retirement, it is at least evident that Melville had lived the great chapter of his life in the Pacific, and that when he had exhausted his memories of that, or lost interest in them, his vitality fell off and his imagination found no other theme large enough to rouse him to action. He sank into lonely thought and wrote nothing. But in his final years, freed from routine and economic anxiety, he produced in *Billy Budd* another masterly short novel which with all his early freshness has also a profound and realistic wisdom that was new to him.

The story of *Billy Budd* was probably suggested by the hanging of a midshipman charged with mutiny on the American brig *Somers* in 1842, of which Melville may have heard while he was in the Navy, but in the novel he lays the scene on a British man-of-war in the year of the great mutiny of 1797. The plot is a subtle moral triangle. Budd, a young foretopman, by his charm and innocence draws upon himself the instinctive perverse animosity of the master-at-arms, Claggart. Claggart falsely accuses him to Commander Vere, who confronts the two men. Budd, outraged by such malice and unable for a moment to speak, strikes Claggart, who dies of the blow. Vere, though he knows that Budd did not intend murder and that Claggart had been the first offender, has no choice under the recent mutiny act but to hang the seaman who has in time of war struck a superior officer, and moreover caused his death. Claggart has been evil and Budd good, but momentary violence and accident have changed the simple contrast. On this ship and at this time, with mutiny threatening, Budd's deed, Vere decides, must be punished whether it had any bad intent or not. Life would go to pieces if its necessary forms were not carried out. Here was a kind of stern understanding beyond the reach of the romancer who had imagined Captain Ahab. Nor is Melville's understanding limited to Vere. It delicately creates Budd in the very image of innocence, without a touch of priggishness or mawkishness, and winds its way through the Iago labyrinth of Claggart's "depravity according to nature." The entire story is closely and beautifully reasoned, full of the most arresting insight into the human heart. Having come at last, it seems, to a full mastery of himself, Melville was master of his imagination and the materials it worked upon.

His death led to renewed attention to his work, but he had

to wait a generation for the excited revival which set him in the rank among major writers which, with some dissent, he still holds. Since 1922 there have been four times as many editions of *Moby Dick* in America and England as during all the years before, and more than ever of all his chief books. He has been at once a hero to literary rebels and the object of much academic research. His life has been investigated in detail, his opinions analyzed, his art minutely studied. His stories have been traced to other sources besides his own experience or observation, even his autobiography shown to have been often invented or taken from his reading. But no discovery of his sources can lessen the wonder of that native power with which he transmuted them, lifting them from flat documents to high magic and lively wit. He remains the best, as he was the first, story-teller of the Pacific, and *Moby Dick* is the epic of the ocean.

VI

BLOOD AND TEARS

THE ROMANCE of the immediate school of Cooper did not die without a struggle, though it had fallen into disuse among most writers of capacity at the time of his death and was rapidly descending into the hands of fertile hacks who for fifty years were to hold an immense audience without deserving more than the barest history. In that very year (1851) Robert Bonner bought the New York *Ledger* and began to make it the congenial home and the hospitable patron of a sensationalism which had been growing upon native romance as its earlier energy had gradually departed from it. Hitherto most nearly anticipated by such a son of blood-and-thunder as Joseph Holt Ingraham, author of *Lafitte: The Pirate of the Gulf* (1836), or by the swashbuckling Ned Buntline, duelist, sportsman, and perfervid patriot, this sensationalism reached unsurpassable dimensions with the prolific Sylvanus Cobb, Jr., who besides *The Gunmaker of Moscow* (1856) counted his successes in this department of literature by scores. From the *Ledger* no step in advance had to be taken by the inventors of the dime novel, which was started upon its long career by the publishing firm of Beadle and Adams of New York in 1860. Edward S. Ellis's *Seth Jones, or the Captives of the Frontier* (1860), one of the earliest of the sort, its hero formerly a scout under Ethan Allen but now adventuring in western New York, is said to have sold over 600,000 copies in half a dozen languages. The type prospered, depending almost exclusively upon native authors and native material: first the old frontier of Cooper and then the trans-Mississippi region, with its Mexicans, its bandits, its troopers, and its Indians,

(103)

who had now for the most part lost the high courtesy of Cooper's and were displayed in the bitter spirit which prompted that Western saying that the only good Indian is a dead Indian. Among the actual heroes of this adventurous world the men who achieved a primacy like that of Daniel Boone among the older order of scouts were Kit Carson, the famous scout, and Buffalo Bill (William F. Cody), who was first put on the stage (1872) by the intrepid Ned Buntline and later capitalized his own personality and reputation in the circus which exhibited its microcosm of the Wild West round the world. The dime novels which suggested such an enterprise, and in turn were furthered by it, were cheap, conventional, hasty—Albert W. Aiken long averaged one a week, and Prentiss Ingraham produced in all over six hundred—but they were exciting, full of incident and innocence, and scrupulously devoted to the popular doctrines of poetic justice. What they lacked was all distinction except that of a rough abundance of invention, and Frank Norris could later grieve that the epic days of Western settlement found only such tawdry Homers.

One successor of Cooper upheld for a time the dignity of the old-fashioned romance. John Esten Cooke (1830-86), born in the Shenandoah Valley and brought up in Richmond, cherished a passion as intense as Simms's for his native state and deliberately set out to celebrate its past and its beauty. Leather Stocking and Silk (1854) and The Last of the Foresters (1856), both narratives of life in the Valley, recall Cooper by more than their titles; but in The Youth of Jefferson (1854) and its sequel, Henry St. John, Gentleman (1859), Cooke seems as completely Virginian as Beverley Tucker before him, though less stately in his tread. All three of these novels have their scenes laid in Williamsburg, the old capital of the Dominion; they reproduce a society strangely made up of luxury, daintiness, elegance, penury, ugliness, brutality. At times the dialogue of Cooke's impetuous cavaliers and merry girls nearly catches the flavor of the Forest of Arden, but there is generally something stilted in their speech or behavior that spoils the gay illusion. Nevertheless, *The Virginia Comedians* (1854) may justly be called the best Virginia novel of the old régime, after *Swallow Barn*, for reality as well as for color and spirit. No other book, of fact or fiction, so well sets forth the vision which in the days immediately before the Civil War Virginians cherished of their greater days on the eve of the Revolution: days the glories of which they thought it possible to bring back and for which if need be they were ready to fight another race of foreign tyrants. During the Civil War Cooke served as captain of cavalry, under Stuart, and had the experiences which he afterwards turned to use in a series of Confederate romances, most rememberable of which is *Surry of Eagle's Nest* (1866). But in this and the related tales *Hilt to Hilt* (1869) and *Mohun* (1869), as well as in numerous later novels, he continued to practise the old manner which grew steadily more archaic as the rough and ready dime novel, on the one hand, and the realistic novel, on the other, gained ground. Toward the end of his life he participated, without changing his habits, in the revival of the historical romance which began in the eighties, but he still seemed a belated dreamer, the last of the old school rather than the first of the new.

Less close to Cooper was another novelist who fought in the Civil War, and who lost his life in one of its earliest battles: Theodore Winthrop (1828-61). Of a stock as eminent in New England and New York as Cooke's in Virginia, he had a more cosmopolitan upbringing than Cooke: after Yale he traveled in Europe, in the American tropics, in California while the gold fever was still new, and in the Northwest. His work at first found so delayed a favor with publishers that his books were all posthumous. Time might, it is urged, have made Winthrop a legitimate successor of Hawthorne, but in fact he progressed little beyond the Gothic qualities of Charles Brockden Brown, whom he considerably resembles in his strenuous nativism, his melodramatic plots, his abnormal characters, his command over the mysterious, and his breathless style. Of his three novels—*Cecil Dreeme* (1861), *John Brent* (1862), *Edwin Brothertoft* (1862)— *John Brent* is easily the most interesting by reason of its vigorous narrative of adventures in the Far West, at that time a region still barely touched by fiction. That Winthrop's talent looked forward in this direction rather than backward to Hawthorne appears still more clearly from *The Canoe and the Saddle* (1863), a fresh, vivid, amusing, and truthful record of his own journey across the Cascade Mountains. His early death closed a promising chapter. Until the arrival of Mark Twain and Bret Harte even California did not enter fiction, and the states further north had to wait still longer for novelists, though the Canadian wilderness just across the border was earlier in being made the scene of dozens of popular romances.

But Hawthorne and Cooke and Winthrop were not the characteristic novelists on the eve of the Civil War. It was the domestic sentimentalists who held the field. A brief decade endowed the nation with its most tender, most tearful classics. Then flowered Mrs. E. D. E. N. Southworth with *The Curse of Clifton* (1853), and subsequently with scores more to the very end of the century. Mary Jane Holmes with *Tempest and Sunshine* (1854) and *Lena Rivers* (1857); Augusta Jane Evans Wilson with *Beulah* (1859) and the slightly belated but no less characteristic *St. Elmo* (1867)— all of these ladies more or less in the *Charlotte Temple* tradition; Susan Warner with *The Wide Wide World* (1850) and Maria S. Cummins with *The Lamplighter* (1854), pious histories of precocious, flirtatious young girls; and—not so far above them—Donald Grant Mitchell (Ik Marvel) with *Reveries of a Bachelor* (1850) and *Dream Life* (1851) and George William Curtis with *Prue and I* (1856), these two

(106)

being, however, young men who thought of themselves as essayists rather than as novelists and who afterwards took themselves to sterner tasks. Professor Ingraham gave up his blood-and-thunder, became a clergyman, and wrote the long popular Biblical romance *The Prince of the House of David* (1855). Timothy Shay Arthur in *Ten Nights in a Bar Room* (1854) mingled weak tears with the strong drink against which his lurid romance was aimed. And these particular successes emerge from a ruck of smaller undertakings which swarmed over literature, coloring the world with pink and white, scenting it with the dry perfume of pressed flowers, quieting it to whispers and gentle sobs, neglecting all the bitter and pungent tastes of life, softening every asperity, hiding every thorn and thought.

Perhaps the best commentary upon this order of fiction is to point out that whereas the dime novels were consumed by boys, and meant for them, sentimental romances fell increasingly into the hands of girls—especially of girls as molded and approved by American Victorianism. And yet it would be idle to declare that none of such books rises above the confectionery level. For a world that accepted the Victorian maiden as an ideal, *The Wide Wide World*, to take a typical instance, was a satisfying account of how she might be shaped out of the plastic material which she was supposed to be at birth. The heroine reads no novels, but she knows Weems's *Washington* and *Hail Columbia* for the sake of her patriotism and hymns and Biblical texts for her piety. The Christian virtues that were supposed to be best for maidens she has steadily dinned into her: resignation, long-suffering, loving kindness, all-embracing faith and charity. She goes through the most pathetic domestic experiences, tempered by all the fires of affliction she is old enough to be scorched by. Perhaps such narratives are little nearer to reality as regards the moods and conduct of the young girls of the time than are the dime novels as regards the actual adventures of their

(107)

brothers, but they must have voiced contemporary aspirations and must have shown in action what was desired by the majority of parents and by many girls themselves. The decade was fighting romance with romance, the romance of blood with the romance of tears.

The tears of the women sentimentalists were the daughters of the tears of Richardson and the Evangelicals; the tears of Ik Marvel and G. W. Curtis were the sons of the tears of the gently secular Irving as exhibited in *The Wife* and *The Pride of the Village*. The Bachelor of the *Reveries* sits dreaming, at his comfortable hearth, the pensive dreams which the maiden of the time imagined he dreamed about the kind of maiden she imagined herself to be. The images which run through his mind are all of snug cottages and soft wives and rosy children and trim servants and lawns and gardens. In *Dream Life* he ventures somewhat further with his dreams and dips a little deeper into the felicities of bachelor reverie, but he is still a Lord of Shalott, sitting before the mirror in his safe tower. He tastes affection but no passion, longing but no ambition, piety but no religion, expectation but no experience. He stands at the very antipodes from the older dream-world of frontier adventure, and of course from the jangling world of the American fifties between the Fugitive Slave Law and the guns of Sumter. His imagination, like the fictive imagination generally, had withdrawn from the cold wind outside and was hugging itself warm over sentimental fires. Had there been less of the spirit of adolescence in its behavior, it might have sounded those richer and more permanent notes which come from the similar withdrawal of Isaak Walton and George Herbert in the seventeenth century, and might have had a larger claim upon posterity than that which lies in its lucid though fragile style and its sweetish taste and fragrance and its steadily-fading colors. *Prue and I* has a larger claim. Not only does it have still less than the Bachelor's evangelical orthodoxy but it has a fuller, firmer,

more masculine style, with certain grave tones lately contributed to the traditionary manner of Irving; and it has rather
more body. The narrator of the story is respectfully married
to an amiable Prue who understands his vagaries, which are
to indulge as a spectator in the luxuries of the world he cannot afford in any other way. Castles in Spain, he argues, are
never costly or impossible, for he himself has dozens. In this
way Curtis, who had already satirized the flamboyant wealth
of New York in *Potiphar Papers* (1853), expressed the disposition of New Yorkers not wealthy or fashionable to take
refuge in an interior life as a protection against the increasing
plutocracy of the city. *Prue and I*, not quite forgotten, fails
of being a genuine classic only by reason of the oversoftness
and oversweetness which characterized the decade from which
it sprang as the decade's finest purely sentimental masterpiece.

The most effective of all these sentimentalists, a writer
whom, indeed, a profound passion once or twice lifted above
sentimentalism though its flavor still clung to her, remarkably represents the clerical aspects of the decade, for she was
daughter, sister, wife, and mother of clergymen. Harriet
Beecher (1811-96), born in Connecticut, was a thorough child
of New England when she went, in 1832, to live in Cincinnati, just across the Ohio River from slave soil. Her earliest
sketches and tales, collected in a volume called *The Mayflower* in 1843, deal largely with her memories of her old
home set down with an exile's affection. In 1850 she returned
to New England, for her husband, Calvin E. Stowe, had
accepted a professorship in Bowdoin College. There, deeply
stirred by the passing of the Fugitive Slave Law, which was
challenge and alarm and martial signal to all conscientious
Northerners, she began *Uncle Tom's Cabin; or, Life Among
the Lowly*, which on its appearance in 1852 met with a popular reception never before or since accorded to a novel. Its
sales went to the millions. Over five hundred thousand
Englishwomen signed an address of thanks to the author;

Scotland raised a thousand pounds by a penny offering among its poorest people to help free the slaves; in France and Germany the book was everywhere read and discussed; while there were Russians who emancipated their serfs out of the pity which the tale aroused. In the United States, thanks in part to the stage, which produced a version as early as September, 1852, the piece belongs not only to literature but to folk-lore.

That *Uncle Tom's Cabin* stands higher in the history of reform than in the history of the art of fiction no one needs to say again. Dickens, Kingsley, and Mrs. Gaskell had already set the novel to humanitarian tunes, and Mrs. Stowe did not have to invent a type. She had, however, no particular foreign master, not even Scott, all of whose historical romances she had been reading just before she began *Uncle Tom's Cabin.* Instead, she adhered to the established native tradition, as old as *Charlotte Temple* and as new as *The Wide Wide World,* the tradition of sentimental, pious, instructive narratives written by women chiefly for women and very largely about women. Leave out the merely domestic elements of the book—slave families broken up by sale, ailing and dying children, Negro women at the mercy of their masters, white households which at the best are slovenly and extravagant by reason of irresponsible servants and at the worst are abodes of brutality and license—and little remains. Many of the pages, too, are purple with melodrama, especially in the conceptions which the parson's daughter and the professor's wife had of St. Clair's luxurious establishment and Legree's filthy menagerie. To understand why the story touched the world so deeply it is necessary to understand how tense the struggle over slavery had grown, how thickly charged was the moral atmosphere awaiting a fatal spark, even though the spark might be naïve and artless. And yet the mere fact of an audience already prepared will not explain the mystery of a work which shook a powerful institution and which, for all its defects of taste and style and construction, still has surprising power. There were other anti-slavery novels, including Metta Victoria Victor's *Maum Guinea* (1861) which because it appeared in the cheap Beadle and Adams series was widely read and critically neglected. But they no longer move, lacking the ringing voice, the swiftness, the fulness, the frequent humor, the authentic passion of the greater book.

It has often been pointed out that Mrs. Stowe did not mean to be sectional, that she deliberately made her chief villain a New Englander, and that she expected to be blamed no more by the South than by the North, which she thought particularly guilty because it tolerated slavery without the excuse either of habit or of interest. Bitterly attacked by Southerners of all sorts, however, she defended herself in *A Key to Uncle Tom's Cabin* (1853), and then, after a triumphant visit to Europe, tried another novel to illustrate the evil effects of slavery, particularly upon the whites. *Dred* (1856), in England known as *Nina Gordon*, has had its critical partisans, but posterity has not sustained them. Grave faults of construction, slight knowledge of the scene (North Carolina), a less simple and compact story than in *Uncle Tom's Cabin*, a larger share of disquisition: these weight the book down, and most readers carry away only fragmentary memories of the black prophet Dred's thunderous eloquence, of Tom Gordon's shameless abuse of his power as a master, and of Old Tiff's grotesque and beautiful fidelity. *Dred* appears to have exhausted Mrs. Stowe's anti-slavery material, though she was, of course, a partisan and a pamphleteer during the Civil War. Thereafter, being now an international figure, she let her pen respond somewhat too facilely to the many demands made upon it till her death; she wrote numerous didactic and religious essays and tales; she was attentive to the follies of fashionable New York society, in which she had had little experience; she was chosen by Lady Byron to publish the scandal by which the poet's wife defended herself against the dead poet.

In another department of her work Mrs. Stowe stood on surer ground, and her novels of New England life do well what there was later a whole school of New England story-writers to do after her. She remained weak in structure and sentimental. Her heroines wrestle with problems of conscience happily alien to all but a few New England and Nonconformist British bosoms; her bold seducers, like Ellery Davenport in *Oldtown Folks* (1869) and Aaron Burr in *The Minister's Wooing* (1859), are villains to frighten schoolgirls with; she wrote always as from the pulpit or from the parsonage. But where no theological or melodramatic idea governed her, she could be direct, accurate, and convincing. The earlier chapters of *The Pearl of Orr's Island* (1862) must be counted, as Whittier thought, among the purest, truest idyls of New England, much as doctrinal casuistry clogs the narrative thereafter. It is harder—impossible, in fact—to agree with Lowell in placing *The Minister's Wooing* first among her novels, and yet no other imaginative treatment so well sets forth the strange, dusky old Puritan world of the later eighteenth century when Newport was the center at once of the ruthless divinity of Samuel Hopkins, the minister of the novel, and of the African slave trade. Mrs. Stowe wisely did not put on the airs of an historical romancer but wrote like a contemporary of the earlier Newport with an added flavor from her own youthful recollections. This flavor was indispensable to her. When her memory of the New England she had known in her girlhood and had loved so truly that Cotton Mather's *Magnalia* had seemed "wonderful stories . . . that made me feel the very ground I trod on to be consecrated by some special dealing of God's providence"—when this memory worked freely and humorously upon materials which it was enough merely to remember and record, she was at her later best. These conditions she most fully realized in *Poganuc People* (1878), crisp, spare (for her), never quite sufficiently praised, and in *Oldtown Folks*, like the other a series of sketches rather than a novel, but—perhaps all the more because of that—still outstanding, for fidelity and point and canny, pawky humor, among the innumerable stories dealing with New England rural life.

Evangelical sentimentalism was carried on with large popular success by the Rev. Josiah Gilbert Holland of Massachusetts and the Rev. Edward Payson Roe of New York until nearly the end of the century, when others took up the perennial burden. That both Holland and Roe were clergymen is a sign that the old suspicion of the novel was nearly dead, even among those petty sects and sectarians that so long feared the effects of it. Holland, whose first novel had appeared in 1857, was popular moralist and poet as well as novelist and first editor of *Scribner's Monthly* (founded 1870). His metrical novels, *Bitter-Sweet* (1859) and *Kathrina* (1867), sweet, soft, warm, and facile, probably caught more readers than any of his tales in prose, Roe contented himself with prose fiction. Chaplain of a regiment of cavalry and of one of the Federal hospitals during the Civil War, he later gave up the ministry in the conviction that he could reach thousands with his beguiling pen and only hundreds with his hortatory voice. His simple formula included: first, some topical material, historical event, or current issue; second, characters and incidents selected directly from his personal observation or from newspapers; third, an abundance of nature descriptions with much praise of the rural virtues; and fourth, plots concerned almost invariably, and never too deviously, with the simultaneous pursuit of wives, fortunes, and salvation. *Barriers Burned Away* (1872), *Opening a Chestnut Burr* (1874), and *Without a Home* (1881) are said to have been his most widely read books, though none fell unheeded from the presses which labored to bring forth enough of them as fast as they were written.

The greatest, however, and practically the ultimate victory over village opposition to the novel was won by *Ben-Hur*

(1880), a book of larger pretensions and broader scope than any of Roe's or Holland's modest narratives, the only American novel, indeed, which can be compared with *Uncle Tom's Cabin* as a folk possession, and one so popular that as late as 1913 an edition of a million copies was called for and distributed. Its author, General Lew Wallace (1827-1905), an Indiana lawyer, a soldier in both the Mexican and the Civil Wars, had already published *The Fair God* (1873), an elaborate romance of the conquest of Mexico which recalled the earlier concerns of Irving and Prescott and Robert Montgomery Bird. A chance conversation with the notorious popular skeptic Robert G. Ingersoll led Wallace to researches into the character and doctrines of Jesus which not only convinced him of the essential truth of Christianity but bore fruit in a tale, grandiose and ornate, which thousands have read who have read no other novel except perhaps *Uncle Tom's Cabin* and have hardly thought of either as a novel at all, and through which still more thousands know the geography, ethnology, and customs of first-century Judea and Antioch as through no other source. Without doubt the outstanding element in the story is the sufficiently un-Christian revenge of Ben-Hur upon his false friend, Messala, a revenge which which takes the Prince of Jerusalem through the galleys and the palæstra and which leaves Messala, after the thrilling (and to the popular taste, the classic) episode of the chariot race, crippled and stripped of his fortune. And yet, following even such pagan deeds, Ben-Hur's discovery that he cannot serve the Messiah with the sword does not seem quite an anticlimax, though the conclusion, dealing with the Passion, like the introductory chapters on the meeting of the Magi, falls below the level of the revenge theme in energy and simplicity. Compared with other romances of the sort, however, with William Ware's or Ingraham's, for instance, *Ben-Hur* easily passes them all, by a vitality which probably has a touch of genius.

(114)

HOWELLS AND REALISM

1~New Frontiers and Old Settlements

AFTER THE weeping fifties came the Civil War, which broke
the pattern, though at the time it contributed little to the
mode of fiction except new materials for the incessant popular romancers who turned their pens from the past to the
present without any change as regards sensationalism. What
the wicked Tory or the fierce Indian had been, the crafty
Confederate or the cruel Federal—it depended upon the section to which the novelist was native—now became. The
cloudy atmosphere and turgid style of the old romance
wrapped themselves promptly around the new events and
assisted in the process which, while the wounds of the struggle were still raw, began to transform it into an epic memory.
That memory, however, had to ripen for a generation before
it achieved any considerable maturity. Meanwhile, another
tendency in fiction dispossessed the sentimentalism which
had dispossessed the school of Cooper.

After the Revolution there had sounded from many literary throats the cry that the new nation ought to have an
epic, as Greece and Rome and medieval Catholicism and
English Puritanism had had; and although nothing great had
been forthcoming the demand persisted until the middle of
the next century. Then it had gradually given way before the
idea that, as Simms pointed out, prose fiction is the modern
epic form. Criticism came therefore to demand the Great
American Novel, not so much to enshrine the national past
as to reflect the national present on a scale commensurate
with the new consciousness. Although this expectation, too,
was disappointed, it undoubtedly had something to do with

(115)

the rapid rise of the fashion of local color which may be thought of as initiated by Bret Harte's story *The Luck of Roaring Camp* in 1868, and which for some thirty years gave a dominant type to imaginative writing in the United States. The war had stirred the surface of various provincialisms which now discovered themselves and one another. Many writers set out, apparently, to furnish the country with an ordnance survey of all its riches of local custom. In the North, where the idea of the Great American Novel had been strongest, a good many writers and readers gave themselves to the new vogue in a romantic enthusiasm for glorifying the total national picture; in the South, the prevailing mood was a passion for displaying the depth and charm of the society which had received a mortal blow from the war. Nevertheless, the episode contributed something to the advance of realism. Scenes could no longer be unlocalized; costume and dialect had to be reported with accuracy; characters and plots must consequently be fitted, more or less, to the actual circumstances among which they moved. The ordinary methods of local color, no less than doctrines of realism imported from Europe, cleared the way for a critical conflict between romance and realism. Granted, controversy finally ran, that real persons and events should of course be represented, ought they to be merely everyday persons and events exhibited to the life or ought they instead to be selected with a view of making more of heightened moments and superior men and women than could be made of commonplace?

Bret Harte, however, and his followers fought no critical battles. Their victory was too easy. When *The Luck of Roaring Camp* was published California was the microcosm and focus of America. Every section was represented there among the gold-seekers who gave the community its picturesqueness. Every section of course read Bret Harte with an interest compounded of curiosity about the unknown and delight in the familiar. The success of the master naturally suggested imitation, not only in regard to the local manners and types of other neighborhoods but in the dimensions of the tales he had begotten. The generation after 1870 practised the short story as no generation had ever done before. Brown and Cooper and Simms and Melville and Hawthorne and Mrs. Stowe had all written short stories, but the novel had called forth their major faculties. Bret Harte, a voluminous author, wrote only one full-length novel; most of his followers are better known for their shorter stories than for their novels or wrote no novels at all. There was still an economic factor, as during the days of Cooper. Until the passage of the international copyright law of 1891 British novels could be freely pirated in the United States and American competition increasingly took the form of short stories, further encouraged by the multiplication of native magazines particularly hospitable to brevity. The novel, in consequence, was left standing for a few years out of the main channel of imaginative production. Those who chose it were likely to do so because of greater seriousness or larger strength than might be needed by the story-writers who were tempted to slighter and yet more profitable undertakings.

During the sixties realism hovered in the air without definitely alighting. Oliver Wendell Holmes, for instance, in *Elsie Venner* (1861) worked his romantic problem of heredity upon a ground of shrewd realistic observation; Bayard Taylor employed a similar composition of elements; Rebecca Harding Davis in *Margret Howth* (1862) and in numerous short stories wanted "to dig into this commonplace, this vulgar American life, and see what is in it"; Louisa M. Alcott in *Little Women* (1868) and Thomas Bailey Aldrich in *The Story of a Bad Boy* (1870) turned away from the watery illusions which in respectable circles had furnished the substance for children's books; at the end of the decade the loud laughter of Mark Twain began to clear the scene. The distinction, however, of writing the first American novel which may be called realistic in a modern sense belongs to John W. De Forest of Connecticut, whose *Miss Ravenel's Conversion from Secession to Loyalty* (1867), as William Dean Howells said, was "of an advanced realism before realism was known by that name." Not half heroic or partisan enough to suit the contemporary feeling about the war, *Miss Ravenel's Conversion* missed the vogue of a war book, and when the tendency in fiction had caught up with it, it seemed too much a war book to fit the new taste. But no other novel of the decade has been less dimmed by a half century of realism. Coldly truthful in its descriptions of battles and camps, crisp and pointed in its dialogue, penetrating, if not over-subtle, in its character analysis, sensible in its plot and in its general temper, it is still almost as convincing as it was once precocious. De Forest wrote other novels but none quite so notable. All of them suffered from the rivalry of local color in its romantic phases.

While these phases originated on the frontier, so often influential in American culture, it was also on the frontier, though in another section of it, that realism took its earliest definite stand. Perhaps some bareness in the life of the Middle West, lacking both the longer memories of the Atlantic States and the splendid golden expectations of California, discouraged romance there and encouraged that bent toward naturalism which descends unbroken from Edward Eggleston (1837-1902) through E. W. Howe and Hamlin Garland, Theodore Dreiser and Sinclair Lewis. At first glance Eggleston looks strange enough in this gallery, for like Holland and Roe he was a clergyman and nourished upon the same soft food as they. As a Methodist on the frontier, though of cultivated Virginia stock, he was even brought up to think of novels and all such works of the imagination as evil things. But his diversified experience as an itinerant preacher, or circuit rider, and his reflective and studious habits lifted him out of these narrow nooks of opinion. It is true that he shared the customary local color motive. "It used to be a matter of no little jealousy with us, I remember," he says, speaking of Westerners, "that the manners, customs, thoughts, and feelings of New England country people filled so large a place in books, while our life, not less interesting, not less romantic, and certainly not less filled with humorous and grotesque material, had no place in literature. It was as though we were shut out of good society." He had a larger and sounder motive. Having read Taine's *Art in the Netherlands*, Eggleston undertook to portray the life of southern Indiana in the faithful, undoctrinaire spirit of a Dutch painter, and wrote *The Hoosier Schoolmaster* (1871). Refusing to follow the violent and yet easy road of the dime novelists, he confined himself to a plain tale of plain men and women, choosing for his scene a backwoods district where true Hoosiers flourished at their most typical, rather than any of the more cultivated Indiana communities. His plot exists almost solely for the sake of the manners described, the backwoods sentiments and dialects, labors and amusements.

These singularities had already been exposed by Bayard Rush Hall in *The New Purchase* (1855), and there was beginning to grow up a modest literature reporting "that curious poor-whitey race which is called 'tar-heel' in the northern Carolina, 'sand-hiller' in the southern, 'corn-cracker' in Kentucky, 'Yahoo' in Mississippi, and in California 'Pike' . . . the Hoosiers of the dark regions of Indiana and the Egyptians of southern Illinois": a people, still not extinct, whom later observers came to think of as the contemporary ancestors of those modern Americans who have outgrown eighteenth-century conditions as the poor whites have not. All of Eggleston's essential novels deal with this aspect of America, whatever the scene: Indiana in *The Hoosier Schoolmaster, The End of the World* (1872), and *Roxy* (1878); Ohio in *The Circuit Rider* (1874); Illinois in *The Graysons* (1887); Minnesota in *The Mystery of Metropolisville* (1873). Light is thrown upon his aims in fiction by the fact that he subsequently aspired to write a History of Life in the United States, which he carried through two erudite, humane, and graceful volumes, with both of them, so abundant was his learning, unable to bring the account beyond 1700. The Hoosier novels, simple in plot, clear-cut in characterization, concise and lucid in language, unwaveringly accurate in their setting, manners, and dialect, are indispensable documents, even finished chapters, for his unfinished masterpiece. What has given the *Schoolmaster* its primacy in reputation is probably nothing but its having been first in the field, though something may also be allowed for its compactness and freshness of substance; *Roxy* is more interesting, and *The Circuit Rider* more realistic. *The Graysons* deserves credit for the reserve with which it admits the youthful Lincoln into its narrative, uses him at a crucial moment, and then lets him withdraw without a hint of his future greatness. The morals of Eggleston's tales, it is true, are over-obvious, though they are not strained. Without any rush of narrative, neither has he verbosity or inflation of style. Even where, in his fidelity to violent frontier habits, his incidents appear melodramatic, the handling is sure and direct, for the reason, as he says of *The Circuit Rider*, that whatever is incredible in the story is true. No novelist, within the range of topics Eggleston touched, is more candid, few more believable. With greater range and fire he might have been a national figure as well as the earliest American realist to leave behind him a settled classic, a folk-book of its neighborhood.

2~William Dean Howells

From the Middle West came the principal exponent of native realism, as an author so prolific during the sixty years between his earliest book and his latest that he amounts almost to a library in himself, as editor and critic so influential that he amounts almost to a literary movement. William Dean Howells was born at Martin's Ferry, Ohio, in 1837, the grandson of a Welsh Quaker and the son of a country printer with a passion for books. Like his friend Mark Twain, Howells saw little of schools and nothing of colleges, and like him he got his systematic literary training from enforced duties as compositor and journalist. But unlike Mark Twain, he fell as naturally into the best classical traditions as Goldsmith or Irving, who, with Cervantes, earliest delighted him. Howells's reading marked his growth. In *My Literary Passions* he delicately recorded the development of his taste. At first he desired to write verse, and devoted months to imitating Pope in a youthful fanaticism for regularity and exactness. From that worship he turned, at about sixteen, to Shakespeare, particularly to the histories; then to Chaucer, admired for his sense of earth in human life; then to Dickens, whose magic, Howells even then dimly saw, was rough though authentic. Macaulay taught him to like criticism and furnished him a temporary model of prose style. Thackeray, Longfellow, Tennyson, followed in due course. Hawthorne for a time dominated him, more completely a passion with Howells than any other American author ever was. Having taught himself some Latin and Greek and more French and Spanish, Howells took up German and came under the spell of Heine, who persuaded him once for all that the dialect and subjects of literature should be the dialect and facts of life.

Poems in the manner of Heine won Howells a place in the pages of the *Atlantic*, then the zenith of his aspiration, and in 1860 he undertook the reverent pilgrimage to New England which he afterward recounted with winning grace in *Literary Friends and Acquaintance*. Already enough of a journalist to have been asked to write a campaign biography of Lincoln and enough of a poet to have published a small volume of poems with his Ohio friend John James Piatt, Howells made friends wherever he went and was finally confirmed in his literary ambitions. At the outbreak of the Civil War he was appointed United States consul at Venice; he was married at Paris in 1862 to Elinor G. Mead of Vermont; and he spent four years of approximate leisure in studying Italian literature, notably Dante, as the great authoritative voice of an age, and Goldoni, whom Howells called the first of the realists. In Italy, though he wrote poetry for the most part, he formed the habit of close, sympathetic observation and discovered the ripe, easy style which made him, beginning with *Venetian Life* (1866) and *Italian Journeys* (1867), one of the happiest of literary travelers. From such work he moved, by the avenue of journalism, only gradually to fiction. On his return to the United States in 1865 he first became editorial contributor to *The Nation* for a few months, and then served as assistant editor and finally editor of the *Atlantic* until 1881.

The literary notices which he wrote for the *Atlantic* during these years of preparation would show, had he written nothing else, how strong and steady was his growth toward his mature creed, by a natural process which included his entire philosophy. From his childhood he had been intensely humane—sensitive and charitable. This humaneness now revealed itself as a passionate love for the simple truth of human life, and a suspicion, a quiet scorn for those romantic dreams and exaggerations by which less contented lovers of life try to escape it. "Ah! poor Real Life, which I love," he wrote in his first novel, "can I make others share the delight I find in thy foolish and insipid face?" Perhaps *Their Wedding Journey* (1871) ought hardly to be called a novel, but it is a valuable Howells document in the method, so nearly that of his travel books, by which he takes a bridal couple on their honeymoon over much the same route, in a reverse order, that he had traveled between Ohio and Boston in 1860, and also in the zeal for actuality which makes him exalt the truth, however tedious, over any unreality however agreeable. "As in literature the true artist will shun the use even of real events if they are of an improbable character, so the sincere observer of man will not desire to look upon his heroic or occasional phases, but will seek him in his habitual moods of vacancy and tiresomeness." Less of such argument, though no less of implicit zeal for veracity, appears in A Chance Acquaintance (1873), more strictly a novel, in which Howells showed that he could not only report customs and sketch characters felicitously but also organize a plot with felicitous skill. A young Bostonian, in love with an intelligent but untraveled inland girl, who returns his love, is so little able to overcome his ingrained provincial snobbishness that he steadily condescends to her until in the end he suddenly sees, as she sees, that he has played an ignoble and vulgar part which separates them, in a subtle dramatic turn by which their relative positions are reversed.

Although, to judge by A Chance Acquaintance, Howells had the art of narrative among his original endowments, he had only gradually discovered it in himself. His first narrative, No Love Lost (1869), had been in hexameters, more or less after the manner of Longfellow and Clough. Besides his life of Lincoln, Howells wrote three volumes of travels or essays before he attempted a novel at all. A Chance Acquaintance made no clean break with his previous experiments, for it deals with a group of Americans traveling in Canada, three of whom had already appeared in Their Wedding Journey. And even the success of his novel did not turn him wholly to fiction. He continued to write criticism and began to write farces, merely enlarging his range as he developed in power. The stream of literature had never before poured from an American writer with such variety and volume. Besides his stated duties for the Atlantic he found time during the seventies to edit a group of autobiographies, and later to write book introductions by the dozen; he translated modern Italian poets; he scanned the entire literary horizon for new planetaries· he was one of the most widely-read of Americans. As

(123)

his curiosity never grew faint, neither did his pen, but kept up its amazing productivity without damage to the smooth surface of his style and the bland cheerfulness of his disposition.

His principal limitation—his chariness of passion and tragedy—did not entirely reveal itself in the novels which he wrote during the *Atlantic* period. Like Henry James in those same years, Howells was at first concerned with the contrast between different manners or grades of sophistication—a conflict to which his own sojourn as an American in Italy and as a Westerner in Boston had made him sensitive. Devoted as all these novels were to the transcription and criticism of the lighter manners of the age, they could hardly be censured for not going deeper, especially since they did what they set out to do with ease, dexterity, revealing humor, shrewd and illuminating comment. It appeared, however, as the series lengthened, that Howells was not doing full justice either to his material or to himself. He who had seldom shown a Bostonian of the traditional order in anything but unlovely attitudes fell too much into Boston habits and confined his art too much within the respectable reticences of Boston. Not without some complaint he accepted the fate of writing largely for women—Boston women. He came to the decision that "the more smiling aspects of life . . . are the more American." He might dare for the sake of truthfulness to represent human beings in their habitual moods of vacancy and tiresomeness but was not willing to represent them in the hardly less habitual moods which make mankind so often illicit or savage or sordid. Yet he never consciously compromised, for he held that the lawless moods of men belong to those heroic or occasional phases which he left to the romancers. His novels in effect pay an extraordinary compliment to civilization. Later and sterner critics called his compliment flattery.

Having resigned his *Atlantic* editorship at forty-four,

Howells in the next half-dozen years brought his Boston period to its summit and conclusion. Besides certain minor novels he wrote *A Modern Instance* (1882), which he thought his strongest, *The Rise of Silas Lapham* (1885), which the public has generally found the best of his novels, and *Indian Summer* (1886), which he himself thought his best. Without the bitter tincture of pessimism which Howells lacked, realism can hardly go further than in these three. The superiority of *A Modern Instance* to all that had come before lies less in its firmer grasp of its materials, for Howells from the first was sure of grasp, than in its larger control of larger materials. Marcia Gaylord, the most passionate of all his heroines, is of all of them the most clearly yet lovingly conceived and elaborated. Her unaccountable impulses and endurances convey an impression that is completely individual. Types do not behave so. In the career of her husband, Bartley Hubbard the journalist, Howells adroitly traces a metamorphosis from selfishness and vanity, fed in this case by Marcia's unreasoning devotion, into contemptible viciousness which has not even a dash of boldness to redeem it. Like the impulses of Marcia, the process hides itself rather too closely from the observer, who as with living persons may now and then be surprised to find that the decay has gone so fast and far with so few outward signs. Writing the winter scenes of the earlier chapters Howells had the advantage of those many pens which in the past decade had wrought at the local color of New England. Although done with an eye intensely on the fact, these scenes have still the larger bearings of a criticism of American village life in general. The subsequent adventures of the Hubbards in Boston, acutely local in setting and incident, are still as universal as any ever laid in that provincial metropolis. Squire Gaylord's arraignment of his son-in-law in an Indiana court room vibrates with a dramatic passion seldom met with in Howells, a passion made the more emphatic by the sickening descent from a tragic occasion which follows immediately afterward in Bartley's virtual offer of his former wife to his former friend. Following such episodes it is difficult to forgive Howells his apparent sympathy with Halleck in the discovery that a New England conscience will now forever hold him from Marcia because he had loved her before she was free. The attentive imagination simply refuses to be convinced; or else it finds itself disgusted at so senseless an ending to a narrative heretofore full of wisdom maturely wielding admirable and enlightening details.

The theme of *Silas Lapham* is one very dear in a republic, that of the rising fortunes of a man who has no aid but virtue and capacity. Lapham, a country-bred, self-made Vermonter, appears when he has already achieved wealth and finds himself being drawn, involuntarily enough, into the more difficult task of adjusting himself and his family to the manners of fastidious Boston. A writer primarily satirical might have been contented to make game of the situation. Howells, keenly as he sets forth the conflict of standards, goes beyond satire to a depth of meaning which comes only from an understanding of the part which artificial distinctions play in human life and a pity that such little things can have such large consequences of pain and error. The conflict, while constantly pervasive in the book, does not usurp the action. The Lapham family has serious concerns that might arise in any social stratum. Most intense and dramatic of these is the fact that the suitor of one daughter is believed by the whole family to be in love with the other until the very moment of his declaration. The distress into which they are thrown is presented with a degree of comprehension rare in any novel, and here matched with a common sense which rises to something half-inspired in Lapham's perception—reduced to words by a friendly clergyman—that in such a case superfluous self-sacrifice would be morbid, and that, since none is guilty, one had better suffer than three. A certain rightness and soundness of feeling mark the entire narrative. As it proceeds, the record

steadily grows in that dignity and significance which, according to Howells's creed, is founded only upon the unadorned
and unexaggerated truth.

As, with the increase of the American population and the
diminution of opportunity for the individual, the self-made
man becomes a less outstanding figure than he was in the
generation to which Silas Lapham belonged, Lapham will still
continue to seem a standard example of his type. But his type
is of New England and not of the United States at large.
In other sections—at least in those not governed by New
England habits transplanted—the adventures of the self-made
have nearly always been more stirring, motivated by less lawful
ambitions, colored by ranker senses. Lapham rises through
the easy and yet compact levels of a homogeneous sectional
society as law-abiding as any in the world. The clang of the
larger America, the sense of the manipulation of vast forces
which give the story of the self-made American its stirring
interest, do not appear in this quiet story. Howells presents
Lapham, for the most part, in his milder hours, with his wife
and daughters in the plainest of households, barely hinting at
the tough struggles with the world to which of course Lapham gave most of his time. Lapham represents the American
magnate only as subdued to New England conditions and
then further subdued to the domestic hearth. Here, Howells
might probably have contended, the true and essential Lapham had his existence, at this central station of human affairs.
One misses, nevertheless, the thrust and clutch and strain and
sweat of actuality. To say that it does not visit the uttermost
deeps of human character is not to say that it plays over the
surface. Howells's imagination has seen through and through
all the persons in *The Rise of Silas Lapham*; it has thought
round and round every situation. There are three dimensions
to the matter; it is a sturdy, tangible, memorable block of life.

That in 1890 he thought *Indian Summer* his best novel
shows how well inclined he was toward the gayer side of his

(127)

character, for in this interlude, lightly, sweetly, pungently narrating the loves of a man of forty, Howells reached his highest pitch of comedy. His touch on each page and sentence is as graceful as his spirit is unfailing from first to last. The scene he laid in Italy; its characters he chose from among those temporarily and voluntarily exiled Americans who in the seventies and eighties of the last century so tempted novelists with any partiality for satire or contrast; the moral hints, as the story unmistakably tells, that for a middle-aged lover there is much more joy and comfort in a woman his own age than in the most entrancing young girl whatever. The easiest and yet wisest badinage flickers continually over the surface of a naturally moving stream of narrative so pellucid that nothing in it, event or motive or insinuation, is ever hidden from the experienced eye. The happy taste which prompted him to name it for the most distinctive and most charming of American seasons no less happily instructed him how to clothe it in a golden, impalpable, enriching haze borrowed apparently from the season. In this autumnal atmosphere the energy of youth in the spring of its love looks awkward; the winter of wisdom is as near as the summer of desire. Only a sage could have carried the story through without falling now and then into the temptation of being too impassioned; only a poet could have done it without now and then becoming cynical and sounding elderly.

In 1882 Howells had gone to England for a visit during which he brought out a series of his works there and with them and himself charmed literary London. He seriously questioned whether he should not settle in Italy for the remainder of his life, but his passion for America proved too strong, and he came back, first to Boston, to a position of almost unparalleled influence in American letters. In his earliest *Atlantic* days he had given Henry James needed encouragement at the outset of the younger man's great career. Then and since Howells had been for Mark Twain the important critical element drawing that tumultuous humorist from burlesque and uproar to the finer art of fiction. By the middle eighties all Boston that read at all was fighting for or against Howells's principles. Promising writers, such as Hamlin Garland and Brand Whitlock, made discipular pilgrimages to him. The decade discovered a vitality and displayed a craftsmanship in novels and tales which the United States had never seen before. Of all this Howells was equally exemplar and critic. If his novels filled the air, so did his doctrines. The monthly articles which he wrote for The Editor's Study in *Harper's Magazine* between 1886 and 1891 adumbrate the labors he performed in behalf of realism. Chiefly discussions of current books, they did not concern themselves merely with aspects of fiction, but also with poetry, history, and biography, applying to them all a calmly rational temper, measuring them by generous but none the less firm canons of truthfulness. What he warred upon particularly was the adulteration of honest literature with false alloys like sentimentalism, pseudo-heroic attitudes, gaudy ornament, theatrical endings; he enjoyed and praised works of pure fancy which do not pretend to paint the fact. Hardly one of the local color writers but passed under his critical or editorial hand, and few of them but in some degree were touched by his creed. The short story as well as the novel responded to his influence; even the theater, ancient home of the tinsel which he hated, had for a time its James A. Herne trying to write plays which should be as real as Howells's stories. Moreover, though as a rule unfriendly to French realists because of his dislike of their fierce candor, Howells was constantly introducing and commending the realists of Spain and Italy and Russia.

Toward the end of the Boston period he had an eager partiality for Turgenev, his art, his poetry, his pity, his wisdom. But about 1886 a change came over Howells through his reading of Tolstoy, who became his final and greatest literary passion. "Tolstoy gave me heart to hope that the world may

(129)

yet be made over in the image of Him who died for it, when all Cæsar's things shall be finally rendered to Cæsar, and men shall come into their own, into the right to labor and the right to enjoy the fruits of their labor, each one master of himself and servant to every other. He taught me to see life not as a chase of a forever impossible personal happiness, but as a field for endeavor towards the happiness of the whole human family." Sincere as was his conversion, however, Howells did not turn preacher as Tolstoy had done, and as his radical admirers expected. At fifty he could hardly undergo any more considerable change than that his sympathies should be enlarged and his utterance even further mellowed by the tides of benevolence and brotherhood which all his life had been rising within him and now knew themselves. Tolstoy's way was impossible to Howells's will because Howells was a saint not of the other world but of this, a walker of amiable, companionable paths, too friendly for the solitude of the natural martyr, too kindly for the battles of the natural warrior. The many books he subsequently wrote show him no less sunny and affectionate than before, though he had now a new eye for social injustice. In his Utopian romances, *A Traveler from Altruria* (1894) and *Through the Eye of the Needle* (1907), without compromise with the economic system under which he had been bred, he threw it incontinently over—though how urbanely and serenely—in favor of the system of his imaginary Altruria, where all work is honorable and servants are unknown, where capital and interest are only memories, where equality is complete, and men and women, in the midst of beauty, lead lives that are just, temperate, and kind. Besides these exotic matters Howells touched closer ones. No man spoke out more firmly or ringingly on behalf of the Chicago anarchists or against the annexation of the Philippines and the attendant saturnalia of imperialism. Had he been by disposition a fighting man he might have become a national voice. Not being that, he led his art if not his nation.

Tolstoy's novels seemed to Howells as excellent as his doctrine. "To my thinking they transcend in truth, which is the highest beauty, all other works of fiction that have been written. . . . He has not only Tourguenief's transparency of style, unclouded by any mist of the personality which we mistakenly value in style, and which ought no more to be there than the artist's personality should be in a portrait; but he has a method which not only seems without artifice, but is so." Howells must have understood that the artlessness of Tolstoy is only apparent, must have learned, then or later, how painfully Tolstoy toiled at his art; still it was hardly more than critical hyperbole to say that, compared to other novelists, Tolstoy was a mirror of nature and had no art but nature's own of growth. Since Howells himself had been in all his novels singularly unartificial, those written after he had read Tolstoy could exhibit no new methods. He merely broadened his field and deepened his inquiries.

A Hazard of New Fortunes (1890), in which Basil and Isabel March, the bridal couple of *Their Wedding Journey*, give up Boston, as Howells himself had just done, for a future in New York, is not content merely to point out the unfamiliar fashions of life which they meet but is full of conscience regarding the evils of the modern social order. He wrote at a moment of hope, at the end of a decade which had disturbed the heavy stagnation following the Civil War: "We had passed," he afterwards said, "through a period of strong emotioning in the direction of the humaner economics, if I may phrase it so; the rich seemed not so much to despise the poor, the poor did not so hopelessly repine. The solution of the riddle of the painful earth through the dreams of Henry George, through the dreams of Edward Bellamy, through the dreams of all the generous visionaries of the past, seemed not impossibly far off." In this mood Howells's theme compelled

(131)

him so much that the story moved forward almost without his conscious agency; "though," he carefully insisted, "I should not like to intimate anything mystical in the fact." A Hazard of New Fortunes, which encountered greater immediate favor than any of his previous novels, outdoes them all, and the subsequent ones too, in its conduct of different groups of characters, in the perfect naturalness with which now one and now another rises to the surface of the narrative and then retreats at the due moment without a trace of management. The episode of the street-car strike, brought in near the end, dramatizes the struggle which has heretofore been in the novel rather a shadow than a fact; Howells employs it as a sort of focal point to which the attention of all his characters is drawn, with the result that, having already revealed themselves generally, they are more particularly revealed in their varying degrees of sympathy.

Howells wrote from the point of view of the older America which in 1890 was mystified by labor unrest and horrified by a strike; the America in which the country had been one with the towns, and the villages had ruled them both; the America which knew the thunder and smoke of the industrial nation less as realities in themselves than as new problems crowding in upon the older order of Americans. So New York was for Howells, in spite of his fine sympathies, a community of established Americans moving somewhat gingerly among its immigrants, and not a new Rome or a new Constantinople for the Western hemisphere. The book partially suggests a volume of travels in a city where the traveler lives with the ruling class, without digging very deeply into the commoner soil of life, except as he encounters some chance individual who belongs with the unpriviliged or who out of conscience consorts with them in the hope of lightening their burdens. Howells's sympathies were as wide as the metropolis, but his knowledge was restricted. For this reason his narrative seems quiet in comparison with the jagged, multicolored, whirling rowdy, gorgeous reality which even then lay under his eyes and which since that day has grown in a hundred respects out of its former likeness.

The thirty years yet remaining of Howells's life brought no marked new development. In 1891 he summed up his critical position in *Criticism and Fiction*, declaring "I am in hopes that the communistic era in taste foreshadowed by Burke is approaching, and that it will occur within the lives of men now overawed by the foolish old superstition that literature and art are anything but the expression of life, and are to be judged by any other test than that of their fidelity to it"; and at the same time declaring, as if to set limits to the naturalism thus implied, that "[if] a novel flatters the passions, and exalts them above the principles, it is poisonous." The next year Howells succeeded George William Curtis in The Easy Chair of *Harper's* and wrote thenceforth monthly articles which, less exclusively literary than those in The Editor's Study, carried on the same tradition. There and elsewhere his light, practised pen kept pace with American literary production, commenting on new authors and tendencies with an unwearied generosity which still never violated his central principles. Reminiscences and travels assumed a larger part in his work. After *A Boy's Town* (1890) and *My Literary Passions* (1895) came *Literary Friends and Acquaintance* (1900), classic account of the silver age of Boston and Cambridge which Howells had lived through. He revisited Europe and left records in various books which occasionally drew his matter out thin but in which he was never dull or untruthful or sour. *My Mark Twain* (1910) is the tenderest of all the interpretations of Howells's great friend. *Years of My Youth* (1916), written when its author was nearly eighty, is the work of a master whom age had made wise and kept strong. In 1909 he was chosen president of the American Academy, and six years later he received the National Institute's gold medal for distinguished work in fiction. Since his death in

1920 the Academy has in a measure been the shadow that he casts.

Howells's later novels make up so long a list that most of them must go unnoted, though all, if not invariably profound, were invariably kind and clear. *The Leatherwood God* (1916), the study of a frontier impostor who proclaims himself a god, as an actual person had once done in early Ohio, best hints at Howells's views of the relation between the real world which he had so long explored and those vast spaces which appear to be beyond it. The maturest Howells, like the Mark Twain whose *Mysterious Stranger* appeared in the same year as *The Leatherwood God*, speculated much upon such matters, but without losing himself in them. In *The Kentons* (1902) Howells most perfectly exemplifies his later reading of the actual world. Returning to the Middle West of his youth he took a family thence to New York and then to Holland, with all the freshness and point of his first period exposing the contrasts between their Ohio manners and those of the other regions which they visit. More than ever he is sage first then satirist. "Remember," says Judge Kenton in a speech which sounds none the less like him for being so much like Howells, "that wherever life is simplest and purest and kindest, that is the highest civilization." Without contending in behalf either of his Ohioans, with their little angularities and large virtues, or of his experienced worldlings, with no angularities at all and their virtues more considerably mixed with manners, Howells interprets both with the lucid intelligence of an angel smiling at a beloved community of men. Only the masters of narrative can tell a story which, like this, is clear yet full, continuous yet unhurried, balanced yet as natural as the flow of water or the movement of clouds across a blue sky. If not a great novel *The Kentons* is still a flawless one.

It is to the difficult distinction between flawlessness and greatness that critical discussions of Howells always finally arrive. With few authors as eminent does it seem so hard to find the master conveniently distilled in a few masterpieces ready for transportation to posterity. His hand worked finely from first to last, but never quite supremely. A Chance Acquaintance, A Modern Instance, The Rise of Silas Lapham, Indian Summer, A Hazard of New Fortunes, The Kentons, all admirable, do not stand more than measurably forth from the remainder of his novels. He must be studied in his total work, as the intimate historian of his age. Geographically, he was limited in the main to Ohio, New England, and New York, and to those parts of Europe and America in which Ohioans, New Englanders, and New Yorkers spend their vacations. He was conditioned, too, by his historical position as editor and arbiter so long in Boston at the declining end of an epoch, when taste ran rather to discipline than to variety or vividness, rather to decorum than to candor, rather to learning than to experience, rather to charm than to passion. Howells rose to meet the new world, contending as well as he could in his natural silver tone with the alternating tones of gold and iron which later dimmed the voice of Boston. But that in his creed which had made him amenable to Boston lay deeper than its influences. On every ground he preferred to walk close to the commonplace, believing that the true bulk and range of life are always to be found there. He was one of the most democratic of novelists. Fenimore Cooper and Hawthorne, both democrats, could still never leave off complaining that democracy lacks the elements of saliency and color upon which they thought the prosperity of the novelist depends. What his predecessors shrank from, Howells ardently embraced, thoroughly satisfied to portray the plain universe that lay before him, in a style which, as he said of that of Jane Austen whom he preferred to all the novelists in English, is "the elect speech of life expressing itself without pretending to emotions not felt, but finding human nature sufficient for its highest effects."

The question is whether Howells's practice matched the

serene consistency of his creed; and the answer is that he shrank from some of its consequences. His gentle nature would not permit him to follow men out of the cheerful sun into those darknesses of the mind and the soul which also belong close to the commonplace. He clung to the day as Hawthorne to the night. Like Emerson, Howells closed his eyes to evil and its innumerable traces. His America, transcribed so fully as it is, is still an America of the smooth surfaces. Great peaks of drama do not rise upon it; passion does not burrow into it nor adventure run over it with exciting speed. Howells employed a selective, a respectable, an official realism. He chose his subjects as a sage chooses his conversation, decently. To state these limitations is to accuse Howells of the uncommon sin of too much gentleness. They challenge the historian to explain whether or why flawless work which lacks malice or intensity, cannot be kept alive by ease and grace and charm, by kind wisdom and thoughtful mirth. Perhaps just Howells's excess of gentleness, like his delicate concern for art, was needed to civilize American fiction by bringing it home from the frontier to the daily life of the settlements.

VIII

MARK TWAIN

OF THE MAJOR American novelists Mark Twain, who hardly thought of himself as a novelist at all, derived least from any literary, or at any rate from any bookish, tradition. Hawthorne had the example of Irving, and Cooper had that of Scott, when they began to write; Howells and Henry James instinctively fell into step with classics. Mark Twain came up into literature from the popular ranks, trained in the school of newspaper fun-making and humorous lecturing, only gradually instructed in the more orthodox arts of the literary profession. He seems, however, less indebted to predecessors than he actually was, for the reason that his provenience has faded out with the passage of time and the increase of his particular fame. Yet he had predecessors and a provenience. As a printer he learned the mechanical technique of his trade of letters; as a jocose writer for the newspapers of the Middle West and the Far West at a period when a well established mode of exaggeration and burlesque and caricature and dialect prevailed there, he adapted himself to a definite convention; as a raconteur he not only tried his methods on the most diverse auditors but consciously studied those of Artemus Ward, then the American master of the craft; Bret Harte, according to Mark Twain, "trimmed and trained and schooled me"; and thereafter, when the Wild Humorist of the Pacific Slope, as it did not at first seem violent to call him, came into contact with professed men of letters, especially Howells, he had already a mastership of his own.

To be a humorist in the United States of the sixties and seventies was to belong to an understood and accepted class.

(137)

It meant, as Orpheus C. Kerr and John Phœnix and Josh Billings and Petroleum V. Nasby and Artemus Ward had recently and typically been showing, to make fun as fantastically as one liked but never to rise to beauty; to be intensely shrewd but very seldom profound; to touch pathos at intervals but not tragedy. The humorist assumed a name not his own, as Mark Twain did, and also generally a character: that of some rustic sage or adventurous eccentric who discussed the topics of the moment keenly and drolly. Under his assumed character, of which he ordinarily made fun, he claimed a wide license of speech, which did not extend to indecency or to any too serious satire. His fun was the ebullience of a strenuous society, the laughter of escape from difficult conditions. It was rooted fast in that optimism which Americans have had the habit of considering a moral obligation. It loved to ridicule those things which to the general public seemed obstacles to the victorious progress of an average democracy; it laughed about equally at idlers and idealists, at fools and poets, at unsuccessful sinners and unsuccessful saints. It could take this attitude toward minorities because it was so confident of having the great American majority at its back, hearty, kindly, fair-intentioned, but self-satisfied and unspeculative. In time Mark Twain largely outgrew this type of fun—or rather, had longer and longer intervals of a different type and also of a fierce seriousness—but the origins of his art lie there. So do the origins of his ideas lie among the populace, much as he eventually outgrew of the evangelical orthodoxy and national complacency and personal hopefulness with which he had first been furnished. The secret alike of his powers and of his limitations must be looked for in the dual, the never quite completed, nature which allowed him on one side to touch, say, Petroleum V. Nasby and on the other William Dean Howells.

Samuel Langhorne Clemens was born in 1835 at Florida, Missouri, a cluster of houses which the boy's father, in something the fashion of Judge Hawkins in *The Gilded Age*, confidently expected to become a metropolis. As it did not, the family soon removed to Hannibal, in the same state, which was on the Mississippi and so daily witnessed if not shared the river's prosperity. There Clemens passed a boyhood and youth nearly as irresponsible as Huckleberry Finn's and nearly as imaginative and mischievous as Tom Sawyer's. Neither studious by nature nor offered even tolerable opportunities for study, he left school at twelve upon the death of his father, and was apprenticed to a printer in the town. For three years with him and later for three years more with his own elder brother, who had bought a newspaper, Clemens worked in this department of literature, beginning as well to write jokes and whimsical skits in the manner approved up and down the river. Then he carried his trade into a larger world, seeing the sights as a skilled workman could then see them in New York, Philadelphia, Washington, Keokuk, and Cincinnati, and finally in 1857 planning, as his visionary father might have done, to go to Brazil to pick up a fortune. Instead, a chance conversation with a pilot on the Mississippi decided him to enter the pilot's profession, to which practically every boy in the river towns then aspired.

If Mark Twain's years as a printer represent a more or less academic aspect of his training, his four years as a pilot are its technical aspect. His *Life on the Mississippi* makes clear how exacting his new profession was; how much erudition it called for to know twelve hundred miles of shifting current by day or night, with absolute certainty; how much responsibility for life and property lay in his hands. His powerful mind absorbed the necessary knowledge easily. His spirit delighted in the authority and prominence which his position gave. He had now a point of vantage from which he could look down on the whole pageant of the Mississippi. That was a spectacle such as modern life has afforded at only a few times and in a few places. An enormous commerce flowed up and down

(139)

the river, attended by every hue and condition of mankind. The United States filed by under the pilot's observation: merchants about their business, planters on their occasional visits to the towns, laborers looking for work, immigrants on the way to new homes, curiosity-seekers and pleasure-hunters, slaves and slave-traders, stowaways and visiting noblemen and sportsmen. So much traffic called for a vast machinery to move it and entertain it and prey upon it: steamboats which competition forced to be swift and beautiful; skilled navigators, with the pilots chief among them; crews for the boats and roustabouts for the landing-stages; shipping agents, shore hotels, musicians, gamblers, and harpies of another sex. All these Mark Twain had an opportunity to observe at an age when most future authors are still at their books. He absorbed them as thoroughly as the lore of his craft. "In that brief, sharp schooling," he later wrote, "I got personally and familiarly acquainted with all the different types of human nature that are to be found in fiction, biography, or history."

The Civil War ended this vivid chapter, and the pilot for whom there was now no longer a vocation, after a brief period of comically bloodless service in the Confederate army, became a wanderer again, starting off by stage-coach across the plains with his brother, lately appointed secretary of the Territory of Nevada. Then followed nine years of travel and adventure by far the most varied which had ever gone into the making of an American novelist. There was too much of the sanguine in his Clemens blood for Mark Twain to resist the temptation to huge and easy wealth which the Far West offered; he tried for gold and silver, bought in mining stock, took up timber claims. There seemed to be little either in himself or in the lax society of the West capable of directing him to the career for which his powers were being assembled. But he did become a writer, picking up local items for the Virginia City *Enterprise* and reporting the sessions of the legislature at Carson City. Here in 1863 he first used the name

Mark Twain, a leadsman's term which he recalled from the Mississippi and which had already been used by another writing pilot. The same year Mark Twain met Artemus Ward, intelligent and original, then lecturing in Virginia City, and was pleased with his praise. The year following, having been forced to leave Nevada by participation in a farcical duel, Mark Twain took himself to San Francisco, where he wrote for various papers and came under the tutelage of Bret Harte. While there he wrote the *Jumping Frog* story which Artemus Ward wanted to use in a volume of his own but which instead appeared in a New York newspaper late in 1865 and tickled the country. A trip to the Sandwich (Hawaiian) Islands still further enlarged Mark Twain's horizon and his journalistic reputation. In 1866 he tried humorous lecturing with unequivocal success, made money, traveled to the East by the way of Panama, convulsed New York at Cooper Union, and in 1867 sailed for the Mediterranean and Palestine on an excursion of which he became the hilarious chronicler in his first important book, *The Innocents Abroad*, published in 1869.

The sudden, the almost explosive fame which the book brought him sharply lights up the taste of the period which produced it. Of the older American schools the Knickerbockers had ceased to exist and Melville was silent; in New England Hawthorne and Thoreau were dead and the creative vitality of their generation had waned. The rising men of genius looked to Europe for their guides: Whistler was established in London; Henry James was being sealed to the Old World; even Howells, loyally native as he was, worked upon his native material with classical tools. Only Whitman had stayed relentlessly at home, and he was still speaking prophecy out of a dim and narrow cloud. Upon this scene Mark Twain burst with a ringing American hurrah, a "powerful uneducated person" of the sort Whitman had promised. Once more the frontier came back upon the older communities as it had done under Andrew Jackson, when David

Crockett was a nine-days' wonder. But Mark Twain was more than a shrewd, barely literate backwoodsman. He had a tumultuous rush of expression; he had, thanks to Artemus Ward and his fellows, a literary mode already prepared for him. Being expected, as a humorist of that type, to employ burlesque, he employed it to make fun of ecstatic travelers, particularly of those whose ecstasy followed the guidebook rather than their own taste and always rose with the reputation of the thing seen. Being expected, too, to be irreverent for humorous effect, he laughed at everything that did not seem to him overpoweringly sacred, and even from sacred moods often extricated himself with a jest. These were the conventions of his order. And as he was individually a husky, unashamed Westerner, when he found much in ancient art and scenery that fell below what he had heard of it, he said so in a loud voice irritating to fastidious ears. His public, however, was not fastidious. Relieved by the absence of that note of breathlessness which had oppressed it in earlier travel books, it gasped and then roared. Here was a writer who scratched the surface of American culture and found beneath it the rough, insouciant, skeptical, hilarious fiber of the pioneer. Undoubtedly Innocents Abroad flattered the mob with the spectacle of free-born Americans romping through venerable lands and finding them on so many counts inferior to America. The practical jokes of the book have lost much of their power to entertain; nor do the purple pages on which Mark Twain set down, in beadrolls of glorious names, his sense of the might and thunder of antiquity now sound so eloquent as they probably sounded in the sixties. But his sweep and vigor and jolting contrasts and pealing laughter are as notable as ever. The book remains an essential document in the biography of Mark Twain and in the history of American civilization.

If confessed mendacity playing around facts can transform them into fiction, both Innocents Abroad and Roughing It, published in 1872, approach the novel. Contemporary readers thought of them as reasonably true, allowing the author, however, the large license of the successful teller of such tall tales as had been the chief literary form developed by the frontier. Now that Mark Twain is no longer in the news his actual exploits concern his readers less and less in comparison with the permanent elements contributed to his work by his elaborating imagination. These elements play a larger part in *Roughing It* than in *Innnocents Abroad*. Having taken down the Old World as measured by the New, he now set up the New in a rollicking, bragging picture of the Great West where he had acquired his standards of landscape and excitement. His account, shaped to look like autobiography, takes him from St. Louis across the plains to the Rockies and on to California and Hawaii. But, unlike the story of the *Innocents*, this was not written day by day with the events still green in the mind. They had had time to ripen in the imagination and to take on a significance which the deepest impression can never have at the first moment. *Roughing It* is uneven in tone and in excellence; the exposition falls below the description, which is often florid, and neither can equal the narration, particularly when it runs lustily across the plains with the rocking stage-coach or when it carries the narrator through his tenderfoot adventures in the mining camps. Although he frequently falls into the burlesquing habits which still clung to him from his days of Nevada and California journalism, he also rises decisively above them, and above all his predecessors in popular humor, with chapters of genuine poetry, of an epic breadth and largeness, commemorating free, masculine, heroic days.

The tumultuous vogue of these books urged Mark Twain to new efforts in which his hereditary ache for sudden wealth —an ache not discouraged by his Western failures—regularly influenced his literary impulses. His marriage in 1870 to Olivia Langdon of New York, by bringing him into a wealthier and more formal circle than he had known before, still further affected him. He made plans for being a sort of captain of letters: he would mine his literary ore for lectures, smelt it into newspaper and magazine articles, refine it into books which he would print, publish, and distribute taking out a large profit for himself for every process. To this extent he shared in the furor of exploitation which followed the war and from which he had no literary ideals to deter him. Energy so immense as his could not lightly be held within bounds. Moreover, he had the contention in himself between his original nature, lyrical, boisterous, and the restraints which he accepted without much question from his fastidious wife and the classical-minded Howells. Between them the two contrived to repress some of his tendencies, those toward blasphemy, profanity, the wilder sorts of impossibility, and also toward satire and plain-speaking. His broad *Fireside Conversation in the Time of Queen Elizabeth,* later known as *1601* (written in 1876 for the amusement of a few friends), was never published though it has several times been surreptitiously printed, and ranks with the similar humorous exercises of Benjamin Franklin. How far Mark Twain was shorn by his wife and Howells of real powers no one can say till his suppressed manuscripts have been studied more thoroughly than they yet have been. It is clear, however, that under these modifying censors he moved from the methods which produced *The Innocents Abroad* to those which produced *Huckleberry Finn* and *Joan of Arc.*

The year after his marriage he went to Hartford, where he lived for seventeen years, with intervals of lecturing and occasional sojourns in Europe. With Charles Dudley Warner, who also lived at Hartford and who to the Mark Twain of that period seemed an important man of letters, he collaborated in a novel, *The Gilded Age,* which appeared in 1873. The more conventional elements in the book, the Easterners and their loves and fortunes, are Warner's; the more original, the sections portraying Western life and satirizing Congress and

Washington, are Mark Twain's. His, too, is the masterly conception of Colonel Beriah Sellers, the man of hope, who lives constantly in the expectation of an avalanche of unearned increment in his direction. From the collaboration of two such different authors nothing unified could come. Warner's chapters are usually tame; Mark Twain's are often noisy and busy with his old burlesque. Neither man shrank from melodrama or hesitated to set it side by side with the most scrupulous realism. But the materials of *The Gilded Age* are better than its art. Perhaps all the more truly because of its lack of balance and perspective does the book reproduce the jangled spirit of the time, its restlessness, its violence, its enthusiasms so singularly blended of the sordid and the altruistic. Colonel Sellers, who has the blood of his creator in him, typifies an entire age which had newly begun to realize the enormous resources of the continent and was mad, was ridiculous, with the fever of desire for sudden riches. The age was gilded. Mark Twain, just arrived from simpler regions, mocked the tedious formalisms and accused the brazen corruptions of the capital. To judge by his share of this joint record he was ready to become a national satirist and to hurl his laughter against a thousand abuses deserving scorn.

He did not become a national satirist, or assume, at least in public, the unpopular rôle of critic of the age. Instead, urged by Howells, he turned back to his Middle Western recollections and wrote for the *Atlantic* in 1875 his *Old Times on the Mississippi*, later included in *Life on the Mississippi* (1883), and *The Adventures of Tom Sawyer* (1876). *Life on the Mississippi* belongs with the most precious American books. The second part, which reports a journey Mark Twain made in 1882 to visit old scenes, rises in parts little above good reporting, though all of it conveys a sense of the deeps of many memories beneath the adventures it recounts. But the first twenty chapters flash and glow as even the highest passages of *Roughing It* had not done. Herein are set down

(145)

with a crowded accuracy warmed by eloquence and affection the impressions of Mark Twain's eager youth, of his old aspirations toward the river, of his struggle to attain mastery over it, of his consummate hours as pilot. The splendor of those days had grown upon him, not faded, and he who had once entered into their events with the flushed passions of an epic hero now wrought at them with the accomplished strength of an epic poet. In his youth observing the river without one thought that he might some day translate it into art, he had had no bias and no self-consciousness. Now he could go back in his imagination to a world seen round and whole, as men of action see their worlds. He remembered a thousand hard actualities of those elder circumstances. He remembered the dialect, the costume, the amphibious river men, half horse half alligator as the old phrase had it, the savagery, the danger, the ardors of the pilot's calling, the thick, stirring panorama of that epoch. He remembered, too, the glamor of those days, the dreams of adventure, the mystery of black nights, the glory of dawn over the yellow water when the atmosphere was full of the songs of invisible birds. And winding through all his memories, like the Mississippi winding through its continent, went the great, muddy, mysterious river which had stirred his imagination for nearly half a century.

The Adventures of Tom Sawyer took Mark Twain from epic to comedy. He first planned to write a play and when he decided upon another form he had in mind a story of boyhood which, like Aldrich's *Story of a Bad Boy*, should emphatically depart from the customary type of Sunday school fiction. But its departure from a type is one of the least memorable aspects of *Tom Sawyer*. Tom and Huck are, indeed, bad boys; they have done more than overhear profanity and smell the smoke of pipes; they play outrageous pranks in the fashion of the disapproved youngsters of all small American towns; their exploits have even caused both *Tom Sawyer* and *Huckleberry Finn* to be at times barred by librarians in whom zeal exceeds imagination. These qualities in the heroes, however, only conform to the general quality of realism which characterizes *Tom Sawyer* throughout. To a delicate taste, the book may seem occasionally overloaded with matters brought in at moments when no necessity in the narrative calls for them. The boyish superstitions, delectable as they are in themselves, may seem to lug *Tom Sawyer* to the documentary side of the line which divides documents from works of art. Nor can the murder about which the story is built up be said to dominate it very thoroughly. The story moves forward in something the same manner as did the plays of the seventies, with exits and entrances not always motivated. And yet a taste so delicate as to resent these defects of structure would probably not appreciate the flexibility of the narrative, its easy, casual gait, its broad sweep, its variety of substance. Mark Twain drives with careless, sagging reins, but he holds the general direction. Most of his readers remember certain episodes, particularly the white-washing of the fence and the appearance of the boys at their own funeral, rather than the story as a whole. The plot of *Tom Sawyer* means considerably less than the characters. A hundred incidents beside those here chosen would have served as well; the characters are each of them unique. Certain of them come directly or indirectly from the life, notably the vagabond Huckleberry Finn and Aunt Polly and Becky Thatcher, the Gang, and Tom Sawyer himself, who, though compounded of numerous elements, essentially reproduces the youthful figure of his creator. Such a mixture of rich humor and serious observation had never before been devoted to the study of a boy in fiction. Mark Twain smiles constantly at the absurd in Tom's character, but he does not laugh Tom into insignificance or lecture him into the semblance of a puppet. Boys of Tom's age can follow his fortunes without discomfort or boredom. At the same time, there are overtones which most juvenile fiction entirely

(147)

lacks and which continue to delight those adults who Mark Twain said, upon finishing his story, alone would ever read it. At the moment he must have felt that the poetry and satire of *Tom Sawyer* outranked the narrative, and he was right. They have proved the permanent, at least the preservative, elements of a classic.

Tom Sawyer cannot be discussed except in connection with its glorious sequel *The Adventures of Huckleberry Finn* (1885). "By and by," Mark Twain had written to Howells when he announced the completion of *Tom Sawyer*, "I shall take a boy of twelve and run him through life (in the first person)"; and he had begun the new book almost at once; but with characteristic uncertainty of taste he had lost interest in it and turned to struggle over a preposterous detective comedy which he wanted to name *Balaam's Ass*. Again in 1880 and finally in 1883 he came back to his masterpiece, published two years later. In spite of this hesitation and procrastination *Huckleberry Finn* has remarkable unity. To tell a story in the first person was second nature to Mark Twain. His travel books had so been told, no matter what nonautobiographical episodes he might elect to bring in. But he was more than a humorous liar; he was an instinctive actor; Sir Henry Irving regretted that Mark Twain had never gone upon the stage. Once he had decided to tell the story through Huck Finn's mouth he could proceed at his most effortless pace. His sense of identity with the boy restricted him to a realistic substance as no principles of art, in Mark Twain's case, could have done. With the first sentence he fell into an idiom and a rhythm flawlessly adapted to the naïve, nasal, drawling little vagabond. "You don't know me without you have read a book by the name of *The Adventures of Tom Sawyer*; but that ain't no matter. That book was made by Mr. Mark Twain, and he told the truth, mainly. There was things which he stretched, but mainly he told the truth." It has been remarked that Huck appears rather more conscious of the charms of external nature than his Hannibal prototype, Tom Blankenship, doubtless was; and of course, strictly speaking, he rises above lifelikeness altogether by his gift for telling a long yarn which has artistic economy and satiric point. But something like this may be said of all heroes presented in the first person. Mark Twain, though for the time being he had relapsed to the shiftless lingo of his boyhood companion, was after all acting Huck for the sake of interpreting him; and interpretation enlarges the thing interpreted. Tom Sawyer acquires a new solidity by being shown here through the eyes of another boy, who, far from laughing at Tom's fanciful ways of doing plain tasks, admires them as the symptoms of a superior intelligence. After this fashion all the material of the narrative comes through Huck's perceptions. Mouthpiece for others, Huck is also mouthpiece for himself so competently that the whole of his tough, ignorant, generous, loyal, mendacious nature lies revealed.

And yet virtues still larger than structural unity make *Huckleberry Finn* Mark Twain's masterpiece. In richness of life *Tom Sawyer* cannot compare with it. The earlier of the two books keeps close home in one sleepy, dusty village, illuminated chiefly, at inconvenient moments, by Tom Sawyer's escapades. But in *Huckleberry Finn* the plot, like Mark Twain's imagination, goes voyaging. Five short chapters and Huck leaves his native village for the ampler world of the picaresque. An interval of captivity with his father—that unpleasant admonitory picture of what Huck may some day become if he outgrows his engaging youthful fineness—and then the boy slips out upon the river which is the home of his spirit. There he realizes every dream he has ever had. He has a raft of his own. He has a friend, the Negro Jim, with the strength of a man, the companionableness of a boy, and the fidelity of a dog. He can have food for the fun of taking it out of the water or stealing it from along the shore. He sleeps and wakes when he pleases. The weather of the

(149)

lower Mississippi in summer bites no one. At the same time, this life is not too safe. Jim may be caught and taken from his benefactor. With all his craft, Huck is actually, as a boy, very much at the mercy of the rough men who infest the river. Adventure complicates and enhances his freedom. And what adventure! It never ceases, but flows on as naturally as the river which furthers the plot of the story by conveying the characters from point to point. Both banks are as crowded with excitement, if not with danger, as the surrounding forest of the older romances. Huck can slip ashore at any moment and try his luck with the universe in which he moves without belonging to it. Now he is the terrified and involuntary witness of a cruel murder plot, and again of an actual murder. Now he strays, with his boy's astonished simplicity, into the Grangerford-Shepherdson vendetta and see another *Romeo and Juliet* enacted in Kentucky. In the undesired company of the king and the duke, certainly two as sorry and as immortal rogues as fiction ever exhibited, Huck is initiated into degrees of scalawaggery which he could not have experienced, at his age, alone: into amateur theatricals as extraordinary as the Royal Nonesuch and frauds as barefaced as the impostures practised upon the camp-meeting and upon the heirs of Peter Wilks. After sights and undertakings so Odyssean, the last quarter of the book, given over to Tom Sawyer's romantic expedients for getting Jim, who is actually free already, out of a prison from which he could have been released in ten minutes, is preserved from the descent into anticlimax only by its hilarious comic force. As if to make up for the absence of more sizable adventures, this mimic conspiracy is presented with enough art and enough reality in its genre studies to furnish an entire novel. That, in a way, is the effect of *Huckleberry Finn* as a whole: though the hero, by reason of his youth, cannot entirely take part in the action, and the action is therefore not entirely at first hand, the picture lacks little that could make it more vivid or veracious.

Huckleberry Finn was, with *The Scarlet Letter* and *Moby Dick*, the third American novel that can be called, simply, great. Of the three only *Moby Dick* offers picture and problem both; *The Scarlet Letter* has in contrast virtually no picture; *Huckleberry Finn*, virtually no problem. Huck undergoes, it is true, certain naggings from the set of unripe prejudices he calls his conscience; and once he rises to an appealing unselfishness when, in defiance of all the principles he has been taught to value, he makes up his mind that he will help the runaway slave to freedom. But in the sense that *The Scarlet Letter* and *Moby Dick* pose moral and cosmic problems, *Huckleberry Finn* poses none at all. Its criticism of life is of another sort. Mark Twain, in the midst of many vicissitudes remembering the river of his youthful happiness, had seen the panorama of it unrolling before him and had been moved to record it out of sheer joy in its old wildness and beauty, assured that merely to have such a story to tell was reason enough for telling it. Having written *Life on the Mississippi* he had already reduced the river to its own language; having written *Tom Sawyer*, he had got his characters in hand. There wanted only the moment when his imagination should take fire at recollection and rush away on its unspeculative task of reproducing the great days of the valley. Had Mark Twain undertaken to make another and a greater Gilded Age out of his matter, to portray the life of the river satirically on the largest scale, instead of in such dimensions as fit Huck's boyish limitations of knowledge, he might possibly have made a better book, but he would have had to be another man. Being the man he was, he touched his peak of imaginative creation not by taking thought how he could be a complete novelist of the Mississippi but by yarning with all his gusto about an adventure he might have had in the dawn of his days. Although he did not deliberately gather riches, riches came.

A *Tramp Abroad* (1880), written about a walking trip which Mark Twain made in 1878 through the Black Forest and to the Alps with his friend the Rev. Joseph H. Twitchell, continued his now expected devices in humorous autobiography, without any important innovations. Certain episodes and certain descriptive passages emerge from the general level, but even they only emphasize the debt his imagination owed to memory. Writing too close to his facts he could never be at his richest. In 1882 he published his first historical novel, *The Prince and the Pauper*, avowedly for children and yet packed with adult satire in its account of how by a change of clothes Prince Edward, later Edward VI of England, and Tom Canty, a London beggar boy, undergo also a change of station and for an instructive period each taste the other's fare. By some such dramatic contrast Mark Twain, the radical American, preferred always to express his opinion of monarchical societies; like the older republican patriots, he set hatred for kings as a first article in his political creed. Of this important side of his nature the most characteristic utterances are to be found in *A Connecticut Yankee in King Arthur's Court* (1889), which deserves also to be considered one of the most thoroughly typical books yet produced by the American democracy. It is typical in method and typical in conclusion. With the brash irresponsibility of frontier vaudeville it catches up a hard, dry, obstreperous Yankee, hurries him back through thirteen centuries, and dumps him, with all his wits about him, into Camelot. Speaking in terms of literary history, the *Yankee* is an anti-romance; it indicates a reaction from the sentimentalism about the Middle Ages which had recently been feeding on Tennyson's *Idylls of the King*, William Morris's *Earthly Paradise*, the Pre-Raphaelites, and Pater, and now was languishing in the sunflower cult of Oscar Wilde. Gilbert and Sullivan had already satirized this cult in *Patience*, by exposing the affectations of the æsthetes who professed it. Mark Twain, partly aroused by the strictures on America of Matthew Arnold, went to work in a more burly way. Let us see, he said in effect, how this longing for the past would work out if gratified. What about the plain man under Arthur? What about plumbing and soap and medicines and wages and habeas corpus? What filth and superstition and cruelty did the pomps of feudalism not overlay? Mark Twain behaves as the devil's advocate in the *Yankee*, candidly ascribing to the sixth century the abuses of other older ages as well as its own. Perhaps, since he habitually read Malory's *Morte d'Arthur* and had a natural tenderness for its chivalric postures, he even exhibits a special animus arising from civil war within himself. At any rate, he let himself run almost without check among sixth-century scenes as he imagined them, ridiculing follies with a burlesque as riotous as that in *The Innocents Abroad*, and adding to it the more serious anger which had grown upon him. To appreciate the fun of the *Yankee* one must have been accustomed to the rowdy modes of American humor; to feel all its censure one must have at least a strain of the revolutionary. And yet persons equipped with neither may perceive the magnificent vigor of the narrative. It ranges from ludicrous to sublime; from the tears of hysterical laughter to the tears of broken pity. With such consequences a barbarian of genius might burst into the court of some narrow principality; he would shatter a thousand delicately poised decorums—many of them harmless enough—and expose a thousand obnoxious shams.

Mark Twain's next and last large experiment in fiction was the *Personal Recollections of Joan of Arc*, published anonymously after long incubation in 1896. His decisive preference for this among all his books may perhaps be ascribed to the unusual labor to which he was put by an unprecedented task; it may also be ascribed to a lifelong interest in Joan which, beginning as a boy's sympathy for a girl's tragic fate, finally

(153)

amounted to a genuine reverence for the Maid which saw in her the symbol of innocence undone by malice and corruption. Like his fierce essay *In Defense of Harriet Shelley* (1894) and his movingly tender *Eve's Diary* (1906), *Joan of Arc* illuminates that region in Mark Twain's nature which practised a sort of secular Mariolatry. Many American frontiersmen by their undoctrinal worship of womankind at large often approached the worship of the Madonna. Of course, this *Joan of Arc* pretends to be narrated by the friend and secretary of the heroine; but the authentic tones of Mark Twain again and again drown the reminiscent treble of Louis de Conte. Against a confused, somber, truthful enough background he raises the white banner of the Maid. She is herself the banner, the quintessence of a cause. He accepts the voices without a question; nor do they seem particularly superhuman by comparison with the radiant sweetness and wisdom with which he endows her. The book constitutes his answer to the charge brought up by the *Innocents Abroad* and the *Yankee*, that he lacked reverence for names made sacred to men by good report; it is proof that he commanded the accents of adoration. In its own right, however, it must rank below an imaginative achievement like *Huckleberry Finn* because it is less thoroughly grounded than that book in any real experience. Over too many chapters of *Joan of Arc* droops the languid haze which accompanied all the historical romances of the American nineties. Only in the final third, which deals with the trial and which masterfully employs the original records, does Mark Twain knit his passion with his facts in the degree which breaks down the boundaries ordinarily only too able to divide romance from reality.

After *Joan of Arc* he wrote nothing equal to it in dimension and ambition. He gave up his house at Hartford and lived somewhat randomly, in various European cities, in New York, at Riverdale-on-Hudson, and finally from 1908 till his death two years later in his new house, Stormfield, at Redding, Connecticut. His sweetness had begun to grow weary and turn more and more insistently to thought which was neither sweet nor gay. His pessimism appears unmistakably in *Following the Equator* (1897), fruit of a lecture tour round the world which at sixty he had courageously undertaken to pay off the burden of debts due to his failure as a publisher. His great schemes for a fortune had failed; a beloved daughter died while he was on his royal progress; the antiquity of Asia appalled him. Though now a national figure, by popular suffrage *the* national man of letters, he had for some years suffered from a diffusion, if not a diminution of his power. *The American Claimant* (1892), returning to Colonel Sellers of *The Gilded Age* for material, and *Tom Sawyer Abroad* (1894) and *Tom Sawyer, Detective* (1896), had none of them fulfilled expectations naturally aroused. Even the better novel *Pudd'nhead Wilson* (1894), defied the efforts he put into it and escaped his control as he wrote. Part of it moved off into unrestrained farce and had to be issued separately as *Those Extraordinary Twins*; part of it developed into the seriously conceived tragedy of Roxana and her son—but a tragedy founded on the conventional device of infants changed in the cradle. It adds something to Mark Twain's documentary value by its picture of Virginians in the West and by its principal character, Pudd'nhead Wilson. As an amateur detective he illustrates the interest which Mark Twain, who liked all sorts of ingenuity, took in stories of the detection of crime, an interest also illustrated by *A Double Barrelled Detective Story* (1902). But Pudd'nhead is more memorable as the village atheist, whose maxims, printed at the head of each chapter in this book and also in *Following the Equator*, so frequently express the tired disillusionment which was becoming Mark Twain's characteristic mood. "Pity," says Pudd'nhead, "is for the living, envy is for the dead."

"I have been reading the morning paper," Mark Twain

wrote to Howells in 1899. "I do it every morning—well knowing that I shall find in it the usual depravities and basenesses and hypocrisies and cruelties that make up civilization, and cause me to put in the rest of the day pleading for the damnation of the human race." Some such despair of mankind had furnished a strain in his constitution from his early days. He had the frontiersman's contempt for the ordinary gestures of idealism. Judged by his simple, though inflexible, code of morals the world fell pitifully short. The human race he observed to be lazy, selfish, envious, given to lying, disposed to disease and vice and crime, fawning in adversity, tyrannical in prosperity, and at all times the dupe of countless errors. "Let me make the superstitions of a nation and I care not who makes its laws or its songs either." At the same time, Mark Twain lacked the fullest outlet of misanthropy; he could not, because of his natural kindliness, help himself by laying his hatred of the race upon his fellows. His hatred came home and condemned him too. "What a man sees in the human race is merely himself in the deep and honest privacy of his own heart." In such a companionship he pitied men more than he hated them. "Everything human is pathetic. The secret source of Humor itself is not joy but sorrow. There is no humor in heaven."

In various unendurable hours, however, Mark Twain did seek something upon which to throw off his burden. In theology a deist of the school of Paine and Ingersoll, with a tincture of modern science added to the iron conscience of old-fashioned backwoods Calvinism, he invented a machine more or less in the image of a god, and held it to account for the blunders of the world. The human individual, he argued in *What Is Man?* (written in 1898 but not printed until 1906 and then at first privately), is a mere automaton, without choice as to his birth or as to any impulse or thought or action, good or bad. Each decision follows irresistibly from precedent circumstances and so on back to the protoplasmic beginnings. Beliefs and resolutions cannot control behavior, which follows instinctively from the temperament with which the individual is endowed and which operates under the sleepless rule of the master-passion, the desire for self-approval. Punishment and censure are consequently meaningless; so is remorse. Mark Twain, who had no more than an amateur's learning in ethical systems, believed his doctrine of scientific determinism to be more novel and contributory than it was. As a matter of fact, not the logical but the personal aspects of his contentions are impressive. By them he unconsciously defended himself from the savage, the morbid attacks of self-condemnation and remorse from which he repeatedly suffered for all his peccadilloes. Only by assuring himself that no one deserves such blame could Mark Twain quiet his raging conscience. The fault lies with the bungled system on which the universe is made; with the intelligences which created it and continue to play wanton pranks upon it; still more upon any competent intelligence, if there is one, which refuses to exercise mercy and destroy the miserable race of men.

Such philosophic nihilism did not constantly possess Mark Twain during the disturbed last dozen years of his life. In *The Man That Corrupted Hadleyburg* (1900) he produced a corrosive apologue on the effects of greed, which here overthrows all the respectable reputations in a smug provincial town. Only one of them wins pity; the others appear not as moral automatons but as responsible thieves and hypocrites. And similarly *The $30,000 Bequest* (1906) traces in a foolish couple the fatal influence of the anticipation of wealth. What Mark Twain had once thought hugely comic in Colonel Sellers he had now come, after his own hot hopes and disappointments, to regard as one of the first of follies, if not of offenses. In neither story, however, are the negligent or malicious higher powers shown at work, unless it is through the poor frailties of the men and women. *Captain Storm-*

field's *Visit to Heaven* (published 1909 but written fully
forty years before) took a very substantial sailor to heaven
as the *Connecticut Yankee* had taken a skeptical mechanic
to Arthur's Court. That Mark Twain originally thought his
fanciful story blasphemous and suppressed it so long shows
how orthodox was the social stratum from which he derived
and which might have been hurt by light references to jasper
walls and pearly gates.

For intellectual energy *Stormfield* cannot be mentioned
in the same breath with *The Mysterious Stranger*, written
during the dark night of Mark Twain's spirit in 1898,
(along, it should be noted, with *What Is Man?* and *The
Man That Corrupted Hadleyburg*) but first published in
1916. The scene lies ostensibly in sixteenth-century Austria
but actually, to all intents, in the Hannibal of Tom and Huck.
Boys like these make up the central group; the narrator, Theodor Fischer, is as much Mark Twain as Tom Sawyer ever was.
To them comes at times a supernatural playmate calling himself Philip Traum but rightly Satan, nephew of the mightier potentate of that name. Though he plays terrible pranks
upon the villagers, he seems beneficence itself as compared
to them, with their superstition and cowardice and cruelty.
And all the time he acts, for the three boys, as commentator
upon the despicable human race, "a museum of diseases, a
home of impurities," which "begins as dirt and departs as
stench"; which uses its boasted moral sense to know good
from evil and then to follow evil. The sole redeeming fact in
human life, Philip assures Theodor in the end, is that *"Life
itself is only a vision, a dream. . . . Nothing exists save empty
space—and you. . . . Strange, indeed, that you should not
have suspected that your universe and its contents were only
dreams, visions, fictions. Strange, because they are so frankly
and hysterically insane—like all dreams, . . . the silly creations
of an imagination that is not conscious of its freaks—in a
word, . . . they are a dream, and you the maker of it."* "I

myself," says Philip, like Prospero breaking his wand, "have no existence; I am but a dream. . . . In a little while you will be alone in shoreless space, to wander its limitless solitudes without friend or comrade forever—for you will remain a *thought*, the only existent thought, and by your nature inextinguishable, indestructible. But I, your poor servant, have revealed you to yourself and set you free. Dream other dreams, and better!"

Although it was out of such deeps of despair that there rose into Mark Twain's work the profounder qualities which lift him above all other American humorists, he nevertheless customarily lived and wrote nearer the surfaces of existence. Heretical as he might be in his theology, he nevertheless employed—when he employed anything of the sort—the Christian images of God and Satan, Heaven and Eden, the patriarchs and the heathen, all of them referred to in a language immediately understood by the populace. So in his political doctrines, though privately he might be now as Utopian as Sir Thomas More and now as realistic as Nietzsche, he spoke in the American idiom as regards the usurping despots of the earth, the rights of the natural man, the superiority of republics to monarchies, the advantages of material well-being, the hope that through individual freedom and public education the human mass might be advanced to a plane never yet reached. He could rage over such abuses as Congressional stupidity and municipal graft, the brutality of the civil mob at home and the military mob in the Philippines, and yet could turn with patriotic fury against foreign detractors, as in his flaying of Paul Bourget for that critic's sharp remarks about the United States. So also the geographical or historical culture taken for granted in Mark Twain's books was that of the average American, who knows more about Palestine than about Greece, more about Rome than about all the rest of the Mediterranean, more about England than about all the rest of Europe, more about the American Revolution and Civil War than about all the rest of history put together; who catches readily any references to Cæsar or Shakespeare or George Washington or Napoleon but not so readily those to Cato or Leonardo da Vinci or Goethe or Darwin. And finally, the typical heroes of Mark Twain's imagined universe are of the sort considered typical in America. They walk the world, like the Yankee in medieval England, the Innocents in the Holy Land, Captain Stormfield in Heaven itself, erect and confident, neither cultivated nor colonial enough to be embarrassed, testing and measuring all things by the simplest standards. They are as clannish as provincials and as cocksure as pioneers. Occasionally obsessed by the Puritan conscience, they lack the eccentric ideals of holiness, mysticism, poetry. Although brave enough in the flesh, they only sometimes have the courage to be original. In the spirit they rise as high as to a certain chivalry toward women, and toward children, and to an occasional fine, heroic altruism; but they do not often rise higher. Their moral concerns are about industry, common honesty, domestic loyalty, good comradeship, sensible habits of mind and body. Profane and irreverent enough, they are generally chaste and considerate. They hold cruelty to be the principal vice and democratic friendliness the principal virtue.

The art of Mark Twain springs hardly less truly than his ideas from the American people as a whole. "I like history, biography, travel, curious facts and strange happenings, and science," he said. "And I detest novels, poetry, and theology." He would have been the last to reflect in what category his own writing fell, and he never suspected that he would come in time to be thought of as having raised the frontier tall tale into literature. As to novelists, he could not stand Henry James or George Eliot or Hawthorne; he found Scott an unendurable snob and Cooper a literary bungler; he developed his loathing for Jane Austen until he came to take a positive delight in uttering it in the most violent language; and his

admiration for the work of Howells must be assigned in part
to his affection for the man. Mark Twain's taste lay wholly
in the direction of large actions, large passions, large scenery.
That he moved so casually over the face of the earth and
through the historical periods he knew is proof enough that
he possessed none of the professed realist's timidity when
on unaccustomed ground. No Franklin ever felt more at home
in ticklish surroundings than Mark Twain did. This same confidence, which deprived him of the austere seriousness of
some men of letters, stood by him also in his methods. He did
not mind a sudden change of key, but could fall from passionate eloquence to burlesque, and climb from farce to
tragedy without even thinking whether this suited the dignity
of literature. Though at times he seems to have respected
academic judgment too much—especially as represented by
Howells and the *Atlantic's* audience—and though he latterly
resented the opinion that he was a humorist merely, he did
depend in his art primarily upon the humorist's technique.

"To string incongruities and absurdities together in a wandering and sometimes purposeless way, and seem innocently
unaware that they are absurdities, is the basis of the American
art," he said of the oral method of humor. The tricks of oral
delivery are those he used most, whether he spoke or wrote.
His rapid improvisation has the effect of flowing speech. To
all appearances—which are borne out by what is known of his
habits of composition—he drove his pen through his sentences
at almost the rate of conversation, and had constantly a physical audience in mind. On it he tried his "wandering and
purposeless" incongruities, his "slurring of the point," his
"dropping of a studied remark apparently without knowing
it, apparently as if one were thinking aloud." When actually
lecturing he could hold, with his inflections and pauses, the
attention of the most fastidious hearers as well as of the ordinary crowd, making capital of his lower moments and shad-
ing down the higher with humorous deprecation. Even in

(161)

the comparative coolness of print his methods were essentially oral. They reveal themselves in his partiality for autobiographical narrative, in his rambling sentence-structure, in his anti-climaxes and afterthoughts. Above all they are revealed in his humoristic device of occupying the stage so much of the time in his own person. For Mark Twain to practise his art was, more than with any other American writer, to exhibit and expound his own personality. The greatness of his personality was the measure of his fame.

Accepted from the first by the public, he was toward the end of his life recognized by universities, with honorary degrees from Yale (1901) and Oxford (1907), and after his death came to be a focus of criticism in an age which brought a new note into American literature. *Mark Twain* (1912), the authorized biography by Albert Bigelow Paine, and *Mark Twain's Letters* (1917) made his life nearly as well known as his work. Advanced criticism fixed upon him as a dark example of the danger of too much concession to the popular taste and of the repression of unpopular ideas in an artist. His career was cited as proof that the United States discouraged originality and candor. *Mark Twain's Autobiography* (1924) had a Preface as from the Grave in which he said: "I speak from the grave rather than with my living tongue, for a good reason: I can speak thence freely. . . . It has seemed to me that I could be as frank and free and unembarrassed as a love letter if I knew that what I was writing would be exposed to no eye till I was dead, and unaware, and indifferent." But the *Autobiography* itself seemed hardly so reckless as he had thought it. Though his sensitive conscience had accused him of playing safe, he had probably spoken out on most of the matters which most concerned him. He was not primarily a thinker, but rather a natural force which had moved through the world laughing, an American Adam with the eye of innocence giving new names to what he saw.

(162)

HENRY JAMES

AMERICAN PATRIOTISM always has contended that America does as well as Europe as a background for fiction, pointing to the epic dimensions and the epic hopes of existence on this continent. Less expansive dispositions long continued to feel that the human past of the country has not been large enough to match the landscape; that the present at any given moment has lacked the stability, the solidarity, which alone might afford the novelist a firm texture of reality in his representations; that the simplicity of American manners, being merely provincial rather than fittingly republican, makes impossible the subtleties and nuances of European fiction. Of the principal novelists of the generation after the Civil War Howells held, on the whole, the most catholic critical opinions. He built, with some limitations, on what he saw before him, not unconscious of Europe but aware that the way to a body of American fiction was action as well as argument and that in the production of a national literature imagination begets imagination. Mark Twain, without much reflection but with powerful instincts in the matter, worked in the fashion of all great autochthons—as if his native land were the center of the world. Henry James, at the other extreme, never ceased to regard America as essentially an outlying region of European, specifically of Anglo-Saxon, civilization. The differing governments of England and the United States were simply nothing to him, who knew and cared so little for man as a political animal. For this craftsman in language it was language which outlined the empire of the English and bound its various parts together in spite of such surface matters as ocean and revolution. He was a loyalist to the tongue of England. And of course speech was for him but a symbol of all the customs which he thought of as centering in or about London and to which he drew near and nearer with a passion of return which implies an atavistic hankering in the blood. In other words, Henry James was a patriot to his race, and his final transfer of citizenship, though immediately called forth by his sense of America's procrastination in the World War, was but the outward sign of a temperamental repatriation already complete.

The process began early under the deliberate guidance of Henry James, Sr., a remarkable metaphysician and theologian, who sought to make his sons citizens of the world by never allowing them to take root in any particular religion, political system, ethical code, or set of personal habits. Born in New York in 1843, Henry James had the most desultory schooling, under the most diverse teachers, in New York, Albany, Geneva, London, Paris, Newport, Geneva again, Bonn, and again Newport, studying now mathematics, now languages, reading a good deal of Latin and a little Greek, dabbling in Fourier and Ruskin, drawing a little, immersing himself in the British magazines and the *Revue des deux Mondes,* and from a very early period writing stories on the model of Balzac. A circle which contained at once the elder Henry James and his son William was out of contact with few of the important ideas then stirring; and the father was accustomed to bringing into the household many of the eminent Europeans who visited the United States from time to time. The Civil War would possibly have enlisted Henry, as it did his two younger brothers, but for a physical disability; and it did without doubt mark him deeply. "It introduced into the national consciousness," Henry James wrote in 1879, by the national consciousness undoubtedly meaning his own as well, "a certain sense of proportion and relation, of the world being a more complicated place than it had hitherto

seemed, the future more treacherous, success more difficult
... [a perception] that this is a world in which everything
happens." His non-participation in the war at first hand appears also to have developed—hardly aroused—in him a sense
that his essential rôle was to be that of a spectator of life.
At any rate, instead of going to war he went to Harvard in
1862, for some reason to the Law School, which touched him
hardly at all in comparison with the men of letters whom he
encountered in Boston or Cambridge, in particular Charles
Eliot Norton and William Dean Howells. Through them he
became a contributor of critical articles to the *Nation* and
the *North American* and of stories to the *Atlantic* and the
Galaxy. The "open editorial hand" which Howells held out
to him from the *Atlantic* during the summer of 1868, Henry
James said, "was really the making of me, the making of the
confidence that required help and sympathy and that I should
otherwise, I think, have strayed and stumbled about a long
time without acquiring. You showed me the way and opened
me the door." New England, however, could not satisfy him.
Early in 1869 he made the passionate pilgrimage to Europe
which, in various forms, provides the theme for so large a
portion of his work: England, Switzerland, Italy, France in
turn met his "relish for the element of accumulation in the
human picture and for the infinite superpositions of history."
Singular contrast between the behavior of the Innocent
Abroad and the Passionate Pilgrim! Without anything like
so deep a sense for history as Mark Twain, Henry James had
not Mark Twain's ignorance to sustain him against the mag-
netic pull of Europe, nor that indigenousness which restored
Mark Twain to his original continent. Lacking any strong
roots in the American soil, Henry James, though he returned
to Cambridge in 1870 for two years, and after a further European sojourn during 1872-1874, for one year more, now suc-
cumbed to the centripetal pull which all along had been acting upon him, and in 1875 finally decided that his future

belonged to Europe. For a year he tried Paris, where he met Turgenev and the Flaubert group: Edmond de Goncourt, Daudet, Maupassant, Zola; but he there felt too much a foreigner for comfort, and late in 1876 he settled for good in London, the natural home of his imagination.

With *Roderick Hudson* (1876) James concluded the long years of experimentation through which, like Hawthorne before him, he seriously ascended to his art. His first novel, *Watch and Ward*, issued as a serial in the *Atlantic* during 1871, was a trivial performance. Of the more than a score of short stories he published before his homesick hegira, he later cared to preserve but three. The discarded trifles betray a strong influence of Hawthorne, particularly *The Romance of Certain Old Clothes*, with its dusky scene laid in eighteenth-century America and its ghostly, inconclusive conclusion; *De Grey: a Romance*, the study of an ancestral curse dubiously inherited by a New York family from its European forebears; and *The Last of the Valerii*, wherein a young Roman noble-man digs up a statue of Venus from his garden and fatally reverts to the worship of her pagan loveliness. No such dominant magic as Hawthorne's, however, quite invests these tales; Henry James belonged to a different universe, with a different heaven and hell. Nor could he even as well as the Hawthorne of *The Seven Vagabonds*, for instance, succeed with little adventures into the picaresque like *Professor Fargo*, with its tawdry traveling showmen. James came nearer to achieving the considered sobriety of George Eliot, whom he admired; and he tucked himself as far as he could under the edge of the mantle of Balzac. In *Travelling Companions* is foreshadowed James's later skill in the description of an-cient landscape and architecture; in *At Isella*, his habit of rounding out a story from the most flying hint; and in *The Sweetheart of Mr. Briseux*, at least in patches, his smoothly ironical, dexterously enwinding style. The stiffness and scrawniness of youth appears more obviously in his purely

American stories than in those narrated against a European
background: the three he salvaged from these days of experiment—A Passionate Pilgrim (1871), The Madonna of the Future (1873), Madame de Mauves (1874). Madame de Mauves
is a sort of American Una among European lions, the snowy
wife of a sinful Frenchman who first hates her because she will
neither "submit basely nor rebel crookedly" and then melodramatically blows his brains out because, when he has fallen
in love with her, she cannot forgive him. Theobald, in the
affecting Madonna of the Future, has for twenty years nursed
in Florence the vision of a flawless Madonna which he means
to paint, only to find out at last that he has dawdled away
his powers and chances: his adored model has grown coarse,
his hand cannot execute his beautiful plan. A Passionate Pilgrim carries an overwrought American to England to claim
a fortune, as Hawthorne's Ancestral Footstep had done. The
plot is nearly as romantic as Hawthorne would have made it;
the chief concern is the sensations of the ardent traveler in
the presence of that charm which maddens, in Henry James,
the "famished race." This concern, too, makes up a large bulk
of Roderick Hudson, the account of a young sculptor who,
thanks to a friendly patron, is suddenly lifted from the naked,
rectangular society of Northampton, Massachusetts, and set
down in Rome in the hope that something great will come of
his genius under circumstances luxuriantly propitious. His
vein proves thin and he goes, with unconvincing promptness,
to pieces, and then on to fall to death over a Swiss precipice.
James later admitted that the element of time in this novel
should have been better handled; that he had borrowed more
from the intensity of the dramatist than, as novelist, he could
offer security for. But he still felt willing to acknowledge as
his own the skill with which he had presented the entire
action—Roderick's aspiration and descent, his unfaithfulness
to Mary Garland and his passion for Christina Light—through
the consciousness of Rowland Mallet, who, though he does

not speak in the first person, renders the narrative something the same service that Miles Coverdale renders in *The Blithedale Romance*. Without at the moment quite understanding it, James was working toward that technique in which he is virtually supreme among novelists: the technique of concentration which makes his novels as compact as tales and which allows his tales to run without dilution of emphasis almost to the dimensions of novels.

Now established in London, James sedulously worked at making himself a purer Anglo-Saxon than he believed he could be anywhere along the periphery of the race, forgetful, it seems, that Anglo-Saxons are explorers and colonizers no less truly than huggers of the insular hearth. As an American with proper introductions he went into penetralia of English society which novelists in the Islands do not easily reach unless they are born to them. He learned, after a struggle and occasional relapses, to like both the weather and the manners of Britain, exposing himself to both those cooling experiences, except for a few brief visits to France and Italy, during five remarkably busy years. The critical doctrines which sustained him he collected and put forth in *French Poets and Novelists* (1888), much of it written during his earlier years on the Continent. "Realism," he said, "seems to us with *Madame Bovary* to have said its last word"; but he felt that for the most part Flaubert's knowledge was greater than his imagination. James admired George Sand's magnificent flow and color, which he oddly compared to that of Spenser in *The Faerie Queene*, but he thought she had too little form and too much optimism: "We suspect that something even better [than optimism] in a novelist is that tender appreciation of actuality which makes even the application of a simple coat of rose-colour seem an act of violence." Balzac, of course, James greatly preferred to either Flaubert or George Sand, for his great range and close texture: "He has against him," James however added, "that he lacks that slight but needful thing—charm." Imagination, substantial texture, charm: all these James found in his great master and favorite Turgenev, whom in 1874, so little had he been translated further west than Paris, it was still possible to include among French novelists. Turgenev had, it seemed to James, "a deeply intellectual impulse toward universal appreciation"; he had form and grace and tenderness and irony. When James says that "the blooming fields of fiction" can hardly show "a group of young girls more radiant with maidenly charm" than Turgenev's, or when he says that these girls "have to our sense a touch of the faintly acrid perfume of the New England temperament—a hint of Puritan angularity," the remark throws a long light ahead on James's own deep concern with the characters of women. And he must have had in mind a parallel between Turgenev and himself when he wrote that "Russian society, like our own, is in process of formation, the Russian character is in solution, in a sea of change, and the modified, modernized Russian, with his old limitations and his new pretensions, is not, to an imagination fond of caressing the old, fixed contours, an especially grateful phenomenon." James still drew considerably, and was long to draw, upon the sprawling continent at his back; but he was fond of caressing the old, fixed contours of Europe.

He sustained his position as an expatriate in his subtle study of *Hawthorne* (1879), which he had been asked by John Morley to contribute to the English Men of Letters series and in which the recent disciple of Hawthorne, while delicately appreciating the master, wrote into almost every page his accusations of provincialism against the entire American nation. "Certain national types," he answered to Howells's comment that it is no more provincial for an American to be very American than for an Englishman to be very English, "are essentially and intrinsically provincial." If James during these acclimatizing years reflected almost constantly upon the international situation it was because he stood in that situation himself. A good deal of what it meant for him may be found ripely remembered in his posthumous autobiographical fragment *The Middle Years*. But he had thousands of companions under the same spell in varying degrees: those of his nationality, who, the Civil War being now over and methods of travel in Europe easier than in the home-keeping days of the Republic, annually swarmed to Europe for vacations of culture. Whether Henry James sympathized with their aspirations or satirized their numerous awkwardnesses in the midst of manners less casual than those of the United States, he could not overlook them or that simplicity which he identified with provinciality. The ground they traversed furnished him a sort of literary terrain which excited his imagination precisely as the frontier, on which another set of Americans had faced the new as these Americans faced the old, had excited the imagination of Fenimore Cooper. Highly ironical as it may seem, it is still not highly fanciful to say that *The American* (1877), begun in Paris in 1875 at a time when James, though delighting in the art and companionship of Turgenev, was yet feeling somewhat excluded from French society, sprang from James's conception of a romantic American gesture like that of Daniel Boone renouncing the settlements, the gesture on which Cooper founded the character of Leather-Stocking. It was, as James subsequently explained, "the situation, in another country and an aristocratic society, of some robust but insidiously beguiled, some cruelly wronged, compatriot: the point being in especial that he should suffer at the hands of persons pretending to represent the highest possible civilization and to be an order in every way superior to his own." But when the opportunity for vindication came, the American, as James conceived him, "in the very act of forcing it home would sacrifice it in disgust," not out of forgiveness but out of so great a contempt for those who had wronged him that he was unwilling to touch them even in a rich revenge. Nor does the plot at large fall, in its romantic

(170)

qualities, below this instigating gesture. Christopher Newman, intensely self-made and American, is in love with the widowed daughter of the intensely ancient and French house of Belle-garde, which, though the daughter loves him in return, snubs him, snatches the lady from him, and drives her into a con-vent. Then, though Newman has found out that her mother and brother murdered her father, the American, making his large gesture, refuses to let the ax descend. Claire de Cintré, lovely as she is made out, belongs with the heroines who are too limp for life though not for romantic tragedy; the mother and brother, James himself admitted, in real life would have been remarkably careful to get hold of Newman's money—through marrying Mme. de Cintré to him if need be—before showing him too much scorn. Nor is Newman excessively convincing; "before the American business-man, as I have been prompt to declare, I was absolutely and irredeemably helpless, with no fibre of my intelligence responding to his mystery." Yet these imperfect elements are tangled in a fine net of charm. Though the style is sparer, sharper than James's style was to become, its texture is here firm with adroit allu-sions and observant wit, while the background of Paris abun-dantly though unobtrusively fills the picture. Vain as it must be to strive for all the perfections of Balzac, Flaubert, George Sand, and Turgenev at once, here still was something that looked toward a synthesis of their excellences—with a singular alloy from the older type of American romance which rejoiced to set the American hero patriotically up above the European crowd.

As if to redress the balance or to atone for this patriotic zeal, *The Europeans* (1878) subjects two charming persons from Europe, though with some of America in their blood, to the deadly seriousness which Henry James remembered as prevailing in the suburbs of Boston. There is caricature in his Wentworths, with their large square house and large square consciences; there is perhaps less of it in the European cousins who find here so little use for the virtues of joy or flexibility; but the conflict of manners is nevertheless presented with nearly as much detachment as brilliance. Following it came two shorter novels—*nouvelles*—also equipoised between the hemispheres. *An International Episode* (1879), which shows an American girl insulted by an English duchess and her daughter and then taking such revenge as she can by refusing to marry the duchess's son, vexed the British, who in such matters were accustomed to look for satire entirely on their own side. *Daisy Miller* (1879) enraged the United States, where it was thought an aspersion upon American girlhood to represent an entirely virtuous but innocently daring young woman from Schenectady as conducting herself in Switzerland and Italy in a manner which confuses, and worse than confuses, a half-Europeanized young American who loves her. Fault was naturally found with Winterbourne, the man in the case, who as an American might have been expected to understand Daisy's behavior as any average American would. But Henry James had done nothing more reprehensible than to make international comedy out of the situation chosen by Milton for his *Comus*. Daisy wears her rustic innocence to the revels, and, though traduced, would have emerged safely had Winterbourne been true to the simple faith of his nation. *Washington Square* (1881) James called "a tale purely American, the writing of which made me feel acutely the want of the 'paraphernalia'" of an established civilization. This want, however, did not keep him from making a dainty masterpiece, lucid and quiet and cool, ironical yet tender, out of his story of how poor dull Catherine Sloper dreamed she had a true lover and then found he was only a fortune-hunter after all. The fashion in which James here constantly explains America to his readers, as if they were of course to be Europeans, hints that he had traveled a long way from his native shores in a half-dozen years, as indeed he had. His concern in the international situation had begun to wear thin.

It was, nevertheless, at this point in his career that he produced the first of his books which may be characterized as magnificent, *The Portrait of a Lady* (1881). Although Isabel Archer belongs in the charming line of those American girls whom James subtly traces through their European adventures, she is more important than any who had gone before her. She is but incidentally American, made so for the convenience of a creator who chose to display her as moving across a scene already lighted by his imagination and familiarized by his art. James saw in her the type of youth advancing toward knowledge of life; of youth at first shy and slight in its innocence but flowering under the sun of experience to the fullest hues and dimensions of a complexity which might under different circumstances have lain dormant; of youth growing irresistibly to meet the destiny which growth compels. Had James belonged to another school he might have preferred a young man for protagonist; as it was he preferred to watch the more subterranean alchemies which, with the fewest possible external incidents, gradually enrich this sort of woman to maturity. The methods of his narrative were suggested by his theme. He would scrupulously keep the center of his subject within Isabel's consciousness, careful not to make her an egoist but equally careful to reveal her qualities by his notation of the delicate refraction which the scenes and personages of her career undergo in passing through her. Working thus, he could not skimp her story. "I would build large," he determined, "in fine embossed vaults and painted arches, as who should say, and yet never let it appear that the chequered pavement, the ground under the reader's feet, fails to stretch at every point to the base of the walls." His scene shifts spaciously from Albany to the Thames, among English country houses more ripe and ample than anything James had yet described, on to Paris, Florence, Rome—"the inimitable France and the incomparable Italy." Nothing hurries the stream of the narrative, which has time for eddies and shallows, broad stretches of noon and deep ominous pools. Isabel, being young and desirable, and like most of James's heroines allowed no career beside that incident to her sex, gets much of her education from being loved: by the too aggressive Bostonian Caspar Goodwood, by the healthy, manly Lord Warburton, by her cousin Ralph Touchett, most light-hearted and charming of all Henry James's men, and by the dilettante Gilbert Osmond. She marries Osmond only to find out finally that she had been coldly tricked into the marriage by Madame Merle, whom Isabel has thought her best friend when the woman is in reality Osmond's mistress anxious to get money for their illegitimate child. Something in the intricate, never quite penetrable fiber of the heroine sends her in the end back to her husband for the sake of her stepdaughter, thinking, it seems, that she thereby encounters her destiny more nobly than in any previous chapter of it. The conclusion, on various grounds, does not satisfy, but it consistently enough rounds out Isabel's chronicle. Praise can hardly exaggerate the skill with which James at first warily investigates as from without the spirit of the fresh young girl, gradually transfers the action to her consciousness, and henceforth with almost no appearance of art reduces his story to the terms of her realization of her fate. In something of this delaying fashion life dawns upon its victims. " 'Tis surely a graceful, ingenious, elaborate work," James wrote of the *Portrait* to Stevenson, who disapproved of it, "with too many pages, but with (I think) an interesting subject and a good deal of life and style." He might justly have said that as to life it was unfailing and as to style all gold and ivory.

In his next two novels, *The Bostonians* (1886) and *The Princess Casamassima* (1886) he relinquished the advantage of international contrast. The first deals with a group of American oddities somewhat stridently set on improving the status of women. Henry James himself belonged with the school of those who hold, in a phrase which he would have given up his position rather than use, that woman's place is the home. He brought to his narrative the tory inclination to satire, and filled the book with sharp caustic portraits and an unprecedented amount of caricature. His Bostonians recall that angular army of transcendentalists whom Lowell's essay on Thoreau hung up once for all in its laughable alcove of New England history. James regards them only too obviously from without, choosing as the consciousness through which they are to be represented a young reactionary from Mississippi, Basil Ransom, who invades this fussy henyard and carries away its prized heroine, Verena Tarrant, on the very eve of her great popular success as a lecturer in behalf of her oppressed but rising sex. By such a scheme James was naturally committed to making his elder feminists all out as unpleasant persons, preying on Verena's youth and charm and enthusiasm, and bound to keep her for their campaign no matter what it might cost her in the way of love and marriage. But more than James's own prejudices and his technical device contributes to a certain insufficiency in *The Bostonians.* It is too largely skeleton, without the blood which might have come from heartier sympathies, without the flesh with which James might have been able to round out a "purely American" tale had he not forgotten so much about American life. He had forgotten, or at least ceased to care greatly about it. Two visits to his native country during 1881-1883 had left him still hungry for Europe, from which after 1883 he was not to return for over twenty years.

The Princess Casamassima is wholly European as to setting and characters. In it the bewildering Christina Light of *Roderick Hudson,* now a discontented princess dabbling in revolution, appears again with a maturer mystery of temperament and an achieved diversity of caprice. The romantic strain which James had lately been repressing here rose unashamed

(175)

to the surface and invented a cock-and-bull yarn about a vast, malignant, ramifying secret society which—not unlike that in Brockden Brown's *Ormond* so long before—was supposed to underlie the whole of modern Europe, ready at almost any moment to break out and set thrones and governments toppling. With the Princess is involved the pathetic Hyacinth Robinson, unacknowledged son of a lord and a book-binder by trade, who falls first into the vicious coils of the anarchists, then into the kindly, though as it turns out no less fatal, coils of the Princess Casamassima, learns to admire the aristocracy, and comes to a tragic end. The story, James said, proceeded directly from his habit of walking the streets of London and reflecting upon the possible lot of some person who should have been produced by this civilization and yet should be condemned, as James decidedly had not been, to witness it from outside: that is, from outside the world of fashion and intelligence. Would not such a humble hero, if sensitive enough, long for all the privileges of such a civilization, plot against them when denied them, fall in love with them when invited to share them even transiently? *The Princess Casamassima* is James's answer to his question; it is, moreover, a remarkable *tour de force*. Although written as from some timid boudoir or club or milder hearth which trembles fantastically at devouring revolutionaries, the book pleases by its variety and swiftness. It has, in the ordinary sense, a plot. And it is evidence too, how thorough was the process of saturation going on in its author, that the background, splendid or sordid, of this novel is crowded with aspects of reality in the still life and racy yet believable characters to an extent that makes *The Bostonians* seem in comparison flat and empty.

If the international novels had shown the "dense categories of dark arcana" of European life threatened by Americans, and *The Princess Casamassima* by revolution, *The Tragic Muse* (1890) showed them threatened by art. Nicholas Dormer resigns his seat in Parliament to become a mere portrait painter, to the horror of his very political mother and fiancée and patron. Parallel to his career is that of Miriam Rooth, who without at first being a lady contrives to become, with the help of genius, a great actress, incidentally refusing, for the sake of her art, a rising diplomat who proposes to make her the most brilliant lady in Europe. The conflict between art and the world had early struck James as "one of the half-dozen great primary motives." That conflict had governed and shaped his own career. So far as he had been a partisan at all in his pictures of life he had sided with the world in its compacter, urbaner phases as against uncivilized crudity and cruelty. But now, standing at the center of the compact, urbane world, he studied the phenomenon of genius which deflects Nick Dormer from all that his caste regards as desirable or even respectable; and which makes Miriam seem important as a human being in spite of her shortcomings as an ornament of society. That singular personage Gabriel Nash, who has no art but the art of living and who has no rôle in the novel but that of chorus, sums up the general problem. "It's the simplest thing in the world; just take for granted our right to be happy and brave. What's essentially kinder and more helpful than that, what's more beneficent? But the tradition of dreariness, of stodginess, of dull dense literal prose, has so sealed people's eyes that they've ended by thinking the most natural of all things the most perverse." Such notes the æsthetic movement in England had been striking for a decade, but only Pater had struck them with the sustained power or linked sweetness of *The Tragic Muse*, and Pater had written about the long past instead of producing, as James here does, a document on the life of art in his own immediate days. Peter Sherringham from watching Miriam arrives at a perception "of the perfect presence of mind, unconfused, unhurried by emotion, that any artistic performance requires and that all, whatever the instrument, require in

(177)

exactly the same degree: the application, in other words, clear and calculated, crystal-firm as it were, of the idea conceived in the glow of experience, of suffering, of joy." Such a statement implies that James had found a new aristocracy to imagine about—an aristocracy essentially more cosmopolitan than the shining barbarians of his perpetual Piccadilly and his innumerable country houses.

This shift in the objects of his imagination was connected with certain external facts. The popular success which James had hardly tasted except in the case of *Daisy Miller* but which he had confidently expected would be won by *The Bostonians* and *The Princess Casamassima*, had failed him. He felt hurt and mystified, for, contrary to the general notion, he desired more numerous plaudits than he got. He wanted money, though he had a comfortable income; he wanted the power that comes from recognition. For these reasons more than any other he gave the five years of 1889-1894 very largely to the writing of plays, working enormously without any substantial reward, and finally concluding early in 1895 that "you can't make a sow's ear out of a silk purse." The same period, and partly the same motive, turned him from full-length novels. "I want," he had written to Stevenson in 1888, "to leave a multitude of pictures of my time, projecting my small circular frame upon as many different spots as possible, . . . so that the number may constitute a total having a certain value as observation and testimony." Of these briefer stories a notably large number deal with problems of the artistic life in its clashes with the world. *The Author of Beltraffio* (1885) had exhibited the wife of that pagan-spirited author as so afraid of her husband's influence upon their son that she actually —if not quite deliberately—lets the boy die to save him from the fearful contamination. *The Aspern Papers* (1888) recounts the strife between the former mistress of the famous Jeffrey Aspern and the critic who wants to publish the poet's letters. In *The Lesson of the Master* (1892) Henry St.

(178)

George's lesson to his disciple is that perfection in art may not normally be hoped for by a man whose powers are drawn away by wife and children. To *The Yellow Book* James contributed three studies richly suited to the purposes of a periodical aiming to erect a temple of art in the midst of British Philistia: *The Death of the Lion* (1894), in which the genius Neil Paraday dies neglected in a country house while his hostess gets credit for being his patron: *The Coxon Fund* (1894), laughably modernizing Coleridge into the parasite Frank Saltram who sponges on the rich and devoted and foolish; *The Next Time* (1895), about poor Ralph Limbert who fails in his struggles to boil the pot because he is incapable of anything less than masterpieces, no matter how hard he tries. This group of stories may be said to end with *The Figure in the Carpet* (1896), with Hugh Vereker explaining to his critics how it is they must look in the whole of a writer's work for the "primal plan," the string his pearls are strung on, the complex figure in the Persian carpet of his art. "If my great affair's a secret," said Vereker, "that's only because it's a secret in spite of itself. . . . I not only never took the smallest precaution to make it so, but never dreamed of any such accident." So Henry James might have reasoned in his own behalf. Obscurity was his destiny not his design. He had set out to record certain subtle relationships that he perceived binding men and women together in the human picture, and he would not call it his fault if his perceptions had proved more delicate than those of the reading public. He had tried to make national contrasts interesting; he had tried to diversify his matter in the great novels of the eighties; he had tried a new literary form in his plays, and had, in his masterly short stories, written about the life of art as no one had ever done in English. Nothing had availed him with the wider audience. He now gave up the battle, reconciled himself to his limited fate, discovered the house at Rye which was to be his permanent residence till the end of his life, and settled down to the untrammeled practice of his art.

Nothing could be more autobiographical, in a sense, than this later work of Henry James, exquisitely reproducing as it so often does the adventures of exquisite souls among thorns and pitfalls. To robuster dispositions he appears, of course, to be making an incredible fuss over nothing to speak of, and he did cease to interest any but that small group capable of caring about passions so delicate as these. But art may be great without being popular, just as now and then some magnificent radiance of personality may light up a narrow corner. A flawless story published in 1895, *The Altar of the Dead*, somewhat forecasts James's final type. It is the tale—almost an apologue—of a George Stransom who at an altar privately maintained in a dim church sets up, one after another, candles for his dead, himself gradually perfected by his worship until at last he can complete the symmetry of his ritual by setting up a final candle to the memory of his bitter enemy, now forgiven. This narrow corner of existence glows with the whitest, purest light of a noble imagination. James's themes, however, rarely rose quite so high. He chose to walk closer to the ground of usual events, expanding and elevating not the deeds of his characters but their sentiments. In *The Spoils of Poynton* (1897) the action is only a sordid squabble between a widow and her son over the possession of a house made beautiful with objects of art which she has collected there for a lifetime but which by the hard English law now belong not to her but to him and the stupid bride he means to take. Round this central strife the story grew from a tale to a novel, from a vivid episode to a drama richly conceived and decorated. Another novelist might have abused the law; some other might have sided with son or mother. Henry James reveals his drama through a third person, the gentle, unselfish Fleda Vetch, who shares the mother's passion for beautiful things but who loves the son. James lacked the moral

(180)

arithmetic which taught Howells in *The Rise of Silas Lapham*
that wisdom prescribes the strictest economy in sacrifice:
Fleda Vetch, though Owen Gereth loves her and not Mona
Brigstock, renounces him without lifting a hand, and condemns, along with herself, son and mother and doubtless
wife to pain—and all seemingly with James's approbation.
But though in this regard sentimental and immoral, *The
Spoils of Poynton* as regards structure, proportion, texture,
style, is accomplished perfection, the result of methods now
matured and working upon their materials with absolute competence, without sign of effort or haste.

It was natural that in imagining the world in its impact
upon tender intelligences, Henry James should have made
use of children as his focuses of sensation. *What Maisie Knew*
(1897) records the disgusting annals of a fast set in London,
through the mystified innocence of Maisie Farange, whose
father and mother, divorced and both married again, toss her
back and forth from one to the other in the intervals of
incessant infidelity. She sees the outer facts of these obscene
ménages—joined together, by the way, through the liaison of
the step-parents—without comprehending their inner horror.
She is like a flower blooming in a filthy pool, by her shy
beauty making the contrast dreadful. That contrast is the
plot. Charming though Maisie appears in her own right, and
ugly as her companions are in theirs, the interest lies essentially in the relations between them and her. The spectator,
aware that in time her innocence will sink down and the
dirty flood overwhelm her, constantly winces. Still worse horrors, however, threaten in *The Turn of the Screw* (1898),
an almost incomparable short novel which, as a sort of moral
sequel to *What Maisie Knew*, exhibits two children so corrupted by wicked servants, now dead and turned to malevolent ghosts, that words will not utter the evil still haunting
the pitiful victims. Although a certain symbolism hints at
the nature of this particular evil, James was careful not to

identify it exactly. Horror multiplies with the vagueness. Maisie is menaced by a bad example which is understood however hated; Miles and Flora appear to have been exposed to dark forces which surround mankind as in the old Puritan cosmos, now and then expressed in actual sin but always huger than anything which can come of them. *The Awkward Age* (1899), also concerned with the young, brought James back from his far explorations to polite comedy again, to the problem of the young girl in a society full of innuendo and intrigue. But Nanda Brookenham's experiences are swathed in such countless folds of reference and gossip that, artfully as the drama is expounded, it comes to the ear with a muffled sound, like agreeable voices heard speaking at a distance which lets the actual words die away on the wind. Five hundred pages of such matter strain the most loyal attention to irritation if not to disgust. And much the same thing must be said of *The Sacred Fount* (1901), which has a soul the size of a short story and a body enlarged to the size of a novel by the solicitude with which James walks round and round his theme, hinting, hinting, hinting.

A consequence of the exuberant insinuation with which he worked in the first five years of his freedom from hope in the public was that the public found itself, by the reports of those who had read these later books, confirmed in its disposition to neglect him. From these years dates the legend that he had consciously, almost spitefully, evolved a style which no one could read but which it was a pleasant game to laugh at. The laughter grew into a cloud which obscured, and still in most quarters continues to obscure, the three superb novels with which, in prolific succession, he brought his art to its peak: *The Wings of the Dove* (1902), *The Ambassadors* (1903), *The Golden Bowl* (1904). As if with some recurrence of his younger interests, he deals in each of the three with the old situation of Americans in Europe, but in a spirit no longer so reproachful toward them as being merely provincial or dowdy. James had ceased to be worried over the petty blunders of his traveling countrymen, now that he felt himself securely European and no longer felt the responsibility which once had caused him compatriotic blushes. Like Mr. Longdon in *The Awkward Age*, an elderly Englishwoman who has retired to the country but is now drawn back to London again, James's Americans in his maturest masterpieces bring into a fast and loose society certain old-fashioned virtues and graces, such as simplicity, truthfulness, monogamy, solvency. Even Lambert Strether in *The Ambassadors*, who, having gone from Woollett, Massachusetts to save a young friend from the naughtinesses of Paris, himself surrenders to the beautifully beguiling universe he has entered—even Strether holds fast to the integrity which has all along given strength to his natural sympathy and which will not allow him to profit by his amiable betrayal of his mission. Strether's being an American who can be contrasted with Europeans does not exhaust his function. He stands also for a common enough human type, the individual brought up in a limited community who discovers too late, or almost too late, what richness, what content, what joy might have awaited him in some fuller existence. "Live all you can; it's a mistake not to," Strether says in a speech which Henry James himself pointed out to be the essence of *The Ambassadors*. "It doesn't so much matter what you do in particular so long as you have your life. If you haven't had that what *have* you had?" With some such precepts Pater had talked of the counted number of pulse-beats and had counseled a life lived at the flame. And in that transcendentalist New England which James partially inherited, Emerson and Thoreau had constantly urged the need of fullness and intensity of life. Strether's situation flawlessly fits James's idea. To get the largest value from them James had of course to make Strether another of his exquisite intelligences—rather too exquisite for his upbringing; he had, too, to make this abundant life into which Strether is initiated a life of lovely line and color, of gorgeous vesture and sweet, subtle, intoxicating atmosphere. All James's old powers came in upon him, with his new freedom. The execution of *The Ambassadors*, which he thought his most perfectly constructed novel, is as richly imaginative as it is deliberate.

James had annually increased the distance between his art and improvisation. He built novels now as architects do cathedrals, planning every stone in advance, testing every material, calculating every stress, visualizing every elevation. Without any impetuous drive of narrative to carry him on, or the clashes of melodrama, he peculiarly needed anxious prevision and conscientious workmanship. *The Golden Bowl* excellently illustrates this. Maggie Verver, an American girl, marries an Italian prince living in London, and her widowed father marries her friend Charlotte Stant. But there had been between Charlotte and the Prince before their marriages a secret intimacy which afterwards is resumed. With the fictive paraphernalia customary to such cases—jealousy, peeping, revelations, revenges—James of course has nothing to do. He would no more have brought the matter into the courts than would Maggie Verver and her quiet father. For James, as for Maggie, the evil of the situation consisted less in the sin of adultery than in the ugliness of stealth and deceit. The problem is to bring the hidden offense into light, and the plot is merely the process by which the various characters, one after another, first only gradually, accidentally, then with suspicions hurrying dreadfully into convictions, discover and are discovered. When the truth has come up into the light, the story ends, with Verver and his wife departing for America. Tenuous as the substance may seem to any first glance, *The Golden Bowl* is still solidly constructed beneath its sumptuous garment of phrases and clauses; careless of moral considerations as it may seem to any moralistic eye, it still glows with condemnation of the ugly facts which here disrupt a charming microcosm. The story suggests the coming of a summer sun after a midnight of slinking ghosts.

In *The Wings of the Dove* the beauty and power of truth and goodness receive a tribute which has rarely been paid them in sophisticated novels. As Isabel Archer in *The Portrait of a Lady* has risen magnificently to meet life, so here Milly Theale magnificently rises to meet death. The book is the drama of her inspired resistance. Without gross or overt agonies, she struggles to experience "as many of the finer vibrations as possible, and so achieve, however briefly and brokenly, the sense of having lived." James made her a New Yorker, the last of her family, rich and free, as the best way he could imagine to endow her with all the ages, and he took her of course to Europe to inherit her domain. There her battle and collapse, since she moves through her fate like a reigning princess, draw a whole circle with and after her; and in the end her tragedy shakes them all. The particular blackness against which she is exhibited is the scheme of Kate Croy and her lover Merton Densher to make Milly believe he is in love with her in order that before her death she may leave him her fortune. Yet so radiant is the whiteness of Milly's character that, though the plot superficially succeeds, the plotters are separated by disgust at their own shame. Every dexterity was required in such a story to keep Milly from seeming a prig or at best a tedious saint. James avoids this fatal defect by revealing her not so much in her words and deeds as in the effect she has on those who devotedly or selfishly surround her. She stands, as it were, in the midst of a splendid hall of mirrors, which give back her beauty from every angle and which themselves report her quest of a crowded existence during her numbered days. As she slowly fades under her malady the mirrors have an increasing task, until at last she is no longer visible except in them, where eventually her image lingers even after her death. Such puissance as hers does not lapse with bodily extinction, but lasts on as a remembered effluence of loveliness. If *The Ambassadors* is the best constructed of these three novels, and *The Golden Bowl* the most subtly suggestive, *The Wings of the Dove* is most elevated, most tender, most noble.

They issued from what might be called the Indian summer of James's career as an American. "Europe," he wrote in 1902, "has ceased to be romantic to me, and my own country, in the evening of my days, has become so." But his longing did not survive the visit which he lustrously chronicled in *The American Scene* (1907). From New Hampshire to Florida, from New York to California, the sensations awakened by the roaring continent overwhelmed him. Like an astronomer come down from his tower into the town, James fled back with his hands to his ears. The remainder of his life was more fragmentary than the rounded period 1896-1904. He resumed for a little while his theatrical ambitions; he wrote more short stories; he worked at the two novels, *The Sense of the Past* (originally begun in 1900) and *The Ivory Tower*, which, though incomplete when posthumously published in 1917, have the special interest that the second of them has an American setting and both are accompanied by the dictated notes which he latterly made to assist him in his composition; and he carried avowed autobiography through *A Small Boy and Others* (1913), *Notes of a Son and Brother* (1914), and the unfinished *The Middle Years* (1917). The war shattered his peace beyond repair. This lover of art who had not taken the trouble to form an opinion concerning the Dreyfus case, who had little more to say of the Boer War than that it doubled his income tax, who had vaguely hoped that the war with Spain might educate Americans as imperialism had educated the English, who had looked with candid contempt upon the Irish aspirations for freedom, now woke to the crisis of the world with a passion which ceased only with his death in 1916. There was nothing complicated in his loyalty, nothing critical in his attitude toward the drama

(186)

being enacted. His Europe—France, England, Italy—had been assailed in utter wantonness; the barbarians were pounding at the gates and might at any moment break in to befoul the pavements and violate the shrines of his sacred city. His own distant country looked on without lifting a helping hand, and he saw no better way to signify his protest and his allegiance than by becoming a British citizen in 1915, declaring "civis Britannicus sum" with a Roman boast, and ending his career, as he had begun it, on the note of romance.

Criticism must take account of the vast gulf across which those who like Henry James view with contempt those who do not, and in return those who do not like him view with incredulity those who do. Common opinion holds that his style by its obscurity has fixed the gulf there. While this does operate with regard to certain of his later works, it can have nothing to do with *The American*, or *The Europeans*, or *Daisy Miller*, or *Washington Square*, or *The Portrait of a Lady*, which are all as pellucid as a clean spring. And even in the elaborate, maturer books the style is obscure only in the sense that it speaks of matters less blunt and tangible than those which most fiction deals with. Nor will the cosmopolitan aspect of his themes entirely explain the hindering gulf, as has been argued by patriots who wish to punish him for his expatriation. The three metropolises—New York, London, Paris—which mark the triangle of his chosen territory are objects of curiosity for an enormous audience. Indeed, nationalism hurts James worse than internationalism: he suffers from the sensitiveness to national differences which kept him concerned too much with them and too little with the universal human likenesses which transcend nationality. He was actually less able to forget his American origin than such an unhesitant son of America as Whitman, for instance, who, taking his native land for granted, could send his imaginations out to all the corners of the world without worrying at the national boundaries thus crossed. Neither may James's failure to touch the wider world he really aimed at be accounted for by his unceasing labors to perfect his technique of representation. These concerned himself alone, or such fellow craftsmen or connoisseurs as find his prefaces to the New York Edition (1907-09) remarkable commentaries on the art of fiction, which he first in English made a thoroughly conscious art.

James's essential limitation may rather accurately be expressed by saying that he attempted, in a democratic age, to write courtly romances. He did not, naturally, go back for his models to the *Roman de la Rose* or *Morte d'Arthur* or Sidney's *Arcadia* or the *Grand Cyrus*. But he did devote himself to those classes in modern society which descend from the classes represented by the romancers of the Middle Ages and the Renaissance. His characters, for the most part, neither toil nor spin, trade nor make war, bear children in pain nor bring them up with sacrifices. The characters who do such things in his novels are likely to be the servants or dependents of others more comfortably established. His books consequently lack the interest of that fiction which shows men and women making some kind of way in the world— except the interest which can be taken in the arts by which the penniless creep into the golden favor of the rich or the socially unarrived wriggle into an envied caste. James is the laureate of leisure. Moreover the leisure he cared to write about concerns itself in not the slightest degree with any action whatsoever, even games or sports. Love of course concerns it, as with all novelists. Yet even love in this chosen universe must constantly run the gantlet of an often incomprehensible decorum. In one of Chrétien de Troyes's romances Lancelot, on his way to rescue Guinevere from a precarious situation, commits the blunder of riding part of the way in a cart and thereby brings upon himself a disgrace which his most gallant deeds can scarcely wipe out. Sensible citizens who may have happened upon this narrative in the twelfth century probably felt mystified at the pother much as do their congeners in the twentieth who stare at the wounds which James's heroes and heroines suffer from blunders intrinsically no more serious than Lancelot's. How much leisure these persons must enjoy, the sensible citizen thinks, to have evolved and to keep up this mandarin formality; and how little use they make of it! Only readers accustomed to such decorums can walk entirely at ease in the universe James constructed. But they have the privileges of a domain unprecedented in modern literature and later matched only by that of Marcel Proust. It is not merely that James is the most fascinating historian of a most elegant society. He is the creator of a world beautiful in its own right: a world of international proportions, peopled by charming human beings who live graceful lives in settings lovely almost beyond description; a world which vibrates with the finest instincts and sentiments and trembles at vulgarity and ugliness; a world full of works of art and learning and intelligence, a world infinitely refined, a world perfectly civilized. In real life the danger to such a world is that it may be overwhelmed by some burly rush of actuality from without. In literature the danger is that such a world will gradually fade out as dreams fade, and as the old romances of feudalism have already faded. Elaborate systems of decorum pass away; it is only the simpler manners of men that live forever.

X

TYPES OF FICTION

THE DECADE 1880-90 produced more good novels than any previous American decade. Howells was then at his height in *A Modern Instance*, *The Rise of Silas Lapham*, *Indian Summer*, *A Hazard of New Fortunes*; Mark Twain in *The Adventures of Huckleberry Finn*, *A Connecticut Yankee in King Arthur's Court*; Henry James in *Washington Square*, *The Portrait of a Lady*, *The Princess Casamassima*, *The Tragic Muse*. It was the decade which saw the beginnings and successes of Francis Marion Crawford, deft story-teller, and Frank R. Stockton, delightful inventor of joyous extravaganza. It was the decade of Wallace's *Ben-Hur*, of Cable's *Grandissimes*, of E. W. Howe's *Story of a Country Town*, of Helen Hunt Jackson's *Ramona*, of Henry Adams's *Democracy* and *Esther*, and John Hay's *Breadwinners*, of Constance Fenimore Woolson's *East Angels*, of Margaret Deland's *John Ward, Preacher*, of Edward Bellamy's *Looking Backward*. In spite of the popularity of the short story, the novel prospered. The publication of novels serially in magazines had not yet begun to decline. Criticism of the art attained a high dignity in the hands of Howells and Henry James; Bayard Tuckerman wrote *A History of English Prose Fiction* (1882) which included American authors; and Sidney Lanier used his lectures on *The English Novel* (1883) as the vehicle for a load of passionate opinions concerning literature. By the eighties practically all the types of fiction known to the United States had been invented and all of them were in use. Domestic sentimentalism of course still walked its way of tears with a sobbing audience. The romance of adventure, though degraded to the dime novel for the most part, asked no quarter from the critical. The historical tale kept up its ancient habits with the past, sweetening and decorating it. The international novel, sometimes rather the exotic romance, was having its day. Local color, tending toward the romantic, divided the principal field with realism, tending away from it. The novel with some sort of purpose continued to be a tool ready to almost every hand. And there were also certain gaily fantastic stories of a sort new to the country if not to the language.

The novels of the eighties cannot be reduced to any such simple formulas as suffice with the romance of Cooper's school or with the tearful tales of the fifties. They show diversities of style and structure, of artistic and moral attitude, as well as topographical variety. In general they represent a decisive advance in simplicity and reality. Characters were now no longer required to speak the stilted language or to feel the quivering sentiments that had once seemed symptoms of nobility of soul. At the same time, but little advance had been made in the direction of studied raciness or strenuous naturalism. Howells's honest decency set the tone for the period. As the master was often saved from seeming thin and tame only by his grace and good temper, the disciples, inferior in these respects, did not always escape thinness or tameness. The preoccupation with local color encouraged love of surfaces, if not a satisfaction with surfaces alone; local color novels suffered from the contagion of triviality. The fiction of the eighties suffered, too, from the delicate contagion of gentility. At the best it imparted daintiness and charm; at the worst, timidity and bloodlessness. The violent currents of political life during the decade, which brought a new party into power for the first time in a quarter of a century; the rising warfare upon established economic privilege; the rapid growth in luxury and sophistication: these but faintly appear in the novels which the decade brought forth, except for those specifically designed to redress grievances or to expose wrongs. Ordinarily, ideas played but a small part. Nor was this want of ideas compensated for, again except in special cases, by large ranges of personality or depths of passion or impressive beauty or truth. The lives which these novels represent had little to do with the clash of the times in religious or moral, any more than in political, matters. Even in the love affairs which make up the great bulk of all such narratives the complications are of the simplest and the psychology simpler still. The very young do most of the loving, innocently, pathetically, hardly ever realistically or tragically. If love is simple, so is livelihood. While many of the novels do indeed concern themselves with the poor, it is the more or less contented poor of the older American villages where little serious poverty existed. In but few cases do the heroes and heroines of the eighties contend with the society in which they live, and then rarely indeed with the approval of their authors. Fiction, in short, had not assumed the heavier burdens laid on it by a subsequent generation, but existed largely for entertainment.

If it was thus limited in certain directions, so was it freed in others. It recognized no obligation to be polemic, though it could be so on occasion. It did not look relentlessly for victims of the social order who might be elevated into champions of a higher truth. It did not feel obliged to take many exceptions to the broad average current of human existence. It chose the simpler emotions for the reason that American character was simple. It preferred to make as much of the cheerful aspects of life as possible, because that was the general American preference, even when there was much unpleasantness to be blinked at. With such a temper prevalent, the style of fiction naturally became lighter and gayer. It discarded the blocks of description which the older romances had admitted and the showers of tears which had immediately preceded the Civil War. Having taken stock of technical methods, it varied its structures with its themes, gave an increased attention to dialect and dialogue, studied the problems of proportion and emphasis. The decade made a highly eclectic use of foreign models. Lanier devoted nearly a half of his study of the English novel to George Eliot, who was influential in many quarters. The writers of local color novels in not a few instances showed traces of Thomas Hardy. *Ben-Hur* recalls both Bulwer-Lytton and Victor Hugo. Aldrich and Cable and Bunner had obviously read such Frenchmen as Merimée, Daudet, Maupassant, though with reservations. Toward the end of the decade Zola began to be heard, though railed at by the orthodox. Henry James and Howells investigated and expounded Turgenev; James added most of the French novelists of the time; Howells added Dostoevsky and his master passion Tolstoy, as well as the Spanish Galdós, Valdés, Valera, and the Italian Verga; while both Howells and James had something to say of almost every eminent European who practised fiction. Though eclectic, the American novel was not unwarrantably imitative. It had certain traditions of its own and followed them. It was faithful to American life, at least to those phases which it chose to record. Its points of view were clearly national. Without achieving methods as distinctive as those of the short story, the American novel was still a distinctively, unmistakably native product.

In the department of domestic sentimentalism the most widely read rivals of E. P. Roe and his kind who appeared in the eighties happened both to be Lancashire women resident in America: Frances Hodgson Burnett, whose *Little Lord Fauntleroy* (1886) moistened millions of uncritical eyes with its account of an American child instructing the British aristocracy in democratic manners; and Amelia Edith Barr, whose swift, kindly pen played over all the fields of fiction except the distinguished. In the romance of adventure Anna Katharine Green Rohlfs made something of a new departure with her very successful detective stories, and Captain (later General) Charles King became the first novelist of the Amer-

(193)

ican army, with his brisk stories of field and camp and military post. The historical novel, for which Howells and James cared so little, suffered some neglect, though Ben-Hur belonged to that form and A Connecticut Yankee burlesqued it; John Esten Cooke worked in it till his death in 1886; Marion Crawford handled past and present with almost equal ease; and at the end of the decade several writers began to point forward to the historical-romantic best sellers which crowded the nineties. The older fashion of sea tales and foreign adventure, now fallen into abeyance, had been succeeded by the milder comedy of international manners, as handled by Howells and James and, more humorously, by Mark Twain.

Novels of foreign life might have flourished if it had not been for the zest with which the rarer materials of existence were hunted for at home. The contrast of the old and new Californian civilizations led Helen Hunt Jackson to write one of the most moving of American romances. In A Century of Dishonor (1881) she had begun her indictment of the United States government for its treatment of the Indians. In Ramona (1884) she carried the indictment into fiction. What Uncle Tom's Cabin had done to make known the wrongs of the black slaves, Ramona attempted to do for the red wards of the nation. It was no longer possible to take Fenimore Cooper's attitude toward the Indian as a romantic figure of the past; since Cooper's day there had been the wars with the Sioux and the massacre of Custer. Mrs. Jackson eluded the difficulty by making Ramona, the heroine, and her Temecula husband Alessandro so near to high caste Mexicans in color and nurture that their wrongs as Indians seem hardly typical of the real grievances of their unfortunate race. They suffer little more from the invading Yankees than do the proudest Mexicans. Indeed, the true conflict and injustice occur between the old Californians, Indian or Spanish, and the predacious vanguard of the Anglo-Saxon conquest. For Mrs. Jackson California had been a splendid paradise of patriarchal estates, in vast fertile valleys, steeped in a drowsy antiquity, and cherished by fine, unworldly priests. Against this rich background she set a story which begins in peace, blackens to hard and ugly tragedy, and then grows at the end to peace again. The pomp of the setting, the strength of the contrasts, the eloquence, the intensity, the passionate color: these dominate, almost submerge, the problem with which the narrative is concerned; but they also tend to lift it above controversy, into those higher regions of the imagination in which particular acts of injustice take on a universal significance.

Ramona was a local color novel which had a passionate aim and a large historical background as well as quaint surfaces. Two novels of the Mississippi Valley, G. W. Cable's *The Grandissimes* (1880) and E. W. Howe's *The Story of a Country Town* (1883), illustrate the range which the type permitted. Cable dealt with the year of the purchase of Louisiana by the United States, but the entire history of the old province lies behind his narrative, constantly showing through; for his scene he chose New Orleans, but action shifts, at least by report, to plantation and bayou, forest and swamp. In the characters there is a mingling of races: French and Spanish and German and Yankee, Creole and quadroon, Indian aborigines, and Negro slaves who speak a strange jargon of French and English but who have the instincts of Africa in their blood. This New Orleans is a city of austere castes and almost incomprehensible customs, never too obviously explained, though hinted at with laughing dexterity. The central plot, which shows the houses of Grandissime and De Grapion at war and then reconciles and unites them by marriage, loses itself, unfortunately, in a maze of episodes. But the episodes glitter under a treatment and a style which is allusive, sparkling, felicitous. In comparison, *The Story of a Country Town* moves with the cold tread and hard diction of a saga. E. W. Howe, whose first book this was, apparently did not know how to give it the sense of locality. It is as if the bare, sunburned Kansas plain, on which the action passes, had no real depth, no mystery in itself, no native motif but the smoldering discontent of an inarticulate frontier. If it lacks locality, so does it lack relief, comedy, poetical touches, and that flowing optimism which was common in the books of that period. *The Story of a Country Town*, stern and grim, was published the same year as Mark Twain's joyous *Life on the Mississippi*. If happiness or gaiety ever lighted up Fairview and Twin Mounds Howe's story does not tell it. Howe wrote about Twin Mounds as Crabbe wrote about the English village—determined, it seems, to paint it "As Truth will paint it, and as Bards will not": a neighborhood as barren of beauty and elevation as of lakes and mountains; dogmatic without being religious, ambitious enough without having any intelligent aims, industrious but futile. A Parisian never wrote more contemptuously of provincial life. And yet beneath this dry exterior, which will not let the narrative or the dialogue be flexible for one moment, lurks authentic power. No shallow mind could have conceived the blind, black, impossible passion of Joe Erring, who loves like a backwoods Othello; no tepid mind could have conducted such a passion through its catastrophe to the purgation and tranquillity which succeed. That Howe, though he wrote another novel or two, ended his career as a novelist almost where he began it, meant a loss to American fiction. He made himself a successful country journalist, a disillusioned and often cantankerous country sage; but the energy of his imagination sought other channels than the novel.

Howe had taken a step beyond Edward Eggleston on the way to that stiffening of the conscience which brought the naturalism of the next decade, but in the eighties he had no colleague in the undertaking except Joseph Kirkland of Illinois, who wrote the crude, truthful *Zury* (1887). Constance Fenimore Woolson (1840-94) during the eighties had a promise that seemed to rank her little below Howells and James. She lived in turn in the Great Lakes region, particularly Mackinac, in the devastated, reviving South of Reconstruction times, and in Italy, applying her art to all of her neighborhoods, both in short stories and in novels. But as she had no such range as Howells and James, neither had she such grace as Cable's or such veracity as Howe's, though her *East Angels* (1886) was a glowing, rich-hued picture of the Florida of the tourists.

Little as most of the novels of the period touched upon its public affairs, some of them were not silent. Albion Winegar Tourgée's *A Fool's Errand* (1879) called attention to the problem of the freedmen in the conquered South. Henry Adams in *Democracy* (1880) drew a caustic picture of society and politics in Washington, a capital which has been strangely neglected in American fiction. His *Esther* (1884), published anonymously and stealthily, dealt with women and religion in a kind of first draft of certain of Adams's later ideas. *The Breadwinners* (1884), also anonymous, by John Hay made a sensation by its defense of property and the old economic order against the increasing claims of labor. Adams and Hay were not at their best in their novels, and did not acknowledge them, but they chose to cast their unpopular arguments in that popular form. Margaret Deland's *John Ward, Preacher* (1888), like the exactly contemporary *Robert Elsmere* of Mrs. Humphry Ward, aroused controversy by its account of a husband and wife so divided on doctrinal grounds that their lives are shattered. In the American novel it is the husband who is orthodox and the wife who is latitudinarian, but here as in the English book stress falls upon the consequences to love of such a difference. In the same year with *John Ward* appeared a work of fiction which caught the immediate public as hardly any novel of its theme had ever done before. The book was Edward Bellamy's *Looking Backward 2000-1887*, and the theme was communism. Hundreds of thousands of copies were sold with a tumult of acclamation; the book went round the world; a political party—the Nationalist—was founded on Bellamy's doctrines. Howells's *A Hazard of New Fortunes* and his Altrurian writings bear witness to the influence Bellamy exerted in literary circles. Reversing the scheme of *The Connecticut Yankee* Bellamy allows his narrator to sleep until the year 2000 and then to wake up in a Utopian Boston which, like the rest of the world, has moved forward, without revolution, to a rational adjustment of production and distribution, and has perfected the conditions of human life. In his glad millennium all capital belongs to the community and all labor contributes to it; the inequality of reward has disappeared, for all men, and women, share alike, however different may be the tasks to which they are assigned by the most careful selection; intelligent planning has increased the wealth of the community, wealth has increased leisure, and leisure has increased joy and goodness. Bellamy's specific solutions of the ancient problem matter less to the history of American fiction than the fact that he found an enormous public ready to snatch from his romance some sort of consolation in a vast discontent.

At the opposite pole from Bellamy was Frank R. Stockton (1834-1902), with his lively fantasy. A Philadelphian, he first worked at wood-engraving but deserted it for literature, which he reached by the unusual avenue of fairy tales and juvenile journalism. As in his fairy tales he had made his fanciful creatures behave, as far as possible, after the manner of the real world, so into his maturer stories of the real world he constantly infused a fairy irresponsibility. His earliest important book, *Rudder Grange* (1879), illustrates all his qualities. To the outward eye the novel resembles realism. The characters look real, they speak like beings who are real enough. But their adventures are the adventures of a Gilbert and Sullivan opera—one rollicking confusion. Stockton's fancy found the short story peculiarly congenial, and the dilemma he invented for his brief tale *The Lady or the Tiger?* (1882)

won him his largest single applause. His masterpiece was the short novel *The Casting Away of Mrs. Lecks and Mrs. Aleshine* (1886), which had a sequel *The Dusantes* (1888). The dauntless Mrs. Lecks and Mrs. Aleshine come directly from the life, from two middle-aged women who knew too little of the world outside of their village ever to be surprised at anything which could possibly happen to them elsewhere. To them in the story it happens that they are wrecked in the Pacific Ocean, paddle themselves in life-preservers, using oars as brooms, to an island which might have been deserted but which instead has a comfortable house on it, and there begin housekeeping as cheerfully as if they were in Meadowville, scrupulously depositing each week in a ginger jar on the mantelpiece a sum for board, minus a fair charge for their services in doing the housework. After a train of incidents which joyfully, though not too obviously, parody all the literature of shipwreck, they are restored to the United States; but they have left behind them a letter which so piques the curiosity of the real owners, the Dusantes, that those migratory personages follow Mrs. Lecks and Mrs. Aleshine and their companions to the United States, especially to return the money which Mr. Dusante is far too hospitable to be willing to keep. Mr. Dusante, who has an adopted mother with him, encounters in Mrs. Lecks a moral principle equal to his own and finds she will not take back the money; the sequel is largely devoted to the fate of the ginger jar. If Stockton's fantastic invention is here at its most luxuriant, so is his manner at its gravest. His tongue is only stealthily in his cheek, and his voice is as calm and level as if he were reciting the multiplication table. Thus inspired liars lie—sailors back from distant voyages and yarning to landlubbers, cowboys stringing tenderfeet with tall tales, Sindbads and Munchausens.

With Stockton may be mentioned Eugene Field, better known for his verse and his comic skits than for his fiction, and yet the author of at least one novel—if it may be called a novel—which has achieved among book-lovers a little immortality. *The Love Affairs of a Bibliomaniac* (1896) chronicles no passions more violent than the desire for books, but it chronicles that desire in forms as diversified as Field's own career as a collector, and in a tone as piquant and engaging as that of his own personality. The tale is packed with episodes and vagaries recognizable by all book-hunters; it exhibits, in an unpretentious way, an unusual erudition playing over the amiable regions of literature which Field himself had explored. But the bibliomaniac of the narrative, though largely studied from Field's own tastes, is also an actual creation, extended, if not enlarged, from the life by the addition of adventures which every book-collector has imagined himself as having, and portrayed with the humor and grace which Field generally reserved for his verse.

Francis Marion Crawford (1854-1909), prolific and long popular, has lost most of his vogue and has come to have little compensating support from loyal enthusiasts. Yet his contemporaries of the decade 1880-90 and later thought him one of the most entertaining and most cosmpolitan of novelists. Born in Tuscany, he was educated in New England, England, Germany, and Italy, became interested in Sanskrit, edited a newspaper in India, and wrote his first novel in 1882 at the request of an uncle who had been struck by Crawford's account of a mysterious Persian he had met. Success came promptly, and the traveler recognized his vocation as a novelist. In six years he had written ten novels of notable variety of subject and setting. Having settled in Sorrento, he spent the rest of his life there, with intervals of traveling, in a full if quiet activity. Except that toward the end he turned from fiction to history he can hardly be said to have changed his methods from his earliest novel to his last. Improvisation was his knack and forte; he wrote rapidly and much—sometimes an entire novel in a month. His imagination, he said, was constantly peopled with a swarming mass of human figures, of whom a group would now and then suddenly come together in a set of relationships and compel him to record them in a novel. His settings he took down, for the most part, from personal observation in the many localities he knew at first hand; his characters, too, were frequently studied from actual persons. In his plots he employed all the devices of melodrama: lost or hidden wills, forgeries, great persons in disguise, sudden legacies, physical violence. Movement, not plot in any stricter sense, was Crawford's primary excellence. He ran through his narratives without breaking or faltering, managing his materials and disposing his characters and scenes without any sign of effort, in a style clear, bright, and shallow. He had few unusual ideas, and he disliked the appearance of unusual ideas in fiction, about the aims and uses of which he was very explicit in *The Novel: What It Is* (1893). Anglo-Saxons had recently been learning—from the critical comments of Stevenson and Howells and Henry James—that fiction has an art that may be studied; that a novel is not merely a novel, as a pudding is a pudding. In answer to such serious critics Crawford declared that novelists were "public amusers," who must always write largely about love and in English-reading countries for the eyes of young girls. Novelists might, he thought, as well be reconciled to the demands of their trade, and by thinking not too highly of it spare themselves the agony that goes with the more apocalyptic arts. For his own part he thought problem novels odious, cared nothing for dialect and local color, believed it a mistake to make a novel too minute a picture of one generation for fear another should think it old-fashioned, and preferred to regard the novel as a pocket theater. He had in mind, of course, the British and American stage in the placid decade before Wilde and Shaw.

With his cosmopolitan training and opinions Crawford held that human beings are the same everywhere and can be made everywhere intelligible if lucidly reported. He knew English, French, German, Italian, Spanish, Swedish, Russian, Turkish, besides Latin, Greek, and Sanskrit. In his novels he seems to have seen every corner of the globe and to have talked with all the natives in their own lauguage. He ranges, with apparent ease though with no great antiquarian knowledge, through time from the days of Belshazzar to the modern United States. His *Khaled* (1891) has something of the color of the *Arabian Nights* and *The Cigarette-Maker's Romance* (1890) is good melodrama. But on the whole his Italian novels are his best, especially the Saracinesca cycle: *Saracinesca* (1887), *Sant' Ilario* (1889), *Don Orsino* (1892), *Pietro Ghisleri* (1893), and *Corleone* (1896). They have helped one another's reputations by the fact that they carry over the same persons from novel to novel and are concerned with the fortunes of one great patriarchal house. Melodramatic, larger than life in valiant deeds and lofty sentiments and eloquent speech, they still convey a sense of generous reality in their version of life in a contemporary Rome which was rapidly changing, to Crawford's regret. His novels come nearer than any others in English to perpetuating that little world. His success with the Roman novels emphasizes the critical point that no novelist can range as widely as Crawford did and yet go deep. Although he called himself an American, he knew Rome best, and where his knowledge was greatest he went deepest. Realism, like charity, must begin somewhere near home.

XI

LOCAL AND HISTORICAL

1~Local Color

THOUGH SUCH eminent figures as Howells, Mark Twain, and Henry James might emerge from the characteristic background of American fiction during the last thirty years of the nineteenth century, the background itself belonged on the whole to local color and romantic history. The local color fashion which began with Bret Harte in California just after the Civil War, gradually broadened out to every state and almost every county. Harte wrote one long novel, *Gabriel Conroy* (1876), and some brief ones, but in these he did little more than expand short stories or string them together on a casual thread. This was true also of his followers. The history of local color must be left primarily to the historian of the short story. And yet the short stories of the fashion have to be borne in mind along with the novels in any account of the growth of the American imagination in the local color decades. It was the total body of local color which, in a country newly discovering itself, served to fit pleasant fiction to stubborn fact in so many regions that the nation came in greater or less degree to see itself through literary eyes and to feel civilized by the sight. This is one of the important processes of civilization. The local colorists were not very realistic observers. Ordinarily provincial, but without the rude durability or homely truthfulness of provincialism at its best, they studied their world with benevolence rather than with passion. Nor were they much differentiated among themselves by highly individual ideas or methods. As with the romancers of the first half of the century, the local colorists fall easily into a topographical arrangement.

The defeated South furnished a romantic subject for the cycle of stories which grew up about the remembered and cherished life of Southern plantations before the war. The mood of most of these was of course elegiac and not too close to historic fact; the motive was to show how much splendor had perished in the downfall of the old régime. Over and over they repeated the same themes: how an irascible planter refuses to allow his daughter to marry the youth of her choice and how true love finds a way; how a beguiling Southern maiden has to choose between lovers and gives her hand and heart to him who is stoutest in his adherence to the Confederacy; how, now and then, love crosses the lines and a Confederate girl magnanimously, though only after a desperate struggle with herself, marries a Union officer who has saved the old plantation from a marauding band of Union soldiers; how a pair of ancient slaves cling to their duty during the appalling years and will not presume upon their freedom even when it comes; how the gentry, though menaced by a riffraff of poor whites, nevertheless hold their heads high and shine brightly through the gloom; how some planter colonel refuses to be reconstructed by events and passes the rest of his life as a courageous relic of his once thriving self. Thomas Nelson Page's *In Ole Virginia* (1887) and F. Hopkinson Smith's *Colonel Carter of Cartersville* (1891) in a brief compass employ all these themes; and dozens of books which might be named play variations upon them. Such stories were most of them kindly, humorous, sentimental, charming. Richard Malcolm Johnston's *Dukesborough Tales* (1871) still had something of the racy humor of the older Georgia, and Opie Read's Kentucky novels such as *The Jucklins* (1895) something of the old Southwest; but most of the post-war versions of Southern life were romantic and notably genteel. Its rougher phases sank out of sight in Southern fiction, not to be revived till well on in the twentieth century.

The South after the Civil War did not restrict itself wholly to its plantation cycle. In New Orleans George Washington Cable, beginning with *Old Creole Days* (1879), daintily worked the lode which had been deposited there by a French and Spanish past and by the presence still of Creole elements in the population. Yet he too was elegiac, sentimental, pretty, even when his style was most deft and his representations most engaging. Quaintness was his second nature; romance was in his blood. Bras-Coupé, the great, proud, rebellious slave in *The Grandissimes*, belongs to the ancient lineage of those African princes who in many tales have been sold to chain and lash and have escaped from them by dying. The postures and graces and contrivances of Cable's Creoles are traditional to all the little aristocracies surviving, in fiction, from some more substantial day. Yet in spite of these conventions his better novels have a texture of genuine vividness and beauty. In their portrayal of the manners of New Orleans they have many points of quiet satire and censure that imply a critical disposition working seriously behind them. That disposition in Cable led him to disagree with the majority of Southerners regarding the justice due the Negroes—and helped persuade him after 1885 to live in Massachusetts. While slavery still existed, public opinion in the South had demanded that literature exhibit the institution as favorably as possible; public opinion now demanded that the problem of the Negro, either past or present, be handled gently and conventionally. But the Negroes were the subject of one group of narratives which promise to outlast all that local color hit upon in the South. These were the stories told by Joel Chandler Harris in *Uncle Remus: His Songs and His Sayings* (1881), *Nights with Uncle Remus* (1883), and several later collections. Uncle Remus is a classic figure, and his stories at once as ancient and as fresh as folk-lore.

Besides the rich planters and their slaves one other class of human beings in the South especially attracted the attention of the local colorists: the mountaineers. Certain distant cousins of this backwoods stock had come into literature as Pikes or poor whites in the Far West with Bret Harte and in the Middle West with John Hay and Edward Eggleston. It remained for Mary Noailles Murfree (Charles Egbert Craddock) with *In the Tennessee Mountains* (1884) and other books, and John Fox with his somewhat belated stories of Kentucky, *A Cumberland Vendetta* (1896) and *The Little Shepherd of Kingdom Come* (1903), to discover the heroic and sentimental qualities of the breed among its highland fastnesses of the Great Smoky and Cumberland mountains. Here again formulas sprang up and so stifled the free growth of observation that, though a multitude of stories was written about the mountain people, almost all of them may be resolved into themes as few in number as those which succeeded nearer Tidewater: how a stranger man comes into the mountains, loves the flower of all the native maidens, and clashes with the suspicions or jealousies of her neighborhood; how two clans have been worn away by a long vendetta until only one representative of each clan remains and the two forgive and forget among the ruins; how a band of highlanders defend themselves against the invading agents of a law made for the nation at large but hardly applicable to highland circumstances; how the mountain virtues in some way or other prove superior to the softer virtues—vices in comparison —of the world of plains and towns. These formulas, however, resulted from another cause than the traditionalism which hated to be disturbed in Virginia and Louisiana. The mountain people, inarticulate themselves, were almost uniformly seen from the outside and consequently studied in their surface peculiarities more often than in their deeper traits of character. And, having once entered the realm of legend, they continued to be known by the half-dozen distinguishing features which in legend are always enough for any type.

In the North and West much the same process went on as in the South among the local colorists, conditioned by similar demands and pressures. Because the territory was wider in the expanding sections, the types of character there were somewhat less likely to be merely local than in the section which had for a time had a ring drawn round it by its past and by the difficulty of outgrowing it. The cowboy, for instance, legitimate successor to the miners and gamblers of Bret Harte and to the frontier scouts of the old dime novels, might derive from almost any of the states and might range over prodigious areas. The notable books dealing with cowboys and their kind came late: Alfred Henry Lewis's racy *Wolfville Days* (1902) and *Wolfville Nights* (1902); Owen Wister's more heroic, more sentimental novel *The Virginian* (1902); Andy Adams's more minute chronicle *The Log of a Cowboy* (1903); O. Henry's more diversified episodes *Heart of the West* (1907) and others of his books. But there had been many dime novel cowboys before these, and Wild West circuses, and the drawings of Frederic Remington. The cowboy long moved on the plane of the sub-literary, as he subsequently returned to it in motion pictures. Like the mountaineer of the South he was largely inarticulate except for his rude songs and ballads. Formula and tradition caught him early and in fiction stiffened one of the most picturesque of human beings—a modern Centaur, an American Cossack, a Western picaro—into a stock figure who in a stock costume perpetually sits a bucking broncho, brandishes a six-shooter or swings a rope, rounds up stampeding cattle, makes fierce war on Mexicans, Indians, and rival outfits, and ardently, humbly woos the ranchman's daughter or the schoolma'am. By 1900 he was ready to be made known to the entire world, wherever men could look at motion pictures even if they could not read.

Formula and tradition marked another type multiplied by local color in one of its humorous aspects: the bad boy. Aldrich's *Story of a Bad Boy* in New England was followed by the rowdy *Peck's Bad Boy* series (1883-1907) of George Wil-

(207)

bur Peck, journalist and governor of Wisconsin. Mark Twain handled the type with such mastery that its later habitat has usually been the Middle West, where a recognized lineage connects Tom Sawyer and Huckleberry Finn with Booth Tarkington's Penrod. The bad boy, it should be noticed, was not really bad; he was simply mischievous. He served as a natural outlet for the imagination of communities which were respectable but which lacked reverence for solemn dignity. He could play wild pranks and still be innocent; he could have his boyish fling and then settle down to a prudent maturity. But his range was limited. In book after book he indulges in the same practical jokes upon parents, teachers, and all those in authority; brags, fibs, fights, plays truant, learns to swear and smoke, with the same devices and consequences; suffers from the same agonies of shyness, the same indifference to the female sex in general, the same awkward inclination toward particular little girls. For the most part he was shown as seen by amused or irritated adults, and seldom studied from within his own life or emotions.

The American business man, though he appeared often enough in the local color novels, hardly became a type. He might be a canny trader in a small town in Edward Noyes Westcott's immensely popular *David Harum* (1898) or either magnate or malefactor. But he was likely, before 1900, to be shown chiefly in his domestic relationships, highly sentimental in affairs of the hearth, and easily susceptible to the influence of good women. He was never quite typical unless he was self-made. The self-made heroes of Horatio Alger's many books for boys (over a hundred between 1867 and 1896) furthered the national legend that the simple commercial virtues lead men from rags to riches. Nor did the American politician become a strongly marked type in fiction. His career was studied by such early realists as Mark Twain in *The Gilded Age* (1873), De Forest in *Honest John Vane* (1875), Henry Adams in *Democracy* (1880); and later by Paul Leicester

Ford in *The Honorable Peter Sterling* (1894), Brand Whitlock in *The 13th District* (1902), Alfred Henry Lewis in *The Boss* (1903), and complacently by Booth Tarkington in *In the Arena* (1905); but local color as a rule made little of the politician. When he appeared he was most often some local figure, boss of his village or city ward. Customarily he held no office himself but sat behind the scenes busy with manipulation. He held one man's mortgage, knew another's guilty secret, and used them for his own ends. He was cynically illiterate, though shrewd, and contemptuous of the respectable classes, with their spasmodic movements toward reform. If he had to he could resort to outrageous violence. Much as he was condemned in novels, he was taken for granted with a kind of fatalism. And he was sometimes a rough Robin Hood, levying on the unworthy rich for the worthy poor.

Among the types of women evolved by local color the young girl was excessively first. As a possible reader she fixed the boundaries beyond which novels were supposed not to go in speaking of sexual matters, and she dominated fiction with her glittering energy and healthy coolness. Some differences appeared among the sections of the country as to what special phases of her character should be preferred. She was ordinarily most capricious in the Southern, most strenuous in the Western, most knowing in the New York, and most demure in the New England novels. Yet everywhere she considerably resembled a bright, graceful boy pretending to be a woman. Coeducation and the scarcity of chaperons made her self-possessed to a degree which might mystify readers unfamiliar with American ways. Though she played at lovemaking almost from the cradle, she managed hardly ever to be scorched: a pretty salamander in the flames. In the earlier novels of the fashion, like *The Wide Wide World*, she inclined to piety to save her; in the later, to a romping optimism, as in Eleanor H. Porter's *Pollyanna* (1913) with a heroine whose name became temporarily proverbial. These qualities gave the young girl, in fiction as in common life, much freedom of action without the penalty of being suspected of designs she probably did not harbor. Daisy Miller, subject of unjust gossip abroad, would have been understood at home. In actual experience even American girls grow up, but popular fiction did its best to keep them forever children. Nothing broke the crystal shallows of their confidence. They were insolently secure in a world apparently made for them. From Hawthorne to the beginnings of naturalism there was hardly a single profound love story written in America. Green girls were the heroines and censors.

The older women created by the local color generation included certain fashionable successes and social climbers in large cities who had more complex fortunes than the young girls, but for the most part these were merely conventional and had to wait for sharper novelists like Edith Wharton and Robert Herrick. The generation came nearer to reality in its representation of a type which is notably characteristic of the United States: the woman who is also a lady, combining in herself the functions both of an active housewife and of an attractive ornament of her society. The shortage of household servants made it necessary and the increase of labor-saving devices made it possible for many American women, while taking care of their houses with their own hands, to keep books and music beside them as pioneer farmers kept muskets near them in the fields, If they had little leisure for intrigue or public affairs, they were still not lost in habitual drudgery. They were almost a new species of women. Local color, however, was too much used to the species to think of laying much stress on it.

Only New England emphasized a distinct type: the old maid. She has been studied in that section as in no other quarter of the world. Expansion and emigration after the Civil War drew heavily upon the declining Puritan stock; and naturally the young men left their native farms and villages more numerously than the young women, who remained behind and in many cases never married. Local fiction fell very largely into the hands of women—Harriet Beecher Stowe, Rose Terry Cooke, Sarah Orne Jewett, Mary E. Wilkins Freeman, Alice Brown—who broke completely with the age-old tradition of ridiculing spinsters no longer young. In the little cycles which these story-tellers elaborated the old maid is likely to be the center of her episode, studied in her own career and not merely in that of households upon which she is some sort of parasite. The heroine of Mrs. Freeman's *A New England Nun* (1891) is an illuminating instance: she has been betrothed to an absent, fortune-hunting lover for fourteen years, and now that he is back she finds herself full of consternation at his masculine habits and rejoices when he turns to another woman and leaves his first love to the felicity of her contented cell.

What in most literatures appears as a catastrophe appears in New England as a relief. Energy has run low in the calm veins of such women, and they have better things to do than to dwell upon the lives they might have led had marriage complicated them. Here genre painting reaches its height in American literature: quaint interiors scrupulously described; rounds of minute activity familiarly portrayed; skimpy moods analyzed with a delicate competence of touch. At the same time, New England literature was now too sentimental and now too realistic to allow all its old maids to remain perpetually sweet and passive. In its sentimental hours it liked to call up their younger days and to show them at the point which had decided or compelled their future loneliness— again and again discovering some act of abnegation such as giving up a lover because of the unsteadiness of his moral principles or surrendering him to another woman to whom he seemed for some reason or other to belong. In its realistic hours local color in New England liked to examine the atrophy of the emotions which in these stories often grows upon the celibate. One formula endlessly repeated deals with the efforts of some acrid spinster—or wife long widowed—to keep a young girl from marriage, generally out of contempt for love as a trivial weakness; the conclusion usually makes love victorious after a thunderbolt of revelation to the hinderer. There are inquiries, too, into the repressions and obsessions of women whose lives in this fashion or that have missed their flowering. Many of the inquiries are sympathetic, tender, penetrating, but most of them incline toward timidity and tameness. Their note is prevailingly the note of elegy; they are seen through a trembling haze of reticence. It is as if they had been made for readers of a vitality no more abundant than that of their angular heroines.

It would be possible to make a picturesque, precious anthology of stories dealing with the types and humors of New England. Different writers would contribute different tones: Sarah Orne Jewett—as in Deephaven (1877) and The Country of the Pointed Firs (1896)—the tone of faded gentility brooding over its miniature possessions in decaying seaport towns or in idyllic villages a little further inland; Mary E. Wilkins Freeman—A Humble Romance and Other Stories (1887), Pembroke (1894)—the tone of a stern honesty trained in isolated farms and along high, exposed ridges where the wind seems to have gnarled the dispositions of men and women as it has gnarled the apple trees and where human stubbornness perpetually crops out through a covering of kindliness as if in imitation of those granite ledges which everywhere break through the thin soil; Alice Brown—Meadow Grass (1895), Tiverton Tales (1899)—the tone of a homely accuracy touched with the fresh hues of a gently poetical temperament. More detailed in actuality than the stories of other sections, these New England plots do not fall so readily into formulas as do those of the South and West; and yet they have their formulas: how a stubborn pride worthy of some supreme cause holds an elderly Yankee to a petty, obstinate course until grievous calamities ensue; how a rural wife, neglected and overworked by her husband, rises in revolt against the treadmill of her dull tasks and startles him into comprehension and awkward consideration; how the remnant of some once prosperous family puts into the labor of keeping up appearances an amount of effort which, otherwise expended, might restore the family fortunes; how neighbors lock horns in the ruthless litigation which in New England corresponds to the vendettas of Kentucky and how they are reconciled eventually by sentiment in one guise or another; how a young girl—there are no Tom Joneses and few Hamlets in this womanly universe—grows up bright and sensitive as a flower and suffers from the hard, stiff frame of pious poverty; how a superb heroism springs out of a narrow life, expressing itself in some act of pitiful surrender and veiling the deed under an even more pitiful inarticulateness. The cities of New England were usually passed over by the local colorists. Boston, the capital of the Puritans, had to depend upon the older Holmes or the visiting Howells of Ohio for its reputation in fiction. After Hawthorne the romancers and novelists of his province took, it may be said, to the fields, where they worked much in the mood of Rose Terry Cooke who called her best collection of stories *Huckleberries* (1891) to emphasize what she thought a resemblance between the crops and the characters of New England: "hardy, sweet yet spicy, defying storms of heat or cold with calm persistence, clinging to a poor soil, barren pastures, gray and rocky hillsides, yet drawing fruitful issues from scanty sources." In the new century the orthodox fashion of local color survived chiefly in the many novels of Joseph C. Lincoln, dry and amusing laureate of Cape Cod. Robert Frost chose verse in which to distill the final essence of New England. Edwin Arlington Robinson in a few brief poems created Tilbury

Town and endowed it with a more haunting and more lasting pathos than that of any New England village in prose.

Through the influence, in important measure, of Howells and the *Atlantic* the modes of fiction practised east of the Connecticut extended their examples to other districts also: to Vermont in Rowland Evans Robinson's many volumes bebeginning with *Uncle Lisha's Shop: Life in a Corner of Yankee-land* (1887); to northern New York in Philander Deming—*Adirondack Stories* (1880)—and Irving Bacheller—*Eben Holden* (1900) and later books; to Pennsylvania in Margaret Deland's truthful, felicitous *Old Chester Tales* (1899) and *Dr. Lavender's People* (1903); to Ohio in Brand Whitlock, deliberately a follower of Howells; to Indiana in Booth Tarkington, who exceeded and outgrew the simpler limits of local color, and Meredith Nicholson who besides his novels wrote a study of the locality in *The Hoosiers* (1900); to Iowa and Arkansas in Alice French (Octave Thanet); to Kansas in William Allen White; to the Colorado mines in Mary Hallock Foote; to Louisiana in Grace King's *Tales of a Time and Place* (1892) and *Balcony Stories* (1893) and Kate Chopin's *Bayou Folk* (1894); to Virginia in the youthful Ellen Glasgow; to Georgia in Will N. Harben and Harry Stillwell Edwards—particularly in Edwards's brief *Aeneas Africanus* (1919) which has become a genuine folk-book of that state; and to other neighborhoods in other neighborly chronicles too numerous and mild to call for mention. New York City and its suburbs had less tender and more incisive habits of fiction. The pace for local color there was set by Henry Cuyler Bunner's brisk *Short Sixes* (1891), Richard Harding Davis's nonchalant *Van Bibber and Others* (1892), and the multitude of inventions by William Sydney Porter (O. Henry) in *The Four Million* (1904). But these New York stories generally resembled those written elsewhere, in their habit of decorum and benevolence. Of all the local color writers none besides O. Henry had so much ironic point and flavor as may still be found in the work of two of them who never thought of themselves as belonging to the fashion or even as writing short stories. Finley Peter Dunne created a true folk-philosopher in his Martin Dooley, a Chicago saloon-keeper who enlivened the current world by his comments on it in *Mr. Dooley in Peace and in War* (1898) and *Mr. Dooley in the Hearts of his Countrymen* (1899) and later collections. George Ade with his *Fables in Slang* (1900) and *More Fables* (1900), and further volumes, packed the folk-wisdom of the entire Middle West, and its familiar ways of life, into his shrewd little narratives.

2~Romantic History

Historical romance flared up about the time of the war with Spain, and produced a score of immensely popular novels. The fashion for history was not exactly new in 1898. It went back a dozen years or more, when it had taken form and doctrine partly from Stevenson's eager preference for Scott and Dumas as against contemporary realists. Within two or three years after Stevenson's *Kidnapped* (1886) and Rider Haggard's *She* (1887), history in the American novel assumed an importance it had not had since Cooper and Hawthorne. Arthur Sherburne Hardy in 1889 published *Passe Rose*, a dainty romance of the time of Charlemagne, and Harold Frederic, the next year, *In the Valley*, a substantial, unaffected narrative of life along the Mohawk at the time of the French and Indian War. The material touched upon by Frederic had already been discovered by Mary Hartwell Catherwood. She probably thought of Stevenson but certainly thought of Francis Parkman, who wrote an introduction to *The Romance of Dollard* (1889) vouching for its historicity. She had discovered a new romantic treasure; the lank heroes of Pike County now gave way before the charm of an older world

(215)

adventuring in the Middle West, noblemen pitted against savages, black-robed Jesuits, coureurs de bois swarming through all the rivers and forests, highbred ladies strayed into the wilderness, innocent Indian maidens, half-breed villains, French villages as little as possible like the Anglo-Saxon towns which had grown up on their ancient sites.

The years 1889-94 forecast almost all the developments of the more fecund years from 1896-1902 which saw the most active school of historical romances the United States had yet produced. Merely to name the more successful performances of the period suffices to show in what fashion the romantic imagination then worked: Mark Twain's *Personal Recollections of Joan of Arc* (1896), James Lane Allen's *The Choir Invisible* (1897), Richard Harding Davis's *Soldiers of Fortune* (1897), S. Weir Mitchell's *Hugh Wynne* (1897) and *The Adventures of François* (1898), Charles Major's *When Knighthood Was in Flower* (1898), Thomas Nelson Page's *Red Rock* (1898), Mary Johnston's *Prisoners of Hope* (1898) and *To Have and to Hold* (1899), F. Marion Crawford's *Via Crucis* (1898) and *In the Palace of the King* (1900), Paul Leicester Ford's *Janice Meredith* (1899), Winston Churchill's *Richard Carvel* (1899), *The Crisis* (1901), and *The Crossing* (1904), Booth Tarkington's *Monsieur Beaucaire* (1900), Maurice Thompson's *Alice of Old Vincennes* (1900), Henry Harland's *The Cardinal's Snuff-Box* (1901), George Barr McCutcheon's *Graustark* (1901), Robert W. Chambers's *Cardigan* (1901), Mary Hartwell Catherwood's *Lazarre* (1901), Gertrude Atherton's *The Conqueror* (1902), Ellen Glasgow's *The Battleground* (1902) and *Deliverance* (1904). Mary E. Wilkins Freeman left her austere tales of rural New England to write a romance of the swashbuckling seventeenth century, *The Heart's Highway* (1900); Edward Bellamy's unfinished early serial *The Duke of Stockbridge* was completed and published as a book aimed at the new fashion (1900). Cable turned away from his forte in *The Cavalier* (1901),

Sarah Orne Jewett in *The Tory Lover* (1901), Stockton in *Kate Bonnet* (1902). After 1902 the type declined, both in energy and popularity. Mary Johnston persisted in romance for several years, but Winston Churchill, Ellen Glasgow, Booth Tarkington moved on toward realism with the times. The writers who had been drawn aside by the episode nearly all of them went back to their former methods. George Ade in *The Slim Princess* (1907) more or less closed the chapter with his parody of Ruritanian, Graustarkian tales.

Such of these narratives as dealt in any way with the present generally took their slashing, skylarking, and robustly Yankee heroes, as in *Soldiers of Fortune* or *Graustark*, off to remote or imaginary regions for deeds of haughty daring and exotic wooing. Elsewhere, even in the romances with a foreign scene, taste ran to the past: to the whirling Paris of the French Revolution as in *François* or to the frilled and powdered Bath of the eighteenth century as in *Monsieur Beaucaire*; or still further to the Tudor sixteenth century of *When Kinghthood Was in Flower* or the French fifteenth century of *Joan of Arc*. The bulk of the romancers, however, as in Cooper's time, kept their imaginations ordinarily at home. *Red Rock* and *Deliverance* chronicled on a large if melodramatic scale the process of Reconstruction in Virginia; *The Crisis*, *The Cavalier*, and *The Battleground* are all transacted during the Civil War in the regions respectively of the middle and lower Mississippi and of Virginia; *Lazarre* revived the old tradition that the Dauphin had been brought to America to grow up among the Indians; and *Kate Bonnet* made its heroine a mythical daughter of that very authentic buccaneer of the early eighteenth century, Stede Bonnet. And yet these belong but to the fringes of the historical fiction of their day. Much as with Cooper's contemporaries, these American romancers exploited the American matters of the Settlement, the Revolution, and the Frontier. As the frontier no longer meant to Americans what it had meant when it still occupied a great portion of the continent, the romancers made less of it than of the other standard matters, and left it to the chroniclers of the cowboys. The mountain regions of local color, in their rough, primitive manners, more or less resembled the frontier of Cooper and Simms. If the matter of the Frontier partially eluded the ardor of the romancers, nothing of the sort happened to the Settlement and the Revolution, which now luxuriantly bloomed again. The hardships of pioneering and warfare were united in *Alice of Old Vincennes*, an account of the expedition of George Rogers Clark, and in *The Crossing*, which dealt with the West during the Revolutionary and Federalist eras, from Vincennes and Kaskaskia on the north and from the Carolinas on the east to the Mississippi and Louisiana. The true territory of romance, however, lay east of the Alleghenies, between New Jersey and Richmond. For every tale concerned with New England or New York there were two or three concerned with Pennsylvania or Virginia. *The Tory Lover* moves from Sarah Orne Jewett's gentle Berwick to Europe and back; *The Duke of Stockbridge* —most realistic of all these romances—is about Shays's rebellion. But *The Heart's Highway* hovers around Jamestown at the end of its first century; *Prisoners of Hope* and *To Have and to Hold* rarely stray far from Tidewater; *Richard Carvel* joins the England of Dr. Johnson with Revolutionary Maryland; *Hugh Wynne* and *Janice Meredith* range from New York to Yorktown, yet the center of their interests is the Philadelphia of the Continental Congress.

Certain distinctions in style and handling of course appear. *Joan of Arc* stands clearly to one side by virtue of a power which none of its rivals displays. *The Choir Invisible* employs history only incidentally in a poetic and sentimental interpretation of human existence. *To Have and to Hold* is more ornate in style, *Monsieur Beaucaire* more graceful and piquant, *The Crossing* more grandiose in its sweep, than the ordinary run. *Janice Meredith* is based upon remarkable erudition and

Hugh Wynne remarkably sums up the traditions of Philadelphia as remembered by the descendants of her Augustan age. In spite of these distinctions, however, the general corpus of such romances forms a singularly unified mass. Certain themes like the importation of wives to Virginia, the fate of gentlemen who desperately came over as indentured servants or convicts, the exploits of John Paul Jones, are repeated again and again. Historical personalities so crowd the scene that a hero or a heroine can hardly step out upon the street or go to dinner without encountering some eminent man—particularly Franklin or Washington, or some one of the colonial governors of Virginia. While intensely American in reporting the conflicts with English rule, the stories almost always sympathize with the colonial and Revolutionary gentry as against the humbler orders, with Washington as against Jefferson, with the aristocratic emigrés from France as against the French revolutionists. Details of costume load the narrative far more than descriptions of landscape. Fine gentlemen, called Cavaliers till the word becomes a byword, flutter and ruffle across the stage, with splendid gestures and delicate points of honor, incomparable at the small sword or the minuet, poetic and patriotic and heroic. With them in all their lighter moments are exquisite ladies, generally very young but with some dowagers among them, who live in spacious, cool houses, in a world of mahogany and silver and brocade; ladies who ardently expect new bales of clothing from London but who joyfully sacrifice all such delights during the Revolution; ladies who rise late, take the air genteelly, play at lovely needlework, and spend their nights at balls of elaborate splendor; and yet ladies who know the saddle and, when need comes, put off their squeamishness and rough it in the most dangerous escapades without a tremor. One formula furnishes something like half the notable plots: an honest American gentleman, mortally opposed to a villain who is generally British, courts a beautiful American girl through

(219)

acute vicissitudes and wins her only in the bitter end just before or after killing his wicked rival in a duel. As if this were a theater of marionettes there are only a few puppets, though there are plenty of handsome costumes to vary the entertainment. As might be expected, the style of all these novels approaches identity, a fluid, languid style, ready to slip into blank verse at the provocation of any heightened moment, and constantly tinctured with a faint archaism of diction and rhythm. "There is an old book my grandchildren love to hear me read to them," says Hugh Wynne in a tone which would fit nearly every novel of the time. "It is the *Morte d'Arthur*, done into English by Sir Thomas Malory. Often when I read therein of how Arthur the king bade farewell to the world and to the last of the great company of his Knights of the Round Table, this scene at Whitehall slip [Washington's farewell to his officers] comes back to me, and I seem to see once more those gallant soldiers, and far away the tall figure of surely the knightliest gentleman our days have known."

The reference to Malory—who in *The Choir Invisible* is cited as the truest teacher of virtue—illuminates the aims and methods of all these rococo romancers. Writing of a time so recent as the Civil War or Reconstruction, they could use a dialect almost contemporary, but the moment they drew near to the Revolution or the Settlement they fell into the language which the nineteenth century had thought the fit medium for medieval deeds. The deeper American past to the romancers seemed a sort of middle age. Their inferiority to the Cooper of the *Leather-Stocking Tales* or to the Melville of *Moby Dick* lies in the fact that whereas Cooper and Melville, much as they might invent, still worked upon a solid basis in a mood not too far from the mood of realism, their successors wrote romance pure and simple, even when they were most erudite. Romance was in the air. Not all the publishing enterprise which developed romances into best sellers and distributed millions of copies could have done so but for the moment of national expansiveness which attended the Spanish War. Patriotism and jingoism, altruism and imperialism, passion and sentimentalism, shook the temper which had slowly been stiffening since the Civil War. Now, with a rush of unaccustomed emotions the national imagination sought out its own past, delighting in it, wallowing in it. Had the romancers who met the mood been more deeply grounded in reality and less sentimental, or had the national mood lasted for a longer time, some eminent masterpiece might have emerged. None did, and the gold lace and gilt of the narratives actually evoked began to tarnish almost as soon as the wind touched them.

Of the novels which belong fully to the fashion *Hugh Wynne* perhaps came closest to permanence, and S. Weir Mitchell (1829-1913) deserves special mention. A Philadelphian, he set aside his youthful literary ambitions on the advice of Oliver Wendell Holmes, made himself a distinguished medical specialist, particularly in nervous diseases, and only after fifty gave much time to the verse and fiction which he wrote henceforth until his death. His professional knowledge enabled him to write authoritatively of difficult and wayward states of body and mind: as in *The Case of George Dedlow* (1880), so circumstantial in its improbabilities, *Roland Blake* (1886), which George Meredith admired, *The Autobiography of a Quack* (1900), concerning the dishonorable purlieus of the medical profession, and *Constance Trescott* (1905), considered by Mitchell his best constructed novel and certainly his most thorough-going study of a pathological mood. His psychological stories, however, had neither quite the appeal nor quite the merit of his historical romances, which began with *Hephzibah Guinness* (1880) and extended to *Westways* (1913). *Westways* is a chronicle of the effects of the Civil War in Pennsylvania, but Mitchell's best work belongs to the Revolutionary cycle: *Hugh Wynne*, the career

(221)

of a Free Quaker on Washington's staff, *The Red City*, a picture of Washington's second administration, and *The Adventures of François*, which stands as close to the American stories as did the revolutionary Paris to the city of Franklin. Philadelphia, so often the center of action, appears under a softer, mellower light than was thrown by contemporary romance upon any other American city. Washington, though drawn as much to the life as Mitchell could draw him, is still a stately demigod.

James Lane Allen (1849-1925) was close to both local color and the historical romance. His earliest collection of tales, *Flute and Violin* (1891), and his commentary on *The Blue-Grass Region of Kentucky* (1892) established the character which his chosen district long had in the world of the imagination. His Kentucky was always conscious of a chivalric past, and *The Choir Invisible* had its scene in and near the Lexington of the eighteenth century. But from the first he had principles of art which would not allow him to consider either local color or history as ends in themselves. He believed they must be employed as elements contributing to some general effect of beauty or of meaning. In this program he was handicapped by various sentimentalisms. The hero of *The Choir Invisible*, loving a woman who though in love with him is bound in marriage to another man, engages himself to a young girl, shortly afterward to find that his real love is free again; yet with a high gesture of sacrifice he holds to his engagement and enters upon a union of duty which is sure to make two, and possibly three, persons unhappy instead of one, though all of them are equally guiltless. In the idyls *A Kentucky Cardinal* (1895) and its sequel *Aftermath* (1896) Allen had only tricks of melodrama to support the true and tragic thesis that Nature holds men in iron hands and may torture them when they struggle for liberty. *Summer in Arcady* (1896) had a richer passion and a sparer form than either of the other idyls, but even it has come to have the dry grace of pressed flowers and valentines. When he says that in June in Kentucky "the warm-eyed, foot-stamping young bucks forsake their plow-shares in the green rows, their reapers among the yellow beards; and the bouncing, laughing, round-breasted girls arrange their ribbons and their vows," Allen brings Theocritus to mind, and the silver ages. He used local color to ennoble it, and made most of the local colorists seem in comparison homespun if not tawdry. But the dewy, luminous style of his better pages could not offset the over-sweetness of too many of them.

The temper called *fin de siècle* in Europe hardly touched the American novel, and Edgar Saltus (1855-1921) stood almost alone in a conscious decadence. He began his career, after a penetrating study of Balzac (1884), with *The Philosophy of Disenchantment* (1885) and *The Anatomy of Negation* (1886), deriving chiefly from Hartmann and Schopenhauer. Saltus's first novels dealt most of them with contemporary life in fashionable New York, melodramatically, unconvincingly. He struck his true, if somewhat trivial, note when he was buried in ancient history or ranged through the fields of time, generally a historian of love and loveliness in sumptuous, perverse phases. In *Mary Magdelen* (1891) he dressed up a traditional courtesan in the splendors of purple and gold and perfumed her with many dangerous essences more exciting than her later penitence; in *Imperial Purple* (1892) he undertook a chronicle of the Roman emperors from Julius Cæsar to Heliogobalus, exhibiting them in the most splendid of their extravagances and sins; in *Historia Amoris* (1906) he followed the maddening trial of love and in *The Lords of the Ghostland* (1907) the saddening trial of faith through the annals of mankind. What especially moved Saltus's imagination was the spectacle of imperial Rome as interpreted by modern Parisians: that lust for power and sensation, those incredible temples, palaces, feasts, revelries, blasphemies, butcheries. Commencing with a beauty which knew no

(223)

bounds, he went on to satiety or impotence for his theme; in the end he brought little but a glittering ferocity to his cold narrative of the czars from Ivan to Catherine, in *The Imperial Orgy* (1920). Occasional wit saved Saltus from utter lusciousness, but there was not enough to preserve his work except in the memory of a few curious readers.

The cosmopolitan career of Lafcadio Hearn, English-Irish-Gypsy-Greek-Arab-Moorish in blood, who was born on an Ionian island and died in Japan, crossed the United States, where he spent most of the years 1869-90, chiefly in Cincinnati and New Orleans, with voyages to the West Indies. Deeply affected by Flaubert, Gautier, and Baudelaire, Hearn lived as writer in exotic regions which he invented if he could not find them, but his short novels *Chita* (1889) and *Youma* (1890) have American settings: *Chita* the story of a tidal wave that swept Last Island, off the coast of Louisiana, and *Youma* the story of a slave insurrection in Martinique. These, with his *Two Years in the French West Indies* (1890), gave Hearn, whatever his technical relations to American literature, a classic standing among the writers who have concerned themselves with the American tropics. With Hearn may be mentioned John Luther Long who, without ever having been in Japan, wrote the short story *Madame Butterfly* (1898). Pathetic tragedy of the Japanese wife of an American naval officer, it was first made into a successful play by David Belasco (1900) and then by Puccini (1904) into his famous opera.

XII

EMERGENCE OF NATURALISM

THE NATURALISM which emerged in the fiction of the last decade of the nineteenth century was not so much a deliberate principle or a definite school as a variety of dissents from the official type of realism favored by Howells. Hamlin Garland (1860-   ) in his *Crumbling Idols* (1894) was the first to outline the critical position of the dissenters. It was no longer enough, they argued and felt, to skim rosy surfaces. The novel, a powerful modern agency for civilization, must go deeper than it had gone in the United States, must turn to the light many ugly realities, hitherto neglected, which were growing more ominous every day. It must deal candidly with political corruption, economic injustice, religious unrest, sexual irregularities, with greed and doubt and hate and cruelty and violence, as well as with more customary subjects. It must assert its right, its obligation, to speak of anything it chose if that thing were true. Garland's statement of principles followed his own practice, already shown in his hard pastorals of the upper Middle West: *Main-Travelled Roads* (1891) and *Prairie Folks* (1893). He was passionately devoted to the war on needless poverty which had already enlisted Edward Bellamy and Henry George, and he stood forth as the chief literary spokesman of the distress and dissatisfaction then stirring along the changed frontier which so long as free land lasted had been the natural outlet for the expansive, restless race.

The prairies and the plains had depended almost wholly upon romance for their literary reputation; Garland, who had tested at first hand the hardships of such a life, became articulate through his dissent from average notions about the pioneer. His earliest motives seem to have been personal. During a youth which saw him borne steadily westward, from his Wisconsin birthplace to windy Iowa and then to bleak Dakota, his own instincts clashed with those of his migratory father as the instincts of many a sensitive, unremembered youth must have clased with the dumb, fierce urges of the leaders of migration everywhere. The younger Garland hungered on the frontier for beauty and learning and leisure; the impulse which eventually detached him from Dakota and sent him on a reverent pilgrimage to Boston was the very impulse which, on another scale, had lately detached Henry James from his native country and had sent him to the home of his forefathers in the British Isles.

Garland could neither feel so free nor fly so far from home as James. He had, in the midst of his raptures and his successes in New England, still to remember the plight of the family he had left behind him on the lonely prairie; he cherished a patriotism for his province which went a long way toward restoring him to it in time. Sentimental and romantic considerations, however, did not influence him altogether in his first important work. He had been kindled by Howells in Boston to a passion for realism which carried him beyond the suave accuracy of his master to a somber veracity. This veracity was more than somber; it was a polemic. Garland desired to tell the unheeded truth about the frontier farmers and their wives in language which might do something to lift the desperate burdens of their condition. Consequently his passions and his doctrines joined hands to fix the direction of his art; he both hated the frontier and hinted at definite remedies which he thought would make it more endurable.

The romancers had studied the progress of the frontier in the lives of its victors; Garland studied it in the lives of its victims: the private soldier returning drably and mutely from the war to resume his drab, mute career behind the plow; the tenant caught in a trap by his landlord and the law and obliged to pay for the added value which his own toil has given to his farm; the brother neglected until his courage has died and proffered assistance comes too late to rouse him; and particularly the daughter whom a harsh father or the wife whom a brutal husband breaks or drives away—the most sensitive and therefore the most pitiful victims of them all. Garland told his early stories in the strong, level language of a man who had observed much but chose to write little. Not his words but the overtones vibrating through them cry out that the earth and the fruits of the earth belong to all men yet a few of them have turned tiger or dog or jackal and snatched what is precious for themselves while their fellows starve and freeze. Tense and unrelieved as his accusations were, he stood in his methods nearer, say, to the humane Millet than to the angry Zola. There is a clear color in his landscapes; youth and love on his desolate plains, as well as anywhere, can find glory in the most difficult existence; he might strip particular lives bare but he clung to the conviction that human life has a dignity which is deeper than any glamor goes and can survive the loss of all its trappings.

Garland never again quite reached the passion and truth of this early cycle of stories in which his imagination worked most eagerly over the materials he knew best. He turned to pleas for the single tax or to exposures of legislative misconduct or imbecility, about which he neither knew nor cared so much as he knew and cared about the actual lives of working farmers. He followed the false light of local color to the Rocky Mountains and began the series of romantic narratives which further interrupted his growth and, gradually, his fame. He who had grimly refused to lend his voice to the legend of the frontier in which he had grown up and who had studied the deceptive picture not as a visitor but as a native, became a visiting enthusiast for the high trails and let himself be roused by a fervor much like that from which he had formerly dissented. In his different way he was as hungry for new lands as his father had been before him. Hamlin Garland thought he had exhausted his old community and must move on to fresher pastures. In a relatively unfamiliar country he came to lay his emphasis upon outward manners and let his plots and characters fall into formula. Again and again he used the theme of a love uniting some vigorous, rude frontiersman and some girl from a politer neighborhood. Pioneer and lady are essentially the same pair in varying costumes; the stories harp upon the praise of plains and mountains and the scorn of cities and civilization.

In *A Son of the Middle Border* (1917), the first of a series of autobiographical volumes, Garland returned to matters closest to him. His enthusiasms might be romantic, but his imagination was not; it was married to his memory of actual events. All along, it now appeared, he had been at his happiest when he was most nearly autobiographical. Those vivid early stories had come from the lives of his own family or of their neighbors. *Rose of Dutcher's Coolly* (1895) had set forth what was virtually his own experience in its account of a heroine—not hero—who leaves her native farm to go first to college and then to Chicago to pursue a wider life, torn constantly between a need for freedom and a loyalty to the father she is forced to desert. In a sense the *Son* supersedes the fictive versions of the same materials; they are the original documents and the autobiography the final redaction and commentary. But the bitterness of the stories has in the *Son* for the most part been lost, in a forgiving, philosophic interpretation of the old frontier, seen in epic dimensions. In Garland's later years he gave much of his time to official support of the American Academy, a kind of successor to Howells.

Stephen Crane (1871-1900) brought to naturalism an authentic young genius and an intensity new to the American novel. Born in New Jersey, son of a clergyman, Crane was a reporter while he was still at school, and after a year at Lafayette and another at Syracuse he gave up formal education, to live precariously by writing for newspapers in New York. Little used to reading, he admired Tolstoi and Flaubert so far as he knew them, but he was impatient of his genteel American contemporaries, whom he called insincere. His own observations in the slums and along the Bowery had convinced him that life was not what books made it out. He was unwilling to look for reality behind accepted forms of manners or art, and too honest to pretend he saw it there. If he could not see life face to face, he did not care to see it at all. Reality, for him, had to be immediate and outspoken. At twenty-one he wrote his first novel, *Maggie: A Girl of the Street,* and borrowed money to have it printed (1893) because he could find no publisher. It was the story of a girl of a brutal Irish family in lower Manhattan who, driven from home by a drunken mother, takes refuge with a lover, loses him to a more practised woman, and drowns herself. The standard form for such a story in the early nineties, if such a story was to be told at all, would have made it sentimental or admonitory. The Bowery was then best known from such slangy, subliterary stories as Edward Waterman Townsend's *Chimmie Fadden* (1895) and other experiments in dialect. When Crane went to the slums he had not gone laughing or slumming, and he would no more preach than he would expurgate. He did not in the least mind that the savagery of his incidents might shock his readers. His method was as direct as his attitude. He arranged his episodes in a simple, natural order, all example and no precept. To his decade Crane seemed heartless when he plunged into forbidden depths and brought up dreadful things without apology or comment. He would have thought it more heartless to intrude his doctrines into Maggie's tragedy.

Though *Maggie* was printed, almost no copies could be sold. But Hamlin Garland quickly recognized Crane and introduced him to Howells, who praised him as a writer sprung into life fully armed. With their encouragement he began another novel and finished *The Red Badge of Courage* (1895), which first appeared as a serial in a Philadelphia newspaper. DeForest had written realistically about the Civil War, and Ambrose Bierce sardonically in the stories first called *Tales of Soldiers and Civilians* (1891) and later *In the Midst of Life*. Crane had not got his chief materials from reading. Ever since Appomattox there had run, side by side with romantic versions of the war, a realistic memory of it, not in books, which former soldiers exchanged in the vernacular and retold to listening boys. Here was Crane's primary source. For his hero he chose an ordinary recruit, fresh from an inland farm, and carried him through his first experiences under fire. Crane had but to imagine himself in a similar danger and recount the moods that he knew would have come over him. As the recruit has no notion of the general plan of the battle, he has to obey commands that he does not understand, that he resents, that he hates. His excited senses color the occasion, even the landscape. He suffers agonies of fatigue and almost a catastrophe of fear. If he seems unusually imaginative, he is not too subtle. He speaks a convincing boyish dialect. His sensations are limited to something like his spiritual capacity. When Crane later saw a battle he found that he had been accurate in his account, not because he had studied military strategy but because he had placed the center of the affair in the experience of an individual soldier. The *Red Badge*, which gave Crane an opportunity to bring his critical ideas to bear upon a matter which he thought had too long been treated with heroic nonsense, gave him also an opportunity to exercise a characteristic art. The soldier is a lens through which the whole battle may be seen, a sensorium upon which all its details may be registered. Being in the fear of death, he is not a mere transparent lens, a mere passive sensorium. The battle takes a mad shape within his consciousness. Since the action of the narrative is laid in his excited mind, it had no excuse for being over-perfunctory or languid. All is immediate, all is intense. The language may with good reason be heightened now and then to the pitch of poetry. And yet the thrill in the narrative does not rise from the language, so tactfully is it elevated. The action and the language fit one another in a clear integrity.

The novel had an instantaneous success in both America and England. Crane's poems, *The Black Riders and Other Lines* (1895), suggested to him by a reading of Emily Dickinson, made little stir, but his prose, with its rapid, flashing movement and its bright, startling phrases, seemed a new note in fiction. Crane went on a journalistic assignment to Nebraska, Arkansas, Louisiana, Texas, and Mexico, desiring most to see the Mississippi, cowboys riding, and a blizzard on the plains. He found materials for numerous short stories, including two of his best: *The Blue Hotel* (1899) and *The Bride Comes to Yellow Sky* (1898). Back again in New York, he published *Maggie* (1896) without disapproval, a milder companion-piece to it called *George's Mother* (1896) and *The Little Regiment: And Other Episodes of the American Civil War* (1896). Because *The Red Badge* was overwhelmingly preferred to *Maggie* Crane wrote thereafter much more about war than about slums. At the end of 1896 he sailed on a filibustering vessel bound for Cuba, was shipwrecked off the Florida coast, and had the adventure which he brilliantly related in another masterly short story *The Open Boat* (1898). By way of London and Paris he proceeded in 1897 to Greece, to report the Turkish war. Having no foreign language he was handicapped and ineffectual, though again he picked up enough with his sharp eyes for his novel *Active Service* (1899), written after Crane had returned to England, and promptly followed by the short novel *The Monster* (1899). The war with Spain called Crane to Florida and Cuba. Purely as correspondent he was no match for Richard

Harding Davis, then at the height of his lively powers, but Davis's reports never rose above good journalism, while Crane's sketches in *Wounds in the Rain* (1900) have touches which belong to literature. Early in 1899 he left New York for England, where he spent the rest of his crowded life in Sussex except for a final month in the Black Forest. He died in 1900, not yet twenty-nine. His poems in *War Is Kind* (1900) were little noted, his satiric romance *The O'Ruddy* (completed by Robert Barr, 1903) was unfinished, and his *Whilomville Stories* (1900), realistic about boyhood affairs, were not properly valued till his *Work* appeared in twelve volumes in 1925-26.

Late in his life Crane came to believe that the *Red Badge* had been too long, and his other masterpieces are all shorter. *The Blue Hotel* shows fate blindly and causelessly interfering, as Crane thought it often does, in the muddled lives of men. *The Bride Comes to Yellow Sky* is an almost unbelievably direct, vivid, and penetrating drama of matter-of-fact heroism in Texas and the discomfiture of a frontier bad-man. *The Open Boat* tells a straight story of adventure at sea with breathless concentration and illumination. *The Monster* exposes the stupidity of public opinion in a small New York town where perhaps no one person could be so cruel as the people are collectively. Crane was often comic, more often ironic, and always pungent. His private indifference to conventional opinions and habits caused him to be credited with legendary wild oats which he would have been too busy to sow even if he had been disposed to. Among the novelists of his decade Crane stood out as Poe had among the poets of the mid-century, with as much scandal as fame in his reputation. There is justice in a comparison of the novelist with a poet. Lucidity like Crane's is poetry. Never obscure, he was an impressionist in prose. He had a poet's charm, which came not only from his shining language but also from his free, courageous mind. He had no burden of nonsense to slow him down. He worked within tangible limits. When his intelligence had brought him close to his materials he felt for them the desire of a lover. His irony did not lessen his passion, only sharpened his understanding and sympathy. Too much a realist to fall in with contemporary romancers, he was too much a poet to follow the course laid down by such systematic naturalists as Zola. Crane's voice was so individual that he did not come into the honor due him till another age, when it became evident that he had spoken with the voice of a generation later than his own. Though he wrote far more than needs to be preserved, yet in the *Red Badge* and a half-dozen or so short stories he is as timeless as any novelist in English. Modern American literature began with him.

Crane's friend Harold Frederic, also a newspaperman, besides his realistic novels of the Revolution and the Civil War wrote *The Damnation of Theron Ware* (1896), a relentless study of a Methodist minister who goes spiritually to pieces because he has only a shallow idealism to sustain him. A nearer contemporary of Crane, Frank Norris (1870-1902), had a larger part in the development of the new school of fiction. A leader in a conscious movement to continentalize American literature as a protest against local color, he was himself one of the least sectional of novelists. Born in Chicago, where he passed his boyhood, a student of art in Paris for two years, student for four years at the University of California and for one graduate year at Harvard, newspaper correspondent in South Africa at the time of the Jameson raid and in Cuba during the Santiago campaign, journalist in San Francisco and New York, Norris had a vision of American life which was geographically very wide. Zola, his chief teacher, and Kipling had taught Norris how much the strength of realism depends upon facts observed in their native places. And though one of his earliest passions was for Froissart, and his first book, *Yvernelle* (1892) was a verse romance upon a medieval French theme, his mature plots were laid almost entirely in settings with which he was familiar. That so many of them are Californian must be explained by his early death; he meant later to turn to other regions.

What gave Norris his continental view of his materials was a certain epic inclination in him. He tended to vast plans and conceived trilogies. His Epic of the Wheat—The Octopus (1901), which deals with the production of wheat in California. The Pit (1903), which deals with the distribution of wheat through the Chicago Board of Trade, and The Wolf, which, though never written, was to have dealt with the relieving of a famine in Europe by American wheat—he thought of as three distinct novels, bound together only by the cosmic spirit of the wheat which comes up from the abundant earth and moves irresistibly to its appointed purpose, guided, of course, by men, and fought and played over by them, but always mightier than they and always their master as well as their sustenance. Another trilogy to which he meant to give years of work would have centered in the battle of Gettysburg, one part for each day, and would have sought to present what Norris considered the American spirit as his Epic of the Wheat sought to present an impersonal force of nature. Such conceptions explain the grandiose manner which Norris never lost and they help to explain, too, the passion of his naturalism.

Trafficking in wheat is a less organic function than either growing or eating it. The Pit, though its success on the stage and its energetic drama of business made it popular, falls in interest and power below The Octopus. The Octopus of the title is the Pacific and Southwestern Railroad which holds the wheat growers of California in its cruel tentacles, able if it likes to deny them access to their natural markets, and consequently a symbol of the control which economic machinery exercises over the elements of life. The book sets forth the drama of Agriculture and Trade locked in a fierce conflict, with Trade for the moment villain and victor. Norris's sympathies lie with the oppressed ranchmen; the Railroad has the iron teeth and ruthless hunger of the Old Witch of juvenile melodrama; in the end, though the ranchers have been defeated, the wheat itself too symbolically pours in upon the agent of the Railroad and destroys him—the wheat "untouched, unassailable, undefiled, that mighty world-force, that nourisher of nations, wrapped in Nirvanic calm, indifferent to the human swarm, gigantic, resistless." And yet these cosmic implications do not remove the story too far from actual existence in California: plowing, planting, harvesting, sheep-herding, merry-making, rabbit-killing, love, labor, birth, death, and certain fine, if not always quite realized, phases of poetry and faith. The style, though often turgid, is strong and full; the movement is nervous and swift; the pictures, though panoramic, are richly alive.

The passion which informs *The Octopus*, a kind of fiery zeal for truth which lifted and enlarged all Norris wrote, is the quality which marked him off from the older realism of Howells. Zola had it, and Norris, who called Zola the very head of the Romanticists, was willing to name his own form of naturalism romantic if he could argue for the use in fiction of deeper and more stirring truths than those minute, surface matters which, in his opinion, were the stock in trade of official realism. The clearest instance in his work of this romantic tendency is the story of Vanamee in *The Octopus*, the sheep-herder who has mystical communion with the spirit of his dead mistress. But equally romantic, in fact, is Norris's constant preoccupation with elemental emotions. His heroes are nearly all violent men, willful, passionate, combative; his heroines—thick-haired, large-armed women, almost all of a single physical type—are endowed with a frank and deep if slow vitality. Love in Norris's world is the mating of vikings and valkyries. The simplest version of such heroic passions may be found in *Moran of the Lady Letty* (1898),

(235)

the story of a civilized young San Franciscan who is shang-
haied upon a Pacific fishing boat and, among many adventures, meets and loves the splendid Norse savage, Moran,
whom he wins with the valor aroused in him by a primitive life. A Man's Woman (1900) and The Octopus and
The Pit only repeat this pair of lovers in varying costumes
and occupations. In McTeague (1899) the man of the pair,
married to a woman of a different type, finally murders her.
But love is by no means the chief concern of Norris's novels,
which were packed with detailed phases of life then unknown
or at least uncommon in American fiction: shark-fishing and
beachcombing; vulgar people in San Francisco and its Bohemian aspects; the perils of Arctic exploration; the enormous
conflicts of trading in the Chicago wheat pit; the ugly dis-
sipations of undergraduates in the posthumous but early Van-
dover and the Brute (1914). Norris set himself to find the
basic elements in human nature and to present them with
unhesitating accuracy. His theories were summed up in his
collected essays The Responsibilities of the Novelist (1903).

The work begun by Crane and Norris was carried on after
their early deaths by writers less gifted than they, but not
less bent on looking beyond the familiar themes of ordinary
fiction. Brand Whitlock in The 13th District (1902) and
Alfred Henry Lewis in The Boss (1903) exposed the mean
crafts of politics. Steward Edward White in The Blazed Trail
(1902) turned from soft life in cities to the rigors of Michigan
lumber camps. Charles D. Stewart in The Fugitive Blacksmith (1905) told a diverting story of a roving artisan who
lives by his mechanic wits among the villages of the lower
Mississippi. The escape to the primitive divided the field
with the exposure of civic abuses. At a time when the journalists called muck-rakers were most active, and historians
busied themselves with reëxamining the past which the romancers had lately done their best to glorify, novelists followed the fashion. David Graham Phillips continued it

through a score of novels in which he hunted for snobbery and stupidity and cruelty and greed, throwing upon them an angry light without much art or charm. He is best remembered for the bulky *Susan Lenox* (1917), the fullest and almost the only full account of an American courtesan.

Jack London (1876-1916), contemporary of Crane and Norris, outlived them long enough to write more books than they but also died young for a novelist. Born in California, of nomadic pioneer stock, he lived as a boy on farms or on the Oakland water-front, and read voraciously in books of romance and adventure. At fourteen he left school to be an unskilled laborer in a dozen occupations, becoming in time oyster pirate and a longshoreman in and near the bay of San Francisco and shipping before the mast at seventeen to go as far as Japan and the Bering Sea. In a mood of disgust induced by overwork he became a tramp at eighteen. He covered ten thousand miles in the United States and Canada during the hard times of the nineties and made up his mind that he could no longer continue in the treadmill which his great bodily strength had regarded as a pleasure and which his reading had told him was a virtue. Home once more, he encountered books which confirmed him in his resolution. A year at the University of California and a winter in the Klondike during the gold rush still further confirmed him: he became a socialist and a revolutionist. With enormous labors he made himself into a popular writer, discovered that the politer world which he consequently entered was not all he had imagined it, and cast in his fortunes with the working class. He visited the East End of London, cruised in the South Seas, acted as correspondent during the Russo-Japanese War and in Mexico in 1914, lectured and traveled and farmed and made large sums of money till the end of his life.

As a propagandist for socialism he wrote *War of the Classes* (1905), *Revolution* (1910), and *The Iron Heel* (1908), a romance recounting an imaginary revolution of 1932. Of his autobiographical writings *The People of the Abyss* (1903), his adventures in the London slums, *The Road* (1907), his life as a tramp, *Martin Eden* (1909), his struggles in learning to write, *The Cruise of The Snark* (1911), a voyage in the Pacific, *John Barleycorn* (1913), his alcoholic memories, are most important, although autobiography colors all his records and inventions. His popularity and his eagerness for money tempted him to write much, especially in the way of short stories, that was below his better level, and he never rose above his first marked success, *The Call of the Wild* (1903). Although he dealt often with ideas in his books, and liked to hint at his learning, he wrote as a rule under the obsession of physical energy. What was elemental in Frank Norris became abysmal in Jack London. He carried the cult of red blood in literature to an extreme at which it began to sink to the ridiculous, as in his lineal descendants of the moving-pictures. His heroes, whether wolves or dogs or prize-fighters or sailors or adventurers-at-large, have all of them approximately the same instincts and the same careers. They rise to eminence by battle, hold the eminence for a while by the same methods, and eventually go down under the rush of stronger enemies. London, with the strength of the strong, exulted in the struggle for survival. He saw human history in terms of the evolutionary dogma, which to him seemed a glorious, continuous epic of which his stories were episodes. He set them in localities where the struggle could be most obvious: in the wilds of Alaska, on remote Pacific Islands, on ships at sea out of hearing of the police, in industrial communities during strikes, in the underworlds of various cities, on the routes of vagabondage. As he had a boy's glee in conflict, so he had a boy's insensibility to physical suffering. *The Sea-Wolf* (1904) represents his appetite for cold ferocity in its record of the words and deeds of a Nietzschean, Herculean, Satanic ship captain whose incredible strength terminates credibly in sudden paralysis and impotence. *The Game*

(1905) celebrates the lust of the flesh as expressed in prize-fighting. *Before Adam* (1906) goes apparently still further afield in a quest for the primitive and moves among the half arboreal ancestors of the race. *White Fang* (1905) reverses *The Call of the Wild* and brings a wolf among dogs.

The Call of the Wild, summary as well as summit of London's achievement, is the story of a dog stolen from civilization to draw a sledge in Alaska, eventually to escape from human control and go back to the wild as leader of a pack of wolves. As in most animal tales the narrative is sentimentalized. Buck has a psychology which he derives too obviously from his human creator; learns the law of the brute wilderness too quickly and too consciously; dreams too definitely of the savage progenitors from whom he inherits, by way of atavism, his ability to contend with a new world. This sympathetic fallacy, however, has behind it a reality in London's own experience which lends power to the drama of Buck's restoration to the primitive. In something of this fashion the young tramp had learned the hard rules of the road; in something of this fashion the gold-seeker had mastered the difficulties of the Klondike face to face with a nature which made no allowance for his handicaps and which apparently desired the destruction of the men who had ventured into the wilderness. Out of his experience he had built up a doctrine concerning the essential life of mankind, and out of his doctrine he had shaped this characteristic tale. But the doctrine is not excessively in evidence, and the experience contributes both an accurate lore and an authentic passion. The narrative is as spare as an expedition over the Chilkoot Pass; it is swift and strong, packed with excitement and peril. Moreover, it has what almost none of Jack London's red blood rivals had, and what he later deprived himself of by his haste and casualness: a fine sensitiveness to landscape and environment, a robust, moving, genuine current of poetry which warms his style and heightens the effect while enrich-

ing it. It is perhaps rather his exciting stories than his explicit doctrines which made him one of the most popular
proletarian writers in the world.

He shared his large international vogue with Upton Sinclair (1878-   ), who was born in Baltimore and who turned
to socialism only after extended literary studies at Columbia
University. His first hero—in *The Journal of Arthur Stirling*
(1903)—belonged to the lamenting race of minor poets,
shaped his beauty in seclusion, and died because it went un-
recognized. In *Manassas* (1904) Sinclair dealt with the battles
called by that name in the South (Bull Run in the North).
The novel was the work of a poet filled with epic memories
and epic expectations, who saw in the Civil War a clash of
titanic principles, saw a nation being beaten out on a fearful
anvil, saw splendor and heroism rising up from the slaughter.
Poetry and history could not keep Sinclair from studying
the troubled present. Having written *The Jungle* (1906),
which made him famous, he assisted in a Federal investiga-
tion of the Chicago stockyards. What struck the public, both
in the committee's report and in the novel, was the evidence
that the meat of a large part of the world was being handled,
at great profit to the packers, in filthy conditions. What
outraged Sinclair was the spectacle of the lives which the
workers in the yards were compelled to lead if they got work
—which meant life to them—at all. Thanks to a conspiracy
among their masters the workers could not help themselves;
thanks to the weight of custom they could get no help from
popular opinion, which saw their plight as something essential to the very structure of society, as Aristotle saw slavery.
Sinclair proclaimed that their plight was not essential, and
he prophesied a revolution.

The revolution did not come as he had foreseen it, but
he continued his exposures of the established order, sometimes in novels—like *The Metropolis* (1908), *King Coal*
(1917), *Oil* (1927), *Boston* (1928), *Co-op* (1936), *Little*

Steel (1938)—which were news made into fiction; and in muck-raking books which looked behind the scenes at the churches, journalism, colleges and schools, literature and the arts: *The Profits of Religion* (1918), *The Brass Check* (1919), *The Goose-Step* (1923), *Mammonart* (1925). In the early years of the century Sinclair's challenging—if not nagging—zeal got him a reputation as a seeker of personal notoriety and he was in effect blacklisted by newspapers which would not even mention his name. Conspired against, he was confirmed in his disposition to see conspiracy everywhere. He saw human life as lying under the hands of dead men, and living men using every device to resist the forces of change. In the arts, he thought, the dead hand held the classics on their throne and rejected new masterpieces; in religion the dead hand clothed the visions of ancient poets in steel creeds and denied that such visions could ever come again; in human society the dead hand welded the manacles of caste and hardened this or that temporary pattern to a perpetual order. As he repeatedly suspected conspiracy where none existed, so he repeatedly suspected deliberate malice where he might as well have perceived stupidity. But stupidity, though the cause of perhaps more evil than malice can contrive, is less employable as a villain: it is not anthropomorphic enough for melodrama. Sinclair's constitution and his method called alike for melodrama and villains. And of course the doctrine of the class struggle furnished him with a multitude of plots.

The times, too, furnished him with a multitude of injustices to detect. The facts he turned up had often the force of propaganda. In the most interesting of his later novels, 100% (1920), he ironically traced the evolution of Peter Gudge from sharper to patriot through the foul career of spying and persecution and incitement opened to his kind of talents by the frenzy of noncombatants during the World War. The book was a disillusioning document, published at a time when many orators were still exclaiming, in the accents of official idealism, over the great deeds and days of the war. Sinclair had already moved to California, where he was for some years his own publisher, an immensely busy writer on various subjects, a gadfly to the respectable, and a repeated though unsuccessful candidate for high office. Long regarded as a crank, he came to be generally tolerated and widely esteemed. His novels were in time more or less lost in his total career. Nor had they the merit as works of art which might have made them permanently stand out. Sinclair created few characters which live on in the memory, and few memorable incidents. He told stories with a running zeal which, exciting or irritating while his books were being read, left in his readers an effect too dispersed to survive with the sharp, clear form of masterpieces. But his work taken as a whole gave him an important standing among the dissident voices of his times.

Robert Herrick (1868-1938), born in Massachusetts, educated at Harvard, long a professor at the University of Chicago, specially voiced a scholar's conscience disturbed by the spectacle of a tumultuous generation which he thought too much undisturbed. Perhaps because of a youth in New England, he was acutely sensitive to the atmosphere of affairs in Chicago, where fortunes came in like a flood before his eyes. Though he was not a local novelist, and laid his scene in many places, Chicago was the chief center of his universe. In that roaring village which so rapidly became a city Herrick was not blown by the prevailing winds. The vision that fired the majority of his neighbors seemed to him a dubious mirage. *The Memoirs of an American Citizen* (1905) follows a country youth of good initial impulses through his rise and progress among the Chicago packers and on to the Senate of the United States. Here was one of the oldest themes in literature, one of the themes most certain to succeed with any public: Dick Whittington, The Industrious Apprentice, over again. Herrick would not merely repeat the old drama or point the old moral. His hero wriggles upward by crooked ways and sharp practices, crushing competitors, diverting justice, and gradually paying for his fortune with his integrity. In a modern idiom Herrick implicitly asked whether the whole world is worth as much as a man's soul. He asked it in *The Common Lot* (1904) in which an architect sacrifices his professional integrity, and again in *Clark's Field* (1914), in which unearned wealth suddenly pours into hands not trained for it, and visits evil upon all concerned. Stories of treasure trove have regularly been romantic. Herrick treated this one realistically and morally.

He differed most strikingly from contemporary naturalists, however, in his attitude towards women. He felt that the elaborate language of compliment traditionally used to them in America, though deriving possibly from a day when women were less numerous on the frontier than men, and therefore prized and praised, had become in large part a hollow language. The pioneer woman earned the respect she got by the equal share she bore in the tasks of her laborious world. Her successor in the comfortable world of the early twentieth century neither worked nor bred as the first women did. The energy so released, instead of being directed into valuable channels, had spent itself upon the complex arts of the parasite. Whether because men had chosen out of vanity to regard women as luxurious possessions and visible symptoms of success; whether because a nation never compelled to save its resources had formed another wasteful habit; whether because women had been quick to seize an advantage after centuries of disadvantage: whatever the cause, America had evolved, Herrick held, a type of woman which lacked the glad animal spontaneity of the girl, the ardent abandon of the mistress, the strong loyalty of the wife, the deep, sure, fierce instincts of the mother, and even the confident impulse to follow her own path as an individual. He had in mind not so much American women in general as the American Woman, that traditional figure of timid ice and dainty insolence, too cherished and remote to let it appear how empty she actually was. He undertook in various novels, by dissecting the pretty simulacrum, to show that it had little blood and less soul. In *Together* (1908), the best of them, crowded with all kinds and conditions of lovers and married couples, he paid particular attention to the type he disliked. Not content, like some novelists, to show her glittering in her maiden plumage, he made it clear that the qualities ordinarily exalted in her were nothing but signs of arrested spiritual development. Hard and willful, she never became mature, and she tangled the web of life with the heedless hands of a child.

Herrick's criticism of the American Woman was but an emphatic point in his larger criticism of American life, and he singled her out essentially, it seems, because her lovely pretences were shallow. It was the shallowness, not the sex, which aroused him. Several of his women demand, more than their men, that they be allowed to live their lives on the high plane of integrity from which the casual world is always trying to pull men and women down. Integrity in love, in personal conduct, in business and public affairs: this Herrick forever urged with a profound, at times a bleak, consistency, an almost mystical rigor which handicapped him as a novelist. His conceptions were somewhat abstract, his imagination somewhat stiff. He wrote with intelligence and conscience rather than with natural art.

XIII

THEODORE DREISER

THE LAGGING triumph of naturalism in the United States belongs as much to the history of public taste as to the history of the art of fiction. Crane and Norris died too young to carry the movement far. Garland turned to romance, London and Sinclair inclined to melodrama, Herrick lacked flexibility and fire. The burden fell chiefly on Theodore Dreiser (1871-), and more controversy than ever on any other American novelist. The charges usually brought against him were that he wrote crudely about disagreeable persons. The truth was that he offended by bringing to the American novel a body of material and an attitude almost wholly strange to the native tradition. Before him all the American novelists had sprung from the older stocks among the people and had, though with occasional dissents, taken for granted certain patterns of life which were, however modified here or there, primarily Anglo-American. Dreiser was the first important American writer who rose from the immigrants of the nineteenth century, as distinguished from those of the seventeenth or eighteenth. Born in Terre Haute, Indiana, he was the son of a Catholic German father who had come to America to avoid military conscription, and a Mennonite Slavic mother from Pennsylvania. The family during Dreiser's childhood and youth was not only poor but also disapproved by their neighbors. The devout father—Dreiser called him bigoted—seemed a tyrant to his sons and daughters, several of whom fell into casual and irregular ways of life. The only one of them who prospered was Paul Dresser (as he chose to spell his name), first a wandering comedian and then a popular song-writer, sentimental and showy. Though he had been disowned by his father, he later helped support his needy parents, and he served as an example of success to his younger brother.

In *A Hoosier Holiday* and *Dawn* Theodore Dreiser wrote with what seems like complete frankness about his family and his youth, upon which he was to draw largely in his books. These early circumstances and experiences profoundly conditioned him. As a boy he thought of himself as looking in, through bright windows, at American life, himself on the outside. But he did not, like London and Sinclair, develop a compensating sense of class conflict. Dreiser desired the world of order and luxury and beauty rather than resented it. Obscure, handicapped, awkward, he was full of longings, full of hopes he hardly dared cherish, full of doubts he could not avoid. Yet outwardly his life was close to the familiar American pattern. He was able to read a good many books. He went to high school, and one of his teachers insisted on lending him money for a year at Indiana University. He did odd jobs, like countless boys, in Indiana and Chicago, to which the family moved when he was sixteen. At twenty-one he became a newspaper reporter, not so much because this might lead to literature as because it might admit him to some kind of exciting, conspicuous life. He followed his trade in Chicago, St. Louis, and smaller towns in the Middle West, and at twenty-three moved on to New York, where Paul Dresser introduced him to the shiny splendors of Broadway. Almost exactly the same age as Stephen Crane, Dreiser had none of Crane's precocious brilliance and intensity, and he did not begin his first novel until a few months before Crane's death. That novel caught the attention of Frank Norris, then reader for a publishing house, and it appeared in 1900.

Sister Carrie was so displeasing to one of the members of the firm, or to his wife, that the book, though it came out according to the letter of Dreiser's contract, was published without enthusiasm and few copies were sold. It had in fact something like the same fate as Crane's *Maggie*. But Dreiser's was, in its naïve decade, the more disturbing book. *Maggie* had come to a mortal end for her offenses, pitiful as they might have been shown to be. Carrie Meeber in the last chapter of her story has already made her name in the theater and has a fine future ahead of her. Readers long accustomed to seeing the lives of women in novels shown under a strict scheme of rewards and punishments were outraged. Such lives as Carrie's ought not to be told about, even if they happened. Dreiser had no sympathy with a moralism that contradicted his observation. The first attractive woman he had ever seen was his brother Paul's mistress. One of his sisters had eloped with a married man in Chicago, to New York, and lived in reasonable comfort. Dreiser had lodged at her house for a time and must have used her as more or less his model for Carrie. If she had had talent she might have risen in her world as Carrie did. If her husband had, instead of losing some of his money, lost it all and gone to pieces, he might have become one of those desolate tramps whom Dreiser saw on the freezing streets and who suggested Hurstwood to him. Here was all the justification Dreiser needed for telling the story. He did not need justification. No punctilio would keep him from telling what he knew. That it was true was all the excuse he needed. These things were true of these people. If nature had made them, he might write about them.

Perhaps the earlier stocks in America were as simple and classical in their behavior as they claimed or assumed. The later race of immigrants had other codes. There was a submerged American world, instinctive and undisciplined, which literature had passed over. For that matter, all America had changed or had—as Dreiser held—never been what academic realism thought. In America as well as anywhere in human society might be studied the blind wills to action. Americans no more than other men and women always counted in advance the profit or loss of what they were to do. They were driven by passions, betrayed by illusions, and hesitant between good and evil. Their true stories could be told only in understanding and pity. In *Sister Carrie* Dreiser tenderly conceived and honestly told the story of a girl who goes from her small town to Chicago, loves first one man and then a second, and outgrows them both, as any number of women have done on their way to the stage. Dreiser's strongest pity was for Hurstwood, the second man, who gives up wife and children and position for love, learns that it is not enough, and gradually deteriorates till he loses Carrie and sinks by way of the bread line to the Potter's Field. Never before in America had any such lives been recounted by a novelist so close to such characters. Dreiser's mastery had no moral condescension in it, nor even much superiority to Carrie and Hurstwood in knowledge and taste. He stood beside them while he told their story.

Sister Carrie was better received in England than in America, where criticism was inept and unimaginative. Neglected by the publishers, it failed to reach the public, and Dreiser was too much discouraged to go on with the second novel he began while the momentum of his first was still upon him. For ten years, during which he was the successful editor of various magazines, he was a kind of legendary figure cherished by a few enthusiasts but generally unread. The publication of *Jennie Gerhardt* in 1911 brought H. L. Mencken into the field as a resounding champion who made Dreiser almost a cause and passionately identified him with the new spirit in American literature. Having made a visit to Europe, recorded in *A Traveler at Forty* (1913), Dreiser rapidly wrote and published *The Financier* (1912), *The Titan* (1914), and *The 'Genius'* (1915). This last within a year was withdrawn from sale by the publishers on a threat from the New York Society for the Suppression of Vice, which aimed at Dreiser the first of its attacks on bold and original books. He did not publish another novel for ten years.

Those years saw him increasingly settled in his permanent place in American fiction, in spite of numerous hostile critics and much public disapproval. It came to be looked upon as his merit that, concerned with wisdom as he was, he lacked the dexterous knowingness of popular story-writers. Not only had he never allowed any one else to make up his mind for him regarding the significance and aims and obligations of mankind, but he had never finally made up his mind himself. A large dubitancy colored all his reflections. "All we know is that we cannot know." The only law about which men could be reasonably certain was the law of change. Justice was "an occasional compromise struck in an eternal battle." Virtue and honesty were "a system of weights and measures, balances struck between man and man." Prudence no less than philosophy demanded that men hold themselves constantly in readiness to discard their ancient creeds and habits and step valiantly round the corner beyond which reality would have drifted even while they were building their houses on what seemed the primeval and eternal rock. Tides of change, Dreiser made it appear, rise from deeps below deeps, cosmic winds of change blow from boundless chaos; mountains, in the long geologic seasons, shift and flow like clouds; and the everlasting heavens may some day be shattered by the explosion or pressure of new circumstances. Somewhere in the scheme man stands punily on what may be an Ararat rising out of the abyss or only a promontory of the moment sinking back again; there all his strength is devoted to a dim struggle for survival. How in this flickering universe shall man claim for himself the honors of any important antiquity or any important destiny? What, in this vast accident, does human dignity amount to?

For a philosopher with views so wide it is difficult to be a dramatist or a novelist. If he is consistent the most portentous human tragedy must seem to him only a tiny gasp for breath, the most delightful human comedy only a tiny flutter of joy. Against a background of suns dying on the other side of Aldebaran any mole trodden upon by a hoof may appear as significant a personage as an Œdipus or a Lear in his last agony. To be a novelist or dramatist at all such a cosmic philosopher must contract his vision to the little island men inhabit, must adjust his interest to finite interests, must reduce his narrative to a comprehensible human scale. The muddle of elements so often obvious in Dreiser's work comes from the conflict within him of large, expansive moods and a conscience working hard to be accurate in its representation of the most honest facts of manners and character. Assuming that the plight and stature of all mankind are essentially so mean, the novelist need not seriously bother himself with the task of looking for its heroic figures. Plain stories of plain people are as valuable as any others. Since all doctrines and ideals are likely to be false in a precarious world, it is best to stick as close as possible to the individual. When the individual is genuine he has at least some positive attributes; his story may have meaning for others if it is presented with absolute candor. Men can partially escape from the general meaninglessness of life by being or studying individuals who are genuine, and who are therefore the origins and centers of some kind of reality.

At a time during the war when any unpopular man might be called pro-German, Dreiser had that label angrily fixed upon him. The accusation more accurately meant that he had gone outside the bounds commonly observed in Anglo-American novels and employed themes more familiar to the Continent of Europe than to the British Isles. In American criticism the term Continental still meant alien. Dreiser was not Anglo-Saxon, though he was American. But in enlarging the territories of native fiction he did not, as international novelists like Henry James had done, deal with the fashionable European world. Dreiser remained at home, close to the ground. And temperamentally he had the characteristics of what for want of a better term may be named the peasant type of mind. Enlarged by genius as he was; open as he was to all sorts of sensations and ideas; little as he was limited by the rigor of habits and prejudices; still he carried with him wherever he went a true peasant simplicity of outlook, spoke with a peasant's bald frankness, and suffered a peasant's confusion in the face of complexity. How far he saw life on one simple plane may be illustrated by his short story *When the Old Century Was New* in the collection *Free and Other Stories*. This, an attempt to reconstruct in fiction the New York of 1801, shows Dreiser, in spite of some deliberate erudition, to be amazingly unable to feel at home in another age than his own. The same simplicity of outlook makes *A Traveler at Forty* so revealing a document, makes the Traveler appear a true Innocent Abroad without the hilarious and shrewd self-sufficiency of an American like Mark Twain. Dreiser's plain-speaking on a variety of topics euphemized by earlier American realists had a conscious intention and was sustained by his literary principles, but his candor came from his nature: he thought in blunt terms before he spoke in them. He spoke bluntly upon the subtle and intricate themes—power and wealth, love and art—which interested him above all others.

The life-story of Frank Cowperwood in *The Financier* and *The Titan*, notoriously based upon that of the financier and magnate Charles T. Yerkes, gave Dreiser a chance to exercise his virtue of immense, patient industry and to build up a solid monument of fact which, though sometimes dull, is notably convincing. The American financier has rarely had, or needed, much subtlety in his make-up. Single-minded, tough-skinned, "suggesting," as Dreiser said, "a power which invents man for one purpose and no other, as generals, saints, and the like are invented," he shoulders and hurls his bulk through a sea of troubles and carries off his spoils. Such a man as Cowperwood presented few difficulties to Dreiser. He understood the march of desire to its goal. He seems to have been intensely curious about the large operations of finance, stirred on his poetical side (like Marlowe in *The Jew of Malta*) by the intoxication of golden dreams, and on his cynical side struck by the mechanism of craft and courage and indomitable impulse which the financier has to employ. Dreiser wrote as an outsider. He simplified the account of Cowperwood's adventures after power and wealth in Philadelphia and Chicago, like a peasant—though a peasant of genius—wondering how great riches are actually obtained and guessing at the mystery. And yet these guesses probably came nearer to the truth than they might have come if either the financier or Dreiser had been more subtle. A poet set to catch a financier is not at all sure of the prize. This Trilogy of Desire was never completed with the third part which was to show Cowperwood extending his mighty foray into London, where Yerkes went to become head of the syndicate which built the subways. Dreiser did not know enough about finance in England, and could hardly have learned. But his trilogy, so far as it goes, is the most substantial epic that American business has yet to show in fiction.

Cowperwood's lighter hours are devoted to pursuits almost as polygamous as the leader of some four-footed herd. In this respect the novels which celebrate him call to mind *Sister Carrie* and *Jennie Gerhardt*, annals of women who yield as readily as Cowperwood's many mistresses to the conquering male. Dreiser, who refused to condemn the lawless financier, did not condemn the lawless lover. He wrote about love with a biologist's freedom from moralism. Love in these novels is a flowing, expanding energy, working resistlessly through all human tissue, knowing in itself neither certain good nor certain evil, habitually at war with the rules and taboos which have been devised by mankind to regulate the amative instincts. To a cosmic philosopher it does not greatly matter whether this or that human male mates with this or that human female, or whether the mating endures for a lifetime. A position so disinterested outraged or upset American readers before the war. They knew how to feel about broad chronicles like *Moll Flanders* or high melodrama like *Tess of the D'Urbervilles*. *Jennie Gerhardt* was a different matter. Dreiser gave no evidence of thinking of her as a fallen woman. Her way of life comes not from self-indulgence but from self-sacrifice. There is nothing in the least monstrous or vicious in her. She is a devoted daughter, a generous rather than a demanding mistress, and passionate only about her child. Dreiser thinks of her as having reached the full measure of her being in spite of her unhappy fortunes. "Shall you say to the blown rose, 'well done'? Or to the battered, wind-riven, lightning-scarred pine, 'thou failure'? In the chemic drift and flow of things, how little we know of either failure or success! Is there either? This daughter of the poor, born into the rush and hurry of a clamant world . . . what a sorry figure! . . . Not to be bitter, angry, brutal, feverish—what a loss! . . . Behold! there are hierarchies and powers above and below the measure of our perception. It is given to us to see in part and to believe in part. But of that which is perfect who shall prophesy? . . . Jennie loved, and loving, gave. Is there a superior wisdom? Are its signs and monuments in existence? Of whom, then, have we life and all good things—and why?"

There can be no doubt that Dreiser underestimated—or did not fully represent—the forces which in civil society do as a rule restrain the expansive moods of love. He dealt with people too obscure to be easily restrained, or too free and restless. One of his favorite situations was that of a strong man, no longer young, loving downward to some plastic, ignorant girl dazzled by his splendor and pliant to his courtship. The spectacle of middle age renewing itself at the fires of youth has of course its romantic no less than its realistic aspects. Dreiser was sometimes romantic about it. He was likely to leave out of account the will and sense of women, and to represent them with few exceptions as kind wax to their wooers, with almost no separate identities till some lover shapes them. If he knew about women of the more resolute kinds he seldom wrote about them in love. Will in his novels almost altogether belongs to men.

Dreiser is said always to have felt a special partiality for *The 'Genius'* among his novels, a massive, muddy, powerful narrative which has little charm. His partiality may be ascribed to his strong inclination toward the life of art, through which his 'Genius' moves, half hero and half picaro. Eugene Witla is impelled by an obsession much like the obsession of Cowperwood. The will to wealth, the will to love, the will to art: Dreiser conceived them all as organic energies with no end except self-realization. This was a new conception to American readers, who in 1915 thought of the arts as forms of education with simple moral purposes. Though Americans in general had forgiven Poe, they regarded his mishaps as misdeeds for which he had been fairly punished. So should a man like Witla be punished for his ruthless conduct, particularly in sexual affairs. But here was Dreiser obviously sympathetic toward Witla in his rank appetite for a life of variety and splendor, unchecked by regulations laid down for smaller men. If such a man came to grief in the world, Dreiser implied, the fault was in the world rather than in the man, and a world which crippled or stifled such men would lose the riches of personality and achievement they might, if left free, have created. Dreiser did not, in Witla, offer a good example of genius. He is said to be a gifted painter, without convincing proofs of it. As Carrie had become a noted actress in a few weeks, Witla not much less rapidly becomes a noted illustrator. Elsewhere in Dreiser's novels there are minor artists who exhibit none of the powers they are credited with. Nowhere does there appear any delicate analysis of a genius's mysterious behavior. Dreiser's artists are hardly persons at all. They are creatures driven, and the wonder lies in the hidden energy that drives them. The cosmic philosopher in Dreiser sees the beginning and the end of the process better than the novelist sees its methods. And the peasant in him, while it knows the world of art as beautiful and great, reports it in terms which are often clumsy and preposterous.

In the ten years after *The 'Genius,'* though Dreiser published no new novel, he wrote much in other forms. *Plays of the Natural and of the Supernatural* (1916) and *The Hand of the Potter* (1918) only barely reached the stage. His dark themes and unrelieved treatment were more troubling to producers than to publishers. His cosmic pity for the psychopathic child-killer in *The Hand of the Potter* made Dreiser feel that an audience need not find the presentation unbearable—as it must have found it. After his voyage to Europe he made the motor trip to Indiana about which he told in *A Hoosier Holiday* (1916), a neglected book which has large value as history and which is invaluable in its account of the soil from which Dreiser sprang. He continued this autobiographical record in *A Book About Myself* (1922) during his years as a newspaperman, and *The Color of a Great City* (1923), sketches of New York in his early years there. *Twelve Men* (1919) showed Dreiser at nearly his best. In that book he set forth the lives and characters of a dozen persons he had been familiar with, all his honesty bent on making his account fit the reality exactly, on presenting the truth without malice or excuses. His studies of his brother Paul, William Muldoon (Culhane, the Solid Man), and Harris Merton Lyon (De Maupassant, Junior) are better known than the others because these men were better known, but all the studies are fresh and alive. In *Hey Rub-A-Dub-Dub: A Book of the Mystery and Terror and Wonder of Life* (1920) Dreiser undertook to expound his general philosophy, but with little skill. He had no faculty for sustained argument. As soon as he began to reason he was less than half himself. He had to have a story to tell, and during these ten years he produced nothing of the sort but *Free and Other Stories* (1918), some of them written earlier. Year after year his publishers announced a forthcoming novel to be called *The Bulwark*. Then in 1925 came *An American Tragedy*, his great masterpiece and his great success.

The story was based upon the actual trial of Chester Gillette for the murder of Grace Brown in 1906. Dreiser so extended and elevated it that what had been a minor tragedy in Herkimer County came to seem a matter for the whole nation. He went back in the life of Clyde Griffiths (as Gillette is called in the novel) to a time when he was twelve, innocent and well-behaved, in the care of pious parents. If he has ambitions, they are no more than every American boy is encouraged to have. He should rise in the world and make his mark in it. But nobody tells him how to rise. His father and mother are unworldly and ineffectual. He has little schooling. His work as a bell-boy in a large hotel in Kansas City brings him every day in contact with careless money and easy habits, tantalizing him. In another country he might have been satisfied with his place in life. In the United States this would have been lack of enterprise. Clyde has no resources in his own mind, nor any work to be deeply interested in. Lacking a definite character, he is pulled here and there by circumstances. He has an indefinite, hungry longing for a world of luxury and beauty from which he feels shut out and which is all the more tempting for that reason. His theory of success, as in itself a merit, confirms his longing. The traditional American ideas of democratic equality and of the worth of plain people have less effect on him than the enormous pressure of modern advertising, which insists that he must have this or that if he is to respect himself or to be happy. Nobody tells him what to be. Everybody tells him what to have.

So far as he can see, rising in the world goes as much by favor as by desert. When he is invited by a rich uncle to come to work in his factory in Lycurgus, New York, Clyde accepts full of hope that his kinship to his new employer may be an advantage. Technically he is in the position, classical in America, of beginning at the bottom with no more than a chance to work up, but actually he is his employer's nephew and distinguished from the other employees in the factory. As employer Samuel Griffiths expects Clyde to earn his own way; as uncle he invites the boy to his house and introduces him to a society he would otherwise not have met. Living in two worlds, Clyde is divided in himself. At his age he naturally finds the two worlds symbolized by two girls: Roberta Alden in the factory, whom he instinctively loves, and Sondra Finchley whom he cannot help aspiring to in fashionable Lycurgus. Baldly stated, this was the shabbiest kind of conflict between love and snobbism. Dreiser would not see it or state it baldly. Clyde's cloudy will, which lets him drag on between the two girls till the situation seems desperate and then leads him to commit a bungling murder, is hardly the affair of a single wicked moment any more than of a long guilty plot. His whole life has prepared him for his dreadful, stupid act. And the whole of America, Dreiser argued, had conditioned and directed Clyde's life. The first volume of the novel traces the confused steps, no one of them criminal, which bring Clyde to the point where he could become a murderer. There is still a second volume needed to tell the full story of how he is condemned and put to death. The civilization which has by precept and example furnished him with a character unable in an emergency to save him from his weakness, turns on him once he has yielded to it and punishes him as utterly as if he had been free to choose and had deliberately chosen to do evil. Nor is his punishment laid on him by even-handed justice concerned only with upholding the law. All the officials active in the case, the journalists who make it a sensation, the public siding with him or against him: these are persons shaped by the same civilization, driven by ambitions, pulled by private sentiments. The course of his punishment is as many-sided and bewildering as the history of his crime.

An American Tragedy was concerned as much with a whole civilization as with a tragic individual. Dreiser, studying Clyde as a figure shaped and compelled and ruined by circumstances, tried to take all those circumstances into account in a vast documentation of the times. No other American crime has ever been examined with such attention to the settings, the subordinate characters, the processes of behavior. And yet the final impression is concerned with Clyde. Whether or not he deserved his penalty Dreiser nowhere says. He has no measure for such a punishment. He wants only to follow, with comprehension and pity, the changes by which a kind-hearted boy could in a few years come to a deed of such cruelty. At no point could Dreiser find that Clyde changes melodramatically from good to bad. He wavers among insidious impulses of which, it seems, the balance might have been shifted as easily to save him as to destroy him. He sins by a hair's-breadth. To read about him is to walk a tight rope over a gulf of imagined experiences, shuddering to think how little separates those who cross from those who fall.

The novel was eagerly and widely read. It was made into an affecting stage play and into a motion picture which, in spite of Dreiser's protests, cheapened the pitiful story. He did not follow his tragedy with another novel, but collected a volume of short stories, *Chains* (1927), and *A Gallery of Women* (1928) which fell short of his *Twelve Men* in interest and value. He went to Russia to observe conditions there. He discussed American affairs in a confused book *Tragic America* (1932). He returned to autobiography and began *A History of Myself* to be in four volumes, of which he published the first as *Dawn* (1931). Living for the most part in semi-retirement in the country, he was still a conspicuous citizen whose actions were watched and whose comments were quoted. He had been the wheel-horse if not the spearhead of American naturalism, and had taught his countrymen a new tolerance toward what might be shown in fiction. After him came followers who were more decisive and more artful than he. But he remains the chief of his school. The awkwardness of his style, his occasional verbosity, his frequent irrelevancies of argument cannot obscure his best effect: that of a large spirit brooding over a world which he deeply, somberly loves. He may miss some of the finer shades of character, particularly in cultivated society. His conscience about telling the plain truth may suffer at times from his systematic refusal to draw lines between good and evil or between beautiful and ugly or between wise and foolish. But he gains, on the whole, as much as he loses by the magnitude of his cosmic philosophizing. These puny souls over whom he broods, with so little dignity in themselves, take on a dignity from his contemplation of them. Small as they are, he has come to them from long flights, and has brought back a lifted vision which enriches his heavy narratives. Something spacious, something now lurid now luminous, surrounds them. From somewhere sound accents of an authority not sufficiently explained by the mere accuracy of his versions of life. Though it may be difficult for a thinker of the widest views to contract himself to the dimensions needed for naturalistic art, and though he may often fail when he attempts it, when he does succeed he has the opportunity, which neater worldlings lack, of ennobling his art with some of the great light of great poets.

XIV

TRADITION AND TRANSITION

1~Stream of Fiction

THE EMERGENCE and triumph of naturalism might be, in the long run, the most important development in American fiction during the first quarter of the new century, but the majority of novelists and novel-readers still preferred less rigorous and more agreeable themes. There was for a decade or so no revolution in the changes of popular fashion. Winston Churchill (1871-   ), of overshadowing popularity before the war, went with the surface movements of the time. Born in St. Louis, within a few weeks of Crane and Dreiser, educated at the United States Naval Academy, Churchill began his effective career with *Richard Carvel* (1899) in the full bloom of historical romance, and continued with *The Crisis* (1901) and *The Crossing* (1904). He had enough erudition to give substance to his narratives, a sense of the general bearings of the epochs he reconstructed, a warm confidence in the future implied by the past, and a feeling for the ceremonial in illustrious occasions. He had a quality of moral earnestness which made his stories have the look of moral significance. Richard Carvel by the exercise of simple Maryland virtues rises above the enervate young sparks of Mayfair during the Revolution; Stephen Brice in *The Crisis* by his simple Yankee virtues makes his mark among the St. Louis rebels during the Civil War; canny David Ritchie in *The Crossing* leads the frontiersmen of Kentucky into the Northwest as the little child of fable leads the lion and the lamb. When Churchill turned from historical fiction he seemed to be following Theodore Roosevelt, who had written heroically about the winning of the West, risen to high enthusiasms

(260)

in the war with Spain, and arraigned civic corruption. In *Coniston* (1906), its action laid in the past century, Churchill dealt with a village boss in New England who has constituents because he holds mortgages. He sentimentally surrenders his ugly power at the touch of a maiden's hand, but he has served as civic example.

In novel after novel Churchill presented some encroaching problem of civic or social life: the control of politics by interest in *Mr. Crewe's Career* (1908); divorce in *A Modern Chronicle* (1910); the conflict between Christianity and business in *The Inside of the Cup* (1913); the oppression of the soul by the lust for temporal power in *A Far Country* (1915); the struggle of women with the conditions of modern industry in *The Dwelling-Place of Light* (1917). He roused much discussion of his challenges and solutions—particularly with *The Inside of the Cup*. This study of the plight and growth of a liberal clergyman in a conservative church was morally strenuous but intellectually belated. Churchill did not get his ideas when they were exciting superior minds but just before the general public caught up with him. Yet though he seems not to have heard the keenest voices of his age, neither did he listen to the dull or base. In all his novels, romantic or realistic, the interest lies in some mounting aspiration opposed to a static régime: the passion for independence among the colonists, the expanding movement of the population westward, the crusades against slavery or public malfeasance, the struggle of enlightened spirits with the burdens of excessive wealth or poverty or orthodoxy. Where the past had been revolutionary he accepted it. He looked for change in the present to come by natural progress, as the Progressives in politics did. His novels were a kind of mass movement, without specific characters or episodes that lasted long in the public memory. After the war he wrote no further novels, and survived only as a pre-war novelist.

Booth Tarkington (1869-) of Indiana was more elastic

(261)

and adaptable. His two earliest books were sentimental romances with such heroes as he was later to satirize. Harkless in *The Gentleman from Indiana* (1899) walks in melancholy because he has been seven years out of college and has not yet set the prairie on fire. Then comes a rush of success and renown and he is elected to Congress by his devoted neighbors. This from the future creator of Penrod, who so often lays large plans for proving to the heedless world that he has been a hero all along. *Monsieur Beaucaire* (1900) was a charming pastiche episode in the life of Prince Louis-Philippe de Valois, who masquerades as a barber and then as a gambler in Bath, is misjudged on the evidence of his own disguises, just escapes catastrophe, and in the end gracefully forgives the gentlemen and ladies who have been wrong, parting with an exquisite gesture from Lady Mary Carlisle, who loves him but for a few fatal days had doubted. This from the future creator of Silly Billy Baxter, who imagines himself another Sydney Carton and after a silent, agonizing, condescending farewell goes out to the imaginary tumbril.

Tarkington soon dropped historical romance, but not the celebration of his native state. Indiana had an indigenous population, not too daring or nomadic. It had been both prosperous and simple-mannered, the home of pleasant pastorals, of a folk-poet like James Whitcomb Riley, of a folk-fabulist like George Ade. Its tradition of realism in fiction descended from *The Hoosier Schoolmaster*, with a full confidence in the rural virtues. In *The Man from Home* (1905), a play written with Harry Leon Wilson, Tarkington glorified another Innocent Abroad, a Hoosier smiling at preposterous Europe. A novelist can of course find a universe folded in any province, if he studies it as Thoreau studied Concord. Tarkington had a less speculative, more sentimental provincialism. Again and again in satirical chapters of his novels he rose above local prejudices and observed with a critical eye. But at a crisis in the building of a plot or the representa·

(262)

tion of a character he was likely to sag down to a sentimental provincial level. Bibbs Sheridan in *The Turmoil* (1915) departs from the Hoosier average by being a poet. Time and the plot drag him back to normality, and to a fortune almost overnight. George Minafer in *The Magnificent Ambersons* (1918) departs from the average by being a snob. Time and the plot drag him back, to a hasty and easy regeneration. The processes are the same, and poetry and snobbery appear to be equivalent offenses. Tarkington brought his wandering heroes home alike at the end and tucked them away in the Hoosier fold.

In *Penrod* (1914) and *Seventeen* (1916) and in subsequent books about their juvenile heroes, Tarkington made a reputation as an expert on boyhood. But these stories often call to mind the winks that adults exchange over the heads of children who are going about their own business, as the adults are not. The pranks of Penrod Schofield, aged twelve, are essentially those of Tom Sawyer repeated in another town, without the poetry or the informing imagination of Mark Twain. The loves of seventeen-year-old William Sylvanus Baxter, diverting as they are, are hardly anything but farce staged for outsiders. Though real adolescence, like any other age of man, has its own passions, its own poetry, its own tragedies and felicities, none of these appears in Tarkington's versions of adolescence. Calf-love in them remains a joke for mature spectators roaring at the discomfort which love causes its least experienced victims. In *Alice Adams* (1922), however, dealing with a young girl alert for marriage, Tarkington wrote with insight and sympathy. Alice is less strictly a tragic figure than she appears to be. She shows no signs of desire in any of the deeper senses; what she loves in Russell is but incidentally himself and actually his assured position and his assured income. Her pretty machinations to enchant and hold him might be farcical if they were ludicrously handled. They are not. Alice's instinct to win a husband is as powerful as

(263)

any instinct she has or has been taught by her society to have. Her struggle, without the help of any contriving mother or tempting dot, becomes increasingly pathetic as the narrative advances; her eventual failure seems to her, and to those who read about her, a definite tragedy. Here for the first time the manners of the young which had always seemed amusing to Tarkington and which he had watched and laughed at as a principal material for his stories, evoked in him a considerate sense of the pathos of youth, though *Alice Adams* is also his best comedy.

Tarkington did not fall in with the critical temper that appeared in the novel after the war, and may be said to have undertaken, in *The Midlander* (1924) and *The Plutocrat* (1927), to correct the versions of the Middle West and the American business man that contemporary satirists presented. In these and later novels he kept close to the level of pleasant —though never profound—entertainment. He wrote with the confident touch of a man unconfused by speculations. His manner was light and allusive. He had a rapid, joyous, accurate eye, invention and good temper. No other native novelist besides Mark Twain has ever been genuinely popular for so long as the forty years between Tarkington's first novel and his latest. Some of his stories were successful on the stage, and later on the screen. Penrod comes near to being a folk-figure.

The strong attachments which made Ellen Glasgow (1874-   ) confine herself chiefly to being a historian of Virginia in fiction had nothing essentially provincial in them. Though she wrote about her native state, she did not regard it—or the South—as an isolated province, but as a part of the whole world of mankind. Virginia's local manners in her novels were simply the special aspects of universal behavior. Some of her precocious early stories had their scenes laid in New York. She returned in fiction, as in fact, to a life spent in Virginia observing and understanding it. In time she

(264)

came to think of her best novels of the years 1900-16 as a social history of the Dominion. *The Voice of the People* (1900) dealt realistically with the rise of a gifted Virginian who was not of the traditional planter class. In *The Battleground* (1902) and *The Deliverance* (1904) she carried her history through the Civil War, with some romantic elements but with a less romantic attitude toward her theme than was then customary in historical novels. In *The Romance of a Plain Man* (1909) and *The Miller of Old Church* (1911) she further extended her account of life in Virginia as lived outside the plantations which had been the subject of almost all Virginia novels. The plain man is a business man in Richmond. The miller follows a matter-of-fact trade in the country. She enriched her Old Church setting with fresh and sweet descriptions of the soft Virginia landscape; she bound her plot together with a fine intelligence. Here was an enlarged and enlightened Virginia pastoral which had none of the narrow dryness or trivial sentimentalism of the local color school. *Virginia* (1913) brought into Ellen Glasgow's social history a note of sharper criticism. The heroine, typically named Virginia, has no equipment for life but loveliness and innocence. She finds that loveliness may fade and innocence may become a bore where wisdom is needed. She loses her husband and gives herself so completely to her children that in the end she has nothing left for herself and is no longer interesting to them. *Virginia* was at once a thorough and a pathetic chronicle of a Virginian—or American—woman as shaped and misfitted by conventional gentility. She was, Ellen Glasgow pointed out, "capable of dying for an idea, but not of conceiving one." *Life and Gabriella* (1916) exhibited a less conventional Virginia woman going to New York and breaking her medieval shell in a successful career.

For nine years, although in that time Ellen Glasgow published three minor books, she did not again find a theme worthy of her talent. But *Barren Ground* (1925) saw her

(265)

renewed and bettered in the first of a series of Novels of Character and Comedies of Manners, as she came to call them. Dorinda in *Barren Ground* has been disappointed in love and takes to farming, in which she prospers. Ellen Glasgow was surprised when her book was thought by the men who read it to be a story of personal triumph. She herself, and her women readers, thought of it as a story of tragic failure. That it could have such different meanings to men and women is proof that it was convincingly true for both of them, whatever their differing points of view. In *The Romantic Comedians* (1926) and *They Stooped to Folly* (1929) she discovered a vein of charming malice at the expense of respectable Richmond. Her comic plots are as intricate as the inner circles of the Virginia capital, with many characters delicately interrelated. But all of them are seen in the clear light of an ironic mind, comprehending though laughing. *The Sheltered Life* (1932) was a brilliant study of how General Archbald could be bound by the women whom he cherished and who thought they were cherishing him. These women, however unaware, exact a great price for their devotion, which is much of it instinctive jealousy. In *Vein of Iron* (1935) Ellen Glasgow turned once more to rural Virginia and the fortitude shown there after the Civil War. Most of her novels were likely to be longer than their materials warranted, but they were always civilized and intelligent, and often bright with irony.

Churchill, Tarkington, and Ellen Glasgow were widely read. Henry Blake Fuller (1857-1929), carrying on a tradition through a long transition, reached only a small audience with his exacting mind and precise art. In the last decade of the nineteenth century, when the international novel and aesthetic criticism were in vogue, he wrote of sentimental pilgrimages to Italy and the Alps, in *The Chevalier of Pensieri-Vani* (1890) and *The Chatelaine of La Trinité* (1892), packing his narratives with affectionate archaeology and presenting them with a Yankee smile. Born in Chicago, Fuller had spent much time in European travel, concerned and yet amused by the contrast between his two worlds. He was, as he said of an American in the *Chevalier*, "between two fires, both of which scorched him; between two schools, neither of which offered him a comfortable seat; between the two horns of a dilemma, each of which seemed more cruelly sharp than the other." But Fuller turned without apparent effort to the study of manners in his native city and wrote *The Cliff-Dwellers* (1893) and *With the Procession* (1895). At a time when local color was glorifying its localities and Hamlin Garland was saying that Chicago must supersede New York as a literary center, Fuller, who was to live all his life in Chicago, nevertheless saw it with eyes which were at once realistic and cosmopolitan. In two collections of short stories, *From the Other Side* (1898) and *Waldo Trench and Others* (1908), he dealt with various Americans traveling in Europe, and in a third, *Under the Skylights* (1901), the life of art as conducted in Chicago.

Speaking of another character of his, in *On the Stairs* (1918), Fuller said: "he wanted to be an artist and give himself out; he wanted to be a gentleman and hold himself in. An entangling, ruinous paradox." Something like this paradox kept Fuller, against his will, a dilettante. In one of the pungent sketches in his free-verse *Lines Long and Short* (1917) he told, more or less autobiographically, of a Midwestern American who has all his life longed and planned to live in Europe but who finds himself ready to realize his wish only in the dread summer of 1914, when he sees there will be no more peace as long as he can hope to live. After 1917 Fuller himself lived in quiet seclusion in Chicago, where fate and his own fatalism had fixed him in spite of his divided impulses. He lacked the passion which might have made him able either to detach himself from Chicago altogether or else to submerge himself in it till he was reconciled. Though

Bertram Cope's Year (1919) adroitly handled the difficult theme of a warm friendship between two men, and *Not on the Screen* (1930) showed a satirical familiarity with the new art of the motion picture, Fuller was withdrawn from the general life. *On the Stairs* was in effect the memoirs, in the form of a novel, of a Chicagoan who can never quite adjust himself to his habitat and who gradually sees the control of life slipping out of his hands to those of more potent, more decisive men. Well as Fuller understood the process, he could not avoid it in himself. Yet he never ceased to exercise a free and penetrating intelligence. He was not jostled out of his equilibrium or swept off his feet by torrents of public emotion. In all he wrote, or all that has been written about him, there is the sense of a living intellect keeping its counsel and yet throwing off rays of suggestion and illumination. Under ironical disguises he produced a notable memoir of himself and a lasting history of the inner life of his city.

There could hardly be a more striking contrast than that between Fuller's reticent art and the energetic knack of Edna Ferber (1887-   ), who was a reporter on a Wisconsin newspaper at seventeen and who made her rapid way to popularity with short stories like those collected in *Roast Beef Medium* (1912) and other volumes in which Emma McChesney, a traveling saleswoman, was the central figure. Fiction had so seldom shown women in business that Edna Ferber for a time had a new field to herself and worked it thoroughly. She did not stay in it too long, but moved on to novels of diverse themes and settings. *So Big* (1924) took for heroine a woman truck gardener. *Show Boat* (1926) was a melodrama of river life on the Mississippi in the days of floating theaters. *Cimarron* (1929) reconstructed the rush of settlement into Oklahoma; *American Beauty* (1931) the conflict and blending of native and immigrant strains in Connecticut; *Come and Get It* (1935) the logging industry in Wisconsin. All these were based on much careful research and full of vigorous entertainment, though the plots and characters were melodramatic and the style occasionally flat or gritty. *Show Boat* was immensely successful on the stage, in a dramatic version by Edna Ferber and music by Jerome Kern. She collaborated with George S. Kaufman in *The Royal Family* (1927), *Dinner at Eight* (1932), and *Stage Door* (1936), also with success. She had narrative speed, she did not mind being sentimental or theatrical. The story of her life and adventures in her autobiography—*A Peculiar Treasure* (1939)—was as interesting as any of her novels.

After 1900 the stream of American fiction was so broad that any brief record of it can do no more than hint at its volume and variety. Since the popular writers did not belong to conscious schools they can be classified only approximately. But most of them worked in kinds of fiction that had been established before them. The domestic sentimentalism with which the American novel had begun was still a staple, though no longer Richardsonian in manner, of Gene Stratton Porter, who piled sentimentalism upon descriptions of nature in soft, sweet heaps, and Harold Bell Wright, who cannily mixed sentimentalism with valor and prudence. They throbbed with all the current impulses; they laughed and wept with the uncritical multitude; and they had the gift of attracting and exciting that multitude with their books in which was displayed, as in a consoling mirror, the rosy, empty features of banality. These two novelists were first among dozens who practised their tearful, perishable mode of art.

The romance of the school of Cooper had not disappeared, though it now had less weight than in his day. The traditional matters of the Settlement and the Revolution persisted, after the falling off of rococo romance, chiefly in tales for boys. There was still a matter of the Frontier, but it was another frontier: the Canadian north and northwest, Alaska, the islands of the South Seas, the battlefields of France, and always the trails of American exploration wherever they chanced

(269)

to lead. Writers like Emerson Hough, Zane Grey, and Rex Beach were on the whole nearer to Jack London than to Cooper, and wrote their novels in red blood. With their spasmodic energy, technical knowledge, stereotyped characters, recurrent formulas, and lack of distinction in style or attitude, they were welcomed by the motion pictures, and Hough's chief novel *The Covered Wagon* (1922) had a huge and influential success on the screen.

The frontier of the loggers, celebrated early in Stewart Edward White's *The Blazed Trail*, saw the rise of a mythical hero in Paul Bunyan, evolved by men in camps from the Bay of Fundy to Puget Sound. Paul is less a patron saint of the loggers than an American (and Canadian) Munchausen, whose fame for years was extended almost entirely by word of mouth among lumbermen resting from their work and contending with one another to see who could tell the most stupendous yarn about Paul's prowess and achievements. The process resembled that in which peoples everywhere have built up enormous legends about favorite heroes, ever since Samson and Ulysses, or before. But the legend of Paul Bunyan is essentially American in its specific geography, its passion for grotesque exaggeration, its hilarious metaphors, its drawling, unblushing narrative method. Exaggeration such as that in some of these stories amounts to genius. When Paul goes west he carelessly lets his pick drag behind him and cuts the Grand Canyon of the Colorado; he raises corn in Kansas prodigious enough to suck the Mississippi dry and stop navigation; he builds a hotel so high that he has "the last seven stories put on hinges so's they could be swung back for to let the moon go by." He finds a river that flows in a circle. He hitches his Blue Ox to a crooked road and pulls it out straight. He accomplishes feats of eating and drinking and working and fighting and loving that make him a rival to Hercules. The legend grew for many years without the help of literature, which it may be said to have entered by the way of advertising booklets issued by a Wisconsin lumber company and Ida Virginia Turney's amusing chapbook *Paul Bunyan Comes West* (1920) published at the University of Oregon. Longer books by Esther Shephard (1924) and James Stevens (1925), both called *Paul Bunyan*, enlarged the saga but were far from exhausting the rich materials.

The Civil War had by 1920 become a fourth matter of American romance. It had not yet had time to equal the Revolution in romantic elements, but it promised to equal if not supersede it in the range of its appeal to readers. The Revolution seemed to concern the past of the thirteen original states, the Civil War the past of all the later states as well. Connected with the Civil War was the most pervasive cult in modern America: the cult of Abraham Lincoln. Immediately after his death he had been thought of as primarily a martyr; then, as the shock eased, emphasis shifted to his humor and a whole literature of anecdotes and retorts and apologues assembled round his name; later he passed into a more sentimental zone and endless stories were multiplied about his natural piety and his habit of pardoning innocent offenders. At about the centenary of his birth there began to emerge a fresh conception of him—though the older conceptions did not altogether fade—as a figure lofty and familiar, sad and witty, Olympian and human. The poets were before the novelists in the new version. Edwin Arlington Robinson in *The Master* (1910) set in words as firm as bronze the hero's reputation for lonely pride and forgiving laughter. In Edgar Lee Masters's *Spoon River* (1915) the most moving lyric was an epitaph upon Ann Rutledge, the girl Lincoln loved and lost. Vachel Lindsay, in Lincoln's own Springfield, during the World War thought of Lincoln as so stirred even in death by the horrors which then alarmed the universe that he could not sleep but walked up and down the midnight streets, mourning and brooding. In this manner in other ages saints have been said to appear at perilous moments, to quiet the

waves or turn the arrow aside. Without these simpler mani-
festations, Lincoln came to live as the founder of every cult
lives, in the echoes of his voice on many tongues and in the
vibrations of his voice in many affections. His chief biographer
in the next decade was again a poet, Carl Sandburg. If the
novelists fell behind the poets, so may they be said to have
fallen behind the people. While the novelists were inventing
plots the people were creating and accepting a cult.

Melville was little remembered and had no followers. Hawthorne though much read was not imitated. Howells, who
lived till 1920, had put forth his critical influence so long
before that it had been absorbed in practice and was taken
for granted rather than recognized. Yet it was he who had
done most to civilize the ordinary run of American fiction,
and however remotely he affected its amiable and decent
realism. The most varied books had something of his spirit
in them: Charles Macomb Flandrau's delightful *Harvard
Episodes* (1897); Alice Hegan Rice's homely *Mrs. Wiggs of
the Cabbage Patch* (1901); William Allen White's Kansas
chronicle *A Certain Rich Man* (1909); even David Gray's
Gallops (1898, 1903), concerned with the parish of St.
Thomas Equinus near New York City and its horse-worship-
ping sportsmen. If the new century had no humorist of the
stature of Mark Twain it still had Booth Tarkington with his
comedies of childhood; Irvin S. Cobb, who continued Mark
Twain's technique of humorous autobiography; and Harry
Leon Wilson, whose *Bunker Bean* (1912), *Ruggles of Red
Gap* (1915), and *Merton of the Movies* (1922) pleased a
hearty public with an excellent fun which has been overlooked
by short-sighted, low-spirited criticism. Although Mark Twain,
alone among first-rate American novelists, had tried his hand
at detective stories, he contributed nothing to the type, which
increasingly flourished after 1900. Craig Kennedy, the scientific
hero in many stories by Arthur Reeve, was perhaps the best
known detective in American detective fiction before 1920,

and Mary Roberts Rinehart the most skillful writer in that ingenious department of literature. The international novel was kept alive by Anne Douglas Sedgwick, who worked closely in the mold of Henry James, and by Gertrude Atherton, who departed from it at many points, covered much time and space in her settings, and was inclined to scolding and sensationalism.

2~*Edith Wharton*

Of the successors of Henry James the most eminent was Edith Wharton, who followed him in dealing as a rule with the leisured, cultivated world of New York, New England, and France, but who had her own distinctive art and attitude and never fell into his complicated subtleties of language. Edith Newbold Jones was born in New York in 1862, and educated scrupulously at home and in discriminating foreign travel. At fifteen she wrote verses which Longfellow recommended to the *Atlantic*. Having married Edward Wharton of Boston in 1885, she for some years divided her life between Newport and various parts of Europe, particularly Italy. Though she began to publish short stories in magazines as early as 1891, she collected only the best of them in *The Greater Inclination* (1899) and *Crucial Instances* (1901). Henry James was pleased with "her diabolical little cleverness, the quantity of intention and intelligence in her style, and her sharp eye for an interesting kind of subject." When she followed these with her long Italian novel *The Valley of Decision* (1902), he insisted that "she must be tethered in native pastures, even if it reduces her to a back-yard in New York." Such counsel came oddly from him, but she wrote no more historical novels like the *Valley*. The current fashion of romance may have suggested that she undertake this full yet lucid study of politics and intrigue in an eighteenth-century dukedom. Her long saturation with Italy aided her. She was not, however, deeply concerned with public affairs, and she had none of the qualities which brought success in the romantic fashion which had diverted her.

She returned to short stories and published, with intervening novels, *The Descent of Man, and Other Stories* (1904), *The Hermit and the Wild Woman* (1908), *Tales of Men and Ghosts* (1910), *Xingu* (1916). About fifty of them all together, they show her swift, ironical intelligence flashing its light into corners of human life not large enough to call for long reports. She could go as far as to the ascetic agonies and ecstasies of medieval religion, in *The Hermit and the Wild Woman;* or as to the horrible revenge of Duke Ercole in *The Duchess at Prayer;* or as to the murder and witchcraft of seventeenth-century Brittany in *Kerfol.* Her ghost stories—like *Kerfol, Afterward, The Lady's Maid's Bell, Pomegranate Seed*—make up so admirable and considerable a part of her work that she assembled eleven of them in her late collection *Ghosts* (1937). *Bunner Sisters,* an observant, tender narrative, tells of the declining fortunes of two shopkeepers of Stuyvesant Square. But more often the locality and temper of her briefer stories were not remote from the center of her special world, in which complex people meet crucial occasions in art or learning or love. Her artists and scholars are likely to be shown at some moment when a passionate ideal is in conflict with an instinct toward profit or reputation: as when in *The Descent of Man* an original scientist turns his feet ruinously into the wide green descent to popular science; or when as in *The Verdict* a fashionable painter of talent encounters the work of an obscure genius and gives up his own career in the knowledge that at best he himself can never do masterly work. Some such stress of conflict marks almost all of Edith Wharton's stories of love, first among her subjects. Love with them in few cases runs the smooth course of untroubled matrimony. It cuts violently across the boundaries drawn by marriages of convenience, and it suffers tragic changes in the objects of its desire.

In the formal world represented by her stories a free, wilful passion has little opportunity. Either its behavior must be furtive and hypocritical or else it must incur social disaster. In one story—*The Long Run*—she seems to imply that there is no ignominy like that of failing love when it comes. In another—*Souls Belated*—she sets forth the costs and the entanglements that ensue when individuals take love into their own hands and defy society. Not love for itself but love as the most frequent and most personal of all the passions which bring the community into clashes with its members: this was the object of her curiosity and research. Her positive conclusions about it, as reflected in her stories, seem to be that love cuts deepest in the deepest natures and yet that no one is quite so shallow as to love and recover from it without a scar. Divorce, to which she gave particular attention, can in her stories never be quite complete. *The Other Two*, an extremely amusing story, shows how the third husband of a woman whose two earlier husbands are still living gradually resolves her into her true elements and finds nothing but what one husband after another has made of her. In *Autres Temps*, the most searching of Edith Wharton's stories, she tells how Mrs. Lidcote, whose divorce long before caused a scandal in New York, realizes that her daughter's similar divorce brings her no serious reproach. But Mrs. Lidcote soon realizes, too, that her own divorce remains the scandal it was in spite of the changed attitude of society. "It's simply," she observes, "that society is much too busy to revise its own judgments. Probably no one in the house with me stopped to consider that my case and Leila's were identical. They only remembered that I'd done something which, at the time I did it, was condemned by society. My case has been passed on and classified. . . . The older people have half forgotten why, and the younger ones have never really known. . . . Traditions that have lost their meaning are the hardest of all to destroy."

As Mrs. Wharton saw the art of fiction it had for its proper aim "the disengaging of crucial moments from the welter of existence." When she was interested in situations, she wrote short stories. When she was interested in characters and their growth she wrote novels. *The House of Mirth* (1905) was for her a drama in the life of Lily Bart. For many readers the book was a revelation of the habits of the circle of New York society then popularly known as the Four Hundred. People outside liked to look at it through the windows of fiction. They had been taught, by novelists who were outsiders too, that the Four Hundred lived in houses of mirth and magnificence. Edith Wharton made it clear that such expected splendors were not the essentials of this strict society. There were circles within circles. The inmost circle was very small, very desirable, and fairly dull. The people in it seemed to one of her later heroes less like aristocrats than aborigines. He called Washington Square the Reservation and prophesied that "before long its inhabitants would be exhibited at ethnological shows, pathetically engaged in the exercise of their primitive industries." Mrs. Wharton represented them as aboriginally resisting the efforts of new Americans to enter the reservation. The new men might not be kept out of Wall Street, but they and their women could be kept from ever entering drawing-rooms and country houses.

The popular novelists had led their readers to suppose that these guarded places were full of revels. Mrs. Wharton showed them as marked by an uncompromising decorum. Lily Bart goes to pieces on the rocks of decorum, though she has every advantage of birth except a fortune, and knows the rules of the game perfectly. She cannot follow them with the sure pace and equilibrium that are required; she has the defect, like an Aristotelian hero, of a single weakness. She hesitates between marrying for power and marrying for love, oscillates, and is

(276)

lost. Once out of her appointed course, she finds, on trying to return to her former society, that it is even harder to enter than if she had never been inside. Her tragedy is exclusion from all that means life to her. Undine Spragg in *The Custom of the Country* (1913), marrying and divorcing with the happy insensibility of those animals that mate for a season only, undertakes to force her brilliant, barren beauty into the circles of the elect. Such beauty as hers can purchase a great deal, thanks to the desires of men, and Undine, insensitive to delicate disapproval, comes within sight of her goal. But in the end she fails. The custom of her country—Apex City and the easy-going West—is not the decorum of New York. Ellen Olenska and Newland Archer in *The Age of Innocence* (1920) neither lose nor seek an established position within the Manhattan mandarinate as it existed in the seventies of the last century. They belong there and there they stay, but only by the sacrifice of instinct and happiness. They go through their drama like troubled puppets; they observe taboos with dread but with respect. They are the victims of the innocence of their generation, and of a formalism which persisted after them.

New York was not the only compact community that Edith Wharton studied during the years of these three New York novels. She dealt with New England in *The Fruit of the Tree* (1907) and with modern France in *Madame de Treymes* (1907) and *The Reef* (1912). All the communities put heavy social pressure on individual impulses, whether they are viewed as sin, ignorance, folly, or unfamiliar manners. She had a special gift for organizing the circumstances in the lives of her characters so as to bring out a strong sense of human beings living in such intimate solidarity that no one of them may vary from the customary path without breaking a pattern or inviting a disaster. Novels written out of this conception are usually partisan, either on the side of the individual in his revolt or on the side of society trying to keep order. Mrs.

Wharton was generally content to let her fine irony play over the spectacle of their clashes. But her attitude toward New York society underwent some changes. In *The House of Mirth* she had touches of the grand style, as if she accepted the authority of the formal world. These hardly appeared in *The Age of Innocence*, as if she had come to question that harsh authority. From the first she had had a satirical flair which at times gave her—as in her short story *Xingu*—the flash and glitter, and the agreeable artificiality, of polite comedy. The many futile women whom she enjoyed ridiculing belong nearly as much to the menagerie of the satirist as to the novelist's gallery. In these moments of satire she indicated her own disposition: her impatience with stupidity and affectation and muddy confusion of mind and purpose; her dislike of dinginess; her toleration of arrogance when well-bred; her little concern with the sturdy or burly or homely, or with broad laughter. She was lucid and detached. Her self-possession held critics, and readers, at arm's length, somewhat as her chosen circles hold the barbarians. No doubt she assigned to decorum a larger power than it often exercises, even in such societies as she wrote about. Decorum is binding upon those who accept it, but not upon passionate or logical natures, who treat it with violence or neglect; neither does it bind those who stand too surely to be shaken. The coils of circumstance and the pitfalls of inevitability with which Mrs. Wharton beset the careers of her characters were in part an illusion deftly employed for their effect. She multiplied them as romancers multiply adventures.

She notably did this in *Ethan Frome* (1911), a short novel often singled out as her best work though she herself did not consider it that. She had begun it as a book to be written in French, some years before she wrote it over and completed it in English. The scene was laid not in her own world but in rural New England, near Lenox in the Berkshires where she had lived in summer. While she knew little at first-hand about people like Ethan Frome, his nagging wife Zenobia, and Mattie Silver whom he loves, Edith Wharton had felt some resemblance between their community and hers. If a metropolis had its hard decorum, so had a village. And in a village there was the further compulsion of a helpless poverty which could bind feet and wings, and dull life to an appalling dinginess. Suppose a man desperately trying to escape from a loveless marriage should by a cruel accident be forced back into it, and have to spend the rest of his years in the same house not only with his vindictive wife but also with the other woman, now a whining cripple. This was essentially a situation, but too large for a short story. The characters would have to be shown both before the accident and long after it, enduring the tragic consequences. But since the characters were to be affected less by natural growth than by a momentary accident, they did not call for a whole novel. Mrs. Wharton told the story in a novel hardly longer than a play. In her brilliant construction the consequences appear first, not understood by the spectator who acts as narrator. Then the early events are told, with a bitter tragic irony in the light of what the spectator increasingly realizes about the horror of the consequences. Nothing is admitted that does not bear on the total tragedy. Event follows event with such a look of iron logic that the reader has no chance to think of possible acts by the characters which might have saved or relieved them. This was far from the episodic art of the local color writers. Edith Wharton handled her material not so much like a collector finding curious stones and calling out about them as like a sculptor setting up his finished work on a commanding hill. The other Berkshire novel *Summer* (1917) was much less memorable.

From 1907 to her death in 1937 she lived chiefly in France, to which she gave devoted and expert service during the World War. In America she came to have more and more the status of a great lady of letters. *The Age of Innocence* had a distinguished career on the stage. The National Institute in 1924 awarded her its gold medal for fiction, awarded before that only once, to Howells. Yale gave her an honorary degree, the American Academy made her one of its few women members. She expounded her theories of her art in *The Writing of Fiction* (1925) and wrote her autobiography in *A Backward Glance* (1934). But after 1920, when the Pulitzer prize went to *The Age of Innocence* in a year remarkable for its novels, Mrs. Wharton added little to the body of her fiction. *The Glimpses of the Moon* (1922) was sentimental, *A Son at the Front* (1923) hysterical. The four short novels called, together, *Old New York* (1924) were more interesting, and *The Old Maid* was a striking story. *The Children* (1928) was a worried story of the children of two persons who had been divorced and remarried. *Hudson River Bracketed* (1929) and its sequel *The Gods Arrive* (1932) took one of her not quite convincing young men from Illinois to New York and on to London and Paris. Only a few of the short stories in Edith Wharton's four later collected volumes equal her earlier ones in brilliance. But she had not lost her skill, and a large collection of her short stories, both early and late, would probably show her at her best and her most lasting. The fashionable world she wrote about changed so much that her novels came to have a somewhat antiquarian flavor, like Henry James's. She had, however, a sharper intelligence than James, and in her stories her perennial irony still lights up a rich variety of crucial situations.

XV

WILLA CATHER

HAWTHORNE DURING his patient apprenticeship to his art could look to almost no native masters for guidance or example. Willa Sibert Cather, serving an apprenticeship as patient as Hawthorne's, had to choose among various predecessors and more or less to reject them all before she found a form natural to her and perfectly suited to her materials. She was born in 1876 near Winchester, Virginia, of a father of Irish descent and a mother of Alsatian. At nine the child was taken to a ranch near Red Cloud, Nebraska. If she had grown up in Virginia, where her people had been long settled, she would have known only the older American stocks. But in Nebraska there were German and Russian and French settlers. The nearest neighbors were Scandinavians, and only a few miles away was an entire township of Bohemians. In frequent rides over the prairie on a pony she grew very fond of the immigrants, particularly of old women who told her about their former homes. Imaginative and generous, she was stirred by the difficult lives of the new Americans, and anxious to make them understood as human beings, not merely as disregarded foreigners. "I have never found any intellectual excitement more intense," she later wrote, "than I used to feel when I spent a morning with one of these pioneer women at her baking or butter-making. I used to ride home in the most unreasonable state of excitement. I always felt as if they told me so much more than they said—as if I had actually got inside another person's skin. . . . Their stories used to go round and round in my head at night. This was, with me, the initial impulse."

(281)

As an undergraduate at the University of Nebraska, where she wrote her first stories about the immigrant settlers, she had no model for what she was trying to do, and fell into sentimental language and artificial forms. Thinking her stories "bald, clumsy, and emotional," she resolved to give up writing of the country and people she felt so strongly about. From the university she went to Pittsburgh, worked on a newspaper, taught in a high school, but in the next ten years spent much time in Colorado, Wyoming, and Nebraska. She had the plains in her blood. "That love of great spaces, of rolling open country like the sea—it's the grand passion of my life." She was desperately homesick for the plains country the whole of her first stay in France. Yet in her early poems *April Twilights* (1903) and her short stories *Troll Garden* (1905) she made little use of the subjects which she knew best and which had been her first love. They lay at the bottom of her consciousness, and continued to feed her imagination, but did not stimulate her. Interested in her own growth and struggles as a writer, she became interested in the general plight of artists in the complex world. She desired to live easily in that world and to write about it. "I think," she afterwards concluded, "usually the young writer must have his affair with the external material he covets; must imitate and strive to follow the masters he most admires, until he finds he is starving for reality and cannot make this go any longer. Then he learns that it is not the adventure he sought, but the adventure that sought him, which has made the enduring mark upon him."

At the university Willa Cather had accepted the principles and admired the methods of Henry James, who seemed to her to do flawlessly what she wanted to aim at. In 1907, when she met Sarah Orne Jewett and her friends in Boston, the young plainswoman felt that she, "an American of the Apache period and territory," might come among them "to inherit a Colonial past." That past was all round them, throwing across them the shadows of memorable events. Though only the echoes of

New England's heroic days were to be heard in Sarah Orne Jewett's stories, they were clear and fresh and simple in their versions of the actual life of the present which lay under that past. Miss Jewett's advice had more effect on Willa Cather than the example of Henry James. The elder woman knew from the first that the younger would sooner or later write about her own country. She must write about the life of the plains as it was, and make a way of her own in which to write. Willa Cather later found her way, in O Pioneers! (1913), by trying to tell the story of her characters as if she were talking about them to Miss Jewett. But the teacher had only a few months to live, and the pupil in her first novel after the meeting had not yet freed herself from the material she coveted. *Alexander's Bridge* (1912) was the story of an engineer divided between two loves symbolized for him by two women: the mistress who kept alive in him the sense of his powerful young ambition, and the wife who was a daily reminder of the complex world into which success had brought him. The ending of the novel was fortuitous and melodramatic. The novel itself was, whether consciously or not, an allegory of the conflict in Willa Cather herself between her instinctive love for her native place and her deliberate appetite for other regions.

O Pioneers! was dedicated to the memory of Sarah Orne Jewett, "in whose beautiful and delicate work there is the perfection that endures," but the title came from Walt Whitman. Willa Cather might have told her pioneer stories with the mild colors of the local novelists, the humor of the cowboy chroniclers, the sensationalism of the red blood romancers, the harshness of the naturalists, the involutions of Henry James. She avoided all these methods. Writing beautifully and delicately, she had large stories to tell, not only in O Pioneers! but in the two books that followed it: *The Song of the Lark* (1915) and *My Ántonia* (1918). The sods and swamps of her Nebraska pioneers defy the hands of labor almost as obstinately as the stoves and forests of old New England had.

Her Americans are fresh from Europe, locked in a mortal conflict with nature. If now and then the older among them grow faint at remembering Bohemia or Scandinavia, this is not the predominant mood of their communities. They go forward on a wave of confident energy, as if human life had more dawns than sunsets in it. For the most part her pioneers are unreflective creatures, driven by inner forces they do not and could not analyze. They are primitive and epic.

These three novels were little epics of women, not merely because women were so often the heroes of the New England stories that Willa Cather admired but because she herself knew more about women than about men. Alexandra Bergson in O Pioneers!, Thea Kronborg in The Song of the Lark, Ántonia Shimerda in My Ántonia: round them as girls and women the actions of their stories chiefly revolve. It is not, however, as other Helens or Gudruns that they affect their universes; they are not the darlings of heroes but heroes themselves. Alexandra drags her dull brothers after her and establishes the family fortunes. Ántonia, less positive and more pathetic, still holds the center of her retired stage by her rich, warm, deep goodness. Thea, a genius in her own right, outgrows her Colorado birthplace and becomes a famous singer with the fierce energy of a pioneer who happens to be an instinctive artist rather than an instinctive manager, like Alexandra, or an instinctive mother, like Ántonia. Because women are here the heroes, neither wars, as among the ancients, nor machines, as among the moderns, determine the principal activities. The moods of the novels have an even more epic air than the actions. Primitive as Willa Cather's scene might be, she filled it with spacious and candid persons who transcend the gnarled eccentricity and timid inhibitions of local color characters. Passion blows through her heroes and heroines like a high and sometimes dangerous wind. It does not, as in ordinary local color, lurk in corners or hide itself altogether. These passions are most commonly seen in home-keeping women, and consequently are close to the core of human experience.

Willa Cather's pioneers are in several respects like the artists of her earlier and later stories. They are alike in their single-mindedness. They work much by themselves, contending with hard obstacles and looking forward, if they win, to a freedom seldom achieved in crowded communities. For her characters, to become too much involved is to lose their quality. There is Marie Tovesky, in *O Pioneers!*, whom nothing more preventable than her beauty and gaiety drags into a confused status and so on to catastrophe. Ántonia, tricked into a false relation with her scoundrel lover, and Alexandra, nagged at by her stodgy family because her suitor is poor, suffer temporary eclipses from which only their superb integrity finally extricates them. Thea Kronborg, troubled by the swarming sensations of her first year in Chicago, has to find her true self again in that marvelous desert canyon in Arizona where hot sun and bright, cold water and dim memories of the cliff-dwelling Ancient Peoples detach her from the stupid faces that have haunted and unnerved her. Pioneers and artists alike are threatened by a world which may trespass upon them. The frontier, for all its vitality, its wild beauty and freedom, has to undergo the coming of clumsy towns. The heroic days endure but a brief period. Then the high-hearted pioneers survive half as curiosities in a new order; and their spirits, transmitted to the artists who are their natural successors, take up the old struggle in new circumstances.

Harsanyi in *The Song of the Lark* says of Thea that her secret is the same as "every artist's secret . . . passion. It is an open secret, and perfectly safe. Like heroism, it is inimitable in cheap materials." It was the secret of Willa Cather's strong yet subtle art. She understood both heroism and passion, not only with her lucid intelligence but also with the help of a rich energy in herself. She had something of Whitman's hearty tolerance, of his exultation over vast distances, of his consciousness of past and future striking hands in the present, of his affection for common men and women. If she did not run on in ungirt dithyrambs like his, but worked quietly with her finely chosen materials, she still knew how to be convincing about the passion of the artist, the heroism of the pioneer. Compared with her artists in the stories collected in *Youth and the Bright Medusa* (1920) most artists in fiction seem to have been imitated in cheap substitutes. Such artists suffer, they rebel, they gesticulate, they pose, they fail through success, they succeed through failure; but only now and then are they breathing and authentic. Willa Cather, who had many friends among musicians, was particularly interested in them, perhaps because a virtuoso must have heroic vitality to arrive at any real eminence. A poet may languish over verses in his garret, a painter or a sculptor over work conceived and executed in a shy privacy. A great singer must be an athlete and an actor, training for months and years for the sake of a few hours of triumph before a living audience. The story of Thea Kronborg is the story of her unspeculative, daemonic integrity. She lifts herself from handicapping conditions almost as an animal shoulders its way through scratching underbrush to food and water. Thea may be checked and delayed by all sorts of human complications, but her deeper nature never loses the sense of its right direction. Ambition with her is scarcely more than the passion of self-preservation in a potent spirit.

Ántonia has less spectacular attributes of heroism, and exhibits the usual instincts of self-preservation hardly at all. She is gentle and confiding, and her strongest impulse is to give well-being and happiness to others. Yet the maternal current is so deep and sure in her that it saves her from mediocrity. Goodness, often negative and annoying, amounts in her to heroic effluence. It touches everything round her with reality. "She lent herself to immemorial human attitudes which we recognize as universal and true. . . . She had only to stand in the orchard, to put her hand on a little crab tree and look up at the apples, to make you feel the goodness of planting and tending and harvesting at last. . . . She was a rich mine of life, like the founders of early races." In actual life Ántonia was a Bohemian girl who was kind to Willa Cather in her childhood. In the novel Ántonia has become so real that, while not in the least a symbol herself, she brings symbols to mind, as only reality can do. It is not easy to say things so illuminating about a human being as Willa Cather says about Ántonia. It is all but impossible to create a character with such sympathetic art that words like these about Ántonia and the apple tree toward the end of the book only confirm and interpret an impression already made.

Jack London, born the same year as Willa Cather, might settle early into repetitious exploitation of his primitive frontier. She found herself more slowly than he, but she continued to grow. Each new book marked an unfolding of her mind or an experiment in method. In *One of Ours* (1922) she undertook to reduce her own apparent share to the minimum, cutting down analysis, description, reflection, and letting the people tell their own story by what they do and say. It was the history of Claude Wheeler, a Nebraska boy born at the end of the century when the pioneer days had passed and a smaller generation had followed the first one. He has no strong bent of his own, but he is out of joint with the time, and he discovers a meaning in life only when he enters the American army to go to France, where he is killed. The subject, being recent, could not have lain long in Willa Cather's memory. In spite of her careful art the book—her longest—seemed a little thin and topical, especially in the parts dealing with the war. In a critical essay on *The Novel Démeublé* published that year she argued that novels had lately been overfurnished and that most of them would be better if shorter and sparer. "The higher processes of art are all processes of simplification. . . . How wonderful it would be if we could throw all the furniture out of the window; and along with it, all the meaningless reiterations concerning physical sensations, all the tiresome old patterns, and leave the room as bare as the stage of a Greek theatre." After 1922 Willa Cather wrote no more novels as long as *One of Ours* or *The Song of the Lark*.

A *Lost Lady* (1923), short and flawless, had no unnecessary furniture. It was again the story of an actual woman Willa Cather had known as she had known the original of Ántonia. But Marian Forrester instead of being another simple farm girl belongs to the aristocracy of the frontier: its planners and rulers and beneficiaries. Married to a man much older than she, she is still too full of youth to be wholly satisfied after he has retired to his farm. She may honor him for giving up his fortune to save the depositors in a failing bank; she may show him loyalty and devotion and make his house charming. She cannot resist the impulses in her blood and nerves. The vitality which passed so soon once the frontier settled into the new order does not ebb in her. Nor after her husband's death can she fill her life with being his widow, and in a sense the frontier's. She must still live, she cannot help loving. In a brighter world suitable to her age and instincts she would have been happy in the natural course of existence. In the fading frontier community she is misfit. Without the stoic heroism of the pioneer, she lacks also the severe passion of the artist. In living, the only art she has, she does not insist on perfection or nothing. She drifts into a shabby and then a shabbier love. Her failure as an artist in life brings her no formal, visible penalty. She dies the wife of a rich and kind Englishman in the Argentine. But she has lost the integrity which Ántonia, a better artist, knew how to preserve. Marian Forrester's penalty is that loss. Her story might have been told in many ways: moralistically, edifyingly, ironically. Willa Cather told it with understanding and pity, setting forth all the essential facts of the lost lady's total character, so mixed,

so often contradictory, and leaving them to be judged by who-
ever is wise enough to judge a bewildered, unhappy woman.

Willa Cather was to return more than once to the frontier
for materials: in the three revealing and touching stories of
Obscure Destinies (1930), episodes of the West of both
country and town; in *Lucy Gayheart* (1935), the story of
another girl who left the frontier for a career in music but
who was passive and pathetic, not conquering like Thea Kronborg. *My Mortal Enemy* (1926), not a frontier story, was
a searching study of another lady lost because she could not
fit her world: Myra Henshawe, favorite of her powerful uncle
in an Illinois town, has made a runaway marriage against his
will. The marriage does not prosper—at least her husband does
not—and Myra finds her life unendurably pinched and dingy.
No doubt she should have been submissively content to lie
in the bed she had made for herself. But, as her understanding
husband says, "she isn't people. She's Molly Driscoll, and
there was never anybody else like her." As she grows older she
becomes more like her uncle. "I can feel his savagery
strengthen inside me. We think we are so individual and so
misunderstood when we are young; but the nature our strain
of blood carries is inside there, waiting, like our skeleton." In
spite of her husband's gentle devotion she comes to feel—at
least on one desperate occasion—that he has been her mortal
enemy. "Violent natures like hers sometimes turn against
themselves—against themselves and all their idolatries." Willa
Cather never handled a more intricate character than Myra,
nor ever made one clearer with what seems utterly artless
handling.

Before *The Song of the Lark* Willa Cather had traveled
sensitively in the Southwest and fallen under the spell of the
ancient Indian civilizations there. In *The Professor's House*
(1925) she took up the theme again. Professor St. Peter, who
lives on Lake Michigan and in whose mind most of the action
takes place, remembers his student Tom Outland, who had

found lost Indian towns on a deserted mesa in New Mexico. They had affected Tom and he had affected St. Peter, not only by helping him with his book on the Spanish adventurers but also by bringing back the sense of the primitive young man he had been long ago in Kansas, before his life grew complicated. Here, as in *Alexander's Bridge*, there was perhaps a touch of autobiography, a hint at a not dissimilar experience in Willa Cather. But as she went on with her Southwestern theme it was not the primitive, heathen Indians who filled her imagination so much as it was the Catholic Church. The Nebraska frontier had passed and almost nothing of it survived. The New Mexican frontier had a kind of survival in the Church as a continuing institution. "The longer I stayed in the Southwest the more I felt that the story of the Catholic Church in that country was the most interesting of all its stories. . . . I had all my life wanted to do something in the style of legend, which is absolutely the reverse of dramatic treatment . . . something without accent, with none of the artificial elements of composition. . . . The essence of such writing is not to hold the note, to use an incident for all there is in it—but to touch and pass on. . . . In this kind of writing the mood is the thing."

Death Comes for the Archbishop (1927) was based upon the lives of two actual prelates: Bishop—later Archbishop— Lamy of Santa Fé, called Latour in the novel, and his vicar general Father Machebeuf, called Father Vaillant. Keeping close to history as to dates and places and the chief persons, Willa Cather rounded out the documents on which the story was based and brought it richly and beautifully to life. She did not work it into a close-knit narrative, but wrote it as a series of scenes and incidents which in historic time may have been years apart. The logic of the story is in the character of the men, deeply founded and yet generously growing in their varied circumstances. Though Kit Carson, known to many Western romances, appears, this is no roaring border chroni-

cle. Adventure and danger, violence and death are only episodes in the resolute advance of a mild culture bringing peace
to the desert. Herself a Protestant, Willa Cather told her
story with full mastery of Catholic opinion and behavior, and
with full sympathy for humane, heroic deeds. Heroism comes
naturally to her heroes, in their day's work. She stresses it no
more than they would have done in talking about it. There
is room for fresh descriptions of landscapes and interiors, food
and clothing, the looks of all the characters, reflections on
conduct and manners, and many big and little happenings, all
told in a quiet tone and in a silver style. The novel was received with general enthusiasm and became at once a special
favorite among her books, along with *My Ántonia* and *A
Lost Lady*. She had made the Catholic Southwest as truly a
territory of her art as the plains had been. She had given as
graceful and exact a form to the lives of holy men as to the
lives of erring women. The history of the Catholic Church
in America includes Canada as well as New Mexico. In
Shadows on the Rock (1931) Willa Cather chose Quebec
for her setting, in the last days of Frontenac. The time is
remoter than in any other of her novels, and she confines
herself to the events of a single year as they appeared to a
child: the shadows of events, not the events themselves. The
body of the book is the things described: the changing seasons, the river, the headland up which the city climbs, the
streets, churches, markets, waterfront, houses, costumes. But
Shadows on the Rock is less rich in pictures than *Death
Comes to the Archbishop* and still less rich in dramatic implications.

"One must know the world so well," Sarah Orne Jewett
said to the younger woman from Nebraska, "before one can
know the parish." Willa Cather was thirty-seven when she
published *O Pioneers!* and had been half her life away from
the Red Cloud neighborhood. "I think," she later said, "that
most of the basic material a writer works with is acquired

before the age of fifteen. That's the important period: when one is not writing. Those years determine whether one's work will be poor or rich." When she began to write novels her materials were no longer raw in her mind, as facts are in a reporter's, but had been turned and worked over for two decades. What was trivial, for her, had been lost, and what was left had taken a shape much firmer and clearer than the most vivid first impressions can have. It was not only the intervening years that had brought about the process. She had studied the larger world in many regions, many people, many arts, many books. Her growth in knowledge and taste had not won her from her first love, only made her able to feel for it a wiser and more proportionate affection. She was never a provincial bragging about a province, but a true citizen of the world who knew why and how a province was beautiful.

"The history of every country begins," she said, "in the heart of a man or a woman." Though she might create a full sense of community life on the plains, in the Southwest and Quebec, and in the cities she touched, she was in effect a biographer. Her novels are life-stories, each novel centered chiefly in a single person. She needed and used time for her characters to turn round in. She was skeptical about those climaxes with which some novelists are content. Men and women after great hours descend to their accustomed levels. The truth about even heroes must have in it some account of what years can do to them. Drama is not so credible as biography. Though Willa Cather admired orderly, comely, fruitful societies, her passion was for heroic individuals. She preferred them to be heroic, she demanded that they be individual. Her characters were too specific ever to be mistaken for types. She drew no caricatures. If she had to choose between form and reality she chose reality. For every novel she tried to find the form that would fit the hero. She had no set formula. Many novelists, having hit upon a formula that seems their forte, thereafter use it again and again, so that their readers may know what to expect. Willa Cather constantly varied her forms. Only her scrupulous concern for reality was unchanging. The realities which interested her were not all equally interesting to others. Some of her books are powerful, some merely graceful. But they are always truthful. And hardly one of them has worn thin with time. They were not written in temporary fashions, and had nothing to lose when fashions passed.

XVI

REVOLT FROM THE VILLAGE

AMERICAN FICTION had regularly celebrated the American village as the natural home of the pleasant virtues. Certain writers, aware of agrarian discontent or given to a preference for cities, might now and then have laid disrespectful hands upon the farm; but even these hesitated to touch the village. It seemed too cosy a microcosm to be disturbed. There it lay in the mind's eye, neat, compact, organized, traditional: the white church with its tapering spire, the sober schoolhouse, the smithy of the ringing anvil, the corner grocery, the cluster of friendly houses; the venerable parson, the wise physician, the canny squire, the grasping landlord softened or outwitted in the end; the village belle, gossip, atheist, idiot; jovial fathers, gentle mothers, merry children; cool parlors, shining kitchens, spacious barns, lavish gardens, fragrant summer dawns, and comfortable winter evenings. These were images not to be discarded lightly, even by writers who saw that time was discarding many of them as industrialism went on planting ugly factories along the prettiest brooks, bringing in droves of aliens who used unfamiliar tongues and customs, and fouling the air with smoke and gasoline. E. W. Howe in *The Story of a Country Town* had made it plain enough that villages which prided themselves on their pioneer energy might in fact be stagnant backwaters. Mark Twain in *The Man That Corrupted Hadleyburg* had put it bitterly on record that villages too complacent about their honesty might have become a hospitable soil for meanness and falsehood, merely waiting for the proper seed. Clarence Darrow in his elegiac *Farmington* (1904) had insisted that one village at least had known

(294)

as much restless longing as simple bliss. But the revolt from the village which brought a new tone into American fiction was most dramatically begun by Edgar Lee Masters's *Spoon River Anthology* (1915).

Though it was not a novel, it was the essence of many novels. Masters had imagined a graveyard such as every American village has and had furnished it with epitaphs of such veracity as no village ever saw put into words. The epitaphs seemed to send up a shout of revelation. Readers felt that they had sat down to an incomparable feast of scandal. Where now were the mild decencies of Oldtown, Tiverton, Old Chester, Friendship Village? The roofs and walls of Spoon River were gone and the passers-by could look into every room; the closets were open and all the skeletons rattled; brains and breasts had unlocked themselves and set their most private treasures out for the most public gaze. Masters was particularly outspoken about love, which had rarely been so secretive anywhere as in the American villages of fiction. But about all aspects of behavior in his village he was impatient, if not violent, toward cautious subterfuges. There is filth, he said in effect, behind whited sepulchres; drag it into the light. Spoon River is slack and shabby. Nor is its decay chronicled in any mood of tender pathos. It has been a general demoralization. Except for a few saints and poets, whom Masters hailed with lyric ardor, the people are sunk in greed and hypocrisy and apathy. While inwardly the village dwindles and rots, outwardly it clings to a pitiless decorum which veils its faults till it can overlook them. Again and again the poet went back to the heroic founders of Spoon River, to the days of Lincoln whose shadow lies little heeded across the sons and daughters of meaner days. The town has forgotten its true ancestors.

There were torrents of controversy about the book. The village was defended, the village was attacked, with every grade of relevance. E. W. Howe answered Masters indirectly and belatedly with *The Anthology of Another Town* (1920). It was not epitaphs in verse for the dead but anecdotes of the living in prose. Howe did not accuse the village at large, nor make a specialty of scandal. He let his memories run through the town, recalling bits of illuminating gossip. Accepting and tolerating its people, he carried on no sentimental tradition. His village is simply a group of human beings of whom some work and some loaf, some behave themselves and some do not, some consequently prosper and some fail, some are happy and some are miserable. His village is not dainty, as in a poem. He believed no village ever was and he knew he had never seen one. Though he appeared to be defending the village, he gave no comfort to those who cherished any idyllic image of it. By 1920 he could have given small comfort if he had tried. The village of the literary tradition had been so long unreal in fact that Masters's angry assault had driven it out of fashion.

The year after *Spoon River* Sherwood Anderson (1876-   ) published his first novel—*Windy McPherson's Son*—and the next year his second—*Marching Men*. In both of them the heroes detach themselves from their native villages to seek their fortunes in some city. In both they succeed without satisfaction, unable to find a meaning in the world which has let them have what they thought they wanted. The novels ache with the sense of a dumb confusion in America. Anderson wrote as if he were assembling documents on the eve of revolution. Village peace and stability have departed; all the ancient American customs break or fade; the leaven of change stirs the lump. In *Winesburg, Ohio* (1919) Anderson turned to a village which he knew as Masters knew Spoon River. But Anderson was less satirical than Masters. The central figure of the Winesburg stories is a young reporter about to leave the place where he has always lived. He has not greatly hated it, and now because he is going he views it with a good deal of tenderness. It seems to him that most of his old neighbors are cramped spirits, repressed by village life. This part of their natures distorted beyond all symmetry, that part wasted away in desperate disuse, they have become grotesques. Their visions have no chance to be realities, and so make visionaries. Their religion, without poetry, is either rigid or cloudy. Love, lacking spontaneity, settles into fleshly habit or is stifled and malicious. Heroism of deed or thought either withers into melancholy inaction or else protects itself with a sullen or ridiculous bravado. If Masters in Spoon River looked cynically at the stealthy life there, Anderson in Winesburg looked sympathetically at the buried life, buried and pitiful.

In the short stories collected in *The Triumph of the Egg* (1921), *Horses and Men* (1923), and the later *Death in the Woods* (1933) Anderson did his most lasting work. Touching American life at many places and always throwing a warm if sad light upon it, the stories had a point and impact which he sometimes lost when he wandered and brooded through novels like *Poor White* (1920), the contorted *Many Marriages* (1922), and *Dark Laughter* (1925), with its rich, deep background of instinctive life among the Negroes who make white life seem thin and dry in comparison. *A Story Teller's Story* (1924) and *Tar: A Midwest Childhood* (1926) have Anderson himself as a hero, but the same kind of hero as in most of the other books. Perhaps there is as much fiction in his autobiography as there is autobiography in his fiction. In any case, his own life was the chief source of his art. Born in Ohio, he had little formal schooling, served in the war with Spain, and settled into business without any definite aim or any consciousness of his gifts or desires. Gradually the conviction came over him that he could no longer find happiness in the routine life of his time. He gave up business, went to Chicago, and wrote stories and novels about heroes like himself, with thoughts like his. The nation, he thought, had reached its goal of material prosperity but did not look ahead to intellectual and spiritual completions. It had grown fat with overfeeding and slowed its march. It was dead-alive. Men ought to be full of vitality, full of beauty and heroism. Anderson went beyond the revolt from the village to an imaginative criticism of the whole American world. But he did not outgrow his earlier confusions. His revolt and his criticism were hardly more than a warning to men not to be too sure and smug in their opinions. After a while, this seemed negative and tenuous. He retired in 1925 to Virginia, became a country editor, and put less of himself into his books, though he still puzzled over how to get at what was true and simple in human life and to make it clear.

The village invented by Zona Gale (1874-1938) of Wisconsin to be the setting for *Friendship Village* (1908) and *Friendship Village Love Stories* (1909), was one of the sweetest of all literary villages. Its views of life were rosy as well as homely, and happy endings were orthodox in its stories of self-reliance and self-sacrifice. But *Birth* (1918) told the story of a man who in spite of a good heart is always inept and unlucky and who bores all who can be bored. No miracle comes to reward him for his genuine merits. Born a blunderer, he dies one. It implied a kind of revolution in village fiction that Zona Gale at no point sweetened or softened her story. In an American village, no less than elsewhere, good hearts might not be enough. In *Miss Lulu Bett* (1920) she brought a delicate malice to bear on the story of the heroine, who is a dim drudge in the house of her silly sister and her sister's pompous husband, but who has a brief adventure into freedom and comes back, though temporarily defeated, better for her rebellion. Zona Gale did not pile up accusations against the town of Warbleton in general. She concerned herself principally with the tedious affectations of the Deacon household. "In the conversations of Dwight and Ina," the husband and wife, "you saw the historical home forming in clots in the fluid wash of the community." With a spare plot and a staccato style Zona Gale set forth a lively, intelligent drama which with few changes could reach the stage and have a striking success. In her later books she did not return to the sweetness of Friendship Village. *Preface to a Life* (1926) was a speculative and mystical novel which deserved more notice than it got, and there were exquisite crisp short stories in *Yellow Gentians and Blue* (1927) and *Bridal Pond* (1930).

The year of *Miss Lulu Bett, Poor White,* and *The Anthology of Another Town* is memorable in the history of American fiction. It was the year also of Upton Sinclair's 100%, Edith Wharton's *Age of Innocence*, Floyd Dell's *Moon-Calf*, F. Scott Fitzgerald's *This Side of Paradise*. It was the year of James Branch Cabell's ironical romance *Figures of Earth* and Sinclair Lewis's epoch-marking *Main Street*. Whatever differences there were among them, they had in common a lively critical temper. That temper had been rising since before the war, and was soon to take a concerted stand in the acid symposium *Civilization in the United States* (1922) by thirty inquiring Americans. The change in attitude toward the village was only one symptom of the general change going on in fiction, and the change in fiction was only one aspect of a wide-ranging shift in accepted values. The simple provincialism of the older America no longer met the needs of the Younger Generation, which had come to think of the country as dusty and dull. They attacked fundamentalism in religion, capitalism in industry, commercialism in education, science, and the arts, chauvinism in international affairs, reactionism in public opinion at large. Most of them had eagerly read George Bernard Shaw and H. G. Wells. The Russian revolution seemed to have shaken the world. Various foreign cultures were held up as examples to backward, standardized America. In particular the native Puritan strain was called responsible for many modern American defects and faults. Mary Austin in *The American Rhythm* (1923) argued that the Indians had understood America better, and had adjusted themselves to it better, than the white men. Stress was laid upon the share of the Negroes in American life—especially its music, dancing, folk-lore—and a group of writers, most of them of African descent, produced the panoramic volume *The New Negro* (1925) edited by Alain Locke.

As the overwhelming bulk of American literature had been written in English, so had it been written by men and women of British stocks. Now there appeared an increasing number of writers who belonged, usually, to the second generation of newer immigrants. They brought qualities not common in the Anglo-American literature; they also insisted that the racial and national diversity of American culture be recognized. The arts were touched by the melting-pot. Some of the immigrants had little literatures in their own language, like the Yiddish in New York and the Scandinavian in Minnesota, as the Germans had long had in Pennsylvania and the French in Louisiana. But the most notable of the immigrant novels before 1920, Abraham Cahan's *The Rise of David Levinsky* (1917), was written in English. It records the making of an American, originally a reader of Talmud in a Russian village and eventually the principal figure in the garment trade in America; it traces the evolution of an industry. In the end Levinsky, with all his New World wealth, lacks the peace he might have had if he had not sacrificed his Old World integrity and faith. This was an immigrant who knew he had lost something by his change of country, and could not be wholly proud of changing or wholly grateful to America for changing him. Sholem Asch, who wrote in Yiddish, and chiefly on European themes, belongs to American literature only by virtue of his later residence in the United States and his high rank among the American writers who have used other languages than English.

The criticism that Cahan implied was clearly stated in *Up Stream* (1922), the autobiography of Ludwig Lewisohn (1883-   ). Though born in Germany, he had come to

America as a child and had grown up in American circumstances. But, a scholar and a critic of learning and taste, he found he could not join in the ordinary immigrant chorus of praise. He liked neither Puritanism nor vulgarity. From being one of the most effective critics of the newer literature he turned to being a novelist. In his powerful *The Case of Mr. Crump* (1926), published only in Paris, he created the most unpleasant woman in American fiction, or perhaps in any. In *The Island Within* (1928), *Stephen Escott* (1930), and *Last Days of Shylock* (1931) he studied with much subtlety, if with occasional melodrama, the relations between Jews and Christians.

The immigrant novels called attention to a new frontier in America. Its pioneers do not, like the earlier ones, face hostile savages and stubborn nature. They are more likely to be set down in shop or mill or mine, herded in slums, exploited by the descendants of pioneers who came first. With the newer stocks an ancient process begins over again. Even those who, like Lewisohn's characters, do not live on the plane of bare survival, have to endure prejudice and insult. Yet one of the immigrants dealt with the old frontier, but dealt with it in a new way. Ole Edvart Rölvaag (1876-1931) came from Norway at twenty to South Dakota, and for most of his mature life was professor of Norwegian at St. Olaf College in Minnesota. He strongly defended the right of Norwegians in America to keep their racial culture, deplored their inclination to drift away from it. The best of his novels, and the best of all immigrant novels in the United States, was written in Norwegian, first published in Norway in two parts (1924-25), and translated into English with the title *Giants in the Earth* (1927). Completely naturalized, the book is as much a part of American literature as of Norwegian. The scene is South Dakota in the seventies. The chief characters are Per Hansa, an inland viking with a fated passion to conquer the wilderness, and Beret Holm, his terrified companion who is always homesick for the land and the folkways she left behind. If the frontier was heroic, so was it tragic. For whatever it gave it asked hard prices, in loneliness, pain, insecurity, barren living. Men must live for the future, and perhaps never see it. A few ruthless wills drive all the rest. Rölvaag dramatized the conflict between the willing and the unwilling pioneers as intensely as that between men and nature. Compared with *Giants in the Earth* most novels of the frontier seem thoughtless romances. But it is, for all its profound realism, rich in matter and magical in style.

XVII

SINCLAIR LEWIS

Spoon river anthology had been a collection of poems, *Winesburg, Ohio* a collection of short stories. *Main Street* (1920) was in the more customary and popular form of a novel, and it carried the protest against the village to an immediate, immense audience. A brief passage in the book became a classic for the decade. Village contentment, the passage ran, was "the contentment of the quiet dead, who are scornful of the living for their restless walking. It is negation canonized as the one positive virtue. It is the prohibition of happiness. It is slavery self-sought and self-defended. It is dullness made God." There was, another passage said, a village virus that "infects ambitious people who stay too long in the provinces." Hundreds of thousands were not content, the book insisted. They were only silent. The book broke up the conspiracy of silence, and the revolt from the village swept across the whole country, with acrimonious attacks and defenses.

It was often charged that Lewis had followed the lead of *Spoon River*. He had in 1920 not even read the book, and his own dissatisfaction with dry provincialism went back to his youth. He was born in 1885 in Minnesota, son of a country doctor who had come there from New England. In the small town of Sauk Centre (original of Gopher Prairie) the romantic boy resented it that Minnesota had no Robin Hoods nor Ivanhoes nor Round Tables. At Yale he found it was not the mellow community he had expected. He held himself chafingly aloof, belonging to no societies, making few close friendships, prowling at night through the back quarters of the town. He first appeared in print with a poem on Lancelot,

(303)

in the college magazine. In the summers of 1904 and 1906 he went to England on cattleboats. During the summer vacation of 1905 he worked in Sauk Centre on a novel to be called *The Village Virus* which he did not finish but which was the preliminary version of *Main Street*. Instead of returning to Yale for his fourth year he spent two months in a socialistic colony in New Jersey, founded by Upton Sinclair, and left it for New York, where Lewis lived in the slums writing sentimental verse. Neither socialism nor Bohemianism satisfied him. He traveled steerage to Panama, to be like one of the dashing heroes of Richard Harding Davis, but came back to Yale to finish the work for his degree in 1908. This year was pleasant, and for a time he thought of going on to become a doctor of philosophy and then a professor of English somewhere. Instinct drove him to more active courses. He became in turn editor of a small newspaper in Iowa, charity worker in New York, reporter in San Francisco, editor in Washington of a magazine for teachers of the deaf. From 1910 to 1915 he was in New York again at various kinds of work for various publishers. Then, supporting himself with stories for magazines, he lived for another five years in Florida, Chicago, Minnesota, New York, Cape Cod, with a motor trip half across the Continent. In Washington he settled down long enough to write *Main Street*, and from its reception discovered that at thirty-five he held up to America what it took, or angrily refused to take, as a mirror to its nature.

Lewis early changed from sentimental verse to realistic-satirical prose, but his novels were his poems in the sense that autobiographical experience lay behind each of them, though none of them was actually autobiographical. The hero of *Our Mr. Wrenn* (1914) is a lonely, restless minor clerk in New York who escapes from his routine life long enough to go to Liverpool on a cattleboat and have timid adventures in exciting England. Una Golden in *The Job* (1917) has to continue in a dreary office such as Lewis hated. He understood them because he had been close enough to their lives to sympathize with them, perhaps in fear that he himself might never rise from those monotonous levels. In *The Trail of the Hawk* (1915), one of the earliest novels with an aviator for hero, Hawk Ericson, born in Minnesota, suddenly leaves college for Panama, learns to fly in California, marries a bewildering girl in New York, finds a settled existence unendurable, and runs with her away from dullness. *Free Air* (1919) goes over the route by which Lewis had motored from Minneapolis to Seattle, and in the Minnesota hero and the Brooklyn heroine represents the difference in manners which had made the young Lewis self-conscious in New Haven and New York.

In *Main Street* he set out to tell a true story about the American village, whether anybody would read it or not, and he was surprised by the tremendous acclamation. He had not reasoned that it was time to take a new attitude toward the village or calculated that it would be prudent. He only put down, dramatically, the discontents that had been stirring in him for at least fifteen years. But there was something seismographic in his nerves, and he had recorded a ground swell of popular thinking and feeling. His occasional explicit comments on dull villages were quoted till they reverberated. Many readers thought there were more such comments than there were. The novelty was less in the arguments of the book than in the story. That violated a pattern which had been long accepted in American fiction. The heroes of Booth Tarkington, for instance, after a brief rebellion of one kind or other, came to their senses and agreed with their wiser elders. But Carol Kennicott, rebelling against the unnecessary ugliness of Gopher Prairie and its smug stodginess, and in the end having to yield to it, yet appears as a heroine. Her discontent has been not folly but a virtue. The village is the villain.

The characters of the story, even Carol, are not remembered as Gopher Prairie is. The most famous incident is Carol's first walk along Main Street, with its detailed description of what she saw. The book is a comic pageant, a panoramic caricature of a small provincial town. Almost every American town had a Main Street as a matter of course. Lewis made the name a symbol and an epithet. Main Street became a synonym for narrow provincialism. People spoke of Main Street minds or customs without needing to explain further what they meant. He could have fixed the epithet so deeply in the national consciousness only by giving it the sharp point of unmistakable ideas. But he reinforced his ideas by innumerable instances. The novel is full of persons, and they are shown in a continuous variety of incidents to illustrate Gopher Prairie's virtues and vices. The vices seemed in 1920 to outweigh the virtues overwhelmingly, because they were shown in a proportion new to American country novels. In time the vices and virtues came to seem more justly balanced. Much praise was at first given to the brilliant accuracy of the dialogue. In time it became clear that the dialogue was partly creation: the American vernacular enlivened by Lewis's own characteristic idiom and cadences.

A complete example of this enlivened vernacular appeared in his next novel, *Babbitt* (1922), in the speech the hero makes before the Zenith Chamber of Commerce. No actual enthusiast ever spoke with such swift and full and revealing glibness. What Babbitt says is quintessential and archetypal. Thousands of such speeches had been undertaken by such men. Here was the speech they would all have liked to make. Babbitt at once became as much a symbol and an epithet as Main Street, and the name Babbitt a synonym for a conventional business man. From the village Lewis had turned to another American tradition. The business man in fiction had been often a hero, sometimes a malefactor. Lewis studied him more fundamentally, in a case that was taken to be a specimen. George F. Babbitt has not prospered according to the familiar maxims about economy, industry, and perseverance. He has more or less blundered into such success as he has had, in a business which was not his first choice, with a wife whom accident chose for him. He has no thorough-going character because he has never needed one. It has been enough for him to do whatever others do, like an indistinguish-able bee in an instinctive hive. But in him, as in Carol Kennicott, though not so strongly, there is possibility of dissent. When one of his friends has come to grief by falling out of step, Babbitt reconsiders his own situation. A troubling love affair makes him reflect on his emotional life as he has never done before. Since he has no gift for thinking, and no original opinions, he cannot go far in his little rebellion. In a temporary resentment he struggles to be himself, without quite knowing what his separate self is. And though he soon drops back into the rhythm of the community, he has learned enough to encourage his son in marrying for love and doing the work he likes best. Babbitt's fling has not been pure folly but a kind of abortive triumph.

His triumph was generally overlooked by readers, who failed to notice that this was a classic experience: a man in the midst of prosperity stopping to weigh and value his possessions. The familiar theme was lost in the volume of evidence as to Babbitt's conformity before and after his adventure. Countless critics saw in Babbitt a proof that the typical American was like a standard part of a machine, always ready to be fitted into the national design. It was easy to get such an impression from the book. Lewis had created a whole city in Zenith, the principal town in the synthetic Middle Western state of Winnemac which is impossibly bounded by Michigan, Ohio, Illinois, and Indiana. Gopher Prairie had been a dusty village; Zenith was an enterprising town. Lewis was as much at home in one as in the other. He built the town according to a minute map he had drawn, even to the plans of houses and offices. The many characters besides Babbitt come and go in Zenith with the most convincing naturalness of movement because their lives had all been painstakingly studied. They

(307)

belong in the town. Their recurrences in the plot confirm the sense that this is the compact community Babbitt feels it to be. Of all Lewis's novels *Babbitt* is the most expertly constructed. Dedicated to Edith Wharton, it made his sprawling Zenith seem as close-knit as her Manhattan, though his vernacular was worlds away from her formal art.

The public expected that after a village and a town Lewis would next write about a large city. He chose not a place but a profession. Grandson, son, nephew, and brother of doctors, he knew the lives of medical families and may have felt, as the sons of American country doctors commonly do, some guilt over not choosing that career himself. There was no current argument about the profession of medicine in which *Arrowsmith* (1925) might take sides. It was the life story of a hero who was successively country doctor, public health official, pathologist in a fashionable clinic, bacteriologist in an institute for medical research, and commissioner sent to fight a plague in the West Indies. The book covers much territory, and it does for an American profession what no other novel has ever done. Carol had been often foolish, Babbitt feeble. Arrowsmith has a more genuine heroism in his passion for scientific integrity. He demandingly looks for it in one grade of his profession after another; when he has despaired of finding it he retires to be a hermit of science in a lonely laboratory in Vermont. There is something Faustian, not to say literary, in Arrowsmith's prayer: "God give me unclouded eyes and freedom from haste. God give me a quiet and relentless anger against all pretense and all pretentious work and all work left slack and unfinished. God give me a restlessness whereby I may neither sleep nor accept praise till my observed results equal my calculated results or in pious glee I discover and assault my error. God give me strength not to trust in God!" There is something true to an honored American tradition in Arrowsmith's retirement. He turns his back on what seem to him worldly confusions and short-sighted compromises, to do his true work in the wilderness, as Daniel Boone and Leather-Stocking in the eighteenth century had turned away from the settlements which they thought crowded and corrupt. This heroic spirit in Arrowsmith gave fire to his story. But the story itself was far from traditional. It was studied from the most contemporary facts, observed by Lewis himself or derived from the first-hand knowledge of Paul De Kruif, who accompanied Lewis on a cruise to the West Indies for material on tropical conditions. Arrowsmith is more than a simple hero of science. He is very much an individual, divided in will, specific in emotions, generous, charming, and irritating. Leora his first wife is the most convincing and affecting of all Lewis's women, and Gottlieb, Arrowsmith's great teacher, seems actually to be great. The book has memorable episodes, as diverse as the roaring burlesque of the Pickerbaugh campaigns and the pathetic death of Leora. Partly with the help of an admirable presentation on the screen, the story of Arrowsmith became one of the best known of modern American stories, known for its characters and incidents rather than for any such brilliant epithets as Main Street and Babbitt.

Between *Arrowsmith* and his next major novel Lewis published the slighter *Mantrap* (1926), its scene the Canadian woods which he had lately visited, and its satirical object a man blustering about his primitive virtues. Then came *Elmer Gantry* (1927) and controversy again. Gantry is a half-educated, vulgar clergyman who is as much a villain in his profession as Arrowsmith is a hero in his. American fiction had seldom been anti-clerical. When clergymen appeared in it they were likely to be gentle village pastors or robust circuit riders on the frontier or worried ministers with worldly congregations. But the iconoclastic H. L. Mencken, to whom *Elmer Gantry* was dedicated, had for years been pointing out that many settled clergymen were ignorant and intolerant, and that there had grown up a tribe of roving evangelists who were noisy and greedy and sometimes vicious. Lewis studied the type, and other kinds of clergymen, like an anthropologist doing field work. In his life-story of Gantry as student in a small denominational college, as traveling salesman, as manager and lover of a woman evangelist, as ordained minister first in the Baptist then in the Methodist church, driving ahead with unscrupulous ambition to larger and richer charges, Lewis presented his shoddy hero in a full knowledge of the details of such a life. Gantry is a bully, a sneak, a liar, a lecher, a drunkard, and an ignoramus. Lewis was accused of attacking religion, of implying that all clergymen are like Gantry. He was only telling the story of a false priest who himself committed the sins he scourged in others. The book was harsh because Lewis hated the falseness. Nothing decent in Gantry relieves his disgusting story. Without sympathy for him, Lewis gave him a character that was almost all caricature, with sensational and melodramatic coloring.

Again there was a minor book, The Man Who Knew Coolidge (1928), a series of monologues by a friend of Babbitt, a leaden treasury of the platitudes he considers to be his own opinions. But in Dodsworth (1929) Lewis was only incidentally satirical. Here more profoundly than in any of his novels he studied the ins and outs of a heart through a crucial chapter of a human life. Dodsworth is a Zenith magnate who retires from business. "He would certainly (so the observer assumed) produce excellent motor cars; but he would never love passionately, lose tragically, nor sit in contented idleness upon tropic shores." His story begins as if he were to be another Innocent Abroad, an American taking his humorous ease in Europe. Though Dodsworth values his own country, and often defends it against any kind of censure, he is no brash frontiersman like the Innocents of Mark Twain. That older kind of traveler had passed with the provincial republic of the mid-nineteenth century. But Dodsworth's travels are complicated by his wife, a pampered woman desperately holding on to her youth, fascinated by what seem to her the superior graces of European society, and susceptible to its men. In her bitter discontent she becomes a poisonous shrew, then deserts her husband for a lover. Long in love with her, and long used to cherishing her in spite of her temper, Dodsworth cannot break off either his affection or his sense of responsibility. She is in his blood. The history of his recovery is like a convalescence of a spirit, and it is told with feeling and insight. Externally Dodsworth is the essence of modern America on its grand tour, neither cocksure like Mark Twain's travelers in Europe, nor quivering and colonial like Henry James's. Himself simple, fair-minded, unhappy, he comes in contact with the more extravagant varieties of Americans abroad. The book is a gallery of expatriates. Without either the traditional comedy or the traditional nostalgia of American international novels, *Dodsworth* is a striking study in contrasts. Yet the essence of the book is almost pure drama. Made into a play by Sidney Howard it had a brilliant run on the stage and was equally effective on the screen. After ten years it was the general favorite among Lewis's novels.

In 1930 he was awarded the Nobel prize in literature, the first American who had received it. His speech of acceptance at Stockholm was a manifesto for the new literature in America, generously naming other writers who might have deserved the honor instead of him. Too few people in his "greatly beloved land," he said, "the most contradictory, the most depressing, the most stirring" country on earth, understood that the United States had "gone through the revolutionary change from rustic colony to world-empire." Too much of its literature was still parochial and timid. Too many of its readers—and writers—were "still afraid of any literature which is not a glorification . . . of our faults as well as our virtues." Its critics and professors of literature too often liked their literature "clear and cold and pure and very dead." But there were "strong young men" who without the support of public standards were "doing such passionate and authentic work that it makes me sick to see that I am a little too old to be one of them. . . . I salute them, with a joy in being not yet too far removed from their determination to give to the America that has mountains and endless prairies, enormous cities and lost far cabins, billions of money and tons of faith, to an America that is as strange as Russia and as complex as China, a literature worthy of her vastness."

It was four years after *Dodsworth*, and the collapse of 1929, before Lewis published another book at all, and six before he once more caught the ground swell of popular opinion. He worked on a novel which was to be about labor in the United States. He could not decide upon a plot. The American labor movement seemed to him to have no form. It was a chaos and tangle of politics full of the conflict of antagonisms which came from Europe. He decided to make his novel perfectly native, the story of three generations of American liberals: a circuit rider on the frontier, a sentimental, heroic socialist, a scientific social engineer. This, Lewis thought, would be his history of a hundred American years. He read a library of books. He drew a magnificent genealogical chart of the family of his first hero, Aaron Gadd. But the story would not take shape in his imagination. More than half of it must run its course in a world of which he could know nothing at first hand. He might by reading find out enough about it for a historian, but not enough for the kind of novelist he was. He gave up the whole enterprise. His *Ann Vickers* (1933) was a full-bodied story of a modern woman in her career, but not Lewis at his best, for the reason that he had not been long or intimately concerned with the material and was not saturated with it. The same defect appeared in *Work of Art* (1934), the story of a hotel-keeper and a procession of hotels.

Seismographic and articulate, Lewis had been more than any other American writer the voice of the liberal decade before 1929. He gave it nation-wide slogans, told it world-wide stories. The depression was confusion for him as well as for his countrymen. The first issue on which he was as clear as in *Main Street* or *Babbitt* was the imperative need of resisting anything like fascism in America. As the dark menace of Hitler rose over Europe it threw an ominous shadow across the Atlantic. All humane men were troubled and apprehensive, but most Americans comforted themselves with the thought that fascism could not reach beyond Europe. Lewis took a common statement for the title of *It Can't Happen Here* (1935). His novel was a prophetic account of what might happen if fascism came to America with the election of a fascist president in the election of 1936. This was only prophecy, which is almost always unsubstantial in fiction, and the details of his forecast seemed at many points copied unconvincingly from events in Nazi Germany. But the book was a tremendous pamphlet, in effect, against tyranny and cruelty, a passionate defense of all that was generous and tolerant in the American way of life. Lewis was taking no position that was novel in him. *Main Street* had been against fascism in the village, *Babbitt* against fascism in business, *Arrowsmith* against fascism in medicine, *Elmer Gantry* against fascism in the ministry. In *It Can't Happen Here* he focused his attention on a possible future in American politics. Countless readers to whom fascism was only a foreign word came to visualize the thing in a native form, ugly and deadly. Made into a play, the story had an unprecedented experience on the stage when the Federal Theater in 1936 produced it with twenty-one companies at the same time throughout the country. For the next three years Lewis devoted himself chiefly to writing for the stage, perhaps, as he believed, learning a new art, and certainly accumulating material for a novel about the theater.

He had become a classic figure in American fiction, and *Arrowsmith* and *Dodsworth* promised to be read by a long posterity. As to the rest of his work, it seemed likely to undergo the same process of selection by time as Mark Twain's had already undergone. The two men had much in common, though Lewis had a better disciplined mind than Mark Twain, and more outspoken courage. Both of them chose large subjects and treated them with high-spirited exuberance. They were fundamentally sensitive and serious, though comedy was for both a natural language. Neither of them excelled in representing women, and neither created memorable lovers, unless the quarreling Dodsworths can be called that. Lewis worked closer to his times than Mark Twain, and produced no such humorous cycle of remembered boyhood as *Tom Sawyer* and *Huckleberry Finn*. Nor did he venture into the past as Mark Twain did in *Joan of Arc* and the *Connecticut Yankee*. Lewis's chief work carried on the kind of examination of the present which Mark Twain began in his *Gilded Age* but did not continue. As this made Lewis the more controversial of the two, and perhaps the more temporary, it also involved him more deeply in living issues. The living issues of one age have a way of living on into another. There can be no question that his books are landmarks in the history of American opinions through two crucial decades. Yet when these opinions come to seem no longer so pressing, the characters who held them will still seem alive because they held them so passionately. The imagined city of Zenith will still have its firm place on the map of the American imagination, Babbitt in Zenith will run through his little year of discontent and turn back to a sorry grace. Arrowsmith, studying medicine at the university a few miles away, will find Leora in a Zenith hospital. Elmer Gantry will carry on his loud crusades in Zenith. Dodsworth, when his peace has been broken and healed in Europe, will think of Zenith as his home. Side by side with actual Middle Western cities, Zenith has appeared to be pure nature. But Zenith is art. When the actual cities have faded or changed, Zenith, with all its crude colors and satiric drawing, will stand up like a monument. A comic energy like Lewis's has a lasting as well as a compelling power.

{314}

XVIII

ROMANCE, COMEDY, SATIRE

1~James Branch Cabell

WHEN THE New York Society for the Suppression of Vice brought James Branch Cabell's *Jurgen: A Comedy of Justice* (1919) into court on the charge of obscenity, the charge was based on a statute of 1873 which had hardly been intended to cover such books but which in 1920 could be invoked by conservatives who disliked the new literature of the decade. Being legalistic, they held that the wit and beauty of *Jurgen* should not be accepted as an excuse for its violation of the statute. Books like persons should be equal before the law. Being moralistic, the conservatives believed that *Jurgen* was immoral, chiefly because it had broken with the nineteenth-century American tradition of reticence about the lighter and more comic aspects of love. Jurgen was an unabashed philanderer, and his story was told with insinuations but not with apologies. The book would have been tolerated, and enjoyed, in almost any century of literature, ancient or modern, except the Anglo-American nineteenth. It seems not to have occurred to the censors that this might imply some critical defect in that century's attitude. Instead, they took it for granted that the late century had been fundamentally right, and *Jurgen* was therefore a vicious book. But it was ardently supported by liberal opinion and the charges against it were dismissed. This meant, in effect, that American literature was freer than it had been before to disregard its provincial limitations and its moral obligation to keep young readers always in mind, and might deal maturely and humorously with any topics which might entertain the mature and humorous. It marked a striking revolution in American literary taste.

Cabell seemed a strange figure among the revolutionaries. Born in Virginia in 1879, he had been educated at William and Mary and had taught Greek and French there, had worked on newspapers in Richmond and New York, engaged in coal mining in West Virginia, and devoted much time to Virginia history and genealogy. His early stories, collected in *The Line of Love* (1905), *Gallantry* (1907), *Chivalry* (1909), *The Certain Hour* (1916), belonged on the surface to the contemporary fashion in historical romance. Most of them have romantic love for their theme, and deal with warriors or poets who at some high moment of valor or renunciation rise to meet it with heroic gestures and ironic language. The stories of *Chivalry* take place in the Middle Ages, those of *Gallantry* in the eighteenth century. The chivalrous heroes, as Cabell explained their code, think of themselves as vicars of God and His representatives in an alien country where they are expected to keep faith by living up to their high rank. The gallant heroes practise a more secular chivalry, but they too live up to a code which makes exacting demands on them. Cabell, though he saw both these codes as comedy, did not on account of that take less interest in the fine gestures of these heroes. Their sense of responsibility leads them to dramatic actions and poetic speech which he reproduced with a delighted if mannered skill in a smiling if formal idiom. In *The Line of Love* and *The Certain Hour* he ranged from the fourteenth century to the eighteenth, in several of the stories choosing episodes about which history is partly silent in the lives of its eminent men and women: a late meeting of Falstaff with a boyhood sweetheart, the forced decision of Villon to turn thief, the final interview of Marlowe with a girl he loves, the apocryphal courtship of Katherine of Valois and Henry V, the philosophical plagiarism of Shakespeare in writing *The Tempest*, the mysterious death of the poet Herrick, the marriage of Wycherley to the Countess of Drogheda and of Sheridan to the irresistible Miss Ogle. Most contemporary

(316)

romancers would have treated these stories in a manner more or less like Robert Louis Stevenson's. Cabell went back to something nearer Congreve's intelligent, insolent grace. The tales in Chivalry, and the longer tale published separately as The Soul of Melicent (1913), were ascribed to a fifteenth-century French romancer whom Cabell had invented, in smiling, scholarly detail.

In Cabell's early novels—The Eagle's Shadow (1905), The Cords of Vanity (1908), The Rivet in Grandfather's Neck (1915)—he told stories of modern life in the towns of Lichfield and Fairhaven, presumably in Virginia. Gallantry appears in the Cords in the series of trifling love affairs of the hero, a minor poet; and chivalry in the Rivet, in the character of a Virginia colonel who is also a genealogist given to the heroics of the chivalrous gentleman of the traditional South. But Cabell's first fully characteristic book was The Cream of the Jest (1917). Though Felix Kennaston lives in comfortable Lichfield much as its more representative citizens live, in the excursions of his imagination he continually visits the medieval country of Poictesme, thinking of himself as a troubadour named Horvendile. His two universes are not separated by any tight wall, but flow one into another by easy transitions. Horvendile may explain his conduct by saying he is a character in a story being written by Kennaston. Kennaston as Horvendile finds himself in a world which compensates and reassures him in intervals between dull stretches of life in Lichfield. He comes to feel most truly at home in Poictesme. This double scheme gave Cabell an opportunity for many comparisons of the realistic world with the logical, symmetrical, satisfying imagined one. He could be a poet and a critic at the same time. The Cream of the Jest, though it did not at first interest the public, quickly caught the attention of influential young writers who greeted Cabell as a colleague in the new literature.

Two years later he published not only Jurgen but also

(317)

Beyond Life, a system of critical ideas ascribed to John Charteris, of Lichfield, who is Cabell's mouthpiece. The most important aim for a writer, Charteris insists, is "to write perfectly of beautiful happenings." Romance may not be left out of literature, because romance is essential in life. Romance is "the first and loveliest daughter of human vanity," by which mankind is deceived, itself eagerly taking part in the deception, and thereby exalted. Only with the help of this persistent self-delusion has the human race been able to endure its actual sorry plight. As the first men rose from the apes by romantically believing they were fated to rise, so the last men will still play ape to their imaginings. Religion, love, art, patriotism, optimism, even common sense are all creations of the passionate human will to better human conditions. Writers of romance in their special way perform a general function when they enrich mankind by entertaining it with distinction and clarity, beauty and proportion, tenderness and truth and urbanity.

Jurgen: A Comedy of Justice was meant to be that kind of entertainment. Cabell pretended to be reconstructing the story of his hero, the famous scapegrace of Poictesme, from old legends. According to them, Jurgen at forty or so is magically permitted to have a year of youth and to move about the world with his old head on his young shoulders, an impish, inquiring Faust. Because his amorous adventures were narrated with fleshly double meanings quite new to American literature in 1919, they seemed to startled, excited, or horrified readers to make up a larger part of the book than they do. They are incidental to the history of Jurgen's search for justice—that is, poetic justice—anywhere in the universe. During his year he assumes the titles one after the other of duke, prince, king, emperor, and pope. As emperor he ventures into hell; as pope he ascends to heaven, where he impudently seats himself on the throne of God. He visits the court of Arthur, the land of Cocaigne, and the country of Pseudopolis which is at war with Philistia. These are the territories of romance, in which great deeds and emotions are supposed to be native. But Jurgen, with his cheeky shrewdness, finds nonsense behind many of the emotions and postures behind many of the deeds. Even in hell there are delusions: the witty devils who inhabit it are kept busy with the torments which men, in the pride of their sins, demand. Living men have been taught to believe in hell, and when they are dead the sinners will be satisfied with nothing else. Heaven, too, is a grand spectacle which the ruler of the universe has sympathetically copied from the human conception of it, so that Jurgen's grandmother will not have to be disappointed when she dies. At the end of his story Jurgen no longer desires to live further in the romantic world of youth. Now less chivalrous than he was, less sensual, and less insistent on perfection, he cannot live on the high plane of fantasies in which he does not believe. Experience nowhere supports the doctrine of poetic justice: that things must somehow turn out as men imagine and wish they would. Poetic justice is an illusion. Jurgen suspects he is a failure for not being able to keep his faith, but he cannot. He turns back from too much sugar to honest salt, and contentedly resumes his humdrum life as a pawnbroker.

The attack on *Jurgen* drew so much attention to Cabell that new editions of all his early books were called for. *The Soul of Melicent* reappeared as *Domnei* (1920). *Figures of Earth* (1921), *The High Place* (1923), *Straws and Prayer-Books* (1924), *The Silver Stallion* (1926), *Something About Eve* (1927) carried on and enlarged the chronicle of Poictesme. Poictesme—its name apparently combined from Poictiers and Angoulesme—became a country of romance which is as inclusive as Spenser's realm of Faerie but more systematic. Cabell evolved a geography, mythology, history, and literature for it, a dynasty, subjects, friends, enemies, a native folk-lore, and international relations. It has two great heroes: Manuel and Jurgen. "Dom Manuel is the Achilles of

Poictesme, as Jurgen is its Ulysses." Manuel, count and redeemer of the province, is also its prime ancestor. His successor Emmerick, Melicent in *Domnei*, Dorothy la Désirée in *Jurgen*, Ettare in *The Cream of the Jest* are Manuel's children by his wife Niafer. The line reaches, by way of Cabell's short stories, down through English and American descendants to Lichfield and Fairhaven. In his own lifetime Manuel is an artist who is forced to be a man of action. What seems to him his one great ambition is to mold out of clay, in the manner of the gods, figures (*Figures of Earth*) in his own image. Instead he must redeem Poictesme from its invaders, rule it, love various women, and keep up appearance. Of the figures he has created the one he most values is Sesphra, whose name is but Phrases respelled. Eventually this hero with the proud heart spends most of his days in the Room of Ageus, which is an anagram for Usage. His life is all appearances and compromises, and his descendants follow his lead through endless generations. But after Manuel's death, as the story is told in *The Silver Stallion*, the legend that grows up about him makes him out a triumphant hero and a salutary example. The hero that Manuel never was civilizes his violent province, which cherishes his memory and expects him to come back to it in glory. This, Cabell implies, is the history of all redemptions. What makes the legend grow is the passion of the human race to forget the past and overlook the present in a blind hope for the future. Manuel may have been barely great enough to hang a hope on. He survives because men desire him to, and, surviving, he becomes for them what they have shaped from the rude original. After they have imagined him, they rise to the level of their own imaginings. If redeemers owe a good deal to men, men cannot do without redeemers.

Jurgen has no such fortune. He does not practise the grand style himself or contribute to it in others. He sees through the Manuel legend, which Jurgen knows took its start from a fib he himself told as a child to get out of a whipping. That so much has come from so little amuses Jurgen. A true ironic poet enjoys the bubbles that he pricks, and may enjoy them so much he will not trouble to prick them. Of all the Cabell characters Jurgen has the most acute and agile mind. It enlightens wherever it touches. Even in *The High Place*, in which Jurgen appears only as the ancestor of Florian de Puysange, the spirit of Jurgen affects the descendant so late as the seventeenth century. Florian by a pact with another devil obtains the Sleeping Beauty in the Wood for his wife, and is soon bored by her, and deceived by her and a priest. Beauty and holiness, that is to say, connive to cheat Florian. Yet he will no doubt go on his cheerful, sinful way without too much distress, for the blood of Jurgen is in him. *The High Place* is the clearest and simplest of all Cabell's major books, a diabolistic fairy tale retold.

In *The Lineage of Lichfield* (1922) Cabell, carefully working out the line of descent that runs through his characters, announced that all his books taken together made up a Biography of Manuel, continuously reincarnated but in each new life playing essentially the old comedy. In his collected *Works* (1927-30) Cabell arranged his novels, tales, poems, plays, and essays in a new order, with the necessary revisions and transitions to round out the total scheme. Then in the final volume, *Townsend of Lichfield*, he closed the Biography. He had done what he set out to do, and at fifty he was content to say farewell to the finished enterprise. On the title-pages of his later books—*These Restless Heads* (1932), *Smirt* (1934), *Smith* (1935), *Smire* (1937)—he called himself only Branch Cabell, as if they were by another author. *Preface to the Past* (1936) was a volume of reminiscence and self-criticism.

His preface of farewell to the Biography was written in the summer of 1929, which was the end of an era. The shock and change that came with the depression cost Cabell the shining eminence he had enjoyed since *Jurgen*. In the hard thirties he was undervalued. The whole Biography, though its eighteen volumes with their humorous apparatus must long remain a delight for scholars with a sense of poetry and irony, was too elaborate to last with readers at large. To them Cabell's plots are likely to seem repetitious, his style luscious, his sly mystifications ponderous. But he created in Poictesme an extremely beautiful world which is also extremely realistic. The characters are not to be judged by their historic costumes or their romantic gestures. Their behavior is human behavior seen by an ironist who preferred to study them not in current daily life but in classical, universal guises. Though the mystifications in *Figures of Earth* and *The Silver Stallion* frequently cumber the narrative, this is less true in *Jurgen* or *The Cream of the Jest* and almost never in *The High Place*. These three promise to outlive all the others, the first place among them to be kept by *Jurgen*. It is the only book of its wicked, witty kind in English, nor is any comparable book—such for example as *Tristam Shandy*—more unmistakably a classic.

2~Lively Decade

The decade 1919-29 was the liveliest in the history of American fiction. The time was flushed with a prosperity which it was said had come to stay. Prohibition, bringing about the most wide-spread disregard for an unpopular law that the United States had ever seen, encouraged a general recklessness. Law-breakers were taken for heroes or comic figures. The critical attack on provincialism had as a rule a metropolitan bias. New York was more distinctly the literary capital than before, though so many writers lived or spent part of their years in France that Paris was almost a second center of American literature. While there were of course novels with regional settings and subjects, the fashion ran to topics and attitudes favored in cities. The blunter virtues were little celebrated, or domestic sentimentalism, or red blood adventures. Cynicism was preferred, or at least detachment, and even a sophistication which was soon nearly as standardized as the dullness it made fun of. Plain-speaking about love was taken for granted. Readers were expected to be reasonably familiar with a large world, both past and present, to be amused with all sorts of ideas, and to accept fantasy as readily as curt realism. Writers were expected to be usually brief, to show originality, grace, charm, or wit, and to write with skill, color, and spice. But no generalization can describe the fiction of the decade so well as a quick survey, year by year, of the typical—for the most part minor—novels and stories of the prevailing fashions.

In 1920, that year of so many novels so widely read, James Gibbons Huneker privately printed his *Painted Veils*, a candid record of the life of art in New York. The next year John Dos Passos in *Three Soldiers* represented the war in unheroic colors; Don Marquis in *The Old Soak* pleasantly ridiculed prohibition; Evelyn Scott in *The Narrow House* studied the raw nerves of an unhappy household; Donn Byrne in *Messer Marco Polo* told a gay romantic story of remote times and places; and Robert Nathan in *Autumn* produced a delicate native pastoral. In 1922 E. E. Cummings used devices of fiction in *The Enormous Room*, his brilliant story of life in a French military prison; Scott Fitzgerald's annual book was called *Tales of the Jazz Age*; Christopher Morley's *Where the Blue Begins* had for its hero a dog living like a man; Carl Van Vechten in *Peter Whiffle* wrote the informal biography of an imaginary American aesthete moving among actual people chiefly in Paris, Florence, and New York; Joseph Hergesheimer's *Cytherea* took a pair of middle-aged runaway lovers to tropical Havana; Waldo Frank's *Rahab* was sultry melodrama; Thomas Beer wrote gracefully about theatrical life in *The Fair Rewards*. In 1923 Beer with his *Stephen Crane* revived the memory of a genius who seemed suddenly contemporary again; Elinor Wylie turned from verse to prose with *Jennifer Lorn*; W. E. Woodward's *Bunk* brought the word debunk into currency; Ludwig Lewisohn in *Don Juan* undertook to naturalize and transvalue the legend in a modern story; Ben Hecht roved like a reporter through 1001 *Afternoons in Chicago*. This was the year also of Robert Nathan's *The Puppet Master*, Carl Van Vechten's *The Blind Bow-Boy*, Willa Cather's *A Lost Lady*, and Fannie Hurst's impassioned *Lummox*.

In 1924 Ring W. Lardner collected the best of his short stories in *How to Write Short Stories* (with *Samples*); Glenway Wescott in *The Apple of the Eye* wrote of rural Wisconsin with a sharp though comprehending exactness; Carl Van Vechten in *The Tattooed Countess* dealt with the dreary years of a heroine retired to a town in Iowa. In 1925 John Erskine humorously reworked a Greek theme in *The Private Life of Helen of Troy*, and Robert Nathan reinterpreted a Biblical character in *Jonah*; Scott Fitzgerald's *The Great Gatsby* had a bootlegger for a hero, and DuBose Heyward's *Porgy* was concerned with the Negro underworld of Charleston; Lardner's *What of It?* was made up of miscellaneous pieces of his fantastic satiric humor; Elinor Wylie's *The Venetian Glass Nephew* had a hero made, and a heroine made over, to order; Thornton Wilder's *The Cabala* was about the social plots of an inner circle in Rome; Gertrude Stein published in Paris her vast cadenced interlocking saga *The Making of Americans*; William Carlos Williams retold stories from the American tradition in the pungent vernacular of *In the American Grain*. In 1926 Ernest Hemingway, suddenly famous that year for *The Sun Also Rises*, about the alcoholic expatriates in Paris, parodied various contemporaries, particularly Sherwood Anderson, in *The Torrents of Spring*; Floyd Dell in *Love in Greenwich Village* celebrated the Bohemian quarter in New York which had become famous throughout America; John Erskine chose a medieval story to retell in

Galahad; Elinor Wylie brought Shelley (as Shiloh) to America in *The Orphan Angel;* Carl Van Vechten revealed a romantic Harlem in *Nigger Heaven,* and Elizabeth Madox Roberts a new poetic Kentucky in *The Time of Man;* Thorne Smith in *Topper* made ghosts his gayest characters. In 1927 Wilder's *The Bridge of San Luis Rey* was read by everybody; Edwin Arlington Robinson's blank-verse *Tristram* was as popular as a novel; Conrad Aiken in *Blue Voyage* employed the method of the stream of consciousness or interior monologue, already attempted by several experimenters; Wescott built up a larger Wisconsin in the family cycle *The Grandmothers.*

In 1928 came Stephen Vincent Benét's verse narrative of the Civil War, *John Brown's Body;* Elinor Wylie in *Mr. Hodge and Mr. Hazard* created a character that was partly Shelley and partly herself; Roark Bradford turned Old Testament stories into Negro folk-lore in *Old Man Adam and His Chillun,* later translated to the stage by Marc Connelly in *The Green Pastures* (1930); in Nathan's *The Bishop's Wife* the bishop had a visiting angel for an archdeacon; Erskine went again to Greece for a subject for *Penelope's Man.* The catastrophic year 1929, when Cabell closed his biography of Manuel, saw a literary decade fading. Elinor Wylie had died, Van Vechten was ready to give up fiction. James Thurber and E. B. White satirized an overworked topic in *Is Sex Necessary?* The brash comedy of Thorne Smith's *The Stray Lamb* was little noted in a year resounding with Hemingway's *A Farewell to Arms,* Evelyn Scott's *The Wave,* William Faulkner's *The Sound and the Fury,* Thomas Wolfe's *Look Homeward, Angel.* The lively decade settled into history, and new opinions came to be held about it.

Joseph Hergesheimer (1880-   ) during the early years of his reputation was often ranked with Cabell, since they were friends and both favored romantic modes. But whereas Cabell was chiefly interested in the behavior of his characters,

Hergesheimer was chiefly interested in the costumes of his. He might excellently reconstruct in *The Three Black Pennys* (1917) three generations of iron-making in his native Pennsylvania, or in *Java Head* (1919) the Salem of the days of clipper ships, or in *Linda Condon* (1920) a world of fashionable hotels and houses. Yet in all these the decoration is likely to be more striking and seem more important than the people or the story. There is a somewhat uniform scheme of contrasts. Ludowika Winscombe, who has always lived at courts, brings exotic graces to the Penny forge in the Pennsylvania forest. Taou Yuen, the Manchu wife of a Yankee skipper, by the bewildering complexity of her costumes and her intricate ceremonial observances makes Salem, which before her had seemed formal enough, after that seem crude and raw. Linda Condon, as lovely as a lyric and as untouchable as a star, moves through tawdry and then correct surroundings, cool herself though the cause of love in others. While now and then genuine feelings and situations emerge, there is not much movement, and the total effect of the stories is rather that of pictures than of dramas. *Cytherea*, two years after *Linda Condon*, was a confusion of unhappy passion and unconvincing symbolism. In his later books Hergesheimer carried his studies of costume and decoration to Cuba, Virginia, Kentucky, and various American cities, but he no longer wrote so richly or so firmly as in his three best novels.

F. Scott Fitzgerald was only twenty-four when he published his first book *This Side of Paradise* (1920). Princeton and the war had separated him from his native Minnesota, and he seemed the voice in fiction of post-war youth, disillusioned and questioning. He wrote of his gilded boys and girls as if traditional decorum existed chiefly to be shocked. There was scandal in his story, to scandalize conservatives who debated whether the new youth was as daring in its behavior as he made out. But all his undergraduates were poets and philosophers, sparkling with challenges. They asked why they should follow the advice of their elders who had let the world fall into chaos. Laughter and liquor and love were more tempting than that hollow wisdom, and might be more solid. *This Side of Paradise* came to no conclusion and ended in weariness and smoke. But it was a document of a whirling time, a beguiling entertainment. The narrative may rise suddenly to delightful verse or glittering comic dialogue. It shifts from passion to farce, from satire to beauty, from impudent knowingness to pathetic young humility. The bright barbarians break the patterns which once might have governed them. And as they play among the ruins of the old they reason randomly about the new, laughing. Fitzgerald set a whole fashion for what was called the Younger Generation, in his stories *Flappers and Philosophers* (1920), *The Beautiful and Damned* (1921), *Tales of the Jazz Age* (1922). And though he so gave himself to the fashion that he passed with it, he wrote in *The Great Gatsby* (1925) a short realistic novel about a romantic bootlegger that remains one of the brilliant books of a brilliant decade.

The novels of Elinor Wylie (1885-1928), better known for her poems, are unsurpassed in modern literature for precise elegance and amused formality of language, structure, and ideas. Descended from New England stock, brought up in Philadelphia and Washington, at home in London and Paris, she had already much experience and even more reading when she wrote *Jennifer Lorn* (1923), which she called "a sedate extravaganza." She laid the action in the eighteenth century not only because she knew that age so well but also because its familiar combination of stiff manners and flexible intellect was delightful to her own temper. With bright, amazing erudition she took her heroine and her husband Gerald Poynyard through England and France, around Good Hope, to India and Persia. Exquisitely picturesque, the book is exquisitely graceful and witty. Gerald, the conquering, opinionated Anglo-Saxon male, is the chief object of the satire, which leaves out

(327)

nothing that any woman has ever thought of such a man. But the satire touches also, with fine-spun ridicule, every kind of human pretense or affectation. In *The Venetian Glass Nephew* (1925), which Elinor Wylie called a moral fairy tale, the object of her satire was an unequal marriage. Her hero Virginio has, so the story says, been made out of glass because the cardinal has no nephew of flesh and blood. But Virginio is married to Rosalba, who has been born not made. Here is a fable of the marriage of art and nature, specifically Christian art and Pagan nature. If this were a mere romantic plot, the ending might be happier and simpler, with the boy of art adapting himself to the girl of nature. Realism like Elinor Wylie's is sadder if truer. Virginio cannot change. In this conflict between art and nature it is nature that must yield. Rosalba, despairing, takes the advice of Casanova, who knows there can be no compromise, only one conclusion, if the pair are to go on being married. Rosalba enters a furnace at Sèvres and comes out porcelain, still the same in color and design but with no troubling instincts of her own. At last she is the right bride for a Virginio. Such a conflict might be dealt with, and has been dealt with, in countless ways by story-tellers. Elinor Wylie's way was to make it into a fairy tale and to bring it to this ironical, oblique solution.

If she ridiculed the hero of *The Orphan Angel* (1926)—called *Mortal Image* in England—it was very gently, for Shiloh was another name for Shelley, whom Elinor Wylie loved above all other men. Suppose, she thought, that drowned, disfigured body found in the Gulf of Spezia had not been Shelley's. Suppose Shelley had actually been picked up by a Yankee ship and brought to America. Her imagination raced at the thought, and she set out to write the history of his adventures across the shaggy continent. With ardent researches she made herself familiar with the roads and rivers, the mountains and prairies, the cities and settlements of 1822. She studied that year in America as if it were her house which Shelley was to visit. The interior and the frontier were more remote from her experience and habits than anything she had written about. She became more formal and fantastic the further west she went with Shiloh, most of all in her account of the white girl Anne living among the Comanches. To Elinor Wylie these western passages seemed partly burlesque, but her intention did not always appear, and to many readers they seemed long if not, for her, flat. Her account of Shelley's mind and character is the most perceptive ever written. She saw the comedy in the life of a man who was a kind of tenderfoot of the world, but she felt no less affection for him because he was sometimes absurd. She knew him as she knew herself. In *Mr. Hodge and Mr. Hazard* (1928) Hazard, though he is not altogether Shelley, comes back to England in 1833 much as Shelley might have come if he had lived, much as Elinor Wylie, though neither was she altogether the model for Hazard, had come back in 1925 after ten years' absence. The book, she said, was "an everyday fable; its historical trappings are slight, and it must remain not a disguised biography but a brief symbolic romance of the mind." It is simply a dramatic clash between a man of imagination like Hazard and a heavy-witted man like Hodge. Outwardly Hodge seems to win, but Hazard has his quiet, pleasant, private revenge.

Each of the four novels continues to have its special partisans on various accounts: *Jennifer Lorn* for its shining extravagance, *The Venetian Glass Nephew* for its precise satiric idea, *The Orphan Angel*—perhaps the least favored of the four—for its version of Shelley in a new world, *Mr. Hodge and Mr. Hazard* for its freedom from fantastic elements and its concentration on credible if subtle human experiences. All of them have been condemned for their brittle style, their elusive attitude, their limited range of interests: that is, for their failure to present life on the broad scale of major novels. They are minor novels. But they are also masterpieces, do

(329)

almost perfectly what they aim to do, and with their enameled surfaces suffer little from the nibbling teeth of time.

Of the two characteristic novelists of the decade who may be mentioned with Elinor Wylie, neither matched her in power of mind or delicacy of art. Thornton Wilder (1897-   ) scrupulously avoided anything like a formula in his themes. After *The Cabala* (1925), with its apparent revelations of gossip and intrigue in modern Rome, he turned to Peru for his setting in *The Bridge of San Luis Rey* (1927). The time is 1714, the central incident the fall of a bridge on the road from Lima to Cuzco. The book pretends to be based on the researches of a contemporary Franciscan who passionately investigated the lives of the victims, to find out if the act of God had been what men could call just. About this perennial problem Wilder told his own stories of the five very different persons who died that day. The Franciscan is burned as a heretic, and Wilder comes, inevitably, to no satisfying conclusion. But his presentation of the ancient vexed argument excited an immense number of readers, his characters live with a gentle freshness, and his book established a little legend. *The Woman of Andros* (1930) went back to Terence's *Andria* for its story; Wilder transformed the original into a beautiful novel full of universal implications. In *Heaven's My Destination* (1935) he took for his hero a traveling salesman who is also an evangelist in the current Middle West and has endless comic adventures. Thereafter Wilder was chiefly interested in the stage, on which his *Our Town* (1939) had both popular and critical success.

Robert Nathan (1894-   ) evolved a form of brief novel which he made his own and which admirably fitted his mild, humane, disillusioned temper. In *Autumn* (1921), *The Puppet Master* (1923), *The Fiddler in Barly* (1926), *The Woodcutter's House* (1927) he laid his scenes in a pastoral or nursery world of kind old men and women, young lovers,

children, puppets, and knowing talking animals. *Jonah* (1925),
telling the story of a single prophet, had much to say about
all prophets, or poets, and their fortunes. In *The Bishop's
Wife* (1928), *There Is Another Heaven* (1929), *The Orchid*
(1931), *One More Spring* (1933) the scene was commonly
the New York of cathedrals, theaters, parks, clergymen,
scholars, artists, and their restless women and agreeable children. Nathan was here as quiet and pellucid as in his pastorals, though his satire came nearer being topical. *One More
Spring*, in which a group of philosophical unfortunates live
in Central Park because they have no place else to go, was a
touching idyl of the depression in its worst year. *Road of
Ages* (1935) imagined all the Jews of Europe, driven from
home, moving in a desperate migration back to Asia. The
doctrinaire critics in the thirties who abused Wilder for not
dealing with what they considered real life, also abused
Nathan. But he had created a charming world and charm-
ingly peopled it, and his little world would lightly outlast,
like the Grimms' or Andersen's, most of the critical controversies.

Criticism regularly overlooked Thorne Smith (1892-1934)
though he had a distinctive talent and an engaging vein. His
novels were all farce and fantasy, perpetual gay adventures
in a fluid universe. In *Topper* (1926) and *Topper Takes a
Trip* (1932) several of the characters, including a dog, are
disreputable, delightful ghosts who appear and disappear in
the story as they like. The hero of *The Stray Lamb* (1929) is
changed with Ovidian facility into a horse or any other convenient animal. Statues from a museum come alive in *The
Night Life of the Gods* (1931) and magnificently enjoy themselves in Manhattan. In *Turnabout* (1931) a husband bears a
child while his wife supports him. In *The Bishop's Jaegers*
(1932) the chance-met passengers on a lost ferry boat find a
bewildering haven in a nudist colony. Anything can happen,
almost everything does. Thorne Smith's favorite hero is a

(331)

man who, settled largely by chance in a dull life, discovers that he has a capacity for pleasure and at once finds opportunities swarming round him. Most of the courting in the stories is done by women, swift, witty, irrepressible daughters of nature who regard men as slow-going creatures that need to be civilized by laughter and love. The books have no problems and no penalties, since the plots are cheerfully irresponsible. They would be shocking if they were not so funny. Though the world Thorne Smith created is not in the least real, it is not remote in time or place. With an instinct for nonsense he took the smart life of his own day and let it run wild and free in his novels.

After 1929 Van Vechten ceased to write about his perverse dilettantes in New York, but Erskine continued his humorous modernizations of heroic stories: *Tristan and Isolde* (1932), *The Brief Hour of François Villon* (1937). Lardner, who called his autobiography *The Story of a Wonder Man* (1927), wrote no novels, but he collected his short stories in *Round Up* (1932) and until his death in 1933 practised the sardonic art which gives him his special place in American humor. He had begun his work as a writer about sports. Damon Runyon, trained in the same school, turned to short stories in *Guys and Dolls* (1932), in that and later collections celebrating the New York underworld, its tough sentimentalists, and its grammarless lingo. In 1929 W. R. Burnett made a stir with *Little Cæsar*, which set a new fashion, at once romantic and tough, for novels dealing with gangsters. The thirties saw toughness by itself developed into a standard fashion, which reached what may be called its high point in James M. Cain's *The Postman Always Rings Twice* (1934). Even the detective story, seldom much touched by literary modes, felt the new influence. The most popular detectives in the fiction of the twenties had been the philosophical Charlie Chan of Earl Derr Biggers, and the posing connoisseur Philo Vance of Willard Huntington Wright (S. S. Van Dine). The most striking detectives of the thirties were the tough agents of Dashiell Hammett, whose *The Glass Key* (1931) and *The Thin Man* (1934) must be named in any history of the American novel. But the decade was not always tough. Mark Van Doren's *The Transients* (1934) told with simple, subtle originality a story of two Olympian visitors in New England. Charles G. Finney in *The Circus of Dr. Lao* (1935) heightened satire with wild fantasy. George Santayana in *The Last Puritan* (1936) brought his long philosophical observations to bear ironically on an American type. Lawrence Edward Watkins in *On Borrowed Time* (1937) made a novel out of a folktale of Death and an apple tree. John P. Marquand, inventor elsewhere of the picturesque detective Mr. Moto, satirized traditional, conventional New England in *The Late George Apley* (1937) and *Wickford Point* (1939).

XIX

NEW REALISMS

1~Post-War

THE CRITICAL decade which followed the World War saw, in the United States as in other countries, many novelists bent on showing how unheroic the conflict had been, how cruel, wasteful, stupid. The most popular American war play, *What Price Glory* (1924) by Maxwell Anderson and Laurence Stallings, exhibited its marines as cheerful rowdies rather than crusaders, and created in the wrangling Flagg and Quirt the best known characters of American fiction surviving from the war. The war novels were likely to be less boisterous, more reflective. After Upton Sinclair's 100% (1920), with its ironical arraignment of war-time civilians, came John Dos Passos's *Three Soldiers* (1921), with its hard account of the effect of the army on the enlisted men; and E. E. Cumming's *The Enormous Room* (1922), which though not a novel has been read largely as one, with its biting narrative of unjust imprisonment in France. *The Enormous Room* is the most brilliant, permanent, and important of all these, but it was the work of a poet who wrote nothing else of anything like its kind. *Three Soldiers* established a new novelist in a distinctive career.

John Dos Passos (1896-   ), born in Chicago of a Portuguese-American father and a Virginia mother, went from Harvard at twenty to study in Spain but, like Cummings, joined an ambulance service in France and saw war at first hand. His *One Man's Initiation* (1919) was a semi-autobiographical story of a young dilettante who drives an ambulance and admires cathedrals. *Three Soldiers* took another dilettante, this time a musician, through his war experiences,

(334)

and with him two average Americans who share his discontent. One of them begins by being ambitious for promotion, but rises no higher than an army kitchen. Another, a mild farm boy, murders an officer who has bullied him. The musician, permitted after the armistice to study in Paris, is so resentful because his final discharge is slow in coming that he deserts and at the end faces a long term in prison. These three soldiers were not typical of the army at large, many shocked readers insisted. Dos Passos held that his story was as true as the romantic versions of the war, with their happy warriors all bravely aware that they were saving democracy. If such instances as he had chosen to present were special, such moods were not. Soldiers were not all heroes, and those who set out to be had a good chance to be disillusioned. John Andrews, the musician and chief figure in *Three Soldiers*, has come from Harvard to the war expecting that he will find peace for his troubled mind in a large, generous cause. Instead he finds slavery and boredom. Like Carol Kennicott, in *Main Street* the year before, Andrews rebels against dullness and pettiness, aimlessness and cruelty. His own impulses are vague: he desires a perfect freedom in which he can compose a symphony on the Queen of Sheba. Once the war is over, and he is free to work in Paris, there is every reason why he should put up a little longer with the minor annoyance of being still technically a soldier. His desertion seems a heedless folly. But he has reached his limit of irritation and thinks he can endure no more. He rebels with a desperate gesture. It was a gesture with which Dos Passos and his decade could sympathize. They resented officers and officials, routine and red tape. The sympathy in *Three Soldiers* lies with the common men, whether they are heroic or not, who do the plain work of the war.

Rosinante to the Road Again (1922) was a book of Spanish travel, *A Pushcart at the Curb* (1922) a volume of verse, *Streets of Night* (1923) another novel about dilettantes. But

(335)

in *Manhattan Transfer* (1925) Dos Passos returned to the narrative method of *Three Soldiers*, applied this time to a metropolis. The narrative is not a continuous story but a flashing procession of incidents in which particular characters often recur, though with only occasional connection. It is several stories, arranged in the hit-or-miss of city life, as if several films had been cut into irregular lengths and all the parts joined together in a jumbled continuity. Some readers were mystified by the sharp impressionism of the style, others repelled by the novel's candor about the hidden lives of its characters. Dos Passos wrote like a newspaper reporter who had gone behind the headlines and had turned the inside of many lives to the light. He moved with ease and knowledge through various social groups, but with special attention to the drifting, rootless people who make up so large a part of New York. The city as a whole might elude him, as it has eluded all novelists, but the parts he touched come in *Manhattan Transfer* to a vast sprawling life.

In the final chapter the poet Jimmy Herf, as much a hero as the book has, leaves New York in disgust to go on an uncertain hunt for reality and freedom elsewhere. Dos Passos had lost interest in the plight of his artists—architect, musician, poet—in the harsh world and grown increasingly concerned with all the victims of the troubled times. In the midst of a flushed prosperity there were fierce industrial wars—strikes—and fierce arguments. The Russian revolution affected American opinion as the French revolution had done in the first decade of the republic. Communists in America looked forward to an international revolution. Dos Passos, who had earlier made the journey to the Near East about which he wrote in his luminous *Orient Express* (1927), went to Russia, Mexico, and Spain to observe the struggles about which he collected his graphic reports in *In All Countries* (1934). He studied the conflicts at home, the trial of Sacco and Vanzetti about whom he wrote his haunting pamphlet *Facing the*

Chair (1927), the various centers of American unrest. Never doctrinaire, Dos Passos belonged to no strict party but preferred, as an old-fashioned believer in liberty, equality, fraternity, he said, to assemble critical documents on the age. His experimental dramas, collected in *Three Plays* (1934), had no success on the stage. After 1929 he gave himself for the most part to his trilogy, published separately as *The 42nd Parallel* (1930), *1919* (or *Nineteen-Nineteen*, 1932), *The Big Money* (1936), and together as *U. S. A.* (1938). His later and slighter *Adventures of a Young Man* (1939) was a topical history of an American radical who finds he is not a European revolutionary.

U. S. A. is a group of life-stories, of six men and six women, sometimes running remotely parallel and sometimes touching or crossing. The time is the first thirty years of the century, and the place the whole United States with parts of Mexico and France. Except when the war draws most of the characters into war activities they go their own ways. Mac, born in Connecticut, learns the printing trade in Chicago, wanders to the Northwest, then south to revolutionary Mexico, and opens a bookstore. J. Ward Moorehouse, born in Delaware, marries one heiress in Philadelphia and another in Pittsburgh, and builds a pretentious career as a public relations counsel in New York. Charley Anderson of North Dakota, a mechanic who becomes an aviator in the war, returns to be a hero, a financier, and a failure in Detroit. Margo Dowling, brought up in American vaudeville, marries a Cuban, runs away from Havana, and rises through calculating adventures in Manhattan and Florida to stardom in Hollywood. Though Dos Passos presumably regarded these and the other characters as typical, he presented them as individuals. Their stories do not fall into the accepted patterns of American fiction, and seem to be dramatic biographies of actual persons. Though his sympathies were strongly on the side of the underprivileged, the neglected, the injured and insulted, he told his stories in a level tone which does not always avoid monotony. But the monotony is systematically broken by a series—or rather, three series—of experimental devices which run through the book. One is a set of vivid, irregular, brief sketches of contemporary worthies who among them exhibit almost every phase of modern America. Another series is called Newsreel and is made up of a torrent of headlines, news items, popular songs and sayings which sweep the country like an inquisitive searchlight. The third series, The Camera Eye, gives a sort of inner autobiography of Dos Passos, of his mind and heart from early childhood to the Sacco-Vanzetti trial: his own comment and his indication of his point of view. These experimental devices interrupt the broad stream of narrative, but they no less lift and enliven it. *U. S. A.* is a collective novel by a novelist who could not write always with dispassion but must now and then escape into irony or rise to poetry.

Since the days of Franklin, more at home in Paris than in London or perhaps even in Philadelphia, Paris had been the favorite city of traveling Americans. The World War, taking thousands to Paris who would otherwise never have seen it, enlarged its charming reputation. The fall in the exchange value of the franc made it possible for Americans to live in post-war France in a comfort and freedom which would have been impossible on their dollar incomes in the United States. Among them, for shorter or longer periods, were most of the young American writers, who in obscure studios or famous cafés on the Left Bank carried on endless literary discussions which led to countless literary experiments. Some of them fell in with Continental modes, and more of them were affected by the overpowering example of James Joyce's *Ulysses* (1922). But as time went on it became increasingly clear that America had a tradition and an idiom of its own, and that American writers could not sound European even if they tried to. Gertrude Stein (1874-   ), though she had been settled in Paris since long before the war, was as obstinately American as Fenimore Cooper had been. Born in Pennsylvania, student of William James at Radcliffe and later student in medicine at Johns Hopkins, she had in her *Three Lives* (1909) written with forward-looking if neglected realism about the inner lives of simple women. The longest and best of the stories—*Melanctha*—was in effect a short novel rich in understanding and sympathy, narrated in prose that had fluid movement and vernacular cadence. Before the publication of *Three Lives* Gertrude Stein had begun what was to be the complete history of a complete American family: *The Making of Americans*, not printed in Paris till 1925 and not published in America (in a shorter version) till 1934. Often praised, this huge novel has seldom been read, nor will it ever be except by enthusiasts who tolerate its tedious, mannered repetitions because of the pleasure they take in the delicate and intricate variety of its sentences. Gertrude Stein's importance, so far as literature was concerned, lay less in her actual writings than in her reforming influence on the tones and cadences of prose. From her practice as well as from her singular discourses *How to Write* (1931) and *Narration* (1936) it appears that words for her had qualities—color and sound—besides their meaning, and sentences had—or ought to have—something like what in music would be called a tune. When she herself wrote obscurely it was because she undertook to do with mere color and sound more than words can do, as if she were humming lovely or witty tunes without pronouncing the words. She did not fall into any ornate or precious classicism. Instead, she evolved her linked, symmetrical, diversified cadences from familiar American speech, much as Mark Twain had done in his tall tales and in *Huckleberry Finn*. Throughout the expatriate decade, and before, she was a living force in Paris. In the United States she was a legend, most widely read in *The Autobiography of Alice B. Toklas* (1933)—actually by Gertrude Stein and chiefly about her. Of her numerous briefer writings only *Four Saints in Three Acts* (1934), made into a beguiling if mystifying opera with music by Virgil Thomson, was widely heard of.

Sherwood Anderson in Chicago, reading her eccentric *Tender Buttons* (1914), had at once become intensely conscious of what he called the perfume of words. Ernest Hemingway (1898-), living in Paris, frequented her house, brought her his early stories for her criticism, and found her, he thought, always right. Unlike the other young post-war writers—Dos Passos, Cummings, Stallings, Scott Fitzgerald—Hemingway had had little academic training. Born near Chicago, he left school to be a reporter in Kansas City, served and was wounded on the Italian front, and in 1921 became European correspondent of a Canadian newspaper. The earliest short story he preserved was written that year. By 1925 he had enough short stories to make up a volume called *In Our Time*. Half of them had their scenes laid among the Michigan woods and lakes where Hemingway had spent boyhood summers, half in post-war Europe, with a series of intervening episodes, unrelated but called Chapter I-XV; brutal miniatures of war and death. Nick Adams, the young American who appears in several of the stories, may be wounded in battle, but he does not feel the pains of disillusionment, like most of the heroes in war stories. He has seen suffering and cruelty in Michigan which prepare him for the hard world he takes for granted. He fights when he must, enjoys hunting and fishing, feels contempt for soft and silly people, and lives according to a gruff stoic code. Hemingway told naked stories in a naked language, which was the same—curt, crisp, fresh—whatever his subject might be. His stories seem to be nothing but facts, set one after another without comment. Every fact makes its point and takes another step in the narrative. There are no superfluous words, no visible rhetoric. But the style of *In Our Time* is not so simple as it looks. The blunt sentences are delicately varied in structure, with the cadences—like Mark Twain's—of familiar speech not of conventional written prose.

If Hemingway had learned about style and cadence from Gertrude Stein, he had none of her obscurity and he used none of her materials. If he had for a time studied Sherwood Anderson, Hemingway went quickly beyond him in precision and form. These naked stories in naked language were something new in English, and they were distinctly Hemingway's.

As if to signalize his independence he wrote *The Torrents of Spring* (1926), an unhappy parody of Anderson and various American contemporaries. *The Sun Also Rises*, published the same year, was better proof of Hemingway's talent. For his motto he took a remark of Gertrude Stein about post-war youth: "You are all a lost generation." His characters are a group of disillusioned, dissolute Americans, with their English friends, drifting about in Paris in a search for a felicity they have never had. Most of them do not work for a living, none of them has any genuine ambition. Accepting their status as lost souls, they get some glory from it. It is romantic to be damned. They drink continually, love promiscuously. Two-thirds of the book are taken up with an expedition to Spain to see bullfights at Pamplona. These bloody spectacles have so much death in them that they touch fundamental nerves, and so much art that they hold and fix the most wandering attention. The decadent visitors from Paris can feel fully alive while they watch animals dying and men in danger of it. The wounds in the ring are hardly more horrible than the things the lost souls say to each other in their quarrels and loves. Paris is their jungle. Hemingway reproduced the Paris of the expatriates with exact detail and introduced characters so much like well known figures that he seemed to be writing directly from the life. He had a terse, cold magic in his story-telling that made Scott Fitzgerald seem flimsy in comparison, Dos Passos loose-gaited. Hemingway and his desperate universe came suddenly into fashion. *The Sun Also Rises*, its title taken from Ecclesiastes, was the decade's way of saying that all is vanity.

(341)

In *Men Without Women* (1927), a second collection of short stories, Hemingway extended his jungle researches to the underworld of the prize ring in *Fifty Grand*, about a fighter who takes money to lose a fight, and *The Killers*, about gunmen hunting for another fighter who has done the same thing. An *Alpine Idyll* is an episode of peasant animalism, *Hills Like White Elephants* an episode of civilized cruelty. In *The Undefeated* an aging bullfighter keeps his self-respect by his loyalty to his craft and his pride in it. All these stories are tense incidents, remembered rather for the things that happen than for the persons they happen to. As if in answer to critics who preferred his short stories to *The Sun Also Rises*, Hemingway wrote another novel, *A Farewell to Arms* (1929), which has been commonly thought his masterpiece. His account of the Italian retreat after Caporetto is his most powerful sustained narrative. The story of the American hero's love for an English nurse, who dies in childbirth, is Hemingway's most moving love story. He looked upon them as a war-time Romeo and Juliet, separated by a malign feud into which they had been fatally born. More humane than any of his earlier stories, this was more popular, and in the year of *Dodsworth* many readers thought that with *Farewell to Arms* Hemingway had succeeded Sinclair Lewis as the first among contemporary American novelists.

It was eight years before Hemingway published another novel. He had come to seem a kind of hero himself, more or less identified with the recurrent hero of his short stories and his novels, who was essentially the same man in slightly differing disguises. Hemingway swaggered through *Death in the Afternoon* (1932), a spectacular history and handbook of bullfighting, and *Green Hills of Africa* (1935), in which he often interrupted his sportsman's narrative with arguments in favor of a strutting individualism. The arguments were generally infantile in themselves and they sounded melodramatically remote from the urgent problems of the depression.

Winner Take Nothing (1933) contained some very expert and revealing short stories, To Have and Have Not (1937) was a sensational and inferior novel. The civil war in Spain drew Hemingway from his detachment, and he went to help the loyalists. His play The Fifth Colum.1, written in 1937, was concerned with rebel espionage and loyalist counter-espionage in Madrid. He had quarreled with Dos Passos over the execution of rebel prisoners; the play presented his ruthless side of the controversy as against the liberal side taken by Dos Passos in his Adventures of a Young Man. In the same collection with the play Hemingway brought all his short stories together with the title The Fifth Column and the First Forty-Nine Stories (1938). Four of these stories were new. The Short Happy Life of Francis Macomber had too much of Hemingway's vulgar virility in it, The Snows of Kilimanjaro an effective touch of fantasy. The Old Man at the Bridge was a naked incident of the Spanish war which showed Hemingway at his best. Taken all together, the collected stories were proof that no American writer had ever equaled him in writing of savage materials with finished art.

2~Thomas Wolfe

Thomas Wolfe (1900-38), sixteen when the United States joined the Allies, felt the conflict only at a magnifying distance, though he was shocked by brutalities he saw at camp in Virginia and later wrote about in a sketch called The Face of the War. In Europe several times during the expatriate decade, he had no impulse to be an expatriate himself. His novels, begun in London or planned in Paris, rose out of his longing for America. He might be affected by Ulysses, but when he came to write he was nearer Whitman. Born in North Carolina, of a Pennsylvania father and a mother of Carolina mountain stock, Wolfe went to the state university, then to Harvard to study playwriting, and for six years (1924-30) taught at New York University. For this simple academic career he was hardly more fitted than Paul Bunyan would have been. A full head taller than ordinary men, Wolfe with his enormous appetites was immensely sensitive. As a boy, he wrote in *Gulliver*, he was agonizingly ashamed of his size, hating the accident of birth which had housed "a spirit fierce and proud and swift as flight, and burning as a flame, in such a grotesque tenement." Before his first book and afterwards he lived and worked in a tremendous solitude, broken in New York or wherever he was by long hours of hungry wandering through the streets, chiefly at night. In the autobiographical sketches in *From Death to Morning* (1935), as in his novels, are numerous street scenes—preposterous or terrible—which he had witnessed. No doubt they often grew in his handling to dimensions which other witnesses would not have perceived. He created always in his own large image.

His whole work was a history of his gigantic desires and desperate frustrations. In the Middle South he had looked forward to impossible great triumphs and satisfactions in Manhattan. But when he had written plays he could not get them on the stage. There was, he found, no magic door to open and let him into the glorious world he had imagined. Nor was Paris or London more hospitable than New York. In the fall of 1926 he began his homesick novel *Look Homeward, Angel* (1929) in London, as if needing to recapture the bitter, wild splendors of his first twenty years. In time he came to resent the common assumption that the book was almost pure autobiography. "I can truthfully say that I do not believe that there is a single page of it that is true to fact." Yet he had been so true to the customary life of his native Asheville (called Altamont in the novel) that the town angrily recognized itself; and he had drawn the Gant and Pentland families of the novel from actual Wolfes and Westalls. *Look Homeward, Angel* is a family chronicle, ranging wide enough to include all the kinsmen and working close enough to show each of them in individual detail. There was a difference between Wolfe and any of the recent novelists who had studied American families in fiction. Instead of writing dryly or cynically, as if to reduce families to the bores and pests it was fashionable to consider them, Wolfe wrote with magnificence. No matter how unpleasant some of the Gants might be, or how appalling, they were not dull. Wolfe in reproducing or creating had not once looked at them with cold disinterested eyes, but with the clannish loyalty in which particular or temporary hatreds cannot bar out a general love. He enjoyed the living reality of the Gants, even if he could not approve their characters. The avarice of Eliza Pentland the mother (Wolfe's own mother was Julia Elizabeth Westall) seems a credible obsession. The roaring violence of Oliver Gant the father (Wolfe's own father was named William Oliver) is gorgeous rather than monstrous. The elder Gant is central to *Look Homeward, Angel* as to the later novels. "The deepest search in life, it seemed to me," Wolfe wrote in *The Story of a Novel* (1935), "the thing that in one way or another was central to all living was man's search to find a father; not merely the father of his flesh, not merely the lost father of his youth, but the image of a strength and wisdom external to his need and superior to his hunger, to which the belief and power of his own life could be united." In *Look Homeward, Angel* Wolfe was searching for the truth about the physical father of Eugene Gant—or of Thomas Wolfe. The story of Eugene, which Wolfe had set out to tell, must be traced back of him to the father in whom his stormy nature had begun. As to Eugene, he belonged to a type often celebrated in contemporary novels: the talented youth trying to rise from more or less commonplace circumstances. But Eugene transcends the restless type by being its most superb example in his time: perhaps mad but certainly magnificent.

In Paris in the summer of 1930 Wolfe was once more overcome with homesickness; "and I really believe that from this emotion, this constant and almost intolerable effort of memory and desire, the material and structure of the books I now began to write were derived." In London, four years before, he had begun his first book with a comparatively simple conception: it was to be a novel about his youth. Now he remembered all America. He ached with "the desire to see it again; somehow to find a word for it; a language that would tell its shape, its color, the way we have all known and felt and seen it. And when I understood this thing, I saw that I must find for myself the tongue to utter what I knew but could not say. And from the moment of that discovery, the line and purpose of my life was shaped." It was hard for him to settle upon a method with which to carry out this grandiose conception. He did not wait to make up his planning mind. In France, Switzerland, and England during the rest of 1930 he was possessed by his materials and poured out scenes, incidents, accounts of characters, notes on his recollections, hymns and visions in enraptured prose. Some of these things he believed would eventually have a place in the work he intended, but many of them he thought of as explorations in the "domain of my resources as a man and as a writer." Back in America in 1931, he soon gave up his early idea that he could pack his materials into a single novel called *The October Fair*. By the end of 1933 he had written enough to make up a dozen novels if he used it all. He could not stop or turn aside. Except for his good fortune in having an editor of patience and courage—Maxwell Perkins—Wolfe might never have gone beyond his explorations. Perkins, who said that he had felt like a man trying to hold on to the fin of a plunging whale, now persuaded, and forced, Wolfe to take stock. Together they found that *The October Fair*, as it then stood, contained "two complete and separate cycles. The first of these was a movement which described the period of wandering and hunger in a man's youth. The second cycle described the

(346)

period of greater certitude, and was dominated by the unity of a single passion." Wolfe worked over the first cycle into *Of Time and the River* (1935), and announced that it would be followed by four further books: *The October Fair, The Hills Beyond Pentland, The Death of the Enemy, Pacific End.* The same year he published *The Story of a Novel*, a remarkable narrative of his literary undertakings; and collected from various magazines the sketches in *From Death to Morning.* Of these *The Web of Earth*—a monologue by Eliza Gant about her husband and children—is one of the mighty fragments Wolfe wrote but could not fit into a completed book. Another fragment, called *A Portrait of Bascom Hawke*, which had appeared in a magazine (1932) but was not among the collected pieces, was cut and fitted into *Of Time and the River.*

Wolfe's course through the three years he lived after *The Story of a Novel* is less clear than through the years before. Becoming dissatisfied with his story of the single passion which dominated his second cycle, he worked it over, changing the name of his hero from Eugene Gant to George Webber, giving him a different outward appearance, a different youth in Old Catawba—which is still North Carolina. At Wolfe's death he left two novels: *The Web and the Rock* (1939) and *You Can't Go Home Again* (to be published in 1940). The change in the hero's name, looks, boyhood meant little. George Webber remained essentially Eugene Gant, as Eugene Gant was essentially Thomas Wolfe. Wolfe like Hemingway —or like Byron or Whitman—was a writer with a single principal hero: himself in one form or another. *Look Homeward, Angel* may be regarded as a kind of prologue, devoted to the young hero in his province. In *Of Time and the River* Eugene goes to Harvard, returns to his father's funeral, lives restless in New York, travels to England and France and back. In *The Web and the Rock* George Webber, after two hundred pages of a youth unlike Eugene Gant's but strikingly parallel

(347)

to it, arrives in New York with an ardent hunger like Gant's to read all the books and know all the people in the world, writes a novel that sounds much like *Look Homeward, Angel*, has an intricate, protracted love affair with an older woman, travels in Europe, and at the end feels, for at least a moment, reconciled to his abnormal body and his human fate.

After Wolfe's death the hymns and visions and radiant catalogues in his writings were brought together in a volume called *The Face of a Nation* (1939). It was prose to match Whitman's poetry, and Wolfe and Whitman would long be remembered together. These rich passages in Wolfe stood out all the more strongly because his great novel—the four are really one—lacked the powerful structure that might have reduced its parts to their due places in the whole. His chronicle of a hero during his first thirty years is a tumultuous series of scenes held together by the unity of a single giant hunger and desire, charging forward without sense of direction, haunted by the perpetual image of time as an infinite river in which men lead their short and trifling lives, so soon forgotten in the universal flood. Again and again Wolfe broke into lyric laments over the terrible brevity of joy. But he was one of the most opulent of novelists, and the whole of America was his theme. There is body to his work as well as wings. Sometimes he wrote at greater length than his materials called for. His passion for fine words made him frequently verbose. He often strained his sentiments and ecstasies. His comic scenes are commonly grotesque. Yet when his emotion was perfectly aroused, as in his account of the prodigious life and even more prodigious death of Oliver Gant, Wolfe was almost incomparable. His fine words all fit, and there are not too many of them. His sentiments and ecstasies are authentic and perennial. Oliver Gant has been too magnificent in life ever to seem grotesque, and there is nothing grotesque about his gigantic death. Perhaps only his son could have told the story. His son told it.

(348)

XX

REVISIONS

THE DECADE 1929-39 saw a wide-spread and searching revision of the picture of American life which American fiction had been drawing since the earliest days. The first half of the nineteenth century had established the heroic and romantic outlines of the tradition; the second half had filled in the standard settings, stories, and types of character which by 1900 had settled into a traditional realism. Before the World War both the romantic and realistic traditions had been disturbed by a naturalism which tried to dig conscientiously beneath the surfaces of American life. After the war there had been a swarm of satirists, ironists, and cynics who were even more disturbing. Soon after the financial collapse of 1929 fiction began to swing away from the themes and attitudes which had recently been fashionable. In place of the dullness which had been the prevailing villain there was a new enemy: poverty. The expatriates came home and rediscovered America. Those who had stayed at home found themselves discovering aspects of America which were either new in its history or else had been neglected by its literature.

Concerted and deliberate effort went into the production of what were called proletarian novels. Before the term became usual there had already been such sympathetic chronicles as Agnes Smedley's *Daughter of Earth* (1929), as much autobiography as fiction; Mary Heaton Vorse's *Strike* (1930), about the textile workers in North Carolina; Michael Gold's *Jews Without Money* (1930), about New York's East Side. Somewhat more explicit doctrines were emphasized in Robert Cantwell's *Laugh and Lie Down* (1931), Fielding Burke's

Call Home the Heart (1932), Grace Lumpkin's *To Make My Bread* (1932), Jack Conroy's *The Disinherited* (1933), William Rollins's *The Shadow Before* (1934). The action was likely to come to its head in a strike, and it took for granted an essential class conflict between the owners and the landless, propertyless workers. The heroes, in a time of unprecedented unemployment, were men desperately looking for work or trying to keep their jobs. The strongest virtue celebrated in the novels was proletarian solidarity. The future, the novelists insisted, lay with the proletariat, which must and would develop a working-class culture. Its literature, like these novels, would be class-conscious, serious, and responsible. The critics of the movement drew up rules by which they thought the coming literature would be directed. Critics had done the same thing in the first years of the United States, looking confidently forward to a republican literature. Whitman had passionately forecast a literature which should be the voice of a true democratic fraternity. It is easier to promise a coming literature than to furnish it. The generous intentions of the proletarian novelists were not enough, and most of their novels were schematic and ineffectual. The best of them was Thomas Bell's *All Brides are Beautiful* (1936), which was less an argument than an idyl of life in the prosaic Bronx. The effective novels which most nearly carried out the plans of the radical critics were by writers who worked with few doctrinaire ideas, with individual talents rather than with collective aims.

The four novels of the decade which overshadowed all others in popularity were, in differing degrees, symptomatic. Pearl Buck's *The Good Earth* (1931) brought to countless American readers an imaginative knowledge of human life on the barest level of subsistence: a life which would once have seemed as remote from them as China but which now seemed a dreadful possibility in the America of the depression. Hervey Allen's *Anthony Adverse* (1933), though chiefly a romance of adventure colored and somewhat confused by metaphysical implications, was incidentally a record of the coming of Europeans to America: to a country which was now thinking about how it had been formed from the varied populations of the earth. Margaret Mitchell's *Gone With the Wind* (1936) not only gave a revised version of the Civil War in the South, so often the subject of more conventional novels, but also told, with remarkable verve and narrative energy, the story of Scarlett O'Hara's rise from the desolate circumstances in which the war had left her and her Georgia community. John Steinbeck's *The Grapes of Wrath* (1939) threw a bitter light on the tragic migrants from the Dust Bowl to California: in America not in China, in the immediate present not in the past of Reconstruction. Among them the four novels said, directly or indirectly, almost everything the fiction of the decade had to say.

Julian Green, born in Paris of Virginia parents, wrote his novels in French and belongs to French literature. Kay Boyle, born in Minnesota, remained in France after the expatriates' return and wrote novels or stories on European or international themes. Elliot Paul's *The Life and Death of a Spanish Town* (1937), if not quite a novel, was like one in its graphic record of the revolution in Spain. But for the most part the decade's characteristic American novels dealt in one way or another with native settings, stories, types of character. Leland Hall's touching *Salah and His American* (1935) took an American to North Africa; Djuna Barnes's brilliant, perverse *Nightwood* (1937) took another American to Paris. Hendrik Willem van Loon's *R. v. R.* (1931)—a novel which was a biography of Rembrandt and a history of his times—extended the action to the New Netherland which became New York. Louis Bromfield turned from his thin chronicles in the manner of a less witty Edith Wharton to the more substantial account of rural Ohio in *The Farm* (1933). Frederic Prokosch, who in *The Asiatics* (1935) and *The Seven Who Fled* (1937) had laid his exotic, brooding scenes and actions in deep Asia,

(351)

told in *Night of the Poor* (1939) of a young American's sensitive progress through the deep United States, from Wisconsin to Texas. The long era during which America seemed the natural home of only homespun fiction had ended, and Prokosch's intricate imagination could find materials for his delicate art in the Mississippi valley.

Though *The Good Earth*, which in as many as twenty languages reached almost the entire reading world, seemed by far the best of the books of Pearl S. Buck (1892-   ), it outdistanced them rather by the timely universality of its theme than by any superiority in its execution. Her work was both abundant and distinguished. Born in West Virginia, she was taken by her missionary parents to China before she was a year old, and lived there, except for her return to college in the United States, till she was past forty. She spoke and wrote Chinese, and thought of China as her country. But in Nanking, where she was a teacher in the university, the anti-foreign troubles of 1927 forced her to realize that to the Chinese she was an alien, and would continue to be. Feeling shut out of a life she loved, she had a stronger impulse toward it than ever, and instinctively began to write about it. *The Good Earth* had a prompt sequel, *Sons* (1932), and then another, *A House Divided* (1935). The united trilogy, called *House of Earth*, followed the whole family of Wang through its rise and triumph and its disintegrating conflicts in the modern world. Before she left China in 1934 she completed and published her fine translation of the great Chinese novel *Shui Hu Chuan* with the English title *All Men Are Brothers* (1933). In America she wrote moving biographies of her mother—*The Exile* (1936)—and her father—*Fighting Angel* (1936), the disappointing *This Proud Heart* (1938) with an American heroine, and another excellent Chinese novel *The Patriot* (1939). The American Academy in 1935 awarded her the Howells medal for the most distinguished work of American fiction published in five years. The Swedish Academy in 1938 awarded her the Nobel prize for her Chinese peasant epics and her biographies.

What was often spoken of as her Biblical style was actually close to the style of Chinese novels, which she used because it fitted her Chinese subjects. She was happiest when she used it in dealing with the common life of China. Fluent and flexible, it was simple in idiom and cadence, like a realistic pastoral or a humane saga. The substance in *The Mother* (1934), the life-story of a Chinese peasant woman, is so slight that the style sometimes falls into a mannered singsong. In *The Good Earth*, with its richer substance, the style is regularly supported by the matter. The style gives an agreeable music to the convincing history. Nor was it more convincing in America, in the midst of the depression, than elsewhere. The depression touched all peoples. Even where they were not threatened with immediate famine, as in the starvation chapters of the book, they saw that complex systems of life had broken down. It was not certain that anything but the land remained. Wang's hunger for land, and his obstinate clinging to it once he had it, touched responsive sentiments in every country. In the United States, which had a special friendly liking for China, *The Good Earth* for the first time made the Chinese seem as familiar as neighbors. Pearl Buck had added to American fiction one of its large provinces.

At the same time native novelists were discovering the depressed regions of America. The Chinese peasant epics were full of Asiatic patience and resignation. Their characters hoped for good fortune, but hardly expected it. They were schooled to live as their fathers had lived, as multitudes round them lived, as their sons would live. In America there was a rooted habit of faith that the future would soon be better. It had been assumed that people who were needy generally deserved to be, for neglecting the opportunities which, it was assumed, existed for them. Or perhaps their poverty made them picturesque, as in local color stories. The novelists of the depression could not be satisfied with these assumptions. They did not find the stamina of fatalism in the American poor. William Faulkner (1897-   ) in *As I Lay Dying* (1930) and *Sanctuary* (1931) showed them to be, in Mississippi, degenerate or debauched. Here was no earth-bound peasantry, always in want and yet kept somehow in order by the customs of the immense class to which they belonged. Faulkner's poor were more likely to be resentful failures living among, or below, the more fortunate. If they were not sluggish they were ferocious. Faulkner drew from their ways of life the sub-human stories he had a knack at telling in his intense, winding prose. Anything could happen, he implied, in the backwoods and backwaters of Mississippi or wherever in America men had fallen out of stride, and been forgotten, and reverted to desperate animalisms. The American standard of living had by no means touched all Americans; nor had the standards of thinking and feeling which were ordinarily regarded as American. In earlier and later novels dealing with different social groups, and in various short stories, Faulkner added to his savage evidence that America had not been able to isolate itself from universal cruelty and misery.

Erskine Caldwell (1902-   ) concerned himself chiefly with Georgia. His *Tobacco Road* (1932) was made into a play which had a longer run on the stage than any other American play had ever had. *God's Little Acre* (1933) was brought into court on a charge of obscenity, but was cleared. The quality in Caldwell which could rouse censors and yet delight an endless public was the grim humor with which he told outrageous stories. With stronger nerves than Faulkner, and a much surer art, Caldwell was not feverish or foggy. He could produce the illusion not only that a story was true but that it was old. For example, the brief *Meddlesome Jack* in the collection called *We Are the Living* (1933) turns on what readers instinctively accept as a folk-superstition. What Caldwell invented sounds like a folk-tale. The term God's acre means a churchyard, but Caldwell makes God's little acre seem always to have meant a part of a farm set aside for the use of the farmer's church. Tobacco Road is nearly as proverbial as Main Street. If, as Hemingway declared, most recent American writers derive from Mark Twain, Caldwell goes back to the early rough popular humor from which Mark Twain derived. Whether or not Caldwell had ever read A. B. Longstreet's Georgia Scenes (1835), he wrote, like Longstreet, without apology about violent or grotesque Georgia manners. Local color, after the Civil War, had diluted and refined Southern literature, laying particular stress on the gentility of plantation life. But life in Georgia had not been confined to genteel plantations, and the less respectable phases of it had survived without ever being touched by literature. Caldwell's stories seem to descend from an older mode because Caldwell's people descend from earlier Georgians. He went below the tradition of literature to a tradition of life. He might feel, as he did, the tragedy and injustice of such wretched conditions, but he told his stories with a hard, ironic comic sense. Besides the short stories collected in We Are the Living he wrote those in two other volumes: Kneel to the Rising Sun (1935) and Southways (1938).

The city poor in the Chicago novels of James T. Farrell (1904-   ) are less destitute than the people of Faulkner or Caldwell. Farrell began his first novel as a study of the consequences of spiritual poverty. Young Lonigan (1932), The Young Manhood of Studs Lonigan (1934), and Judgment Day (1935)—later published together as the trilogy Studs Lonigan (1936)—are both tough and tender in their record of a hero whose good impulses are discouraged in his gross neighborhood and who has no satisfactions except crude longings which he would be ashamed to have anybody know about. Outwardly a hoodlum, he is really as much of a poet as he knows how to be. But Studs is no conventional ruffian with a heart of gold. He is individual, convincing, and pathetic.

(355)

With *A World I Never Made* (1936)—its title from *A Shrop-shire Lad*—Farrell began what was to be tetralogy concerned with the career of Danny O'Neill, who was plainly Farrell himself. At the end of the second novel, *No Star is Lost* (1938), Danny was still only eleven, and the rough narrative was beginning to seem too long. Farrell turned aside to write *Tommy Gallagher's Crusade* (1939), a short novel exposing the sodden motives behind anti-Semitism. In seven years he had produced six novels, three volumes collected as *The Short Stories of James T. Farrell* (1937), and *A Note on Literary Criticism* (1936) in which he argued against narrow Marxist ideas about literature. "The living stream of literature is a process, intertwined with other processes in society. The products of this process give us understanding; they enable us to feel aspects of life more deeply; and they afford us pleasure." Understanding, sympathy, pleasure: Farrell aimed at all of them in his detailed and outspoken stories. And he thought it important for Americans to realize how drab and vicious the under-life—not the underworld—of their cities had become in the confusing times.

Angry readers who called Faulkner, Caldwell, Farrell merely obscene and sordid did not perceive that they were making valuable if disagreeable discoveries about American life, and that they were doing what American novelists had been doing ever since *Uncle Tom's Cabin* forced millions of Americans to imagine what it might be like to be a slave. Garland and Crane, Dreiser and Sinclair Lewis and Dos Passos and Rölvaag, Hemingway and Wolfe had all revealed new regions and layers of experience. If these things were American facts they had a right to appear in American fiction. America could not be understood so long as only a part of it was known. It had changed and was changing faster than general opinion guessed. Novelists could no more refuse to notice than mirrors to reflect new faces in front of them. No doubt the novelists of the depression decade gave a picture which, in spite of what they argued, was less than the whole of America. If a tenth of the people were unemployed, nine-tenths had work; and if a third were badly housed and nourished, two-thirds were not. The comfortable and orderly majority had less than their share of representation in contemporary novels, which were a minority report.

The depression decade saw new forms of what had once been called local color but was now called regionalism. The differences between them could be accounted for by the changes in literary attitude and taste over fifty years. There were after 1929 still local or regional patriotisms at work, eager to make neglected sections known to the country at large; still simple ambitions to find fresh literary resources and profitably exploit them. But regionalism looked for robust drama rather than for picturesqueness, and preferred epic to idyllic dimensions in its stories. In the days of local color it had been customary to use one idiom for the past and another for the present, and seldom to bring them both into the same novel. The regional novelists often studied their regions through long periods of time, interested in learning how this present had come from that past. Several local color writers had turned from stories about their localities to systematic comment on them, keeping the two kinds of writing separate. A good many regional writers combined descriptive surveys with illustrative fiction in a mixture difficult to classify. The *American Guide Series*, undertaken by the Federal government on a tremendous national scale, began to be as indispensable to writers as to travelers. Constance Lindsay Skinner planned—and edited to her death in 1939—a series called *Rivers of America* which was to reinterpret American history and culture by fixing attention on natural not arbitrary divisions of the map.

To move across the map of the regional novelists was to observe many recent alterations. Dorothy Canfield in Vermont continued to celebrate, with generous intelligence, the sound provincial virtues. New Hampshire was the scene of *The Devil and Daniel Webster* (1937) in which Stephen Vincent Benét created a brief legend fit to stand with *Rip Van Winkle*. But Esther Forbes reconstructed colonial Massachusetts with a realistic precision new to Massachusetts novels, and Kenneth Roberts in his chronicles of New England wars—particularly *A Rabble in Arms* (1933) and *Northwest Passage* (1937)—made less use of the stately historical tradition than of the exciting picaresque. Victoria Lincoln in *February Hill* (1934) told a racy, bawdy story of low life in Fall River, about such people as the local color writers, if they knew about them, seldom mentioned and never touched.

In upstate New York the Erie Canal, long a quiet memory, came to roaring life in Walter D. Edmonds's *Rome Haul* (1929). Carl Carmer, who wrote *The Hudson* (1939) for the *Rivers of America*, worked much history and many legends into *Listen to a Lonesome Drum* (1936). New York City had novels and short stories about almost every aspect of its multifarious life: finance, business, the theater and the arts, sports, the underworld. If no history of a family in the decade quite matched Thyra Samter Winslow's little classic *A Cycle of Manhattan* (1923), Albert Halper's *Union Square* (1933) set a new mark for novels dealing with quarters of the town. John O'Hara was probably the best of the writers who dealt with the shifting circles known as cafe society. In suburban New Jersey Josephine Lawrence—*Years Are So Long* (1934), *If I Have Four Apples* (1935)—was firmly unsentimental about themes in the domestic-sentimental tradition. William Carlos Williams in *Life Along the Passaic River* (1938) wrote with curt realistic precision, as in his novel of New York and Vermont, *White Mule* (1937). Elsie Singmaster wrote about the Pennsylvania Germans as a local color writer might have done, but John T. McIntyre investigated the rougher side of life in Philadelphia. Washington still had little fiction written about it.

(358)

Regionalism in the Old South was based partly on the arguments of a group of able critics who in the symposium *I'll Take My Stand* (1930) insisted that the agrarian Southern culture must not be absorbed by the industrial Northern; but the actual novelists no longer gave themselves up to glorifying the traditional plantations. While there were novels about the Civil War, and some about the age before it, most Southern novels dealt with later times. Local patriotism appeared in a loyal affection for the South, and occasionally in poetic feeling. There was less romance than realism in the New South. If Faulkner and Caldwell were franker than any local color novelist would have thought of being, so—though not so frank as these two—were Julia Peterkin in *Scarlet Sister Mary* (1928) and DuBose Heyward in *Mamba's Daughters* (1929): both of them life-stories of Negro women in South Carolina who lived according to their own large natures. Zora Neale Hurston, herself a Negro, told the truest and most charming of such life-stories in *Their Eyes Were Watching God* (1937), its scene in Florida. Something of the local color manner survived in Marjorie Kinnan Rawlings's story of a Florida boy in *The Yearling* (1938). Carl Carmer in *Stars Fell on Alabama* (1934) mixed history and folk-lore as in his regional book on New York. In Roark Bradford's Negro versions of Bible stories—*Old Man Adam and His Chillun* (1928) and *Ol' King David and the Philistine Boys* (1930)— the landscape and customs seem naively like those of Louisiana, where the books were written. Bradford's *John Henry* (1931) took a famous legendary Negro for its hero. Most of John Henry's exploits in the book are connected with the Mississippi river. Somewhere along the river, or near it, the Negro Richard Wright placed the actions of *Uncle Tom's Children* (1938), four fiery stories of Negroes who defy and resist white injustice. The life of the river people, the boatmen and their families, was the happy subject of Ben Lucian Burman's pleasant *Blow for a Landing* (1938). The most

famous of Tennessee heroes took new life in Constance
Rourke's *Davy Crockett* (1934) which made full use of the
legendary elements in the Crockett saga. Here may be mentioned a group of books about other legendary heroes who,
wherever in America they might be supposed to have lived,
had all sprung from the tradition of tall tales first developed
on the old Mississippi and Southwestern frontier: *Mike Fink:
King of Mississippi Keelboatmen* (1933) by Walter Blair and
Franklin J. Meine; *Up Eel River* (1928) by Margaret Prescott
Montague, about Tony Beaver of West Virginia; *Legends of
Febold Feboldson* (1937) by Paul R. Beath, about a legendary Nebraskan; *Pecos Bill: The Greatest Cowboy of All Time*
(1937) by James Cloyd Bowman. Frank Shay collected native
hero tales in *Here's Audacity!* (1930) and Carl Carmer in
The Hurricane's Children (1937). Vincent McHugh in his
hilarious *Caleb Catlum's America* (1936) lamented the passing of the great race that had lived in tall tales.

Special qualities of style and method appeared in two Kentucky writers. Jesse Stuart's *Head o' W-Hollow* (1936) was a
book of stories in which a mountain-born poet seems to be
telling, in an easy vernacular, about all the people in the
hollow where he lives. Elizabeth Madox Roberts (1886-   )
beautifully stylized Kentucky. Her method was simplest in
Black Is My Truelove's Hair (1938), which was in effect a
prose folk-ballad with a title from an old song. Dena James, a
girl tricked by a false lover, comes back to her home, outgrows
her grief and fear, and finds a new love. The plot is as bare
as a ballad, but the novel is not. Its formal design is graceful
with lovely landscapes and characters sensitively conceived.
The narrative as well as the dialogue is a vernacular refined
and lifted to poetry without essential loss of its natural flavor.
A *Buried Treasure* (1931) is nearly as simple, though dramatically more tense. *The Great Meadow* (1930) is historical,
the richest and loveliest of all narratives of the settlement of
Kentucky. Diony Hall the heroine has read metaphysics in

(360)

Virginia and ventures into the wilderness with a sense that the world exists only as she perceives it. Kentucky is in her mind. There it takes the shape and color it was to have in Elizabeth Roberts's imagination when she wrote her first novel *The Time of Man* (1926), in which Ellen Dresser lives in a timeless folk-world localized in a Kentucky which is another Arcadia. Compared with James Lane Allen, who also had seen Kentucky as Arcadian, Miss Roberts was intelligent not sentimental, poetical not rhetorical. Her version of Kentucky superseded his and promised to endure much longer. She had not merely used Kentucky materials; she had transmuted them. Besides these and other novels she wrote verse in *Under the Tree* (1922) and short stories in *The Haunted Mirror* (1932).

North of the Ohio there were fewer regional novels of distinction after 1929. Zona Gale added little and Glenway Westcott nothing to their Wisconsin cycles. Harold Sinclair in *American Years* (1938) traced the rise of a typical Illinois town. Don Marquis in the uncompleted posthumous *Sons of the Puritans* (1938) dealt ironically, compassionately with another Illinois town at the end of the past century, with comic episodes which local color would have expurgated. The favorite state of Middle Western local fiction ceased to be Indiana and became Iowa, across the Mississippi. Herbert Quick's trilogy of the migration and settlement—*Vandemark's Folly* (1921), *The Hawkeye* (1923), *The Invisible Woman* (1924)—had set a fashion. Ruth Suckow, beginning with *Country People* (1924), studied contemporary life with honest realism, and in her long *The Folks* (1934) came nearer than any other writer has done to representing the whole of American life on farms and in small towns. Phil Stong's more pungent *State Fair* (1932) became at once a rural classic. In Missouri Josephine Johnson wrote the finished, somewhat mannered *Now in November* (1934). George Milburn in his short stories *No More Trumpets* (1933) and his novel *Cata-*

(361)

logue (1936) wrote sharp satiric sketches of local life in Missouri and Oklahoma.

The great plains from Texas to Montana, the old range country now too much of it under the plow, produced no new regional novels as good as Rölvaag's or Willa Cather's, and not many of any merit. But there was no falling off in the number of routine stories about cowboys and the Wild West. Commonly known as westerns, such novels rivaled detective stories, known as mysteries, for first place in sub-literary popularity. Their types of plot and character were almost always stereotypes, used over and over as in the motion pictures which eagerly welcomed westerns and incorrigibly standardized them. Of the later novelists who dealt with cowboys Eugene Manlove Rhodes was the most truthful and the least conventional. The most amusing of all cowboy books was *Bowleg Bill* (1938) in which Jeremiah Digges retold sailors' yarns from the Massachusetts coast about a cowboy who was said to have left Wyoming to go to sea and become a nautical Paul Bunyan. James Boyd of North Carolina, whose *Drums* (1925) is a notable romance of the American Revolution, wrote in *Bitter River* (1939) a novel of Wyoming's cowboy past which transcends the standard westerns. As a rule the facts about cowboys were more interesting than the fictions. Struthers Burt's *Powder River* (1939) accurately and dramatically caught the spirit of Wyoming in the cowboy age, and J. Frank Dobie's *A Vaquero of the Brush Country* (1929) that of Texas.

Dobie did not write novels, but he has a secure place in the history of American fiction on account of *Coronado's Children* (1931) and *Apache Gold and Yaqui Silver* (1939), which are folk-stories of Texas and the Southwest about buried Spanish treasure. Though no such lost riches had ever been found, there were many Southwesterners who genuinely believed they might be some day. Dobie hunted not the treasure but the treasure-hunters, traveling anywhere to hear their fanatic proofs that the legendary hoards must exist, their agile explanations why they had not yet come to light. Stories about buried treasure are always magical. The magic in Dobie's stories gains more than it loses from the shrewd, humorous, reasonable telling. Katherine Anne Porter, another Texan by birth, called her *Pale Horse, Pale Rider* (1939) three short novels, though they were hardly longer than the longest of her short stories in *Flowering Judas* (1931, with additions 1935). While the settings are usually Southern or Mexican, the novels hardly belong to regional fiction. There are three violent deaths on a Texas farm in *Noon Wine*, but the essential story is about the states of mind of the farmer who kills a man without quite intending to, and then kills himself because he can neither be sure that he is innocent nor bear the neighbors' suspicion that he is guilty. Most of the novels and stories are chiefly about women, particularly about women at moments of doubt or instinctive decision. Miss Porter told her stories with lucid insight in a style of brilliant simplicity.

In the farthest west regional novelists turned fresh attention to the established stories of early explorers and settlers. Archie Binns's *The Land Is Bright* (1939) followed the Oregon Trail. H. L. Davis's fine *Honey in the Horn* (1935) vigorously revised the local heroic legend of the Oregon country. George Stewart of California retold the dark story of the Donner catastrophe in *Ordeal by Hunger* (1936), and in his novel *East of the Giants* (1938) the tumultuous story of California before and after the discovery of gold. Vardis Fisher of Idaho who had written *In Tragic Life* (1932) and other neurotic romances found a magnificent theme in the rise and migrations and settlement of the Mormons: as astounding a story as any in American history. *Children of God* (1939), which is national as well as regional, neither exalted the Mormons as their own pious tradition did nor abused them in the tradition of their ignorant enemies. Without denying that the Saints were heroes, Fisher saw them as flesh-and-

THE AMERICAN NOVEL

blood moving through the old frontier, of which his novel is
an heroic panorama and a vast realistic comedy. In the far
Southwest, still the home of many westerns, distinguished
regional fiction was likely to be about the Pueblo Indians, of
whom for a reflective and effective lifetime Mary Austin
had been the most widely known interpreter—of them and the
country in which they live. With her first book—*The Land of
Little Rain* (1903)—her last promised to be her most memorable: *One-Smoke Stories* (1934), such stories as Indians tell
no longer than a cigarette will burn. Oliver La Farge's *Laughing Boy* (1929), a Navaho novel, was the most understanding
and touching study of an Indian hero since *Ramona*.

John Steinbeck (1902-   ) kept pace with the depression
decade. Born in California, he left Stanford without his degree,
worked on ranches, wandered to New York and was dissatisfied there, and once more in California wrote his first novel
Cup of Gold (1929), a romantic story of Henry Morgan the
buccaneer which was considerably like Cabell. In *Pastures of
Heaven* (1932) Steinbeck, who had been unsuccessfully writing short stories, made a novel out of short stories, loosely
joined, about various families living in a California valley
near Monterey. *Tortilla Flat* was like nobody but Steinbeck.
The paisanos of Monterey—that is, the descendants of the
original Mexican population—were for him "good people of
laughter and kindness, of honest lusts and direct eyes, of
courtesy beyond politeness." His novel recounted the exploits
of three amiable paisano rogues who find it as difficult to be
law-abiding as to be unkind. If *Tortilla Flat* might be called
a regional novel, *In Dubious Battle* (1936) might be called
proletarian, though Steinbeck was too individual to be so
baldly classified. He had been assigned by a newspaper to write
articles about transient labor camps in California. What he
learned furnished him the materials for the most absorbing
strike novel of the decade. A straightforward though slightly
romantic narrative, it was less popular than *Of Mice and Men*

(364)

(1937), a short novel which Steinbeck tried to make like a play, and of which he produced also a version for the stage the same year. There was something theatrical as well as pitiful in the moron Lennie who is dependent on his friend George, but there was also an aching timeliness in the plans they make to have somewhere a small farm of their own and be secure. The novels of the prosperous twenties had perpetually ridiculed people who desired no more than enough to eat and a place to sleep. A novel of the depressed and unemployed thirties could make touching heroes of men for whom such desires were now Utopian.

The Long Valley (1938) contained the beautiful short story The Red Pony and others which had little to say about the times. But in Steinbeck's passionate, salty masterpiece The Grapes of Wrath (1939) he returned to the plight of men desperately looking for a living. His scene was larger than California. The soil had been blown away by the winds in the Dust Bowl and starving farmers set out for California, where they were told they would be welcome. Steinbeck traveled over the route from Oklahoma, studying the conditions they left behind, the hard details of the migration, their disillusionment at the end. Of course no people in possession of good lands have ever welcomed migratory tribes pouring in upon them. Men will fight as hard to hold land as to obtain it. But Steinbeck could not see this movement of Americans from Oklahoma as a migration on primitive terms. He believed that injustice had helped drive them from their farms, that injustice helped keep them homeless beyond the desert. Certainly here were hundreds of thousands of men and women destitute in plain sight of abundance. They were men and women, not mere factors in an economic situation. Statistics could not tell their story. Steinbeck told it as an intimate history of the Joad family in their wanderings. Readers who had thought of migrant workers as so many negligible thousands on the road or at work in masses, now suddenly realized they were not that at all. The Joads might have been any ordinary farm family uprooted and turned out to drift over the continent. This was not only a regional affair. The whole nation was involved. *The Grapes of Wrath* did more than any other depression novel to revise the picture of America as Americans imagined it. And *The Grapes of Wrath* had the benefit of the twenty years during which novelists had worked to make the American novel a full, free expression of human life.

BIBLIOGRAPHY

General

THE FOLLOWING lists have been rigorously selected from the mass of material available. The principal emphasis is laid upon literary history, biography, and bibliography, and less upon criticism except when incidental to these. Students who wish to carry their researches further will find admirable guidance in *American Literature: A Period Anthology* (5 vols., 1933) edited by Oscar Cargill: *The Roots of National Culture: To 1830* edited by R. E. Spiller; *The Romantic Triumph: 1830-1860* edited by T. McDowell; *The Rise of Realism: 1860-1888* edited by L. Wann; *The Social Revolt: 1888-1914* edited by O. Cargill; *Contemporary Trends: Since 1914* edited by J. H. Nelson. There are excellent bibliographies (pages 448-664, compiled by Harry Hartwick) in *A History of American Letters* (1936) by W. F. Taylor. For any extended study of American literature the *Dictionary of American Biography* (20 vols. and *Index*, 1928-37) is indispensable.

Adams, O. F. *A Dictionary of American Authors* (1897, revised 1905).

Alderman, E. A., and others (editors). *A Library of Southern Literature* (17 vols., 1908-23).

American Literature, published quarterly by the Duke University Press since 1929. Publishes lists of publications on the subject and of researches in progress.

Benét, W. R., and N. H. Pearson (editors). *The Oxford Anthology of American Literature* (1938). Useful selections and biographical and bibliographical notes.

Blair, W. (editor). *Native American Humor 1800-1900* (1937). Excellent selections and bibliographies.

Boynton, P. H. *The Rediscovery of the Frontier* (1931). *Literature and American Life* (1936).

Branch, E. D. *Westward; The Romance of the American Frontier* (1930). *The Sentimental Years, 1830-1860* (1934).

Brooks, Van W. *The Flowering of New England 1815-1865* (1936). Classic record of the period.

(367)

BIBLIOGRAPHY

Brownell, W. C. *American Prose Masters* (1909). Austere studies of Fenimore Cooper, Hawthorne, Henry James.

Clark, Emily. *Innocence Abroad* (1931). Graceful first-hand accounts of recent writers, chiefly Southern.

Cleaton, I. and A. *Books and Battles: American Literature, 1920-1930* (1937). Lively, superficial.

Cowley, M. *Exile's Return* (1934). Useful, typical account of the Lost Generation. Cowley edited *After the Genteel Tradition* (1937). Essays on writers after 1910, chiefly by younger writers.

Dondore, D. *The Prairie and the Making of Middle America* (1926). Chiefly the literature of the region.

Du Breuil, A. J. *The Novel of Democracy in America* (1923).

Dunlap, G. A. *The City in the American Novel, 1789-1900* (1934).

Edgar, P. *The Art of the Novel from 1700 to the Present Time* (1933).

Erskine, J. *Leading American Novelists* (1910).

Foster, R. A. *The School in American Literature* (1930).

Frank, W. *Our America* (1919). *The Re-discovery of America* (1929). Comments on cultural materials.

Fullerton, B. M. *Selective Bibliography of American Literature, 1775-1900* (1932). Notably accurate as to dates.

Gabriel, R. H. (editor). *The Pageant of America: A Pictorial History of the United States* (15 vols., 1926-29). Incidentally illustrates much of American fiction.

Gaines, F. P. *The Southern Plantation* (1924). Valuable study of the facts and the fictions.

Griswold, W. M. *A Descriptive List of Novels and Tales Dealing with American Country Life* (1890). *A Descriptive List of Novels and Tales Dealing with American City Life* (1891). *A Descriptive List of Novels and Tales Dealing with the History of North America* (1895).

Gruening, E. (editor). *These United States: A Symposium* (2 vols., 1923-24). Regional studies of states.

Hansen, H. *Midwest Portraits* (1923). Good account of Chicago writers.

Hartwick, H. *The Foreground of American Fiction* (1934). Useful for information, confusing as criticism.

Hatcher, H. *Creating the Modern American Novel* (1935).

Hazard, L. L. *The Frontier in American Literature* (1927).

Herron, I. H. *The Small Town in American Literature* (1939). Highly detailed, with valuable bibliographies.

Hicks, G. The Great Tradition (1933). Emphasizes the radical elements in American literature since the Civil War.

Hubbell, J. B. American Life in Literature (2 vols., 1936). Valuable.

Johnson, J. G. Southern Fiction Prior to 1860: An Attempt at a First-Hand Bibliography (1909).

Keiser, A. The Indian in American Literature (1933).

Leisy, E. E. The Novel in America; Notes for a Survey, in Southwest Review, XXII (1936), 88-99.

Lewisohn, L. Expression in America (1932, revised as Story of American Literature, 1939). Important criticism.

Loggins, V. The Negro Author: His Development in America (1931).

Loshe, L. D. The Early American Novel (1907, revised 1930). Pioneer work still valuable for period before 1830.

Macy, J. (editor). American Writers on American Literature (1931). Useful, though the 37 chapters are of uneven merit.

Manly, J. M., and E. L. Rickert. Contemporary American Literature: Bibliographies and Study Outlines (1921, revised 1929). Highly useful.

Meine, F. J. (editor). Tall Tales of the Southwest (1930). First in its field.

Michaud, R. The American Novel of To-day (1928).

Millett, F. B. Contemporary American Authors (1939). Based on Manly and Rickert above but goes much beyond that work.

Modern Language Association, Publications of. Prints in issue of March each year a list of books and articles on American literature, compiled by N. Foerster and G. L. Paine.

Mott, F. L. A History of American Magazines (3 vols., 1930-38). Invaluable record to 1885; to be continued.

Nelson, J. H. The Negro Character in American Literature (1926).

Parrington, V. L. Main Currents in American Thought (3 vols., 1927-30). Indispensable for fiction as for other forms of literature.

Pattee, F. L. A History of American Literature Since 1870 (1915). The New American Literature, 1890-1930 (1930). The First Century of American Literature (1935).

Pearson, E. Dime Novels (1929).

Pulitzer Prize novels. List from the beginning published annually in The World Almanac.

Quinn, A. H. American Fiction: An Historical and Critical Survey (1936). Full, detailed, moralistic; includes short stories.

Rourke, C. American Humor: A Study of the National Character (1931). Very important.

BIBLIOGRAPHY

Rusk, R. L. *The Literature of the Middle Western Frontier* (2 vols., 1925). Searching and thorough.

Shurter, R. L. *The Utopian Novel in America, 1888-1910*, in *South Atlantic Quarterly*, XXXIV, 136-44.

Singer, G. F. *The Epistolary Novel: Its Origin, Decline, and Residuary Influence* (1933).

Speare, M. E. *The Political Novel: Its Development in England and America* (1924).

Stanton, T. (editor). *A Manual of American Literature* (1909). Chapter on Novelists by C. S. Northup.

Stedman, E. C., and E. M. Hutchinson (editors). *A Library of American Literature* (11 vols., 1889-90). Still valuable for selections.

Sullivan, M. *Our Times: The United States, 1900-1925* (6 vols., 1926-35). Useful chapters on current literary fashions and best sellers.

Tandy, J. R. *Crackerbox Philosophers in American Humor and Satire* (1925). Popular humorists.

Trent, W. P. *A History of American Literature, 1607-1865* (1903).

Trent, W. P., J. Erskine, S. P. Sherman, and C. Van Doren (editors). *The Cambridge History of American Literature* (4 vols., 1917-21); reissued in 3 vols., 1933, without the extensive bibliographies. The chapters on Fiction in this work, written by C. Van Doren, served as a basis for the first edition of *The American Novel*. The bibliographies accompanying the chapters were much more detailed than those in the book.

Turner, L. D. *Anti-Slavery Sentiment in American Literature Prior to 1865* (1929).

Van Doren, C. (editor). *Modern American Prose* (1934). Includes fiction.

Van Patten, N. *An Index to Bibliographies and Bibliographical Contributions Relating to the Work of American and British Authors, 1923-1932* (1934).

Walbridge, E. F. *Romans à Clef: Real People Behind Fiction Characters*, in *The Author's Annual* (1929) edited by H. W. Lanier.

Weeks, E. A. *Best Sellers Since 1875*, in *Publishers' Weekly*, CXXV (1934), 1503-06.

Wegelin, O. *Early American Fiction, 1774-1830: A Compilation of the Titles of Works of Fiction* (1902, revised 1929).

Wendell, B. *A Literary History of America* (1900).

Whipple, T. K. *Spokesmen: Modern Writers and American Life* (1928). Superior criticism.

Whitcomb, S. L. *Chronological Outlines of American Literature* (1894). Should be revised and brought down to the present.

Woestemeyer, I. F., and J. M. Gambrill (editors). *The Westward Movement* (1939). Useful selections and bibliographies on the changing frontier.

Wright, L. H. *American Fiction, 1774-1850: A Contribution toward a Bibliography* (1939). Remarkably detailed and accurate.

Zabel, M. D. (editor). *Literary Opinion in America* (1937). Concerned with the period since the World War, including its theories of fiction.

Chapter I

W. H. Brown's *The Power of Sympathy* was reprinted in facsimile (2 vols., 1937) with a bibliographical note by M. Ellis. For Hopkinson see G. E. Hasting's *The Life and Works of Francis Hopkinson* (1926). C. M. Newlin's *The Life and Writings of Hugh Henry Brackenridge* (1932) is valuable, and his critical edition of *Modern Chivalry* (1937) invaluable, for any study of Brackenridge. Mrs. Foster's *The Coquette* was reprinted in facsimile with an introduction by H. R. Brown (1939). F. W. Halsey's edition of *Charlotte Temple* (1905) was superseded as to bibliography by R. W. G. Vail's *Susanna Haswell Rowson: A Bibliographical Study* (1933). Charles Brockden Brown's novels were collected in six volumes (1887). Three of them later appeared in good critical editions: *Wieland* edited by F. L. Pattee (1926), *Edgar Huntly* edited by D. L. Clark (1928), *Ormond* edited by E. Marchand (1937). The materials in these editions supplement William Dunlap's *The Life of Charles Brockden Brown* (2 vols., 1815) and his shorter *Memoirs of Charles Brockden Brown* (1822). For the myth-making Weems see H. Kellock's *Parson Weems of the Cherry-Tree* (1928) and *Mason Locke Weems: His Works and Ways* (3 vols., 1928-29) by P. L. Ford and E. E. F. Skeel. The actual Indians may best be studied in their treaties with the whites, most conveniently in *Indian Treaties Printed by Benjamin Franklin* edited in facsimile by Julian P. Boyd with an introduction by Carl Van Doren (1938). For the Indians in early fiction see Keiser (title under General above).

Chapter II

Of the numerous collected editions of Cooper the most notable are the one illustrated by F. O. C. Darley (32 vols., 1859-61) and the one with introductions by Susan Fenimore Cooper (32 vols., 1876-84). Of Cooper's non-fiction, *Letter of J. Fenimore Cooper to Gen. Lafayette* was reprinted (1931, in facsimile) with a note by R. E. Spiller, and *Gleanings in Europe* (France and England) with an introduction by the same editor (2 vols., 1928-30); and *The American Democrat* with an introduction by H. L. Mencken (1931). Spiller's editions of *James Fenimore Cooper: Representative Selections* (1935) and (with J. D. Coppock) of *Satanstoe* (1937) are invaluable for bibliographical details. Cooper's *Correspondence* was edited by his grandson J. Fenimore Cooper (2 vols., 1922). The earlier *James Fenimore Cooper* (1883) by T. R. Lounsbury and *James Fenimore Cooper* (1913) by Mary E. Phillips are supplemented by H. W. Boynton's *James Fenimore Cooper* (1931) and R. E. Spiller's *Fenimore Cooper: Critic of His Times* (1931). Useful monographs are E. R. Outland's *The "Effingham" Libels on Cooper* (1929); J. F. Ross's *The Social Criticism of Fenimore Cooper* (1933); D. Waples's *The Whig Myth of James Fenimore Cooper* (1938). The classic but exaggerated *Fenimore Cooper's Literary Offenses* may be found in Mark Twain's *How to Tell a Story and Other Essays* (1897).

Chapter III

For Neal see his *Wandering Recollections of a Somewhat Busy Life* (1869). For Judd see Arethusa Hall's *Life and Character of the Rev. Sylvester Judd* (1857). For Thompson see J. F. Flitcroft's *The Novelist of Vermont* (1929). For Paulding see W. I. Paulding's *Literary Life of James K. Paulding* (1867) and A. L. Herold's *James Kirke Paulding, Versatile American* (1926). For Kennedy see H. T. Tuckerman's *The Life of John Pendleton Kennedy* (1871) and the valuable editions of *Swallow Barn* by J. B. Hubbell (1929) and of *Horse-Shoe Robinson* by E. E. Leisy (1937). Simms's *Border Romances* were collected in 17 volumes (1859, and numerous reissues). For Simms see W. P. Trent's *William Gilmore Simms* (1892); Parrington's *Main Currents*, II (title under General above); and A. Cowie's critical edition of *The Yemassee* (1937). For Bird see C. E. Foust's *The Life and Dramatic Works of Robert Montgomery Bird* (1919) and *Nick of the Woods* edited by Mark Van Doren (1928). For Tucker see *The Partisan Leader* edited by C. Bridenbaugh (1933). For Herbert see *The Sporting Novels of Frank Forester* (4 vols., 1930) with a memoir by H. W. Smith.

Chapter IV

The *Complete Works* of Hawthorne were edited by G. P. Lathrop (12 vols., 1883, and various reissues). N. Arvin edited *The Heart of Hawthorne's Journals* (1929). R. Stewart edited *The American Notebooks* (1932) from the original manuscript, restoring passages omitted by Hawthorne's wife. Of the many books about Hawthorne these may be listed: *Hawthorne* (1879) by Henry James; *Nathaniel Hawthorne and His Wife* (2 vols., 1885) and *Nathaniel Hawthorne and His Circle* (1903) by Julian Hawthorne; *Memories of Hawthorne* (1897) by Rose Hawthorne Lathrop; *Nathaniel Hawthorne* (1902) by G. E. Woodberry; *N. Hawthorne: sa vie et son oeuvre* (1905) by L. Dhaleine; *Hawthorne and His Publisher* (1913) by Caroline Ticknor; *The Rebellious Puritan* (1927) by L. Morris; *Hawthorne* (1929) by N. Arvin; *Romantic Rebel* (1932) by Hildegarde Hawthorne. Among many monographs: E. L. Chandler's *A Study of the Sources of the Tales and Romances Written by Nathaniel Hawthorne before 1853* (1926); A. Turner's *Autobiographical Elements in Hawthorne's Blithedale Romance*, in *University of Texas Studies in English*, XV (1935), 39-63; R. Stewart's *Hawthorne and Politics*, in *New England Quarterly*, V (1932), 237-62. Full and explicit bibliographical details are to be found in *Nathaniel Hawthorne: Representative Selections* (1934) edited by A. Warren.

Chapter V

The only full edition of Melville is the *Works* (London, 16 vols., 1922-24). The *Sea Tales* were edited by A. Stedman (4 vols., 1892), the principal *Romances* collected in one volume (1928). Raymond Weaver wrote introductions for *Israel Potter* (1924), *Redburn* (1924), *Moby Dick* (1925), *Mardi* (1925), and *Shorter Novels* (1928); and edited *Journal up the Straits October 11, 1856-May 5, 1857* (1928) from the manuscript. Rockwell Kent's illustrations for *Moby Dick* (1930) have a classic reputation. *Pierre* was edited by J. B. Moore with an introduction by H. M. Tomlinson (1929) and by R. S. Forsythe (1930). For the best account of Melville editions and materials see *Herman Melville: Representative Selections* (1938), an excellent anthology, including letters, with an indispensable critical and bibliographical introduction. Raymond Weaver's *Herman Mel-*

BIBLIOGRAPHY

ville: Mariner and Mystic (1921) was not superseded by the biographies by J. Freeman (1926) and L. Mumford (1929), but C. R. Anderson's *Melville in the South Seas* (1939) added enormously to the knowledge of Melville during the Pacific years, and of the sources of his tales. H. H. Scudder's *Melville's Benito Cereno and Captain Delano's Voyages*, in *Publications of the Modern Language Association*, XLIII (1928), 502-32, and R. P. McCutcheon's *The Technique of Melville's Israel Potter*, in *South Atlantic Quarterly*, XXVII (1928), 161-74, further illustrate Melville's use of his sources. J. N. Reynolds's *Mocha Dick*, a probable source of *Moby Dick* published in *Knickerbocker Magazine*, May 1839, was reprinted with an introduction by L. L. Balcolm (1932). C. Olson's *Lear and Moby Dick*, in *Twice a Year*, I (1938), 165-89, is notable among the many discussions of the novel. Carl Van Doren's *Lucifer from Nantucket*, first published in the *Century*, CX (1925), 494-501, has been drawn upon for Chapter V above.

Chapter VI

Edmund Pearson's *Dime Novels* (1929) is the fullest account of the type and its history. For Cooke see J. O. Beaty's *John Esten Cooke, Virginian* (1922); for Winthrop, Laura Winthrop Johnson's *Life and Poems of Theodore Winthrop* (1884). E. D. Branch's *The Sentimental Years, 1830-1860* (1934) is useful. *The Life of Donald Grant Mitchell* (1922) by W. H. Dunn is more detailed than *George William Curtis* (1894) by Edward Cary. *E. P. Roe: Reminiscences of His Life* (1889) by Mary A. Roe and *Lew Wallace: An Autobiography* (1906) are the principal sources of information about these writers. Mrs. Stowe's *Writings* were collected in 16 volumes (1896). There were biographies by C. E. Stowe (1889), Annie Fields (1897), C. E. and L. B. Stowe (1911). L. B. Stowe's *Saints, Sinners, and Beechers* (1934) contains the most recent discussion of Mrs. Stowe, and Constance Rourke's *Trumpets of Jubilee* (1927) the best.

Chapter VII

The Great American Novel was discussed by J. W. De Forest in *Nation* for 9 January 1868; by T. S. Perry in *North American Review* for October 1872; by Lew Wallace in *Old and New* for February

1874. For Bret Harte see Bibliography for Chapter XI. De Forest's *Miss Ravenel's Conversion* was reprinted, from a text revised by the author, with a valuable introduction by G. S. Haight (1939). There are accounts of Eggleston in G. C. Eggleston's *The First of the Hoosiers* (1903) and in M. Nicholson's *The Hoosiers* (1900). Mildred Howells edited *Life in Letters of William Dean Howells* (2 vols., 1928). Further information appears in the *Letters of Mark Twain* (1917) and of Henry James (1920) and in Howells's autobiographical writings, particularly *My Literary Passions* (1895), *Literary Friends and Acquaintance* (1900), *Years of My Youth* (1916). Biographical and bibliographical details are to be found in the critical studies, each called *William Dean Howells*, by D. G. Cooke (1922) and O. W. Firkins (1924). For Howells's place in the development of critical ideas see Parrington (title under General above) and B. Smith's *Forces in American Criticism* (1939).

Chapter VIII

Mark Twain's Writings (25 vols., 1899-1910) have been often reprinted as a whole and in separate volumes. *The Family Mark Twain* (1935) in one volume is a convenient selection. Albert Bigelow Paine edited *Mark Twain's Letters* (2 vols., 1917), *Mark Twain's Autobiography* (2 vols., 1924), *Mark Twain's Notebook* (1935), and wrote the authorized *Mark Twain: A Biography* (3 vols., 1912). W. D. Howells's *My Mark Twain* (1910) was the record of a great friendship. Van W. Brooks's *The Ordeal of Mark Twain* (1920, revised 1933) was a severe judgment, and B. De Voto's *Mark Twain's America* (1932) a robust defense. Clara Gabrilowitsch in *My Father: Mark Twain* (1931) wrote as a daughter, S. Leacock in *Mark Twain* (1932) as a fellow-humorist. E. C. Wagenknecht's *Mark Twain: The Man and His Work* (1935) is a sensible critical study. More specialized works are M. M. Brashear's *Mark Twain: Son of Missouri* (1935) and F. C. West's *Folk-Lore in the Works of Mark Twain* (1930). Constance Rourke's *American Humor* (1931) has valuable comments on Mark Twain, and *Native American Humor* (1800-1900) edited by Walter Blair fully illustrates the literary tradition from which Mark Twain sprang.

Chapter IX

Henry James collected most of his novels and tales for the New York Edition (26 vols., 1907-09, 1917) for which he wrote his famous prefaces. These were published separately as *The Art of the Novel: Critical Prefaces by Henry James* (1934) with an introduction by R. P. Blackmur. For the complex history of James's whole work see Le R. Phillips's *A Bibliography of the Writings of Henry James* (1906, revised 1930). There is no authorized biography, but the *Letters* (2 vols., 1920), and the autobiographical *A Small Boy and Others* (1913), *Notes of a Son and Brother* (1914), and *The Middle Years* (1917) contain much information; as do also the *Letters* of Robert Louis Stevenson (1899), Charles Eliot Norton (1913), William James (1920), and W. D. Howells (1928). The memoir *Alice James: Her Brothers* edited by A. R. Burr (1934) contains interesting family material. C. H. Grattan's *The Three Jameses* (1932) studies the father and his sons. There are numerous critical studies: *Henry James* (1916) by Rebecca West; *The Method of Henry James* (1918) by J. W. Beach; *Henry James at Work* (1924) by T. Bosanquet; *The Pilgrimage of Henry James* (1925) by Van W. Brooks; *Henry James: Man and Author* (1927) by P. Edgar; *Henry James's Criticism* (1929) by M. Roberts; *The Early Development of Henry James* (1930) by C. P. Kelley; *Homage to Henry James* by Marianne Moore and others, in *Hound & Horn*, VII (1934), 361-562; E. Wilson's *The Triple Thinkers* (1938) with an ingenious essay *The Ambiguity of Henry James*.

Chapter X

For H. H. Jackson see Ruth Odell's *Helen Hunt Jackson* (1939), C. C. Davis's and W. A. Alderson's *The True Story of Ramona* (1914), and G. F. Whicher's *This Was a Poet* (1938)—this last for its account of the friendship of Mrs. Jackson and Emily Dickinson. For G. W. Cable see L. L. Bikle's *George W. Cable* (1928) and E. L. Tinker's *Cable and the Creoles*, in *American Literature*, V (1934), 313-26. For E. W. Howe see his *Plain People* (1929) and *The Story of a Country Town* (1924) with an introduction by Carl Van Doren. Some of Howe's miscellaneous writings were selected by

H. L. Mencken as *Ventures in Common Sense* (1919). There are books about *Constance Fenimore Woolson* by Clare Benedict (1930) and J. D. Kern (1934). For Henry Adams's novels see R. E. Spiller's introduction to the facsimile reprint of *Esther* (1938) and Speare (title in General above). For Bellamy see S. Baxter's introduction to *Looking Backward* (1929) and the article in the *Dictionary of American Biography*. Stockton's novels and stories were collected in 23 volumes (1899-1904). See M. I. J. Griffin's *Frank R. Stockton* (1939). For Field see his collected works (12 vols., 1896-1900), S. Thompson's *Eugene Field* (2 vols., 1905), and C. H. Dennis's *Eugene Field's Creative Years* (1924). For Crawford see his collected works (30 vols., 1919) and M. H. Elliott's *My Cousin: F. Marion Crawford* (1934).

Chapter XI

For Bret Harte see his collected works (19 vols., 1896-1903, and reissues), his *Letters* (1926), edited by G. B. Harte, and G. R. Stewart's excellent *Bret Harte: Argonaut and Exile* (1931). For the plantation cycle see Gaines (title under General above). For Page see R. Page's *Thomas Nelson Page* (1923). For Cable see Bibliography for Chapter X. For Harris see Julia Collier Harris's *Life and Letters of Joel Chandler Harris* (1918). For cowboys in life and in literature see P. A. Rollins's *The Cowboy* (1922, revised 1936). For political novels see Speare (title under General above). For Sarah Orne Jewett see her *Best Stories* (2 vols., 1925) with a preface by Willa Cather, and F. O. Mathiessen's *Sarah Orne Jewett* (1929). For Dunne see *Mr. Dooley at His Best* (1930) edited by E. Ellis. For George Ade see Carl Van Doren's *Many Minds* (1924). For Mitchell see A. R. Burr's *Weir Mitchell: His Life and Letters* (1929). For Allen see J. W. Townsend's *James Lane Allen* (1928) and G. C. Knight's *James Lane Allen and the Genteel Tradition* (1935). For Saltus see M. Saltus's *Edgar Saltus the Man* (1925). For Hearn see E. Bisland's *Life and Letters of Lafcadio Hearn* (2 vols., 1911) and E. L. Tinker's *Lafcadio Hearn's American Days* (1924).

Chapter XII

For Hamlin Garland see his collected *Works* (12 vols., 1922) and his autobiographical writings: *A Son of the Middle Border* (1917),

A Daughter of the Middle Border (1921), Memories of the Middle Border (1926), Trail-Makers of the Middle Border (1926), Back-Trailers from the Middle Border (1928), and later volumes. For Crane see his Work (12 vols., 1925-26) edited by W. Follett with introductions by various writers; H. G. Wells's Stephen Crane, in North American Review, CLXXI (1900), 233-42; T. Beer's Stephen Crane (1923) with an introduction by Joseph Conrad; Carl Van Doren's Stephen Crane, in American Mercury, I (1924), 11-14—partly reproduced in the present book. For Bierce see C. McWilliams's Ambrose Bierce (1929). For Harold Frederic see R. M. Lovett's introduction to The Damnation of Theron Ware (1924). For Norris see his Complete Works (10 vols., 1928) and F. Walker's Frank Norris (1932). For Phillips see I. F. Marcosson's David Graham Phillips and His Times (1932). For Jack London see his Complete Works (21 vols., 1924); his autobiographical writings cited in the text above; Charmian London's The Book of Jack London (2 vols., 1921); I. Stone's Sailor on Horseback: The Biography of Jack London (1938); Joan London's Jack London and His Times (1939). For Sinclair see his autobiographical The Brass Check (1919) and American Outpost (1932); and F. Dell's Upton Sinclair: A Study in Social Protest (1927). For Herrick see H. Hansen's Midwest Portraits (1923), L. Mandel's Robert Herrick (1927), and the fuller account in Carl Van Doren's Contemporary American Novelists (1922).

Chapter XIII

Dreiser's works have not been collected nor his letters published. Of his projected History of Myself he published Dawn (1931) and Newspaper Days (1931, a reissue of the earlier A Book About Myself, 1922) and announced two to follow: A Literary Apprenticeship, Literary Experiences. His Twelve Men and his travel books are full of autobiography. He authorized the biography Forgotten Frontiers: Dreiser and the Land of the Free (1932) by Dorothy Dudley. See also Burton Rascoe's Theodore Dreiser (1925); G. J. Nathan's Intimate Notebooks (1932). H. L. Mencken's defense of Dreiser appears particularly in A Book of Prefaces (1917), and S. P. Sherman's attack in On Contemporary Literature (1917). In a selection of The Living Thoughts of Thoreau (1939) Dreiser expounded many of his own ideas.

BIBLIOGRAPHY

Chapter XIV

For Churchill see Carl Van Doren's *Contemporary American Novelists* (1922). For Tarkington see his collected *Works* (27 vols., 1922-32), and especially the autobiographical *The World Does Move* (1928); and R. C. Holliday's *Booth Tarkington* (1918). For Ellen Glasgow see the collected Virginia Edition (12 vols., 1937-38) and its admirable prefaces; and D. L. Mann's *Ellen Glasgow* (1927). For Fuller see C. M. Griffin's *Henry Blake Fuller* (1939). For Edna Ferber see her autobiography *A Peculiar Treasure* (1939). The Hitchcock Edition of David Gray (3 vols., 1929) includes his *Gallops I, II*. For Edith Wharton see her autobiographical *A Backward Glance*, her critical *The Writing of Fiction*, and her preface to *Ethan Frome* (1922). See also Henry James's *Letters* (1920); K. F. Gerould's *Edith Wharton: A Critical Study* (1922); R. M. Lovett's *Edith Wharton* (1925); B. De Voto's introduction to *Ethan Frome* (1939).

Chapter XV

For Willa Cather see her collected Autograph Edition (12 vols., 1937-38), her prefaces to *Alexander's Bridge* (1922) and *The Song of the Lark* (1932), and her *Not Under Forty* (1936), critical and autobiographical pieces; and R. Rapin's *Willa Cather* (1930).

Chapter XVI

For Masters see his autobiographical *Across Spoon River* (1936), and J. C. Chandler's *The Spoon River Country*, in *Journal of the Illinois State Historical Society*, XIV (1921-22), 252-329. For Howe see the Bibliography for Chapter X. For Anderson see his *A Story Teller's Story* (1924), *Tar* (1926), *Sherwood Anderson's Notebook* (1926); H. Hansen's *Midwest Portraits* (1923); C. Chase's *Sherwood Anderson* (1927); N. B. Fagin's *The Phenomenon of Sherwood Anderson* (1927). For Zona Gale see her *Portage, Wisconsin, and Other Essays* (1928). For Lewisohn see A. Gillis's *Ludwig Lewisohn: The Artist and His Message* (1933). For Rölvaag see his *Giants in the Earth* (1929) with introduction by V. L. Parrington. For Ameri-

(379)

can writers in German, French, and Yiddish before 1921 see *Cambridge History of American Literature* (title under General above), IV, 572-609, 813-26.

Chapter XVII

For Lewis see Carl Van Doren's *Sinclair Lewis: A Biographical Sketch* (1933) with a bibliography by H. Taylor; Van Doren's *Three Worlds* (1936) for invaluable letters from Lewis on his early work, pages 146, 153-59; *Why Sinclair Lewis Got the Nobel Prize* (1931) containing his speech before the Swedish Academy; G. J. Nathan's *Intimate Notebooks* (1932).

Chapter XVIII

For a lively popular account of the lively decade see Cleaton (title under General above). For Cabell see the Storisende Edition of his works (18 vols., 1927-30) with its prefaces and accompanying matter; *Between Dawn and Sunrise: Selections* (1930) edited by J. Macy; the autobiographical *Preface to the Past* (1936). See also C. Van Doren's *James Branch Cabell* (1925, revised 1932) with a map of Poictesme drawn by Cabell; H. L. Mencken's *James Branch Cabell* (1927); J. P. Cover's *Notes on Jurgen* (1928); W. A. McNeill's *Cabellian Harmonics* (1928). For Hergesheimer and Fitzgerald see Taylor-Hartwick (title under General above). For Elinor Wylie see her *Collected Prose* (1933) with introductions by C. Van Vechten, C. Van Doren, S. V. Benét, I. Paterson, W. R. Benét; W. R. Benét's *The Prose and Poetry of Elinor Wylie* (1934), by her husband; N. Hoyt's *Elinor Wylie* (1935), by her sister; C. Van Doren's *Three Worlds* (1936) containing a personal record and unpublished letters, pages 215-41. For Wilder see Taylor-Hartwick (title under General above). For Nathan see his *The Barly Fields* (1938), five novels collected with a preface by S. V. Benét. For Thorne Smith see *Thorne Smith: His Life and Times* (1934), a pamphlet by Smith, R. Young, and others; and *Topper* (1939, Pocket Books reprint).

Chapter XIX

For Cummings see *The Enormous Room* (1934) with a preface by the author. For Dos Passos see his *Three Plays* (1934), his collected travels *Journeys Between Wars* (1938), *U. S. A.* (1939, Modern Library reprint), all with prefatory comments by the author; Sinclair Lewis's *Manhattan at Last* (1925), a pamphlet review of *Manhattan Transfer*; J. Chamberlain's *John Dos Passos* (1939), a pamphlet. For Gertrude Stein see her *The Autobiography of Alice B. Toklas* (1933) and *Everybody's Autobiography* (1937); *Three Lives* (1933) with an introduction by C. Van Vechten; *The Making of Americans* (1934) with an introduction by B. Faÿ. For Hemingway see his preface to *The Fifth Column* (1938); G. Stein's *Autobiography of Alice B. Toklas*; E. Wilson's *Ernest Hemingway*, in *Atlantic Monthly*, July 1939—the best critical article on him. For Wolfe see his *From Death to Morning* (1935) and *The Story of a Novel* (1935). His one-act play *The Return of Buck Gavin* may be found in *Carolina Folk-Plays, Second Series* (1926) edited by F. H. Koch; and another play, *The Third Night*, in *Carolina Play-Book*, XI (1938), 70-75, with a note on *Thomas Wolfe: Play-Maker* by F. H. Koch.

Chapter XX

For the proletarian novel see varied discussions in *Proletarian Literature in the United States* (1935) edited by G. Hicks and others; *American Writers Congress* (1935) edited by H. Hart; and *A Note on Literary Criticism* (1936) by J. T. Farrell. For Pearl Buck see her Nobel lecture *The Chinese Novel* (1939); R. J. Walsh's *A Biographical Sketch of Pearl S. Buck* (1936). For Faulkner see his preface to *Sanctuary* (1932, Modern Library reprint) and Taylor-Hartwick (title under General above). For Caldwell see his note to the dramatic version of *Tobacco Road* (1934) by J. Kirkland and Caldwell, and his preface to *God's Little Acre* (1934, Modern Library reprint). The fifth and later printings (Viking) of *God's Little Acre* have an appendix on the prosecution and acquittal of the book. For Farrell see his introduction to *Studs Lonigan* (1938, Modern Library reprint) and *A Note on Literary Criticism*. For regionalism see C. McWilliams's *The New Regionalism in American Literature* (1930);

BIBLIOGRAPHY

J. C. Ransom's *The Esthetic of Regionalism*, in Zabel (title under General above). For Heyward see H. Allen's *DuBose Heyward* (1927). For Julia Peterkin see Clark (title under General above). For Stuart see his *Beyond Dark Hills* (1938). For Elizabeth Madox Roberts see G. Wescott's *Elizabeth Madox Roberts: A Personal Note* (1930) and Mark Van Doren's *Elizabeth Madox Roberts*, in *English Journal*, XXI (1932), 521-29. For the Iowa novelists—not the most recent—see *A Book of Iowa Authors* (1930) edited by D. Murphy. For Rhodes see M. D. Rhodes's *The Hired Man on Horseback* (1938). For Dobie see J. W. Rogers's *Finding Literature on the Texas Plains* (1931) with a bibliography—by Dobie—of books on the Southwest. For Katherine Anne Porter see G. Wescott's *Praise*, in *Southern Review*, V (1939), 161-73. For Mary Austin see her autobiographical *Earth Horizon* (1932) and H. M. Doyle's *Mary Austin: Woman of Genius* (1939). For Steinbeck see his introduction to *Tortilla Flat* (1937, Modern Library reprint); *Of Mice and Men* (1938, Modern Library reprint) with a biographical and critical introduction by J. H. Jackson; C. McWilliams's *Factories in the Field* (1939), a study of migrant workers in California.

INDEX

(383)

INDEX

INDEX

Caesar, 160, 223
Cahan, Abraham, 300
Cain, James Mallahan, 332
Caldwell, Erskine, 354-55, 356, 359, 381
Caleb Catlum's America, 360
Caleb Williams, 10-11
Call Home the Heart, 350
Call of the Wild, The, 238, 239-40
Camera Eye, 338
Canfield (Fisher), Dorothy, 357-58
Canoe and the Saddle, The, 106
Canterbury Pilgrims, The, 61, 62
Cantwell, Robert, 349
Canty, Tom, 152
Captain Smith and Princess Pocahontas, 20
Captain Stormfield's Visit to Heaven, 157-58
Cardigan, 216
Cardinal's Snuff-Box, The, 216
Carlisle, Lady Mary, 262
Carmer, Carl, 358, 359, 360
Carson, Christopher (Kit), 104, 290
Carton, Sydney, 262
Carvel, Richard, 260
Carwin, 13
Casanova, 328
Case of George Dedlow, The, 221
Case of Mr. Crump, The, 301
Cassique of Kiawah, The, 55
Casting Away of Mrs. Lecks and Mrs. Aleshine, The, 199
Catalogue, 361-62
Cather, Willa Sibert, 281-93, 324, 361, 379
Catherine the Great, 224
Catherwood, Mary Hartwell, 215, 216
Cato, 160
Cavalier, The, 216, 217
Cecil Dreeme, 106
Celebrated Jumping Frog of Calaveras County, The, 139
Celestial Railroad, The, 65
Century of Dishonor, A, 194
Cereno, Benito, 98-99
Certain Hour, The, 316
Certain Rich Man, A, 272
Cervantes, 3, 121
Chainbearer, The, 40
Chains, 258

Chambers, Robert William, 216
Chan, Charlie, 332
Chance Acquaintance, A, 123, 135
Chansons de geste, 45-46
Charlemagne, 16, 215
Charlemont, 55
Charles Egbert Craddock. See Murfree, Mary Noailles
Charlotte Temple (Charlotte), 8-9, 106, 110
Charteris, John, 318
Chatelaine of La Trinité, The, 266
Chaucer, 121
Chevalier of Pensieri-Vani, The, 266-67
Child, Lydia Maria, 45
Children, The, 280
Children of God, 363-64
Chillingworth, Roger, 68-71, 83
Chimmie Fadden, 229
Chingachgook, 26, 29, 37
Chippings with a Chisel, 61
Chita, 224
Chivalry, 316, 317
Choir Invisible, The, 216, 220, 222
Chopin, Kate, 214
Chrétien de Troyes, 188
Christmas Banquet, The, 65
Churchill, Winston, 216, 217, 260-61, 266, 379
Cigarette-Maker's Romance, The, 202
Cimarron, 268
Cincinnati, Society of the, 6
Cintré, Claire de, 171
Circuit Rider, The, 119, 120
Circus of Dr. Lao, The, 333
Civil War (fourth matter of romance), 115, 230, 271
Civilization in the United States, 299
Claggart, John, 101
Clarel, 100
Clark, George Rogers, 218
Clark, William, 19
Clark's Field, 243
Clay, Henry, 32
Clemens, Olivia Langdon, 143-44
Clemens, Samuel Langhorne, 106, 117, 121, 128-29, 133, 134, 137-62, 163, 165, 190, 194, 196, 203, 208, 216, 251, 263, 264, 272, 294,

(386)

INDEX

INDEX

INDEX

Following the Equator, 155
Fool's Errand, A, 197
Foote, Mary Hallock, 214
Forayers, The, 53
Forbes, Esther, 358
Ford, Paul Leicester, 208-09, 216
Foresters, The, 5
Forrester, Marian, 288-89
42nd Parallel, The, 337
Foster, Hannah Webster, 8, 371
Four Hundred, 276
Four Million, The, 214
Four Saints in Three Acts, 339-40
Fourier, 164
Fox, John, 206
Frank, Waldo, 323
Frank Forester. See Herbert, Henry William
Franklin, Benjamin, 3, 5, 9, 18, 19, 32, 98, 144, 161, 217-18, 219, 222, 338
Franko, 87
Frederic, Harold, 215, 233, 378
Free Air, 305
Free and Other Stories, 251, 256
Freeman, Mary Eleanor Wilkins, 211, 212, 216
French, Alice, 214
French Poets and Novelists, 168-69
Friendship Village, 298
Friendship Village Love Stories, 298
From Death to Morning, 344, 347
From the Other Side, 267
Frome, Ethan, 279
Frome, Zenobia, 279
Froissart, 54, 233
Frontenac, 291
Frontier (matter of romance), 15, 19-20, 25, 43, 44, 46, 51, 52, 55, 103-04, 118, 136, 269-70
Frost, Robert, 213
Fruit of the Tree, The, 277
Fugitive Blacksmith, The, 236
Fuller, Henry Blake, 266-68, 379
Fuller, Margaret, 75

Gabriel Conroy, 203
Gadd, Aaron, 312
Galahad, 325
Galaxy, 165
Galdós, 193

Gale, Zona, 298-99, 361, 379
Gallantry, 316
Gallery of Women, A, 258
Gallops, 272
Game, The, 238-39
Gant, Eliza Pentland, 345, 347
Gant, Eugene, 345, 347-78
Gant, Oliver, 345, 347-48
Gantry, Elmer, 309-10, 314
Garland, Hamlin, 118, 129, 225-28, 229, 245, 267, 356, 377-78
Garland, Mary, 167
Gaskell, Elizabeth Cleghorn, 110
Gates, Horatio, 52
Gautier, 224
Gaylord, Marcia, 125-26
Gaylord, Squire, 125
Genêt, Edmond Charles, 5
'Genius,' The, 248-49, 254-55
Gentle Boy, The, 62, 65
Gentleman from Indiana, The, 261
George, Henry, 131, 225
George (Milton), 365
George Eliot, 160, 166, 193
George Sand, 168, 171
George's Mother, 231
Georgia Scenes, 354
Gereth, Owen, 181
Gerhardt, Jennie, 253
Ghosts, 274
Gilbert and Sullivan, 152, 198
Glasgow, Ellen, 214, 216, 217, 264-66, 379
Glass Key, The, 333
Glimpses of the Moon, The, 280
Giants in the Earth, 301-02
Gil Blas, 7
Gilded Age, The, 139, 144-45, 151, 155, 208, 314
Gillette, Chester, 256
Gods Arrive, The, 280
God's Little Acre, 354
Godwin, William, 10-11, 13, 43
Goethe, 160
Gold, Michael, 349
Golden, Una, 304-05
Golden Bowl, The, 182, 184-86
Goldoni, 122
Goldsmith, Oliver, 121
Goncourt, Edmond de, 166
Gone with the Wind, 351

(390)

INDEX

INDEX

INDEX

Marble Faun, The, 78-80
March, Basil and Isabel, 131
Marching Men, 296
Mardi, 86-87
Margaret, 48
Margaret Smith's Journal, 58
Margret Howth, 117
Marion, Francis, 16, 51, 53
Mark Twain. See Clemens, Samuel
  Langhorne
Mark Twain (Paine), 162
Mark Twain's Autobiography, 162
Mark Twain's Letters, 162
Marlowe, 252, 316
Marquand, John Phillips, 333
Marquis, Donald Robert Perry, 361
Martin Eden, 238
Martin Faber, 51
Mary Magdalen, 223
Master, The, 271
Masters, Edgar Lee, 271, 295-96,
  297, 379
Mather, Cotton, 112
Matiwan, 52, 54
Matters of American romance, 14-20,
  271. See also Civil War, Frontier,
  Revolution, Settlement
Maum Guinea, 111
Maupassant, 166, 193
Mauves, Madame de, 167
Mayflower, The, 109
Mayo, William Starbuck, 45, 46
Maypole of Merry Mount, The, 62
Mead, Elinor G. (Mrs. William
  Dean Howells), 122
Meddlesome Jack, 354
Meeber, Caroline (Carrie), 247-48,
  254
Meine, Franklin J., 360
Melanctha, 339
Melicent, 320
Mellichampe, 52
Melville, Elizabeth Shaw, 87, 91
Melville, Herman, 72, 84-102, 117,
  141, 220, 272, 373-74
Memoirs of an American Citizen,
  The, 242-43
Men Without Women, 342
Mencken, Henry Louis, 248, 309
Merimée, 193
Merle, Madame, 174

Merton of the Movies, 272
Mervyn, Arthur, 11
Messala, 114
Messer Marco Polo, 323
Messiah, The, 114
Metropolis, The, 240
Middle Years, The, 170, 186
Midlander, The, 264
Mike Fink, 360
Milburn, George, 361
Miles (Turn of the Screw), 182
Miller, Daisy, 172, 210
Miller of Old Church, The, 265
Millet, 227
Milton, John, 69, 172
Minafer, George, 263
Minister's Wooing, The, 112
Miriam Coffin, 88
Miriam (Schaefer), 79-80, 83
Miss Lulu Bett, 298, 299
Miss Ravenel's Conversion, 118
Mr. Crewe's Career, 261
Mr. Dooley in Peace and in War, 215
Mr. Dooley in the Hearts of his
  Countrymen, 215
Mr. Hodge and Mr. Hazard, 325, 329
Mrs. Wiggs of the Cabbage Patch,
  272
Mitchell, Donald Grant, 108, 374
Mitchell, Isaac, 20
Mitchell, Margaret, 351
Mitchell, Silas Weir, 216, 221-22,
  377
Mitford, Mary Russell, 49
Moby Dick, 87-97, 100, 102, 151,
  220
Mocha Dick, 88-89
Modern Chivalry, 6-7
Modern Chronicle, A, 261
Modern Instance, A, 125-26, 135,
  190
Mohun, 105
Moll Flanders, 253
Monikins, The, 34
Moon-Calf, 299
Monsieur Beaucaire, 216, 217, 218,
  262
Monster, The, 231, 232
Montague, Margaret Prescott, 360
Montresor, John, 8-9
Moorehouse, J. Ward, 337

INDEX

(397)

INDEX

Saltus, Edgar, 223, 377
Samson, 270
San Dominick, 99
Sandburg, Carl, 272
Sancho Panza, 6
Sanctuary, 354
Sant' Ilario, 202
Santayana, George, 333
Sanutee, 52
Saracinesca, 202
Satan, 158
Satanstoe, 40, 49
Sawyer, Tom, 139, 146-50, 158, 208, 263
Scarlet Letter, The, 58, 65-71, 73, 74, 76, 79, 151
Scarlet Sister Mary, 359
Schofield, Penrod, 208, 262, 263, 264
Schopenhauer, 223
Scipio Africanus, 32
Scott, Evelyn, 323, 325
Scott, Sir Walter, 7, 14, 24, 26, 27, 32, 41, 42, 43, 47, 51, 55, 110, 137, 160, 215
Scout, The (The Kinsmen), 52, 53
Scribner's Monthly, 113
Sea-Wolf, The, 238
Sedgwick, Anne Douglas, 273
Sedgwick, Catherine Maria, 16
Select Party, A, 65
Sellers, Beriah, 145, 155, 157
Sense of the Past, The, 186
Septimius Felton, 81
Sesphra (Phrases), 320
Seth Jones, or the Captives of the Frontier, 103
Settlement (matter of romance), 15, 17-19, 43, 46, 52, 217-18, 269
Seven Vagabonds, The, 61, 63, 73, 166
Seven Who Fled, The, 351
Seventeen, 263
Shadow Before, The, 350
Shadows on the Rock, 291
Shaheen, Bryan, 10
Shakespeare, 51, 61, 121, 160, 316
Shaw, Elizabeth (Mrs. Herman Melville), 87, 91
Shaw, George Bernard, 201, 299
Shaw, Henry Wheeler, 138

Shay, Frank, 360
Shays's rebellion, 218
She, 215
Sheba, Queen of, 335
Shelley, 11, 325, 328-29
Sheltered Life, The, 266
Shepherd, Esther, 271
Sheridan, Bibbs, 263
Sheridan, Richard Brinsley, 316
Sherringham, Peter, 177
Shiloh (Shelley), 328-29
Shimerda, Antonia, 284-87, 288
Short Happy Life of Francis Macomber, The, 343
Short Sixes, 214
Short Stories of James T. Farrell, The, 356
Show Boat, 268, 269
Shropshire Lad, A, 356
Shui Hu Chuan (All Men Are Brothers), 352
Sidney, 188
Silver, Mattie, 279
Silver Stallion, The, 319, 320, 322
Simms, William Gilmore, 43, 45, 50-55, 57, 58, 104, 117, 218, 372
Sinclair, Harold, 361
Sinclair, Upton, 240-42, 245, 246, 299, 304, 334, 378
Sindbad, 199
Singmaster, Elsie, 358
Sir Charles Grandison, 4
Sister Carrie, 246-48, 252
Six Nations, 18, 39
1601, 144
Skinner, Constance Lindsay, 357
Sky-Walk, 11, 13
Sleeping Beauty in the Wood, 321
Slim Princess, The, 217
Sloper, Catherine, 172
Small Boy and Others, A, 186
Smedley, Agnes, 349
Smire, 321
Smirt, 321
Smith, 321
Smith, Francis Hopkinson, 204
Smith, John, 20, 51
Smith, Thorne, 325, 331-32, 380
Smollett, 3, 4, 5, 27, 31, 43
Snow Image, and Other Twice-Told Tales, 72

INDEX

INDEX

INDEX